Praise for *Affiliate Program M...* *An Hour a Day*

Social is sexy, search is cool, a hundred other things seek our attention. Yet for a number of companies, affiliate marketing remains the trusty workhorse diligently producing amazing results. In this book, Geno shares, in extraordinary detail, how to effectively engage the affiliate channel for your company.

> —AVINASH KAUSHIK, Author of *Web Analytics 2.0* and *Web Analytics: An Hour a Day*

This is the best affiliate marketing guide available. No one knows the field like Geno Prussakov, and his book breaks down affiliate marketing into manageable chunks that get you up and running in no time, armed with "insider" know-how so you can launch and manage your program successfully. Learn from the master, and start tapping into this lucrative marketing channel for online sales and leads.

> —ANITA CAMPBELL, CEO, Small Business Trends

Affiliate Program Management: An Hour a Day is the book you need if you want to start and manage a successful affiliate marketing campaign. It's all here, from what to do and why to do it and then exactly how to do it, step-by-step. This book will ensure you have the knowledge you need to get it done the right way, the first time.

> —JIM KUKRAL, 10-year affiliate marketing veteran and author of *Attention! This Book Will Make You Money*

As technology advances and publishers become more diverse, managing an affiliate program becomes an even more complex task. In this book, Geno successfully dissects the many intricacies of setting up and critically growing a profitable transparent relationship.

Avoid common mistakes that threaten long-term relationships as Geno expands on the previously unwritten rules of engagement, motivation, conversion strategy, and communication.

Jam-packed with actionable strategies and real-life examples to help you leapfrog your competitors, Affiliate Program Management: An Hour a Day will no doubt become the first point of call for any serious business wanting to start an affiliate program.

> —MATTHEW WOOD, founder, Affiliates4u.com and a4uExpo Conference & Exhibition

Launching an affiliate program? Or simply hoping to run yours better and more profitably? Then pick up this indispensable handbook. Affiliate marketing guru Geno Prussakov takes you by the hand and walks you, day-by-day and step-by-step, through every aspect of running a successful and lucrative affiliate program.
> —REBECCA LIEB, digital marketing consultant and author of
> *The Truth About Search Engine Optimization*

Much of what is written about affiliate marketing is by affiliates for affiliates. There's nothing wrong with that, but there has long been a need for a practical guide on getting the most from affiliate marketing for marketers managing affiliate programs. Geno's book more than fills the gap, stepping merchants through the questions they need to ask to improve their program and showing where to find the answers.

You'll learn the pillars for successful management of an affiliate marketing program through examples, checklists, and practical advice based on Geno's many years immersed in affiliate marketing.
> —DR. DAVE CHAFFEY, CEO, SmartInsights.com and author of
> *Internet Marketing, Strategy, Implementation, and Practice*

This is an extremely thorough and insightful guide about how to do affiliate marketing for any entrepreneur or individual who wants to do this properly and maximize their success. The book is at the same time meticulous and engaging to read, with a step-by-step approach to mastering this digital discipline. After an initial introduction and overview of the industry, Geno guides online businesses on how to set up, measure, and optimize their business performance. He does an admirable job of highlighting the most important considerations while also providing advice on how to avoid common pitfalls.
> —LINUS GREGORIADIS, research director, Econsultancy

Well-written and completely comprehensive, Geno Prussakov's new book Affiliate Program Management: An Hour a Day *is a must-read for merchants who want to expand brand awareness and increase sales through affiliate marketing. From competitive market analysis through affiliate program setup, launch, and management to avoiding the program-killing mistakes that affiliate program managers make, Geno has covered it all in detail. Some of my existing merchants and program managers should read this book now!*
> —ROSALIND GARDNER, speaker and affiliate marketing consultant
> and author of *The Super Affiliate Handbook and Make a Fortune*
> *Promoting Other People's Stuff Online*

Perhaps no other area of Internet marketing has more potential to grow online sales than affiliate marketing yet has so much room for online retailers to improve. Affiliate Program Management: An Hour a Day is the go-to guide for anyone who is looking to start or tune up their affiliate program. Its comprehensive, up-to-date advice on how to attract good affiliate partners, motivate and keep them happy, and protect yourself in the process is greatly needed in the industry.

—LINDA BUSTOS, director of ecommerce research, Elastic Path
Software and author of GetElastic.com ecommerce blog

Affiliate program management is a necessary and critical component of a successful affiliate marketing strategy. In this book, Geno provides a comprehensive, step-by-step guide that any business owner or affiliate manager can use to build and manage a profitable affiliate marketing program. I highly recommend this book to anyone looking to take advantage of the multibillion industry known as affiliate marketing.

—KRISTOPHER B. JONES, founder and former president and CEO of
Pepperjam Network, and author of *Search Engine Optimization:
Your Visual Blueprint to Effective Internet Marketing*

If there were ever a bible and A to Z guide on affiliate marketing, this is it. Affiliate performance marketing is one of the fastest-growing and important segments of Internet marketing. It's also the most misunderstood and complex because it touches every aspect of Internet marketing's traffic channels and transaction types. Geno has created a must-read that allows anyone to understand the affiliate marketing ecosystem and how to best apply affiliate marketing to their business. Most people entering the industry find it to be overwhelming because of the vast universe of moving parts, reach, breadth, and depth. Affiliate Program Management: An Hour a Day distills the infinite realm of performance marketing possibilities into easy-to-understand chapters that empower the reader to not only better understand performance marketing but also how to enter the industry, build a business, or add a new channel to their marketing programs.

—PETER BORDES, CEO, MediaTrust

Geno Prussakov has authored an absolute gem of a book! Affiliate Program Management: An Hour a Day is a must-read, not only for those new to affiliate marketing but also for the vast majority of marketers currently managing affiliate programs. Step-by-step, easy-to-understand instructions enable you to really grasp the essence of setting up and managing a world-class affiliate program. With no stone left unturned in his analysis, I was able to identify past mistakes made in previous affiliate programs I had set up. Now, with Affiliate Program Management: An Hour a Day by my side, I feel confident that I'll get the best results from my next affiliate program. I highly recommend this book to anyone getting ready to set up an affiliate program, whether for a small, home-based business or a Fortune 1000 ecommerce site.

—KEVIN GOLD, publisher, Search Marketing Standard magazine and
director of Marketing, iNET Interactive

Geno Prussakov has written the only book an affiliate program manager needs. In Affiliate Program Management: An Hour a Day, *he provides an in-depth and comprehensive guide to designing, implementing, and running an affiliate marketing program. Over the course of 18 chapters, he covers the entire process, from competitive market analysis and how to determine payment models all the way through to handling fraud and important mistakes to avoid.*

Throughout, he brings his years of experience to bear yet writes with humor and insight in order to keep things simple and easy to understand. Examples and screenshots are included to show how things are done in the real world. He even includes sample templates for email messages to affiliates. It's an impressive effort.

Affiliate marketing should be part of any merchant's online marketing strategy. And whether that company has a lot of experience in the field or none whatsoever, Geno Prussakov's book should be the next thing they read. If you want to sell your products online, buy this book. Highly recommended.

—CHRIS TRAYHORN, founder and publisher, *Revenue Performance* magazine

In Affiliate Program Management: An Hour a Day, *Geno Prussakov has written the most up-to-date and practical how-to guide to affiliate marketing I have ever read. With an experienced hand, Prussakov guides the prospective affiliate program operator through each decision they'll need to make and empowers them to make educated choices. Including topics such as conceptualizing the program, deciding on program structure, choosing the right platform for giving a program the best shot for success, rolling out a program in a way that will attract attention for the right reasons, and setting up promotions that will encourage active promotion without giving away the farm, this book is packed full of tips for the beginning manager to the "old hand" alike. I've been managing affiliate programs for 11 years, and I was making notes on items I look forward to putting into place in my current project.* Affiliate Program Management: An Hour a Day *is a must-read for any business owner who'd like to get more out of their online business.*

—WADE TONKIN, affiliate manager, FootballFanatics.com

I wish I had this book at the onset of my affiliate career. Not only is it chock-full of relevant information that is organized in an easy-to-digest format, but the suggestions that Geno provides are real-world tips that can be implemented immediately. I've already discovered several ways I can improve the performance of my own affiliate program. Furthermore, his in-depth look at the industry demonstrates the impact that affiliates have on ecommerce and business at large. This book should be given to every affiliate manager and network in the industry.

—CHELSEA OSOLING, affiliate marketing specialist, CowBoom.com/Best Buy

Geno Prussakov's book Affiliate Program Management: An Hour a Day *is an excellent resource for both new and seasoned affiliate professionals. Mr. Prussakov begins by explaining the basics of affiliate marketing and digs deeper into each topic with real-life examples and tips. He outlines his book based on the stage of the program, from preparing for a program launch to post-launch advanced management and analysis. This makes it convenient for busy readers because they can start with the chapter that's most relevant to them.*

Mr. Prussakov covers topics in great detail, down to the strategic and tactical levels, which every merchant needs to understand. For example, he discusses the pros and cons in deciding between running an affiliate program in-house vs. through an affiliate network, which is an underlying decision for any merchant. He also outlines how-to's and potential pitfalls of various tactics, from designing creatives to communicating with affiliates.

Seasoned affiliate managers should not dismiss the book because it provides a great way for them to step back and rethink their program strategy. Mr. Prussakov also provides a comprehensive list of affiliate vendors, from affiliate networks by geographical area to data feed providers. Regardless of your experience in the affiliate world, it certainly is helpful to have a list of affiliate vendors handy when you are exploring specific program needs.

I highly recommend all affiliate professionals read this book. Whether you are just starting out as an affiliate manager or looking for new strategies to improve your mature affiliate program, you'll find recommendations and examples from this book that you can apply to real-life situations.
    —MIA VALLO, online advertising manager, Network Solutions

There is so much information—and so many opinions—that many online retailers and marketers are too intimidated to even launch or expand their own programs, thus leaving millions of dollars on the table.

Finally there is a way to cut through all the noise: Affiliate Program Management: An Hour a Day. *Geno has done the near-impossible task of making all aspects of successful affiliate program management easy to understand. Even better, he has broken down the steps to affiliate program success into simple, actionable steps any online marketer can execute, even with their already overwhelming schedules.*

I'm buying copies of Affiliate Program Management: An Hour a Day *for all of my clients and associates, and I highly recommend you do the same!*
    —MARTY M. FAHNCKE, professional revenue developer,
    FawnKey & Associates

Affiliate marketer since 2001 and advisory board member and speaker/trainer for the Affiliate Summit conference, Geno has done it again! This book includes comprehensive and easy-to-understand strategies for novices and experts alike that can be applied successfully across industry types! In a week you will have caught up on the last 10 years in affiliate marketing.

    —MALCOLM COWLEY, CEO, Performance Horizon Group,
      and former cofounder, buy.at

This is the most complete resource ever for new and experienced affiliate managers. From understanding affiliate marketing fundamentals to getting set up to tracking and management, you'll find everything you need to build and maintain a highly profitable affiliate program.

    —PETER HAMILTON, VP of marketing, HasOffers.com

Affiliate Program Management: An Hour a Day is the perfect book to lead you through all pitfalls of starting and managing a successful affiliate program.

You get detailed information about how to prepare and launch your affiliate program together with advanced management tips. This book is not about theory; it is about building your real affiliate program, which will earn you real money!

I recognized Geno Prussakov as an affiliate marketing trend spotter about two years ago, when I started reading his blog. Since he started to blog about affiliate marketing in 2007, he has researched nearly every single problem of affiliate marketing. The years of research that Geno put into writing his blog and Affiliate Program Management: An Hour a Day certainly paid off.

I strongly recommend this book to everyone who wants to dive into affiliate marketing and swim through all the pitfalls waiting for you while you build a successful affiliate program.

    —VIKTOR ZEMAN, CEO and affiliate software architect, Quality Unit

Affiliate Program Management

An Hour a Day

Affiliate Program Management

An Hour a Day

Evgenii "Geno" Prussakov

Wiley Publishing, Inc.

Senior Acquisitions Editor: WILLEM KNIBBE
Development Editor: ALEXA MURPHY
Technical Editor: MICHAEL COLEY
Production Editor: DASSI ZEIDEL
Copy Editor: KIM WIMPSETT
Editorial Manager: PETE GAUGHAN
Production Manager: TIM TATE
Vice President and Executive Group Publisher: RICHARD SWADLEY
Vice President and Publisher: NEIL EDDE
Book Designer: FRANZ BAUMHACKL
Compositor: JOANN KOLONICK, HAPPENSTANCE TYPE-O-RAMA
Proofreader: REBECCA RIDER
Indexer: JACK LEWIS
Project Coordinator, Cover: KATIE CROCKER
Cover Designer: RYAN SNEED
Cover Graphic: ALEXBET.COM

Dear Reader,

Thank you for choosing *Affiliate Program Management: An Hour a Day*. This book is part of a family of premium-quality Sybex books, all of which are written by outstanding authors who combine practical experience with a gift for teaching.

Sybex was founded in 1976. More than 30 years later, we're still committed to producing consistently exceptional books. With each of our titles, we're working hard to set a new standard for the industry. From the paper we print on, to the authors we work with, our goal is to bring you the best books available.

I hope you see all that reflected in these pages. I'd be very interested to hear your comments and get your feedback on how we're doing. Feel free to let me know what you think about this or any other Sybex book by sending me an email at nedde@wiley.com. If you think you've found a technical error in this book, please visit http://sybex.custhelp.com. Customer feedback is critical to our efforts at Sybex.

Best regards,

Neil Edde
Vice President and Publisher
Sybex, an imprint of Wiley

To my parents, Igor Prussakov and Svetlana Prussakova

 # Acknowledgments

First and foremost, my thanks go to my parents for always believing in me, regardless of the circumstances. The content and contexts that they have provided during the early years of my life have greatly contributed to shaping me into who I am today. For this, and their never-quenching love, I am and will be eternally grateful.

Second, I'd like to thank my precious wife, Lena, for her perennial encouragement and support—both during my work on this volume and in the course of my work and study in general.

Next, this book of mine could not have been the same without invaluable input from a friend and fellow affiliate marketer, Michael Coley, the technical editor of this volume. His patience, constructive criticism, and sharp mind have contributed greatly to this book.

For making this volume a reality, my thanks also go to the book's development editor Alexa Murphy, as well as to the whole Wiley/Sybex team that was involved in it, especially Willem Knibbe, Pete Gaughan, Jenni Housh, Connor O'Brien, and Dassi Zeidel.

But most of all, no one has given up more than my little Princess Anastasia, who was three when I wrote my very first book and who turned seven while I was completing this one. Once again, she has involuntarily sacrificed countless hours of play with her father and should definitely be mentioned here.

About the Author

Evgenii "Geno" Prussakov was born and raised in Kishinev, Republic of Moldova—back in the years when it was still part of the Soviet Union. He studied linguistics, English, and translation at the State University of Moldova, philosophy at Oxford, psychology in the United States, and international relations at Cambridge. At the time of this book's writing, he is pursuing his doctorate studies, focusing on leadership, on motivation, and particularly on the challenges of leading such independent "workers" as affiliate marketers.

In 2007 Geno authored his first book on affiliate marketing, *A Practical Guide to Affiliate Marketing: Quick Reference for Affiliate Managers and Merchants,* which quickly became (and to this date remains) the bestselling volume in the niche of affiliate program management. In 2008, his *Online Shopping Through Consumers' Eyes* came out. In 2010, a good number of his articles on leadership, motivation, and affiliate program management were included in *Internet Marketing from the Real Experts.* And today you're holding in your hands his largest and most comprehensive book out of all of them, *Affiliate Program Management: An Hour a Day.*

With more than a dozen years spent in digital marketing, Geno has built up several online businesses of his own (both retail- and service-oriented ones), as well as the highly regarded AMNavigator.com affiliate marketing blog, which is an educational resource that currently contains more than 1,000 articles on affiliate program management, leadership, mobile marketing, and every possible area of digital marketing. His blog was voted number-one affiliate marketing blog in 2010's Search & Social Awards by SearchEngineJournal.com. Geno was named among the three finalists in the Best Blogger category of Affiliate Summit's Pinnacle Awards, the industry's most prestigious awards, for two years in a row: 2010 and 2011.

Besides being an award-winning blogger, Geno is a well-known international speaker who has spoken at such conferences as Affiliate Summit, a4uexpo Affiliate Marketing Conference, eMetrics Marketing Optimization Summit, Internet Marketing Conference, PubCon, eComXpo, and other venues. He is also the senior editor for the affiliate marketing section of the *Search Engine Marketing Journal* and is a regular contributor to numerous periodicals on digital marketing such as *Website Magazine, Search Marketing Standard, Visibility Magazine, FeedFront,* and Econsultancy.com's blog.

Geno was voted the world's Best Outsourced Affiliate Program Manager for three years in a row (2006–2008) by the largest online affiliate marketing community, ABestWeb.com. Over the years he has launched more than 50 different affiliate programs, managing programs and consulting with such top brands as Forbes, Nokia, Hallmark, Warner Music, Skype, Forex Club, and multiple others. He recently founded a new affiliate program management company, Affilinomics (as in "affiliate-driven economics"), which offers outsourced solutions for full affiliate program management, affiliate recruitment, and affiliate marketing consulting.

He resides in Northern Virginia with his wife and daughter and continues to write, speak, manage affiliate programs, and actively contribute to the industry.

Contents

CONTENTS

Foreword

Word of mouth. Referrals. Pay for performance. There is hardly anyone who isn't in favor of making money on the efforts of others. This is the basis for affiliate marketing. However, it isn't as easy as it sounds.

Affiliate marketing requires solid planning and smart work to yield the optimal results. Amazon.com, which captures approximately 25 cents of every ecommerce dollar in the United States, is the poster child for affiliate marketing, with well over a million affiliates. Amazon.com developed a program that made it easy for people to share the products they enjoyed, recommend their network to that product, and direct that traffic to the Amazon.com website, where those people would buy the product and the affiliate would get paid for sharing. You may not become the next Amazon.com, but plenty of others are making a lot of money from affiliate marketing.

In a June 2010 Harris Interactive poll, when asked what sources "influence your decision to use or not use a particular company, brand, or product," 71 percent claim reviews from family members or friends exert a "great deal" or "fair amount" of influence. Fifty-three percent of people on Twitter recommend companies and/or products in their tweets, with 48 percent of them delivering on their intention to buy the product, according to the ROI Research for Performance from June 2010. And according to a 2009 Manage Smarter report, 83 percent of online shoppers said they are interested in sharing information about their purchases with people they know, while 74 percent are influenced by the opinions of others in their decision to buy the product in the first place. Do you have a plan in place to take advantage of these trends?

Don't worry. Geno Prussakov will give it to you in *Affiliate Program Management: An Hour a Day.* I've known Geno for years, and he eats and breathes affiliate marketing day and night. Geno was voted the "Best Outsourced Program Manager of the Year" for three years in a row (2006, 2007, and 2008) by the largest online affiliate marketing community, ABestWeb.com. His blog was voted the top affiliate marketing blog in 2010.

Follow Geno's plan to understand what it takes to develop a program that affiliates want to participate in, no matter what your competitors may be doing in the same space. Learn how to recruit affiliates who will bring you oodles of traffic, how do develop creative and persuasive communications that keep them motivated, and how to give your affiliates the tools they need to maximize their efforts. You'll also learn how to spot what you are doing well so you can keep doing more of it, and you'll learn how to avoid the costly mistakes that most merchants with affiliate programs make.

Trust me, invest an hour a day in *Affiliate Program Management: An Hour a Day* before your competitors do.

BRYAN EISENBERG

New York Times *and* Wall Street Journal *best-selling author of* Waiting for Your Cat to Bark?, Call to Action, *and* Always Be Testing, *as well as popular speaker*

Introduction

Conceived of slightly more than a decade ago, affiliate marketing has come a long way. It has grown from just a handful of affiliate programs in the late 1990s to a multibillion-dollar worldwide industry.

Affiliate marketing is essentially performance-based advertising, whereby affiliates promote a merchant's product/service and get remunerated for every sale, visit, or subscription sent to the merchant. The most frequently used payment arrangements include pay-per-sale, pay-per-lead, pay-per-call, and pay-per-click. Affiliate marketing is one of the most powerful and effective customer acquisition tools available to an online merchant today. The merchant decides what commission to pay and pays only when the results (sales, leads, and/or clicks) are there.

The mainstream concept owes its creation to CDNow.com and Amazon.com. In November 1994, CDNow started its Buyweb program—the first online marketing program of its kind. Amazon continued this pattern in July 1996 with its Associates program. Amazon claims that currently the number of its affiliates worldwide exceeds 1 million.

Today nearly all online retailers from the Internet Retailer's Top 500 list have an affiliate program. Forrester has forecasted the U.S. affiliate marketing spend to grow from $1.9 billion in 2009 to $4 billion by 2014. This is natural, because with its low-entry costs and performance-based compensation models, no other method of marketing can compare to affiliate marketing.

Amusingly, regardless of affiliate marketing's wide popularity, which it earned by the incredibly effective performance-based advertising model described earlier, there are a surprisingly small number of quality books written on the subject. This is especially true when it comes to comprehensive step-by-step manuals on how to start and develop affiliate programs of your own. That is where *this* book comes in. By the time you finish it, not only will you easily understand all the ins and outs of the industry and be able to speak the professional lingo, but you will be truly well-equipped to run an affiliate program of your own or to oversee one run for you by in-house staff or an outsourced affiliate program manager.

Who Should Read This Book

Almost anyone involved in digital marketing will benefit from reading this book. However, since it is primarily intended to help you create and manage your affiliate marketing program, its target audience falls into three basic groups:

- Business owners whose companies are either already online or are looking at developing an online presence and benefiting from digital marketing

- Marketing professionals working in or with companies that are actively interested in the digital space (for example, ones that have websites targeting prospective customers or that are interested in launching web marketing campaigns with the purpose of making sales)
- Affiliate program managers—new and seasoned—who will pick up a lot of tips and information on how to build and run fruitful affiliate marketing campaigns

Finally, although this book is primarily focused on affiliate marketing as a method of generating sales for online advertisers, affiliates should also find it of interest. After all, unless you know what makes up a good affiliate program, how will you be able to tell a good one from a bad one?

What You Will Learn

Affiliate Program Management: An Hour a Day is written as a step-by-step manual on how to use affiliate marketing effectively to advertise your online business and generate new sales. The book will help you launch and build a successful affiliate marketing program, walking you through every aspect of affiliate management. I have organized it in a way that helps you learn the ropes of affiliate program management by spending approximately an hour a day on each task.

The chapters are structured in a fashion that will walk you *all the way* from an introduction to affiliate marketing to advanced affiliate program management and analysis. Here is a quick breakdown of what to expect from the book:

Part I: History, Terminology, and Introductory Remarks

Chapter 1: Understanding Affiliate Marketing   explains what exactly affiliate marketing is and how it exists at the intersection of all other types of online marketing and involves all possible forms of online advertising. In this chapter, I will lay the foundation on which to build your knowledge about this type of marketing, looking at its history, basic terminology, and all the main components involved.

Chapter 2: Budget, Payments, and Related Considerations   looks at the financial component of your affiliate program. Additionally, I will touch on the subject of interaction between affiliate marketing and other online marketing channels you may be utilizing.

Part II: Month 1: Pre-Launch Research and Analysis

Chapter 3: Week 1: Perform Competitive Marketing Analysis   equips you to analyze the past, the present, and the future, arriving at conclusions of what weaknesses need to be strengthened, what advantages should be used to your business's further benefit, and how adding an affiliate program can help you advance in your battle with competitors.

Chapter 4: Week 2: Understand Tracking and Reporting looks at the very skeleton of your affiliate program, including the platform on which it will operate (whether in-house or network-based), as well as the way everything will function, such as various payment options, cookies, and their role in affiliate marketing.

Chapter 5: Week 3: Evaluate Program Management Options demonstrates the importance of proactive affiliate program management; looks into the basics, key terms, responsibilities of managers, and your sourcing options; and covers other important elements you want to know.

Chapter 6: Week 4: Finalize Payment Models and Cookie Life shows real-life examples of how various merchants have set up their programs. You will also decide whether a two-tier program is right for you, as well as learn about cookie life. By the end of this week, you will have a good idea of what and how you will be paying your affiliates.

Part III: Month 2: Setting Your Affiliate Program Up

Chapter 7: Week 1: Develop Creative Inventory is devoted to the important subject of affiliate creatives. You will learn everything you need to know about banners and text links, and at the end of this week, you should have a creative arsenal to be proud of.

Chapter 8: Week 2: Data Feeds, Coupons, and Plug-Ins discusses data feeds (their purpose and structure, as well as tools for their creation and import into affiliate sites), coupons, widgets, and video.

Chapter 9: Week 3: Research and Develop Program Policies guides you while you are working on your affiliate program agreement, including describing both general considerations and very specific policies, such as the use of trademarks, necessity of disclosures, specific types of marketing employed to promote your brand and your products, and other important topics.

Chapter 10: Week 4: Final Brushstrokes looks at such things as your tracking implementation and testing, email templates, program description page, text of the announcement email, and more. At the end of this week, you will be taking your program live.

Part IV: Month 3: Program Launch and Affiliate Program Management

Chapter 11: Week 1: Launch the Affiliate Program and Recruit concentrates on very specific topics: announcing your program to the affiliate marketing world, developing and rolling out your affiliate recruitment campaigns, and charting the guidelines of your program's social-media strategy, as well as other recruitment-related questions.

Chapter 12: Week 2: Plan Your Affiliate Communication walks you through the best practices of communication with affiliates, getting you equipped to handle this important component of program management in the way it should be handled.

Chapter 13: Week 3: Program Management teaches you where to start, what to look out for, how exactly to manage, and what kind of affiliate manager it takes to succeed in the uneasy task of managing a program driven by an unmanageable "workforce."

Chapter 14: Week 4: Affiliate Motivation tackles the fascinating subject of stimulating affiliates and motivating both those who are confident and willing and those who may not be interested, who are not capable, or who have burned themselves in the past. You will learn about the differences between extrinsic and intrinsic motivation, learn about contingency theory, and arrive at an optimal approach.

Part V: Month 4: Advanced Management and Analysis

Chapter 15: Week 1: Study and Learn to Deal with Parasitism and Problematic Affiliates helps you develop a systemic approach to the evaluation of affiliate applications, discusses the problems of affiliate parasitism (a topic the importance of which cannot be overemphasized), and addresses problems of coupon and content theft.

Chapter 16: Week 2: Master Affiliate Program Analytics and Optimization focuses on affiliate marketing analytics, ongoing testing and optimization, and competitive intelligence. During this week I will also discuss alternative tracking solutions and compensation models and show how to develop an approach to progress analysis.

Chapter 17: Deadliest Mistakes to Avoid describes 40 mistakes you want to avoid while managing your affiliate program. The mistakes are split into two groups: those committed by merchants and those made by affiliate program managers.

Chapter 18: Affiliate Program Promotion Ideas provides you with more than two dozen practical ideas on affiliate program promotion.

Glossary of Abbreviations defines the acronyms and abbreviations that each affiliate marketing manager should be comfortable using.

How to Contact the Author

I warmly welcome feedback from you about this book or about books you'd like to see from me in the future. You can reach me by emailing geno@amnavigator.com.

For more information about my educational work, please visit www.amnavigator.com. With questions related to affiliate program launch and management, you may reach me at 1-888-588-8866 or via www.affilinomics.com.

I can also be found on Twitter at www.twitter.com/eprussakov where on a daily basis I tweet tips on digital marketing, advertising, and everything that interests me. I would love to connect with my readers via LinkedIn or Facebook. You may find me there at www.linkedin.com/in/eprussakov and www.facebook.com/prussakov, respectively.

History, Terminology, and Introductory Remarks

I

One of the world's greatest authors, French philosopher and writer, Voltaire, is known for saying, "If you wish to converse with me, define your terms." This is exactly where we will start our journey, defining affiliate marketing itself, and all of the key terms, participants, and processes. We will also discuss how affiliate marketing fits into your overall marketing mix, how affiliate programs work, and how affiliates differ by the promotion methods they use.

Understanding Affiliate Marketing

1

With its heavy focus on performance, affiliate marketing is a model of advertising that, regardless of its young age, has already gained great popularity among multiple online businesses, including many of the largest brands. It exists at the intersection of all other types of online marketing, and it involves all possible forms of online advertising. In this chapter, I will lay the foundation for your knowledge about affiliate marketing, including looking at its history, its basic terminology, and all its main components.

Chapter Contents

What Is Affiliate Marketing?

Affiliate marketing is performance-based marketing, whereby a product or service gets remunerated for every sale, visit, or subscription sent to the merchant. Because of this performance-based component, which is the cornerstone of affiliate marketing, it is also sometimes called *performance marketing.* The payment arrangements used include pay-per-sale (or cost-per-sale), pay-per-lead (or cost-per-lead), pay-per-click (or cost-per-click), pay-per-call (or cost-per-call), and other similar action-dependent compensation patterns. They are also frequently referred to as cost-per-action (CPA) payment models. Cost-per-action means affiliates' compensation is wholly dependent on their performance. CPA is a type of remuneration that essentially says, I'll pay you when there is action. In most cases, advertisers have to choose one of the payment models, but in some cases there is room for more than one type of compensation in one affiliate program. For example, a merchant can use the cost-per-sale (CPS) and cost-per-lead (CPL) models together, paying 10 percent commission on each sale (CPS) as well as $0.50 for each newsletter sign-up (CPL). Or an advertiser may decide to employ both the CPL and pay-per-call (PPCall) models within one program, by paying both for lead-generating forms filled out on their site and for phone calls referred by affiliates.

Origins of Affiliate Marketing

Mainstream affiliate marketing owes its birth to CDNOW.com and Amazon.com. In November 1994, CDNOW started its BuyWeb program, which was the first online marketing program of its kind at that time. Amazon continued this pattern in July 1996 with its associates program. Amazon claims to have more than 1 million associates worldwide as of 2010.

An affiliate (marketing) program is a business arrangement whereby one party (the merchant or advertiser) agrees to pay another party (the affiliate or publisher) a referral fee, bounty, or commission for every occurrence of a desirable (to the advertiser) action. Examples of such actions include sales and leads that occur in the event of the end customer clicking the affiliate link prior to completing the sale/lead. It is important for the advertiser to define what will make the end user's actions qualify for affiliate remuneration. That's where we get the lingo of *valid leads* and *confirmed orders.* You don't want to pay for fake, or fraudulent, "referrals." I will discuss this topic in more detail in the following chapter.

Depending on the merchant's preference, an affiliate program may also be called an associate, commission, revenue-sharing, bounty, or partnership program. The payment pattern is always a pay-for-performance pattern: When there is qualified action, there is payment.

Since most of the traditional scenarios involve compensating affiliates for sales and leads, these will be the main examples used in this book. Also, although there are different terms for affiliates (see the next section), I will stick to the terms *affiliate* for the marketers who get compensated based on performance and *merchant* for the advertiser who the affiliate has their performance marketing relationship with.

Affiliates, Subaffiliates, and Superaffiliates

Now let's turn to three terms you need to be comfortable with as far as different affiliates go: affiliates, subaffiliates, and superaffiliates. It is important to understand what these terms mean, how they differ, and what they have in common.

Affiliates

Sometimes also called *associates* or *publishers*, affiliates are essentially independent marketers who may choose to promote a business and be paid according to one of the previously described performance-based models. They are the sales force for your affiliate program. I like to think of affiliates as dealers or your most valuable partners who promote your brand and your business, investing their own money to sell your product/service.

Affiliates are *independent* marketers who choose what affiliate programs to promote, what programs to drop, what merchants to push more aggressively, and on what merchants to spend less effort. They are self-managed and in the vast majority of cases are not accountable to merchants for performance. All of this makes them very different from the traditional business definition of an affiliate. On the other hand, the freedom that undergirds their very business existence allows affiliates to develop into an extremely self-motivated workforce. I will talk about it more in the following chapters, but at this stage, you should understand that this lack of top-down influence and control does not hurt affiliates' productivity. In fact, the freedom that's embedded in affiliates' hearts helps them achieve heights that would have been otherwise impossible.

What I Don't Mean by *Affiliate*

The term *affiliate* can be easily mistaken for something that it is not. Flipping through literature on business and economics, you will see the following definitions:

- *Compilation of State and Federal Privacy Laws* tells us that the term "means any company that controls, is controlled by, or is under common control with another company" (Privacy Journal, 2002).

- Michael R. Lavin in his *Business Information* points out that the term "can be used as a generic word to indicate either a subsidiary or division" (Oryx Press, 1992).

- Arvind V. Phatak in his *International Dimensions of Management* writes that terms such as *affiliate* and *subsidiary* should be (and are) "used synonymously" (Dame Publishing, 1994).

Continues

> **What I Don't Mean by *Affiliate*** *(Continued)*
>
> - Finally, in their *Security Analysis: Principles and Technique* volume, the infamous Benjamin Graham and David Dodd make an observation that *affiliate* is more indefinite than *subsidiary*. They write that "an affiliate may be a company effectively controlled—perhaps jointly with others—though ownership is less than 50%. Or the relationship may exist through control of both companies by the same owning group or 'parent,' with resultant close commercial or operating ties." Also, "in some cases a company may be called an affiliate although it really is a subsidiary." (McGraw-Hill, 2005)
>
> None of these is even close to what the term *affiliate* means in the context of affiliate marketing. Looking at the mentions of common ownership, control, and "close commercial or operating ties," you can conclude that one *affiliate* can justly be characterized as an *antonym* of the other. Not one of these elements is present in the context of the affiliate-merchant relationship.

Subaffiliates

Subaffiliates are your second-tier affiliates, or affiliates who have joined your program by a referral from an affiliate you already have on board. Some affiliate programs choose to pay both the subaffiliate and the affiliate who sent them to you on a first- and second-tier commission basis. You will learn about the pros and cons of such a setup in the section called "Tuesday: Determine Whether You Need a Two-Tier Program" in Chapter 6, "Week 4: Finalize Payment Models and Cookie Life."

Figure 1.1 reflects a self-description provided by an affiliate who wants to act as a first-tier affiliate, redistributing profit between his subaffiliates. In this case, the merchant does not have a second tier in its program, but the affiliate has set up a system to make this possible. You'll learn more about this later in the book.

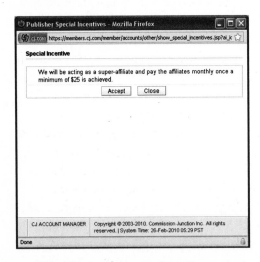

Figure 1.1 Affiliate self-description. They will be considered a first-tier affiliate rather than a subaffiliate.

Superaffiliates

Superaffiliates are affiliates capable of generating a substantial amount of traffic and sales for merchants. I like to define superaffiliates in terms of the following three characteristics, in order of priority:

Maturity Superaffiliates generally manifest high levels of professional and psychological maturity. They are able and confident in what they do.

Potential One such affiliate can turn a whole affiliate program around. From what I have seen in the programs I have managed and also in the statistics reported by other outsourced program managers (OPMs), it is not unusual for one to three such affiliates in the program to drive 50 percent to 70 percent of all affiliate program sales.

Income They are steadily making at least five figures a month in gross profit and are normally involved in affiliate marketing full-time.

Although some people may mention "preferential treatment" as a characteristic of superaffiliates, this factor has no place in the definition. Private offers, co-branded landing pages, and other manifestations of the "preferential treatment" are consequences of superaffiliates being what they are, not determinants.

In addition to the previously mentioned characteristics, it is important to address a topic that I call the "problem of superaffiliate recruitment." One of the questions that is most frequently asked by merchants—both those who have just launched an affiliate program and those who have already been in this business for some time—is, "Where and how can I recruit some of those superaffiliates?"

Superaffiliates are not your easy-to-catch type of fish. It often takes years of relationships development, networking in the right circles, attending the right events, and making contact with the right people before you can recruit a superaffiliate. Additionally, every merchant should be aware of two factors. First, many superaffiliates are often focused on particular niches and do not sign up for programs that are functioning outside their niches of interest. Second, superaffiliates generally partner with affiliate programs that have a proven track record and a solid conversion rate that can be verified through third parties (normally, affiliate networks).

If your affiliate program is new or underdeveloped, you have little to no chance of recruiting an existing superaffiliate. There is, however, a solution.

I believe that any affiliate manager can help a new affiliate grow to a superaffiliate status. If your product/service sells online, it should also sell through the affiliate channel. What you need is either a marketing expert (paid search marketer, SEO specialist, video or mobile marketer, and so on) who would be willing to work with you on a commission basis or a website that already has the traffic you are targeting, and then you need to convince them to try your affiliate program by putting up a link or two on their site. Both of these methods have worked for me in the past. I have seen skilled online marketers, who have never tried an affiliate program before, turn into top affiliate producers, and I have also seen popular content websites that were attracting the same audience as my clients become the best affiliates in the program.

So, even though talking an established superaffiliate into working with your program may be challenging, there is another way, and it's one that successful affiliate program managers have been using for years: A manager can help a newbie become a superaffiliate.

Affiliate Marketing vs. Multilevel Marketing

The amount of business and even e-commerce literature that equates affiliate marketing to multilevel marketing (MLM) is substantial enough for me to address this common misconception in the very first chapter of this book. Paul Ford, for example, in his *Multi-Level Marketing* brochure, states that affiliate marketing is just another term for MLM, a name that appeared because of recent changes in legislation regulating businesses that employ multilevel systems (Real World Real Money, 2010). Shah and Erickson in their *Dictionary of E-Commerce* state that affiliate programs use "a multilevel marketing concept where consumers (affiliates) attract additional consumers" (J.L. Kumar for Anmol, 2003). As explained, affiliates are most often not consumers but marketers and, frequently, professional marketers. Also, the "multilevel marketing concept" is utilized only when a program has the previously described second tier, which allows affiliates either to earn a one-time bounty on every affiliate they refer to the merchant (for example, you may decide to pay your existing affiliates $1 for every new affiliate signup) or be paid a lifetime second-tier commission on all sales generated by the affiliates they refer (for example, a merchant may be paying a 10 percent commission on the first tier and 2 percent on the second tier). It is this last possibility that confuses some people, and it is important to mention that it is extremely unusual for any affiliate program to have more than two commission tiers (most have only one).

In her *Riches in Niches* book, Susan Friedmann warns affiliates about being trapped into MLM type "affiliate" programs, especially those that charge affiliates to join the program (Career Press, 2007). Just as the sign-up fee should immediately raise a red flag in the affiliate's head, so should the presence of multiple tiers.

Another interesting point is being raised by Scott Dacko in *The Advanced Dictionary of Marketing*. Dacko states that the scope of network marketing (also known as *matrix marketing* or *multilevel marketing*) overlaps "with many aspects of affiliate marketing." He writes that the basic approach of both affiliate and MLM is united by "the use of an interconnected system of firms or other individuals outside the organization who essentially act as agents of the firm in facilitating the distribution of the firm's offerings and in securing sales from end customers" (Oxford University Press, 2008). The author is only partially right—both affiliate and MLM use outside people to market a product/service. However, the outside sales force that is "interconnected" in MLM programs is not in any way interlocked in affiliate marketing programs. Additionally, although the primary goal of most MLM schemes is to create (and profit from) pyramids of resellers, the main idea behind affiliate marketing is the creation

Universality of Affiliate Marketing

Affiliate marketing is *universally applicable*, and any online business can be enhanced by running an affiliate program. Since the essence of affiliate marketing is in placing the main emphasis on the actual consumer action that occurred, it is always a no-lose situation for the merchant (unless you pay for clicks, of course). When starting an affiliate program, you may decide to remunerate affiliates for clicks sent to you. This is only one option. In fact, most affiliate programs do *not* do this. Most merchants tie the compensation of affiliates solely to the registered and confirmed sales or leads (fraudulent, duplicate, and other unqualified actions do not count).

If you're hesitant, go to any search engine, and see what your competition is doing. Basic competitive intelligence has never hurt anyone. Chances are that upon querying any major search engine by using a "<your product> affiliate program" key phrase, it will be much easier for you to make your decision.

Another aspect of universality that is important to point out is that affiliate marketing is universal by its very nature. It exists on the crossroads of all other types of online marketing. I frequently underscore that affiliate marketing is not a type or kind of marketing. It is more appropriate to understand it as a special marketing context, the undergirding principle of which is its performance-based remunerating model. This model works with any type of marketing: display, contextual, video, social media, and other types of advertising, as well as search engine marketing (SEM), email marketing, and other methods. The only difference with the pre-affiliate model is that advertisers *post*-pay and do it for the actions of their choice, as opposed to *pre*-paying for the actions of the publisher's choice (for example, you can run an ad on a content publishing network and not pay them by thousands of impressions [CPM] but for the actual conversions that these impressions generate).

Marketing Channels and Types of Affiliates

Since I have touched upon the subject of universality, it seems appropriate to now expand the topic and look at types of affiliates. Successful affiliates seldom exist in a pure form but are more often incorporating several marketing approaches in their strategies. However, for you to better understand how things work, it is helpful to break down the more popular approaches into groups. They all cover an online marketing channel, and I like to split them into the following five groups.

Content Publishing

Affiliates who employ this method build content-saturated websites (as in our example in Figure 1.2) and monetize them by featuring merchants' links on those properties. Links should be understood as all possible types of affiliate links: banners, widgets, text links, video, product links, and so on. The ways in which a content affiliate may advertise a merchant range from in-text links to sidebar ads to separate sections devoted to merchants' banners to even a product selection. Examples of content publishers would include both large portals like Forbes.com and smaller content producers like bloggers.

Figure 1.2 About.com is a classic example of a content publisher.

Couponing

Multiple affiliates are already using this method of promotion, and with projections on online coupon use anticipated to increase further, new coupon websites should be expected to spring up. These affiliates play on the human psychology of trying to find a product at a discounted price if possible. To satisfy this demand, these affiliates put together collections of coupons from different merchants (see Figure 1.3). Since the number of coupons gathered "under one roof" can easily exceed several thousand, the key to success is in the convenient categorization of deals. The more successful coupon affiliates segment their coupons by vertical markets, holidays, lowest price markdowns, expiration dates, types of coupons (for example, deal of the day, free shipping, buy two...get third free), and so on.

Figure 1.3 Example of a coupon affiliate website

Data Feeds

A whole segment of affiliates work with merchants' product feeds. They are generally selling products of multiple merchants "under one roof" (see Figure 1.4), importing product information into their websites via the use of data feeds that merchants make available to them.

A subgroup of *comparison shopping affiliates* should definitely be mentioned here. Adding the convenient function of cross-merchant price checking or feature checking to their online engines, they add value by simplifying the product search and comparison process for the end user.

Figure 1.4 Shopzilla is a data feed–driven website

Email Marketing

Any individual or organization that has a mailing list of targeted prospects who have opted in to be contacted can make an excellent email affiliate. Here, just as is the case with any type of affiliate, it is important to emphasize that merchants safeguard their own brand and reputation by partnering with acceptable marketers. It must be made explicitly clear that advertising considered spamming or unsolicited commercial email (UCE) is unacceptable and will be penalized. Let your emailers know they may use mailings to customers and opt-in e-mail lists only so long as the recipients are already customers or subscribers of the affiliate's services or websites and that recipients have the option to remove themselves from future mailings.

Paid Search

Many PPC marketing experts turn to affiliate marketing to monetize their skills and expertise. Such affiliates bid on merchant-specific keywords and key phrases at Google (Figure 1.5), Yahoo!, Bing, and other search engines, and they send the PPC traffic either directly to the merchant's website or via an in-between page of their own (depending on their own goals and the restrictions imposed by the merchant). In multiple situations, paid search affiliates can replace either the merchant's in-house paid search marketing expert or an outsourced solution. As with every affiliate, the main benefit is that the PPC affiliate invests their own resources and costs the merchant only when the desirable action occurs.

Figure 1.5 Google AdWords ad units

Loyalty Marketing

Loyalty marketing has been around for a while. It became especially popular when airline companies started using it. Airlines would reward their customers with "frequent flyer miles," which are, essentially, points that, once accumulated to a certain threshold, qualify the customer to obtain a free airfare or other product/service. Now, while traditional loyalty marketing aims to "reward loyal customers for making *multiple* purchases" (*Essentials of Marketing*, 2008), loyalty affiliate websites focus on one sale/transaction at a time. Loyalty affiliates (also known as *incentive affiliates*) facilitate the desired user action by offering them an incentive. Cash-back/rebate offers, donations to charitable organizations, and contributions to scholarship funds are by far the most popular forms of incentives used by this type of affiliates (see Figure 1.6). FatWallet.com, BigCrumbs.com, and CashBaq.com are classic examples of incentive affiliate websites. The idea behind such a business model is simple: Share a part of the revenue you receive from the affiliate program with the end consumer.

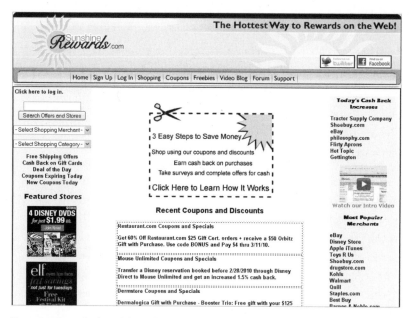

Figure 1.6 Example of a cash-back affiliate

Many merchants and affiliate program managers do not know what loyalty affiliates are and how they operate. This, in some cases, results in low-quality affiliate program performance, whereas in others, it may bring about unwanted customer activity. To illustrate how it works when it does work for the merchant, look at the following example:

- Merchant A pays 10 percent commission on all orders.

- The incentive affiliate offers its visitors a 5 percent cash-back reward.

- Everyone (customer, merchant, and affiliate) is happy.

However, there are instances when partnerships with incentive affiliates do *not* work (and cannot work) for the advertiser/merchant. I'll model three contexts to illustrate such a situation. If one of the following performance-based payment models describes your current or prospective affiliate program, you want to explain in your program's terms and conditions that you do not work with loyalty affiliates and screen affiliate applications carefully to look for sign-up requests from incentive/loyalty affiliates.

Scenario 1

- Merchant B (hosting company) pays 50 percent or $25 (whichever is greater).
- The incentive affiliate offers $15 cash back on all orders.
- Problem: Customer signs up for only one month of hosting at $6.95.

Scenario 2

- Merchant C (diet supplements merchant) pays $35 per sale (including orders for free trials).
- The incentive affiliate offers $20 cash back on all orders (including free trials).
- Problem: Customer orders a free trial.

Scenario 3

- Merchant D (credit relief company) runs a PPL affiliate program paying $20 per lead.
- The incentive affiliate offers $10 cash back to everyone who fills out the form on the merchant's website.
- Problem: Obvious.

The marketing model used by incentive/loyalty affiliates can work for you when your affiliate program's specifics allow for this type of online marketing. In certain contexts—such as the three scenarios—affiliate program managers should keep the incentive affiliates out of their programs. In essence, the problem in all three cases is in the misalignment of merchant and affiliate interests. Loyalty affiliates can work extremely well in scenarios where merchants are paying a percent of sales rather than a bounty or a per-lead amount.

Additionally, in cases when there is room for a merchant's partnerships with incentive affiliates, affiliate program managers should regularly monitor their behavior. Some incentive/loyalty affiliates are known for using cookie-overwriting toolbars, forcing clicks, and engaging in other unethical behavior. I will discuss these problems later in the book to equip you to police and fight such behaviors.

Partnerships with acceptable incentive affiliates can bring additional sales to your affiliate program. Conversely, partnerships with the wrong types of incentive affiliates can do your program much damage. It will simply not grow beyond the level of sales that a handful of unethical affiliates can refer to you, interfering with the performance of your other online marketing channels; in addition, no decent affiliate will want to work with you. This principle applies not only to this particular type of affiliates but to any rogue affiliate in the program (be they a paid search or a loyalty affiliate).

Social Media

This area is quickly gaining popularity among Internet users, and affiliates are happily leveraging this growing acceptance of forums, microblogs, social networks, and other social media channels. Some affiliates are putting together Facebook apps and monetizing them through affiliate marketing, others are tweeting deals on Twitter (with the help of tools like the one in Figure 1.7), while yet others are creating social shopping engines where users can interact with each other, helping each other shop. The more sophisticated and innovative the method is, the more successful the affiliate generally is. Just as it is with other types of affiliates, make sure you partner with marketers that have ethics on their side and are helping you build your brand.

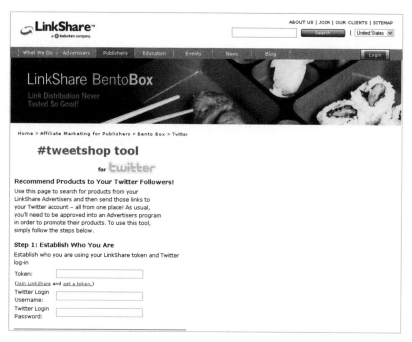

Figure 1.7 TweetShop Tool by LinkShare affiliate network encourages affiliates to market on Twitter.

Video

Online video is a technology that is enthusiastically accepted by end users. However, the number of affiliates using it is still relatively small. If the affiliate program platform allows for it (as in Figure 1.8), you want to provide affiliates with any video creatives (that would track referring clicks and credit commissions when they are due) or allow them to use their own (encouraging them to produce video clips for marketing use). In the least sophisticated scenario, encourage them to at least embed YouTube (or Viddler) videos into the pages of their blogs/websites, complementing the video with search-engine-friendly text and linking it to you through an affiliate link.

Figure 1.8 Video creatives by Legacy Learning Systems offered through ShareASale affiliate network

Any of these methods can be generic or niche-oriented. When an affiliate chooses to be "niche," they specialize in a particular niche (or niches) only, optimizing their website in such a way that it gets most of that targeted traffic. Examples of popular affiliate niches are apparel, shoes, entertainment, books and magazines, and sports.

Note also that my list does not include those I call wanna-be affiliates (banner farms are the best example). Each of the groups has its superaffiliates. You need to understand the way each group works, what problems and challenges they encounter, what factors they are considering while looking for an affiliate program to join, and what they want you as an affiliate program manager to help them with once they are on board with your program.

The famous Peter the Great was known for striving to learn everything first-hand, from the inside out. With this philosophy in mind and disguised as a common man (even though he was the emperor of Russia), he traveled to the Netherlands and England to study shipbuilding and sailing. This knowledge and experience helped him build Russia's first navy, which was instrumental in his wars against the Ottomans and the Swedes. I always encourage affiliate program managers to follow the emperor's example and start affiliate accounts with all major networks. Take your time to try them yourself in the capacity of PPC affiliate, mall affiliate, coupon affiliate, and so on. Try various affiliate tools provided by the networks and third parties. You will gain invaluable experience in the process. Do not quit those accounts. You'll need them later for ongoing competitive intelligence.

Popularity

Affiliate marketing is one of the most powerful and cost-effective customer acquisition tools available to an online merchant today. You decide what commission to pay and pay only when results (sales, leads, and/or clicks) are obvious.

Remember that unlike with other channels of distribution, affiliate marketing hardly has any advertising and marketing expenses involved yet often shows the best return on investment (ROI). With affiliate marketing, you pay only for the desired performance. With most other advertising, however, you get no performance guarantee, and generally the results aren't as good.

If you are not yet utilizing the affiliate marketing channel, I'm glad you're holding this book in your hands. It will teach you the ins and outs of affiliate program management and help you start and run your own affiliate program. I know you won't regret it.

Budget, Payments, and Related Considerations

In this chapter, you'll look at the financial component of your affiliate program, learning the answers to such questions as these: What investment will be required to get it all rolling? What compensation models are most popular, and how are other advertisers using them? What happens if invalid sales/leads get referred?

Additionally, this chapter will touch on the interaction between affiliate marketing and other online marketing channels you may be utilizing.

Chapter Contents

Budgeting

Performance-Based Models

Interaction with Other Channels

Reversal Policies and Related Considerations

Budgeting

Like any marketing endeavor, your affiliate marketing program requires a budget. In comparison with the majority of other types of online advertising, affiliate marketing generally requires a significantly smaller budget to get things rolling; however, it does require one. Additionally, besides the up-front expenses, you'll want to be aware of other ongoing costs.

The following is a breakdown of expenditure points you'll want to be aware of right from the planning phase. You can handle these tasks in-house or outsource them.

Platform You will have to pay for the platform on which your affiliate program will be run. There are essentially two options: going with an affiliate network or going with affiliate program tracking/management software. This chapter will cover the differences, similarities, pros, and cons of each, but at this time, you need to know that you will either be charged some setup fees or have a choice of one-time or monthly fees, depending on what platform you go with.

Creative Inventory You will want to put together a creative inventory for your program. These will be your banners, text links, and possibly even Flash and video creatives. Out of all of these, only creating text links does not require many additional skills. As far as graphics and video go, you may have to hire someone to do this for you. If so, this will be an additional investment.

Product Feed If you are an online retailer, you will want to supply your affiliates with a detailed product feed. If, on the other hand, you will be using your affiliate program to generate leads, you'll want to experiment with different landing pages. Depending on your in-house capabilities, this may cost you something in programming or web design and conversion optimization fees.

Management Most importantly, you will need to have someone manage your affiliate program (from its announcement and the recruitment of first affiliates through the ongoing policing of affiliate compliance with your program's rules, as well as the activation of stagnant affiliates, the ongoing work of keeping the program fresh and attractive, and other responsibilities that we will look at in later chapters). Not managing your program is not an option. You can have one of your in-house staff handle this or hire an outsourced affiliate program manager to work on your program.

The sum total of all four expenditure points can vary anywhere from a few hundred to a few thousand dollars. In the past, I have launched programs with up-front investments of as little as $300 on some and as much as $9,000 on others. The maintenance of your affiliate program will encompass supporting the latter three points and may range from anywhere between a couple hundred to tens of thousands of dollars. Again, as mentioned earlier, *much* will depend on your (or your company's) own involvement in the affiliate program's setup, launch, and ongoing management.

Performance-Based Models

In Chapter 1, "Understanding Affiliate Marketing," I defined affiliate marketing as performance-based marketing where your affiliate partner gets paid only when a qualified action takes place. Let's take a look at the remuneration models that are most frequently employed in affiliate marketing relationships. The models are tied to action-based payment scenarios and can be used with virtually any type of online marketing. I will also briefly describe the possible actions that you, as an advertiser, may choose to target.

The following are the four main affiliate compensation models in more detail; each is illustrated with an example to make things even more practical:

Pay per Sale/Cost per Sale (PPS/CPS) This is the most widely used affiliate payment model, used by up to 80 percent of affiliate programs (AffStat, 2007). A good parallel would be looking at this model through a revenue share perspective. Just as you would pay your salespeople a percentage of the sale that they drive in, you pay your affiliates a percentage of the *sale*. See Figure 2.1 for an example of a PPS program.

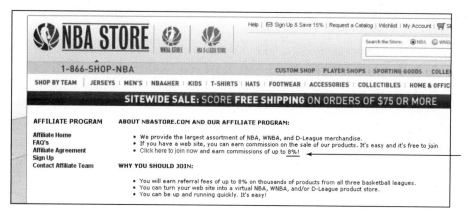

Figure 2.1 NBAStore.com's affiliate sign-up page

Pay per Lead/Cost per Lead (PPL/CPL) According to the previously quoted AffStat report, close to one-fifth of all affiliate programs use a PPL compensation model exclusively or in combination with other models (when there is a combination, it normally adds the PPS method into the mix). You can find an offline example of this in the tourism business. Travel agents and bus drivers frequently get a bounty for getting you to one store over the other. Sometimes it is sales-based; however, with more targeted *leads*, it is a flat amount paid for every customer (or prospective customer). Another example of how it works in the offline space is in the medical industry, where doctors receive payment for suggesting that their patients order complementary services or products. This is exactly the way it works in PPL affiliate programs too. See an example in Figure 2.2.

Figure 2.2 QualitySmith.com's affiliate sign-up page

Pay per Click/Cost per Click (PPC/CPC) This particular payment model was dying out (in great degree because of a large volume of fraud) until eBay revived it with its quality click pricing (QCP) in August 2009 (Figure 2.3). This CPC model was called to do something previously unprecedented: to "take into account the *incremental* value of that traffic to eBay, i.e., whether a sale happened as a direct result of the publisher's actions" (eBay Partner Network, "Announcing Quality Click Pricing," 2009; italics mine) and reward the affiliate accordingly.

eBay's QCP model is quite different from traditional CPC. eBay has developed a system where the per-click rate changes daily based on the value of affiliate-referred traffic to the company. However, to date this is the only major merchant that uses this model. Things have been different at the dawn of the industry, but at the time of this writing very few affiliate programs employ CPC.

Unless you have a good system of click fraud prevention in place, I do not recommend making the CPC model available for all affiliates in your affiliate program. Choose from the previous two options instead.

Pay per Call (PPCall) This is still a fairly new technology that serves the purpose of generating hot leads—those that are either calling the advertiser directly or leaving their phone number for an immediate callback. This marketing vertical is developing quickly, and PPCall advertising spending already comprises several billion dollars. Extending this payment model into the affiliate marketing realm, companies such as RingRevenue (Figure 2.4) and KeyMetric bridge the gap between the online and offline, making it possible for affiliates to drive phone leads too.

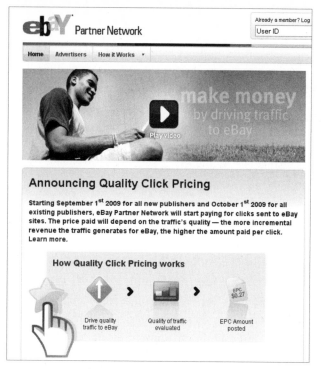

Figure 2.3 How eBay's quality click pricing works

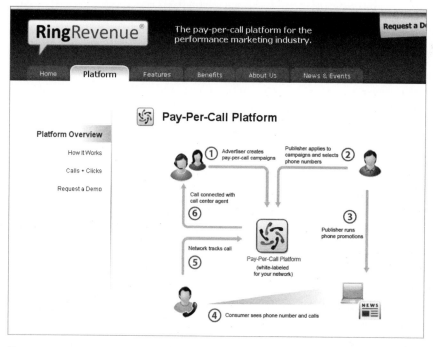

Figure 2.4 How the RingRevenue performance-based platform works

As mentioned previously, advertisers may successfully combine more than one model within one affiliate program, and PPCall is a perfect addition to most CPS and CPL affiliate programs, filling in a "phone number leak" that most affiliates will have a problem with. If you have a phone number listed on your website and it is displayed to affiliate-referred visitors, they could call in and place their order over the phone, bypassing the order confirmation webpage (which triggers affiliate payout), which means the affiliate will get no commission. When uncommissionable activity like this happens, affiliates say that the traffic "leaks." I will discuss this in greater detail in future chapters, but at this stage just know that PPCall is an excellent solution to phone leaks.

Interaction with Other Channels

On more than one occasion I have heard marketers and web analysts bring up the subject of "conflict" between affiliate marketing and other online marketing channels. The primary area of concern has always been the attribution of online sales. What is it that *really* helps close a sale or land this or that prospect? Is it a paid search campaign, an organic listing, advertising through a comparison shopping website, or a banner with a compelling message? Or has an affiliate presold the customer skillfully and enticingly enough for them to place the order through?

- First, it is important to reemphasize that affiliate marketing is not a marketing "channel" but, rather, a way of remunerating a marketer (based on performance). Hence, affiliate marketing really exists on the crossroads of a number of online marketing channels and works with nearly all of them.

- Second, why does it have to be an "either/or" question and not a "both/and" one instead? Just as a merchant's own paid search campaigns work well alongside organic traffic, so can affiliate paid search, inclusion in affiliate shopping comparison websites, and content websites beautifully complement other merchant's online campaigns.

- Third, I believe such debates to be akin to a debate between an existentialist and a utopian. The latter believes in building a perfect human society, while the former focuses on the existence of each individual, believing each person to be fully responsible for giving their own life meaning and making the most out of it. Not widening this allegory any more than we have to, I believe that in the question of online marketing attribution, it seems that either side can be argued at any time. Although we should definitely strive for appropriate remuneration of every marketer and channel involved in the presale process, the perfectibility of online attribution has yet to be achieved. There are various solutions in the works (see "Alternative Compensation Models" part of Chapter 16, "Week 2: Master Affiliate Program Analytics"), but not one is universally accepted yet.

So, instead of arguing, it seems sensible to follow the example of the larger brands and strive for the widest online presence possible, reaping the fruit ripened from an array of marketing channels. You can think of your search engine optimization efforts as fertilizing the soil, social media marketing and branding as the rain, while reviews, comparison shopping, paid search, coupons, loyalty marketing, and other channels—be they handled with or without an affiliate marketing payment model in place—as the sun that brings about the desired outcome, which is that sale or lead you are ultimately seeking to land. Utilize *all*, measuring and improving all at all times.

In 2008, as I was working on my book *Online Shopping Through Consumers' Eyes*, analyzing the responses of survey takers, I found one particular distribution of votes of interest (Figure 2.5). I asked, when shopping for products requiring ongoing replenishing (such as grocery, ink, bank checks, and so on) and receiving satisfactory service, would you still compare your retailer's offer to other offers next time you need their product? The vast majority of the survey respondents said they will still shop around regardless of the quality of service received with their first purchase.

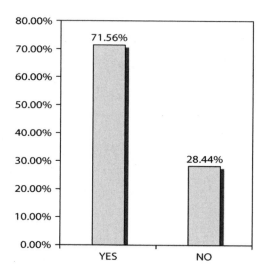

Figure 2.5 Some 72% of satisfied customers would still shop around before committing to a repeat purchase.

In a trading environment as aggressively competitive as the Web, consumers who receive satisfactory service once still compare you with the competition before they add *your* product to their shopping cart next time. No wonder the Wal-Marts and the Best Buys of the online world are employing every possible advertising opportunity available, especially affiliate marketing.

Reversal Policies and Related Considerations

In most cases, affiliates are being credited their commission as soon as a qualified action takes place. What about cases when an order gets canceled or a merchant sells something that is no longer in stock?

First, make sure it is not possible for the customer to order something that is out of stock. Once it sells out, it should be removed from your website *and* your affiliate data feed, or at least the order function should be disabled. Second, the short answer to the previous question is no, you will not have to pay affiliate commissions on orders that either get canceled by the customer or are in any other way invalid for you. In fact, it is a good practice to clarify in your affiliate program's terms and conditions that you compensate affiliates for valid sales/orders/subscriptions/leads, defining what exactly *valid* means for you.

Normally affiliate transactions are being voided (or reversed) when any of the following behaviors are registered:

Customer Behavior
- Payment authorization failed
- Fraudulent sale
- Returned order or unclaimed shipment
- Repeated/duplicate order
- Canceled order

Affiliate Behavior
- Fraudulent transaction
- Test transaction
- Self-referral (if you've specified in your Affiliate Program Agreement that you do not pay commission on self-referred leads/orders)

Merchant Behavior/Circumstances
- Test transaction
- Order nonfulfillment

The previous lists may be longer depending on your affiliate program agreement/restrictions, but they cover the most popular reasons for reversals. Beware that an affiliate may request that you provide proof of these issues. Do not leave such affiliate requests unattended, because this will undermine their trust in you and the transparency of your affiliate program. Also, when you place a test transaction at your website and you do not want to test a particular affiliate link, make sure you have cleared your cookies before placing the order. Otherwise, a commission may be credited to the affiliate account whose link you clicked last.

A word of warning is also necessary here: Do not abuse your right to void sales. Some online industries—hosting, for example—are sadly known for a large volume of reversed affiliate transactions. Excessive numbers of such reversals often breed suspicion in affiliates' minds, thus compromising trust, which is a cornerstone of any merchant–affiliate relation.

Duplicate Orders

Duplicate customer orders mean just that—two identical orders placed in a row by the same customer. This happens rarely, and when an identical duplicate takes place, you do not pay the commission twice.

Also, merchants new to affiliate marketing sometimes confuse duplicate orders with something else. At the time of my writing of this book, an etailer who was setting up an affiliate program emailed me:

> I wanted to see if you knew what happened if a shopper has more than one cookie from different affiliates and then makes a purchase. I think this would be very likely to happen and was wondering who would get the commission, etc.

This is actually a very good question for someone new to affiliate marketing to ask. The way things work with virtually all affiliate networks (and affiliate program software applications) is that the *last* referring affiliate's cookie overwrites the previous affiliate's one. So, the previously mentioned scenario is generally impossible. Simply put, the end user has only one affiliate cookie on their computer, and it is always the cookie set by the last affiliate that referred the shopper to you. This rule is also known as "the last cookie wins" rule.

Locking Periods and Lock Dates

To ensure there is clarity on when exactly the credited payment becomes irreversible, locking periods are set. When setting up your program on affiliate networks, you will be able to choose when exactly you want affiliate commissions to lock.

Let's look at two examples. The first one will come from ShareASale (SAS). On this particular affiliate network, the lock date is always the 20th of the following month, and the merchants can see the lock date for every transaction in their reports (see Figure 2.6).

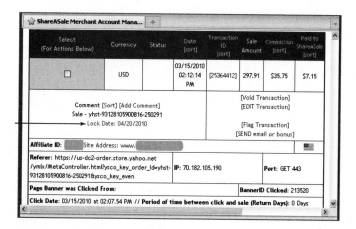

Figure 2.6 ShareASale transaction recorded on merchant's end

Affiliates, on the other hand, see both the lock date and the transaction status (Processing or Locked). In Figure 2.7, you can see how the previously quoted transaction will look on the affiliate end.

Figure 2.7 ShareASale transaction recorded on affiliate's end

For the second example, let's look at Commission Junction (CJ). On this network, affiliates see the lock date/period data in each particular program's terms. Figure 2.8 shows you how it looks in Overstock.com's affiliate program.

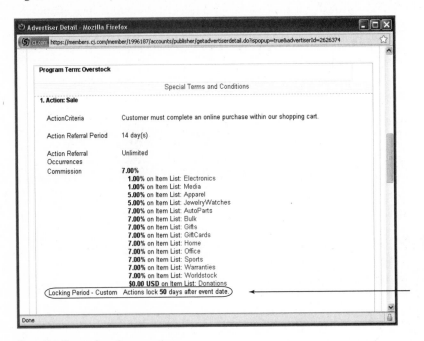

Figure 2.8 Overstock.com's program terms

Whether it's called a locking period or a lock date, we're talking about the same thing—the period of time that merchants give themselves to review and make any necessary adjustments to affiliate-referred transactions. As mentioned, affiliate commissions can get voided for a whole number of reasons, but once the locking period has passed or the lock date has come, the commission gets permanently locked in the affiliate account, and the merchant can no longer do anything to that transaction (voiding, editing, and so on).

Most affiliate networks allow merchants to choose the length of time within which they want to be able to edit/void affiliate commissions (based on how quickly they can verify the validity of sales, on their experience with returns, or on whatever other reasons may influence the commission reversal/adjustment). For example, the CJ's default locking period/date is the 10th of the following month, whereas on SAS it's the 20th of the following month. However, as evident from Figure 2.8, merchants may also choose custom lengths for those locking periods, and Overstock.com has decided to tie it to the number of days past the order placement.

Again, although it is fair for advertisers/merchants to have locking periods, you want to be extremely careful not abuse this right. Do what makes business sense to you, but please keep in mind that longer locking periods are less preferred by affiliates because they cause payment delays.

Consider a Nonreversal Policy

Some merchants, regardless of the vertical they operate in, decide to have a nonreversal affiliate policy. Some void only those transactions resulting from fraudulent activity (Figure 2.9), while others do not void any at all (Figure 2.10).

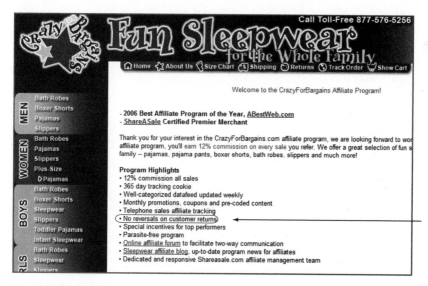

Figure 2.9 CrazyForBargains.com does not reverse commissions when customers return products.

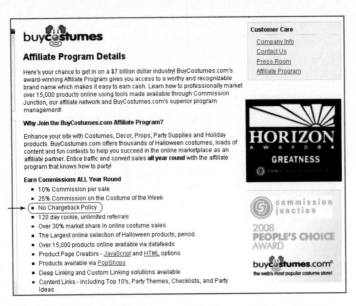

Figure 2.10 BuyCostumes.com's "No Chargeback Policy" makes the company stand out.

I greatly commend such an approach. After all, you are getting a customer referred to you, and how you satisfy them is out of your affiliate's control. Having a nonreversal policy will really make you stand out as an affiliate-friendly program. You don't have to do it, but it is definitely something worth considering.

Month 1: Pre-Launch Research and Analysis

II

In preparation for entering the exciting world of affiliate marketing, we have a lot of ground to cover. You'll want to make sure you have thoroughly studied the competitive landscape, understood how tracking and reporting works, and decided on the program management route to choose. In the course of the following four weeks, you'll get all of these sorted, as well as finalize the core structure of your future affiliate program.

Week 1: Perform Competitive Marketing Analysis

You will spend this week analyzing the past, the present, and the future, arriving at conclusions of what weaknesses need to be strengthened, what advantages should be used to your business's further benefit, and how the addition of the affiliate program to your marketing mix will help you advance in your battle with competitors.

This will be achieved by using a Strengths, Weaknesses, Opportunities, Trends, Threats (SWOTT) analysis. You will learn how to present your case to the boss or client. Finally, planning for the future, you will also look at developing a robust competitive intelligence strategy for your company.

3

Chapter Contents

Monday: Understand SWOTT Analysis

Strengths, Weaknesses, Opportunities, Threats (SWOT) analysis is a widely used method of strategic planning, formulated on the basis of research performed at the Stanford Research Institute in the 1960s and 70s. The method was originally developed to better understand situations in which corporate planning failed. You can think of this analysis as a doctor. There are two things both are called to do: Diagnose the situation and prescribe solutions.

Regardless of its seemingly old age, SWOT is still being used as an efficient tool for understanding and making decisions in various business contexts, particularly those where new business ideas are introduced. Affiliate marketing is still very much a "new business idea" for many businesses. So, it will be of great benefit to look at the possibility of starting an affiliate program through the prism of an overall SWOT breakdown— analyzing your business' current strengths, weaknesses, opportunities, and threats.

I know you're wondering about that second *T* in this section's title. No, it's not a typo but rather an addition to the model. The second *T* stands for Trends—an extremely important factor for online businesses that exist in a dynamically changing environment. I will discuss trends when I talk about opportunities.

Before you start your SWOTT analysis, I'd like to warn you about two mistakes that marketing professionals frequently commit when working their way through such analyses. The first mistake is to make the process akin to an academic exercise of classifying data and collecting information. The second problem stems from the first one and is the boiling down of the process to a list without serious empirical consideration of the issues you're working on. Right from the start, you should approach your SWOTT analysis with a desire to make it productive and beneficial to your business. So, in the course of the next three days, look at everything you discover through a prism of practical application. How will you be able to use this for the benefit of your online business? What can you change in your business to turn a strength into a competitive advantage and a weakness into an opportunity? Stay focused and grounded. Flee from generalizations and theory. Think practice! SWOTT is all about developing a competitive advantage, and in this task, thinking pragmatically is a must.

Let's take ShoeBuy.com's setup, for a general (and simplified) example. Its strengths include the website's ease of use (navigation, images, one-page checkout, and so on), the breadth of selection, offers such as a "free shipping both ways" (Figure 3.1), an aggressive coupon strategy, and impeccable customer service.

Figure 3.1 ShoeBuy's "free shipping both ways" offer in the header of the website

A possible weakness is that it does not have traditional retail outlets where customers can buy shoes, but the "free shipping both ways" offer (in other words, free shipping to the customer and return shipping covered by the merchant as well) neutralizes that "weakness." An opportunity for growth is to sell handbags (which are commonly purchased with ladies' shoes) and accessories, and the site is actively exploring this area. Its threats are the direct competitors—Zappos.com being the major one, which also offers free shipping and free returns and aggressively utilizes various online media for promotion. On the affiliate side, the ShoeBuy.com affiliate program looks more attractive both as far as the basic terms and performance statistics go (Figure 3.2).

Advertiser	3 Month EPC (USD)	7 Day EPC (USD)	Network Earnings	Sale	Lead	Click					
Shoebuy.com » View Links » View Products	$31.37	$38.37		Sale: 17.00% USD Performance Incentive							
Zappos.com » View Links » View Products							$28.55	$34.65		Sale: 5.00% - 12.00% USD Performance Incentive

Figure 3.2 In comparison with the Zappos.com affiliate program, ShoeBuy.com's program offers better commission rates and has better EPC (affiliate earnings metric).

To reiterate, while performing your own SWOTT analysis over the next few days—looking at things through the prism of adding an affiliate marketing campaign to your already-existing bouquet of marketing endeavors and seeing whether you can capitalize on the untapped opportunity—you want to *focus on the practical*.

In addition to this, you want to keep the following guidelines in mind:

Search Extensively for Competitors This entails looking not only at the major brand competitors but at everyone else who may be involved in the space (or who may get involved in it).

Collaborate with Other Functional Areas When performing your analysis within the organization (as an in-house employee), share information and perspectives across different departments. Cross-pollination of ideas often results in more creative and innovative solutions.

Examine Issues from the Customer's Perspective This is especially important in the transparent context of electronic commerce. Look at customers' beliefs, perceptions, preferences, and tendencies.

Look for Causes, Not Characteristics When preparing your analysis, do not simply list characteristics of internal or external environments; dig down to the true causes for the strengths, weaknesses, opportunities, and threats.

Separate Internal Issues from External Issues If an issue would exist even if the firm did not exist, the issue should be classified as external. This is extremely important to understand, because affiliate marketing will exist regardless of whether any given online merchant decides to utilize it. So, make sure you separate marketing options, strategies, and tactics from opportunities in your analysis. There will be overlaps, but underscore the undependability.

Keeping all of this in mind, you are now ready to dive into the fun of observation and analysis.

Tuesday: Identify Strengths and Weaknesses

Today you will look at the first two parts of the SWOTT analysis: strengths and weaknesses.

Strengths

While looking at all five components of the SWOTT analysis, you should remember that the goal of this exercise is to analyze the merchant's capabilities against the realities of both the immediate business/competitive environment and the broader context of ecommerce. The end goal of your analysis is to come up with a plan of how to gear your strategy based on the findings of your SWOTT analysis.

While working on the list of the company's (and its online property's) current strengths, you may find the following questions of help:

- What are your major sources of revenue and profit, and how actively are using the Internet for sales/distribution?
- In what ways are you superior to competitors (that is, what are your competitive advantages)?
- How strong is your brand name (brand awareness)?
- What about your reputation among customers?
- How competitive is your pricing? What about quality?
- What are your unique selling points (UPIs)?
- What about product/services selection (in comparison with competitors)?
- What works especially well in your marketing?
- Are you staffed with online marketers? If so, what type (paid search, SEO, landing page optimization specialists, email marketers, and so on)?
- What other experience, knowledge, tools, or technologies do you possess in-house?
- Does your company/personnel possess the ability to adapt and change?
- Is the company's personnel flexible and open to learning?
- How efficiently are you currently utilizing the online media for marketing?

Weaknesses

Looking at weaknesses, be objective. Don't try to disguise anything, and remember that the weaknesses you discover aren't bad. They produce opportunities, and you must get a clear understanding of what you're not doing right, or what you're not doing at all, to be able to look at things realistically and constructively.

Also, the absence of strengths mentioned earlier may be viewed as weaknesses, and you want to automatically include the negative answers to any of the questions in the strengths list in the weaknesses list. Conversely, an absence of a weakness may be a considerable strength. So, it is absolutely fine if you find yourself working on the two lists simultaneously.

In addition to the previous, here are some further questions to establish your weaknesses:

- What gaps in capabilities do you have?

- What are your vulnerabilities?

- What do your customers complain most frequently about?

- What marketing channels you're utilizing show the lowest return on investment?

- In what other areas is your business not able to recover costs?

- What are the company's current biggest expenditures?

- Is your business losing out to competitors on the technology front, especially when it comes to online marketing?

Wednesday: Evaluate Opportunities, Trends, and Threats

Let's look at the opportunities and trends, as well as the threats (internal and/or external) that exist.

Opportunities and Trends

Nearly all opportunities in online marketing (and ecommerce in general) will be tied to the trends that exist in the market. It is because of this reason that I am not separating the two, providing you with one list of questions for both:

- Are there any unfulfilled customer needs to which you aren't attending?

- What new technologies are you not utilizing? (See Figure 3.3.)

- Are there any regulations that have been loosened, resulting in an opportunity? (If the answer is negative, jot this one down for the list of threats).

- Are you tapping into the international market?

- How geotargeted are your marketing campaigns?

- Are you catering to the different ethnic markets? (See Figure 3.4.)

- Are there any emerging trends that fit your company's strengths?

- What are the current online marketing trends, and how is your company positioned to take on those trends?

- Are there any areas that your competitors have not covered (even if it requires innovation)?

- What favorable circumstances are you now facing?

Figure 3.3 Besides the already-traditional "Email to a friend" sharing function, Macy's also encourages such forms of social-media sharing as Facebook, MySpace, and Twitter.

Figure 3.4 Skype offers extensive affiliate creative inventory in foreign languages (in French, Russian, German, Spanish, and other languages)

Threats

It is now time to dig into the threats that any of the internal or external circumstances/realities may be causing to your company in general and its online presentation in particular. The following questions should help you compile your list of threats. Just remember to stay focused and as objective as possible. Your ultimate goal is to make your company better, and this phase is similar to the work of a surgeon. Just as a surgeon who works on removing a life-threatening tumor, you may have to induce pain in order to heal the areas that may otherwise kill your business.

- Have there been any recent shifts in consumer tastes that resulted in consumers drifting away from the company's products/services?
- Have any new competitors emerged recently?
- What threats do the current competitors pose?
- Are there any existing or expected trade barriers?
- Are there any other external trends that amplify any of your weaknesses?
- What obstacles do you face?
- What is your competition doing?
- Are any changes in the online space threatening your position?

Once you are done with the list, you are ready to move on to the final phase of the analysis, where you will put all pieces of this big SWOTT puzzle together.

Thursday: Present Your Analysis to Your Boss/Client

Whether you are an in-house marketing person who has been commissioned by the company to look into a possibility of starting an affiliate program or you are an out-sourced agency or affiliate marketing consultant, there will come a time for you to present the results of your analysis to your boss or prospective client.

Now that you have the SWOTT analysis in your hands, you want to present your case for the introduction of the affiliate program into your marketing mix, being guided by the following five principles:

- Build on your strengths.
- Resolve weaknesses.
- Exploit opportunities.
- Take advantage of trends.
- Avoid and/or mitigate threats.

The most traditional way to present a SWOT analysis is a SWOT matrix, which represents a table with two rows and two columns. With the addition of Trends into our analysis, you want to add trends into the Opportunities cell, making the final product look like Table 1.1.

I know that I sound like there is no possibility that your analysis will speak *against* the introduction of an affiliate program into the company's marketing mix. That's because if you're doing business online, there really is no possibility that an addition of an affiliate program won't benefit your marketing efforts.

▶ **Table 1.1** SWOTT matrix

	Strengths	Weaknesses
Opportunities and Trends	Pursue opportunities and trends that fit well with your strengths.	Overcome weaknesses, exploiting opportunities and responding to trends.
Threats	Identify ways for the company to use its strengths in response to vulnerabilities and threats.	Put together a plan of defense to make the company resilient to threats.

Adapted from http://quickmba.com/strategy/swot/

I am a firm believer that any business can benefit by launching an affiliate program. What have you got to lose if you'll be paying only for performance? In 2006 when writing *A Practical Guide to Affiliate Marketing*, I narrowed things down to online businesses only: "Any online business will surely be enhanced by running an affiliate program. Since the essence of affiliate marketing is in placing the main emphasis on the actual sale that occurred, it is always a no-lose situation for the merchant."

There has been much progress since then. The performance marketing (or affiliate marketing) industry has gone well beyond online businesses. Pay-per-call platforms like that of RingRevenue now also track mobile (for example, Offermobi network) and even offline (billboards, print, and so on) campaigns, while companies like Impact Radius (Figure 3.5) allow the performance-based models to work both with online channels and with such traditional media channels as TV, radio, and press.

It still goes without saying that any online business can benefit from affiliate marketing (because it's not a marketing method but a way to make multiple methods work via performance-centered models), but now brick-and-mortar business are also highly encouraged to look into performance marketing.

Although the SWOTT analysis is not a mandatory step for the prelaunch phase of your affiliate marketing campaign, it will help you get a complete picture of where your business currently is and where it should be going. As pointed out earlier, affiliate marketing is not a type of marketing (such as social-media marketing, PPC, content, display, SEO, email marketing, and so on) but rather a name for the type of business relationship/partnership between a marketer and an online (or now even offline) business being marketed—one where the former is being paid by the latter based on the performance/conversions driven in. With an affiliate program, you can successfully patch the gaps found through your SWOTT analysis. For example, if you've discovered that your competitors are actively utilizing comparison shopping engines and you're not, you can partner with many of them through affiliate marketing relationships. So, the analysis is a good step to undertake to develop an educated approach to fixing what needs to be fixed and strengthening what you're already strong in.

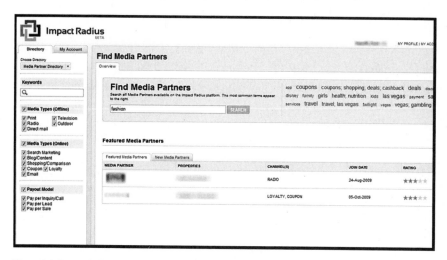

Figure 3.5 Impact Radius's media partner directory

Friday: Develop a Competitive Intelligence Strategy

Examining your strengths and weaknesses and analyzing opportunities, trends, and threats is only the beginning. Now you want to turn this into an ongoing exercise, and the best approach is to develop a competitive intelligence strategy.

From all the definitions of *competitive intelligence*, I like Christopher West's version in his book *Competitive Intelligence* best of all. He eloquently defined it as "the process by which companies inform themselves about every aspect of their rivals' activities and performance" (Palgrave Macmillan, 2001).

There are multiple areas in which you will want to monitor your competitors. These include, but are not limited to, the following:

- Technologies used
- Product/service features
- Price levels
- Customer-oriented promos, discounts, and rebates
- Distribution channels

- Delivery methods

- Perceptions they create for their brand

- Means of creating perceptions online

- Online marketing methods employed

- Affiliate-oriented promos

- Affiliate program specifics (commission, cookie life, performance incentives, and so on)

Online competitive intelligence is actually quite a bit of fun and easily automatable too. Although there will be things that you will want to do "by hand," many processes can be automated.

Competitive intelligence is also an ongoing task. It is not something that you can afford to do once a week or even every other day of the week. You have to monitor in *real time* (minute by minute), keeping a close eye on every step your competitors (or those affiliated with them in any way) make. How? Read on.

Join Affiliate Programs

One of the easiest ways to spy on your competitors (even before you have started your own affiliate program) is to join their affiliate programs as an affiliate. It may mean you'd have to create a basic website (or at least a blog), but the time you'll put into this will pay off with knowledge otherwise unattainable.

I always encourage merchants to open affiliate accounts on all major affiliate networks and then join their competitor's affiliate programs, as well as affiliate programs of any related merchants. If the receipt of their affiliate newsletter is contingent on a subscription, make sure you subscribe to it too. Also join the in-house affiliate programs your competitors run, requesting to be notified of any and all promotions. As with any kind of marketing, competition analysis and monitoring is an essential part of good affiliate marketing. Monitor what your competitors do, and ensure that your future affiliate program offers at least equally attractive (or preferably, much more attractive!) affiliate conditions, promotions, bonuses, prizes, commission increases, and so on.

Follow Competitor in Other Ways

Besides joining the competitor's affiliate program and following their affiliate newsletters and promotions, follow them in all other ways possible. These would include, while not be limited to, the following:

- Register with them as a customer, and sign up to receive their offers and newsletters.

- Join their Facebook fan page.

- Follow them on Twitter.

Keep a close eye on what they're doing via these channels and methods to see where your company has room for improvements.

Set Up Automatic Monitoring

A number of online tools will help you monitor your competitors' brands free of charge:

- Google Alerts
- Social Media Firehose (by Yahoo!)
- TweetBeep
- BuzzMonitor
- Collecta.com
- BackType
- Omgili
- boardreader
- Whos Talkin
- Social Mention
- BlogPulse

All of these work according to the same pattern: You set up the tool to monitor a particular word or key phrase, and every time the monitored word or phrase is mentioned online, the tool notifies you of the mention with the link to the page where it may be found. Looking at Google Alerts (Figure 3.6), for example, you can select your search terms, choose the type of online media you want to monitor (everything, or something as specific as news, blogs, forums, or video), select the frequency of how often you want to receive your alerts, select the maximum number of alerts to be included in the email, and select the delivery address.

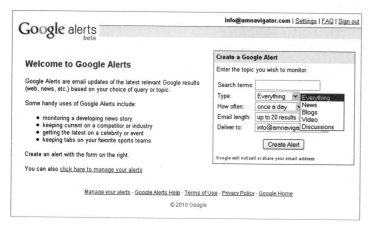

Figure 3.6 Google Alerts setup screen

In conclusion, it is important to mention that all of these tools can and should also be used to monitor *your own* brand online. Many businesses (both online and offline ones) have yet to understand the importance of monitoring what is being said about them online (in reviews and on microblogging platforms, blogs, forums, and so on) and reacting to the mentions of their brand. Besides the obvious benefits, such an approach greatly facilitates the finding of new marketing opportunities.

Employ Traffic Monitoring Tools

Among the traffic measuring tools that you want to employ in your research, I recommend utilizing the following:

- Alexa
- Compete
- Hitwise
- Quantcast

Out of these four, Compete and Quantcast get my highest votes.

Compete (Figure 3.7) gives a lot of great analytic information on competitors. Besides such generic data as the number of unique visitors (UVs) and their time on site, it evaluates visitor attention, provides complete demographics for a desired time period, tracks all subdomains (on more advanced packages), analyzes referral sites, provides data on "search share" of each keyword that leads to a site, lets you see audience profiles (if the analyzed merchant added CompeteXL tracking code to their site), and is packed with other invaluable data. When skillfully used, the data that Compete provides is capable of driving a significant increase in a merchant's conversions (see the "Compete: Exemplary Competitive Intelligence Solution" sidebar).

Quantcast (Figure 3.8), on the other hand, allows you to have not merely a bird's-eye view of your competitors' traffic but also provides insight into the site's demographics (gender, age, household income, ethnicity, head of household education, and children in household), audience keywords, and "siteographics" (other sites an audience frequents, which helps you analyze life styles and behavioral traits).

Analyzing the competitor's traffic will help you arrive at conclusions about who to target more closely, as well what type of offers to push and what websites to partner with.

Figure 3.7 Compete's site profile for Target.com

Figure 3.8 Quantcast's summary report for CafeMom.com

Compete: Exemplary Competitive Intelligence Solution

Compete is a good example of an online intelligence solution. It offers a number of robust competitive intelligence tools (all in one online interface) to help online businesses improve their marketing "based on the online behavior of millions of consumers." One such tool is their referral analytics dashboard, which allows you to perform detailed analysis of nearly any website's referral traffic. The graphic shown here gives a vivid example portraying how Compete shows data about who is driving traffic to Netflix.

This gives you only a general look at things. When you go to the Traffic Details tab, you may actually review details of all 32,250+ websites that refer traffic to Netflix.

With the help of tools like these, merchants may effectively uncover your competitors' online strategies, monitor and analyze performance of their websites, and consequently benchmark their own online performance against immediate competitors and plan their marketing campaigns to be equipped with invaluable competitive intelligence data.

Although some of the previously mentioned intelligence data may not seem to be directly connected to affiliate marketing programs, it is. Everything that may help you improve your customer experience and improve conversion is connected with your affiliate program. You may have the best affiliate offer in the world (highest commission payouts, longest cookie life, and so on), but it won't matter if your website converts poorly. This is why I'm advising you not only to run a SWOTT analysis but also to develop a competitive intelligence plan.

Week 2: Understanding Tracking and Reporting

Now is the time to learn about what will be the very skeleton of your affiliate program: the platform on which it will rest and operate, as well as the exact way everything will function. In this chapter, you will look into the different types of affiliate program platforms available to merchants, analyze payment options, and also explore cookies and their role in affiliate marketing.

Chapter Contents

Monday: Evaluate Affiliate Networks
Tuesday: Understand CPA Networks and How They Work
Wednesday: Assess In-House Solutions
Thursday: Analyze Payment Options
Friday: Understand the Importance of Cookies

Monday: Evaluate Affiliate Networks

This chapter starts with a look into the types of platforms you may run your affiliate program on. Some call these *affiliate program management solutions* or *affiliate tracking platforms*, but neither of these really gives an accurate description of what these platforms are. Any solid affiliate marketing solution will not only help you work with your affiliates or track the program's performance but will provide for an array of other important elements. So, I will be calling these *platforms* or *affiliate marketing solutions*.

As I mentioned in Chapter 2, "Budget, Payments, and Related Considerations," when it comes to affiliate program platforms, the choice essentially comes down to two options: Go with an affiliate network or acquire some affiliate marketing program software so you can run your affiliate program in-house. Let's turn to affiliate networks first.

Affiliate Networks

Affiliate networks are essentially mediators connecting affiliates with affiliate programs and providing tracking and maintenance services—such as hosting creatives and data feeds, providing technical support, providing reporting and marketing tools for affiliates and merchants, taking care of affiliate payments, and so on—to the latter. They are sometimes also called *affiliate solution providers* (ASPs), because no additional software is required for the merchant to run an affiliate program if they decide to use an affiliate network. During the whole process of setting up an affiliate program with a network, you are generally guided through the setup stages, which include but are not limited to implementing tracking (frequently with close technical support from the network's technical staff), uploading your program agreement, adding creatives, and adding program description, approval, and denial emails. Figure 4.1 gives you a general idea of the process.

Figure 4.1 ShareASale—one of the world's most popular affiliate networks, heavily focused on small and medium businesses (SMBs).

Affiliate networks are numerous. Some are country-specific or heavily focused on one geographical region only, while others (as in the example in Figure 4.2) are fairly global. Table 4.1 lists affiliate networks arranged in alphabetical order. It is also not my goal to publish a comprehensive list of affiliate networks. I've done my best to bring you the major North American (mostly U.S.), U.K. (as is the one in Figure 4.3), European, and Asia-Pacific affiliate networks currently in operation.

Figure 4.2 Commission Junction—one of the world's largest affiliate networks, preferred by many larger brands

▶ **Table 4.1** Affiliate networks

North American Affiliate Networks	
AffiliateFuture	LinkShare
AvantLink	oneNetworkDirect
buy.at	Offermobi (mobile affiliate network)
ClickBank	Pepperjam Network
clickXchange	ShareASale
clixGalore	Share Results
Commission Junction	Video Performance Network (video)
Google Affiliate Network (formerly Performics)	Webgains US
Impact Radius (multichannel affiliate network)	Zanox.com
LinkConnector	
South American and Hispanic Targeting Networks	
7reach.com (Argentina & Brasil)	Fox Netwoks
AdverLatin	Harren Media
Batanga Network	MediaCom (Brasil)
Filiado.com	

Continues

UK Affiliate Networks	
Advertising.com	OffersQuest
Advortis	OMG Network
Affiliate Advantage	Paid On Results
Affiliate Window (see Figure 4.3)/buy.at	Profitistic
AffiliateFuture UK	QwertyTrade.com
affilinet	R. O. Eye
Afform	Silvertap
clixGalore	SmartQuotes
Commission Junction UK	TML Affiliates
GlobalDirectMedia.com	TradeDoubler.co.uk
LinkShare UK	Webgains UK
Netklix	Zanox.co.uk
French Affiliate Networks	
Advertising.com	PublicIdees
Commission Junction France	TradeDoubler
MobPartner (mobile)	Webgains
Netaffiliation	Zanox
OMGfr.com	
German Affiliate Networks	
Advertising.com	Sponsormob (mobile)
Affili.net	SuperClix
Belboon.com	TradeDoubler
CommissionJunction.de	Webgains
OMGde.com	Zanox
Scandinavian Affiliate Networks	
7reach.com (Denmark)	Double.net (Sweden)
Advertising.com (Denmark, Norway, Sweden)	TradeDoubler (Denmark, Finland, Norway, Sweden)
Affiliator (Sweden)	Webgains (Denmark, Sweden)
Commission Junction Sverige (Sweden)	Zanox (Denmark, Finland, Norway, Sweden)
Eastern European Affiliate Networks	
eHub.cz (Czech Republic)	Kavanga.ru (Russia)
Potenza.cz (Czech Republic)	MiraLinks.ru (Russia)
AffiliateMotion.gr (Greece)	MixMarket.biz (Russia)
Linkwise (Greece & Cyprus)	UltimateCash.ru (Russia & Kazakhstan)
Afilo (Poland)	Adnations.co.uk (multiple countries)
NetSales.pl (Poland)	AechMedia.com (multiple countries)
TradeDoubler (Poland)	Click2Sell.eu (Lithuania)

Zanox (Poland)	Sworp.com (UK-based, covering Slovakia, Poland, and Czech Republic)
Affiliation.ro (Romania)	
2Parale.ro (Romania)	
Australian Affiliate Networks	
CheckMyStats.com.au	CoProsper
clixGalore (also New Zealand)	DarkBlue.com
Commission Monster	dgmMarketing.com.au (also New Zealand)
Indian Affiliate Networks	
AffiliateCurry	DGM-India.com
clixGalore	
Asia-Based Affiliate Networks	
8Affiliate.com	ClickValue.cn (China)
AccessTrade.net (Japan)	clixGalore (Japan)
AdForBest.com	JANet (Japan)
Alimama (China)	LinkShare (Japan)
Allyes.com (China)	LuckyPacific.com
AsiaClickz	U2Mee.com (China)
Baidu Union (China)	ValueCommerce (Japan)
Chinese AN (China, Hong Kong, Taiwan)	Zanox (Japan)
Other Countries	
AdsMarket.com (Israel)	TradeDoubler (multiple European countries)
Advertising.com (Spain)	TrafficSynergy (South Africa)
OfferForge.com (South Africa)	Webgains (Ireland, the Netherlands, Spain)
SprinTrade.com (Italy)	Zanox (multiple European countries)

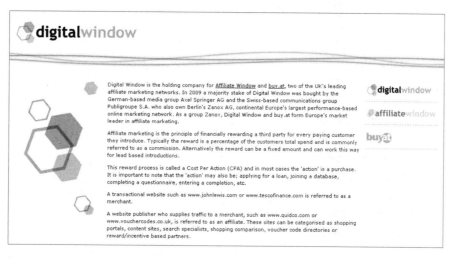

Figure 4.3 Digital Window owns the UK's largest affiliate network.

Each network has its own rules and regulations, terms of service, way of operating, and fee structure. Although the general way all affiliate networks work is very similar, there are differences, and you want to make sure you thoroughly study a network prior to signing up with it.

Cost Involved

With the majority of affiliate networks, regardless of the country were they are located, you should be aware of the following fees:

- Setup/activation fee
- Minimum deposit
- Transaction fees
- Other charges (for example, monthly minimums)

The setup/activation fee and the minimum initial deposit are self-explanatory, and they constitute one-time investments. In addition to these, there are also ongoing expenses that you should know about.

Most of the affiliate network's money is made on transaction fees. In the United Kingdom where this fee is more frequently known as an *affiliate override*, the very name of it illustrates what it is. It's a fee that overlaps what you are paying affiliates. Most frequently, transaction fees (or affiliate overrides) are calculated as a percentage of each affiliate payment, which is subtracted from your account *in addition* to the affiliate commission. You can think of it as similar to a credit card processing fee. Just as credit card processing companies charge 2 percent to 4 percent of the transaction amount to process it, so do affiliate networks charge you a fee on every transaction, with the only difference being that the fee is not tied to the sale amount but to the transaction amount that happens between the merchant and the referring affiliate. So, for example, if an affiliate network charges a 25 percent transaction fee, you should be prepared to pay one-fourth of all affiliate payouts to the network. In other words, if you set the affiliate commission at $10, keep in mind that the actual amount debited from your affiliate network account will be 25 percent larger, or $12.50 ($10 to the affiliate and $2.50 to the network). Similarly, a 10 percent commission then will increase to a total of 12.5 percent in merchant expenses.

In addition to transaction fees, there may be other ongoing fees charged by affiliate networks. One of the most widely adopted fees is a monthly minimum fee, or the amount you are charged by the network if the minimum sales or payment threshold is not met in any given month. Moreover, I have seen some networks charging fees for monthly access, for sending out affiliate circulars and a data feed, and for other maintenance-related fees. Familiarize yourself scrupulously with all expenses that may be involved so that you don't get any unpleasant surprises after the launch of the program.

To give you a general idea of the fees, I have compiled a side-by-side comparison of some of the major U.S. affiliate networks (Table 4.2).

Name	Setup fee	Deposit	Transaction fee	Other
AvantLink	$2,000	$500	3 percent of gross sale	
Commission Junction	$3,000	$3,000	30 percent of commission or $0.3, whichever is greater	$500 monthly minimum
Google Affiliate Network	$1,000	Varies ($1,000 to $5,000)	25 percent of commission	$500 monthly minimum
LinkShare	$1,000	$3,000	2 to 3 percent of a sale's total	$500 monthly minimum
ShareASale	$550	$100	20 percent of commission	$25 monthly minimum

With some of these networks, the setup fee includes such things as assistance with tracking integration, technical and automatic configuration of daily data feed updates (AvantLink is known for that), additional exposure for newly launched programs, and account management interface training. Table 4.2 is in alphabetical order and is not meant to rank, but only compare, the affiliate network information. Experience shows that it is not unusual for the pricing to change; so, it is always best to check for the most up-to-date information with the affiliate network directly. Table 4.2 should be used as a preliminary introduction to the ranges of fees.

In conclusion, it is worth mentioning that when it comes to larger brands, networks are generally open to negotiating their fees.

Affiliate Networks and Affiliates

As you evaluate affiliate networks, you should also consider the relationship between each network and its affiliates. To this end, you should ask the following two questions about each network you evaluate:

• What are the network's rules for affiliates?

• Who owns the relationships with affiliates?

Let's first look at what an affiliate network's agreement with affiliates is. Not to be confused with the agreement you as a merchant will want to set in place for your affiliate program, this is actually somewhat different. Sometimes also called affiliate/publisher service agreement, affiliate membership agreement, operating agreement, and affiliate terms of use, it is an agreement between affiliates and the affiliate network they are applying to join. Such agreements contain the terms and conditions that govern the relationship between the affiliate and the network.

Here are a few example agreements:

• AvantLink: www.avantlink.com/terms_and_conditions.php

• Commission Junction: www.cj.com/psa.html

- LinkShare: www.linkshare.com/affiliates/terms.shtml
- ShareASale: www.shareasale.com/agreement.cfm

First, study this agreement thoroughly to ensure that your affiliates will be comfortable working with your network of choice. Prior to joining your program, they will have to first sign up with the network and only then apply to *your* program. Therefore, it is essential that the network's agreement with affiliates doesn't hinder your own goals in any way.

Second, and equally importantly, realize that in many cases affiliate networks own the relationship with affiliates. In other words, since all affiliates that are recruited by you into your affiliate program first sign up with the network, it is the network that has their full contact information, and in many cases you will not have direct access to it. There are, however, some networks that give you full access to affiliate contact information, which you may use for your purposes.

I personally do not view the fact that some networks keep affiliate contact information proprietary to them as a disadvantage. I keep a database of affiliates of my own, and every time I come in contact with a new affiliate, I add them to my database and ask them if they would also like to be on my mailing list.

Finally, there exists a misconception that it is possible to compare one network to another based on the highest number of strong affiliates on the network. I have had a number of merchants asking me this question at the stage of choosing an affiliate network. My answer to such merchants is always twofold: Most affiliate networks will not disclose such information anyway, but it is somewhat irrelevant, because most significant/strong affiliates have accounts with *most* major affiliate networks.

Some affiliates may prefer to work with one network only, but this is seldom the case, especially when we are talking about strong affiliates. Smaller affiliates may prefer to stick only with one affiliate network for the purpose of consolidated payments across different affiliate programs they promote. But even smaller affiliates have to join different networks when they decide to promote multiple brands/merchants (even in the same vertical). Looking at the famous online malls, for example, you will see that the Overstock.com affiliate program is now operating on Commission Junction (CJ), Walmart.com is on LinkShare (Figure 4.4), Target.com is with the Google Affiliate Network (GAN), and Amazon.com runs an in-house affiliate program. Looking at the insurance sector as another example, you will see that Insure.com runs its affiliate program through buy.at, InsureMe.com is with CJ, Medex is with GAN, and QHealth.com is with ShareASale.

It is not the number of affiliates within any given affiliate network that you should focus on but rather the quality of the network (this includes but is not limited to tracking and reporting, unique tools and technologies, level of their technical and customer service support, overall reputation among merchants and affiliates, and how their offer fits into your existing marketing plan, budget, and strategy).

Figure 4.4 Wal-Mart affiliate program sign-up page

How Do You Choose an Affiliate Network?

With an obvious multitude of options out there, the decision doesn't always come easy. However, I'll offer some guidelines.

First, I'll emphasize once again *what* you are really selecting at this stage. When looking for an affiliate network, you are looking for a vendor that will handle all of your affiliate program's tracking, reporting, and affiliate payments.

At the very outset, every merchant must understand that while selecting an affiliate network, they are not selecting an agency that will run the affiliate program by recruiting affiliates and driving in sales/leads. Although some affiliate networks do offer management as add-on service, none does this by default.

It regularly appears that some merchants are merely extending the definition of advertising networks to include affiliate networks. Just like ad networks, affiliate networks do connect advertisers with publishers; they do not ensure that the advertiser actually gets advertised.

In most scenarios, it is the advertiser's own responsibility to manage the affiliate program and recruit affiliates, and you will look into the different options in the very next chapter. At this stage, just know that the affiliate network does/will not manage your program, and unlike ad networks, affiliate networks do not guarantee ad placements.

So, whichever affiliate network you decide to go with, make sure you are clear on the expectations and have someone to manage the program. I'll talk more about that in the next chapter.

Speaking of the decisive factors for choosing an affiliate network, I believe there are five against which you want to compare each candidate (Figure 4.5).

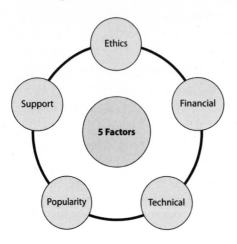

Figure 4.5 Five factors to keep in mind while picking an affiliate network

Ethics Nothing is more important than partnering with an ethical affiliate network that takes a clear stand against adware, spyware, and rogue affiliate techniques.

Financial There will be setup/integration fees, minimum monthly fees, and other charges. Get this data from different networks and analyze it, and you will see the difference.

Technical It is extremely important to find out what additional capabilities, tools, and technologies are made available. To name but a few, it's worth mentioning phone order tracking, video creatives, data feed import tools, dynamic product and/or coupon feeds, and so on.

Popularity You want to partner with a network that is loved and respected by affiliates.

Support It is no secret that many affiliate networks provide poor merchant and affiliate support. Do your due diligence to pick a network that cares.

Lastly, a word of warning about free-to-join affiliate networks: Do your homework in researching the network prior to joining it. There could be good ones among them, but as the famous Italian couturier Aldo Gucci used to say, "The bitterness of poor quality is remembered long after the sweetness of low price has faded from memory."

Tuesday: Understand CPA Networks and How They Work

In addition to the traditional networks mentioned earlier, you must also look into CPA networks. There is a plethora of them on the affiliate marketing landscape, and it is crucial that merchants fully understand what they are and how they operate.

Contrary to how it may appear on the façade of things, CPA networks and affiliate networks are actually two different species.

Most affiliate marketing professionals treat CPA networks and the traditional affiliate networks as two *separate* branches of affiliate marketing. The "CPA" part in the CPA network name is what is misleading many. "CPA" generally stands for cost-per-action. Cost-per-action is basically the very idea behind affiliate marketing as a method of advertising/marketing. It is a type of remuneration that essentially says I'll pay you when there is action. However, the abbreviation "CPA" is actually *not* the best way to describe "CPA networks." The more appropriate name for them is subaffiliate networks. Whereas a traditional affiliate network is functioning as a mediator between merchants/advertisers and affiliates/publishers, CPA networks are working as yet another link in the chain between the merchant and the affiliate. Figure 4.6 illustrates the difference between a traditional network and a CPA network.

**Affiliate Networks
vs.
Subaffiliate Networks**

Merchant

Affiliate Network

$20

Affiliate

Merchant

Affiliate Network

$30

Subaffiliate Network
(aka *CPA Network*)

$22

Affiliate

Figure 4.6 Traditional vs. subaffiliate networks

If a merchant were running an in-house affiliate program, the subaffiliate network will be a link between the merchant and the affiliate, receiving commissions from every sale that the affiliate sends. Whether it is with and in-house or with an affiliate network program, the affiliate becomes a subaffiliate. On the other hand, the CPA network is the affiliate that is paid a "preferred" or "private offer" (read: higher) commission (or per lead bounty, which is the preferred payment model for subaffiliate networks) and can afford to pay their subaffiliates a higher commission/bounty than the default commission/bounty that the affiliates would get if they went directly to the merchant. Why "preferred" commission? Being an affiliate with a large volume of subaffiliate traffic and sales, they are essentially perceived as power affiliates or superaffiliates.

This raises several problems. Three of the main ones deserve our attention: conflict of interest, shady marketing, and loss of transparency.

Conflict of Interest Being an affiliate itself, the CPA network is in direct competition with its subaffiliates. The conflict of interest is there, and no serious affiliate will disclose their techniques and methods to a competitor by working under them as a subaffiliate. Hence, if a merchant decides to run their affiliate program on a CPA network, they should not expect any superaffiliates to join their program. Furthermore, they should be aware of the lower quality of leads they will receive through the CPA network, as opposed to a managed affiliate program on a traditional network.

Shady "Marketing" Practices History testifies to the fact that it is not uncommon for CPA networks to tolerate (or even partake in) email spam, adware, fraudulent "leads," cash-for-freebies websites, or other activity you do not want in your affiliate program.

Loss of Transparency Unlike with the traditional affiliate networks, in cases with some CPA networks, transparency is a rare commodity. It isn't unusual for merchant to be totally unaware of who the subaffiliates are and what they are doing to "market" your "offer." Access to detailed and transparent reporting should always be one of your highest priorities while choosing a network to work with. Otherwise, ending up with affiliates who engage in spam, adware, and deceptive marketing or who employ other questionable techniques may become a sad brand-damaging reality.

Having said all of that, I don't mean to imply that all CPA networks are bad. However, when choosing to partner with a subaffiliate network, do a thorough due diligence to fully understand who you will be partnering with, and if the reputation of the network leaves no ground for doubt, ensure that the marketing approach proposed by the CPA network is going to work for *your* business model. It is a common practice with CPA networks to insist that the merchant/client runs an offers-centered affiliate program or one that consists of one or more marketing offers. Some will advise you that the offers that work best must include distribution of free trials or samples of products or services. As discussed in Chapter 1, "Understanding Affiliate Marketing" (see the "Loyalty Marketing" section), such methods do not work for all types of merchants, and you want to carefully weigh all pros and cons before starting any offer-centered affiliate campaign.

At the moment, in North America alone there are more than 150 CPA, lead generation, and similar networks (see Table 4.3), and new ones are springing up nearly monthly. Among the top 10, a 2010 ranking by *Revenue Performance*—based on feedback of more than 5,000 affiliates, merchants, and industry experts—lists such names as Epic Direct, NeverBlue, Market Leverage, ClickBooth, and MediaTrust (see Figure 4.7). Do thorough research on any given network before entering into an agreement.

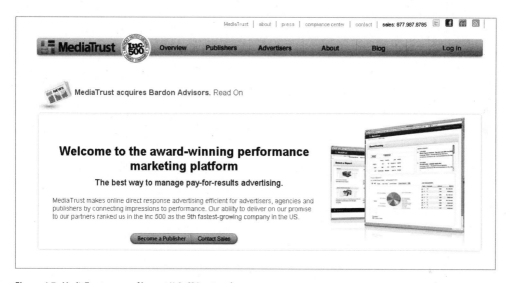

Figure 4.7 MediaTrust—one of largest U.S. CPA networks

▶ **Table 4.3** North American CPA, lead generation, and other networks

AdCanadian	IncentReward.com
AdCommunal.net	Income Access
AdDrive	InstantDollarz Media
AdFoundry.net	Intela
AdMarketers	.com
AdPaid.com	Kolimbo
Adreporting	LeaderMarkets
Ads4Dough.com	LeadExpose
Adscend Media	LeadFlash
Adteractive	LeadGen Marketing
Advertising.com	LeadHound.com
AdZacta	LeadPoint.com
Affiliace	LevelClick
Affiliate Fuel	LinkProfits.net

Continues

Affiliate.com (formerly CPA Empire)	LinkRads.com
AffiliateBot.com	Logical Media
Affiliateer.com	MarketHealth (formerly JoeBucks)
AffiliateNetwork.com	MarketLeverage
Affiliopolis	MaxBounty
AffNet	MediAdNet
Agami Media	MediaTrust (formerly AdValiant)
AKMG	MediaWhiz
Alliance Health Networks	ModernClick.com
Amped Media	NDemand Affiliates
Andes Network	ndustry Clix
Aquasis Media	NeverBlue
ATM Interactive	OfferFusion
Axill	OffersDirectADS
AzoogleAds (Epic Advertising)	OffersQuest.com
BlinkAds.com	Monetizeit.net
Blue Phoenix Media	MoreNiche
Bridaluxe	Motive Interactive
BulletAds.net	OfferPal
Cake Marketing	OfferWeb
CanadianSponsors.com	Panthera Network
CapitAll Network	PartnerWeekly
ClickBooth	PayDotCom.com
ClickSector (formerly Revenuecpm)	PeerFly.com
CommissionSoup.com	PerfectPayCheck
Convert2Media	PerformLine
COPEAC	PermissionData.com
CoProsper Network	PrimaryAds
CPA eMarket	ProfitKingsMedia
CPA Junction	Prospectiv
CPA Storm	Q Interactive
CPA Thunder	QuinStreet
CPA Universe	ReferBack
CPABoo	RegNow
CPABooster	Revenue 500
CPALead.com	Revenue Street
CPAPark	Revenue Wire
CPAShine	RevenueAds
CPX Interactive	RevenueGateway
CutsPM.com	RevenueLoop

CyberBounty.com	RevenuePilot.com
Dale! Network	RevResponse
DirectAssociate	RevShareNow
DirectLeads	Rextopia
DirectResponse	RocketProfit
DirectROI	ROI Rocket
CX Digital Media (form. IncentaClick)	Rowise
DMi Partners	Saveology
DrumCash	Search4Clicks.com
Epic Edge Media	SearchCactus
Epicenter.net	SellShareware
eTology	SFP Network
Express Revenue	ShareBucks.com
Firelead	ShareCPA
FlexOffers.com	TattoMedia
Float Interactive	ThinkAction
FloppyBank	TrafficSynergy
FluxAds.com	Triad Media
FosinaOffers.com	TriAd Media Solutions
FusionWhiz	Trienta
Global Ad Revolution	Unique Leads
GptMedia	ValueClick Media
Guppy Media	VHMnetwork
Healthy Payout	Vintacore
Hydra Network (formerly LynxTrack)	WebSponsors.com
iCommissions.com	XY7
iDrive Interactive	Yep! Revenue Network
iMediaTeam	z-Mirage

Wednesday: Assess In-House Solutions

Not all affiliate programs are based on affiliate networks. Many are being run in-house on self- or remotely hosted (and sometimes even internally developed) software. Amazon and eBay, for example, run their affiliate programs in-house and on their own software.

Although larger brands can afford to build their own affiliate program platforms, most of us would be looking for a tried and tested software package to purchase and get going. (See Figure 4.8 for an example.) All of these applications are made in a way that makes it easy to integrate them with your current shopping carts and ecommerce platforms. Some will charge you a monthly access fee, others will charge an annual license fee, while others will charge a one-time payment.

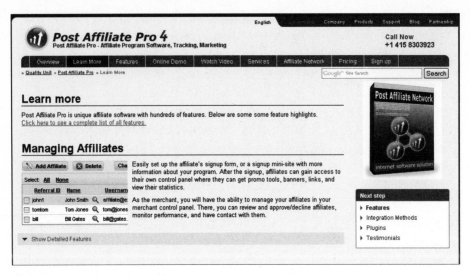

Figure 4.8 Post Affiliate Pro by QualityUnit—a popular platform for in-house programs

Table 4.4 lists software options to consider, including various affiliate tracking platforms, in alphabetical order.

▶ **Table 4.4** Affiliate tracking software options

AffiliatePro	JROX Affiliate Manager	PartnersManager
AffliateShop	iDevDirect	Performance Horizon
AssocTrac	Interneka	Post Affiliate Pro
AffiliateWiz	Leadhound Network	PHPAffiliate (for PayPal)
AffiliateTracking.com	LinkTrust	ShareResults software
ClickInc	MPA3	TWSC Affiliate Lite
DirectTrack	MyAP	QualityClick
eLitius	MyReferer	Ultimate Affiliate
HasOffers	NATS	
HitPath	OSIAffiliate	

In addition to these solutions, you will also see that some shopping platforms and shopping carts have affiliate program support functions built in as well. Table 4.5 lists such platforms.

▶ **Table 4.5** Shopping platforms with affiliate-program functions

1AutomationWiz	eAffiliatePro	QuickPayPro
1ShoppingCart	eCartsoft	RelyAffiliate
3dCart	Fortune3	Synergyx (for digital products)
BigCommerce	Magento	Volusion
CoreCommerce	MemberSpeed	WebmasterCart
E-junkie	osCommerce	X-Cart

Just as a side observation, it is interesting to see that the bigger of these players (for example, Volusion, 3dCart, BigComerce, and CoreCommerce) run their own affiliate programs on affiliate networks, and not on their own software.

Making the Choice

Yes, from first glance, it may seem to be more effective to run an affiliate program in-house. But there are pros and cons to both methods of running an affiliate marketing program. In-house affiliate programs help you save money on network fees, while network-based affiliate programs allow for a broader exposure to an already-existing base of affiliates. Being on a network also often allows for numerous affiliate recruitment opportunities. As mentioned, networks also take away the burden of check-writing, banner serving, reporting, and affiliate technical support. However, some networks spell it out in their terms of service that the relationship with all affiliates is the property of the networks (despite the fact that many of your own affiliates will be recruited by you), and I have touched upon this question as well. The advantages and disadvantages of having a program on the network or running it in-house must be carefully weighed, and the decision should be made according to your individual need.

Affiliates work both with network-based and with in-house affiliate programs. Econsultancy's 2009 U.S. Affiliate Census revealed that roughly "two-thirds of affiliates (68 percent) work with at least one merchant that runs its own in-house" affiliate program "compared to just under a third of affiliates (32 percent)" who said that they prefer not to work with merchants directly (Figure 4.9).

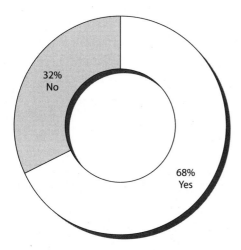

Figure 4.9 Do affiliates work with in-house affiliate programs?

Affiliate Summit's 2010 AffStat Report, which worded its related question somewhat differently, discovered the data on affiliate preferences. It was reported that 47.4 percent of affiliates favor network-based affiliate programs vs. 14 percent who prefer in-house programs, while the remaining 38.6 percent do not have any stringent preferences (Figure 4.10).

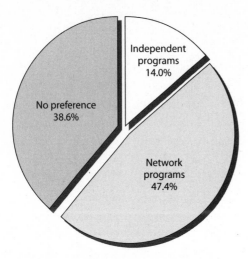

Figure 4.10 Which affiliate program do affiliates prefer?

My recommendation for new affiliate programs is usually to launch on an affiliate network first and add an in-house option in the future—when and if it makes business sense for you to pursue this route.

Thursday: Analyze Payment Options

While deciding whether to go with an affiliate network or build an in-house-based affiliate program, you also want to look into the various affiliate payment options. With networks, affiliate payment settings are generally preset by a network. In cases with in-house affiliate programs, it is normally the merchant that decides on these questions.

What Do Affiliates Prefer?

Payments are a highly sensitive area, and you want to approach the topic with all your diligence and care. Regardless of what platform your affiliate program is going to be based on, you want to be attentive to the following three subjects: payments threshold, frequency, and preferred methods.

Payment Threshold

Turning to the Affiliate Summit's 2010 AffStat Report, you can see that 15.2 percent of affiliates prefer not to have the threshold in place and be regularly paid whatever they earn. The rest of the pie chart is divided fairly equally between $25, $50, and $100 thresholds (Figure 4.11).

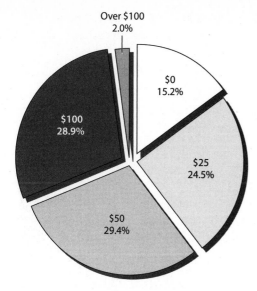

Figure 4.11 Affiliate-preferred payment thresholds

The majority of affiliates (58.3 percent) are comfortable with the $50 to $100 range for the threshold, while most of the rest (39.7 percent) desire to be paid when their commission reaches $25 or less. Keep this data in mind when you set up your program.

Payment Frequency

When it comes to the payment frequency, a vast majority of affiliates (73 percent) prefer weekly payments to bimonthly or monthly ones. I believe this is conditioned by the fact that many affiliates have to bear substantial and frequent investments to get merchants promoted effectively, and the sooner they get paid, the better (Figure 4.12).

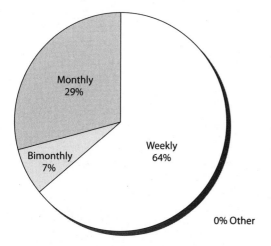

Figure 4.12 Affiliate-preferred payment frequency

It appears that international affiliates are generally the ones that prefer monthly payments, primarily because of the fees they incur when receiving international wire transfers or cashing international checks.

When possible, give the *affiliates* a way of configuring their minimum threshold payment amounts and setting their payment frequency by themselves. In cases with overseas affiliates, for example, less frequent but larger payments are generally preferred over smaller but more frequent ones. Smaller other affiliates, on the other hand, may want to be paid more frequently regardless of the amount.

Payment Methods

Going back to the findings of Affiliate Summit's 2010 AffStat Report, you can see that the vast majority of affiliates (62.1 percent) prefer direct bank deposits. The other two popular payment methods (17 percent each) are checks in the mail and PayPal (Figure 4.13).

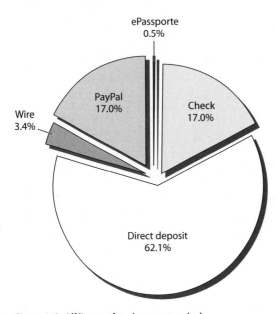

Figure 4.13 Affiliate-preferred payment methods

Bank wire transfers are one of the least preferred affiliate ways of receiving payment. So, when choosing an affiliate network or setting up your own in-house affiliate program, ensure you offer affiliates direct deposit, check payments, and, if possible, PayPal too (international affiliates will often prefer it to the former two payment options).

Outsourced Payment Solutions

If you decide to go with an in-house affiliate program but do not want to complicate things with payments and would rather outsource the payment part to a third party, there are such solutions out there.

There are several outsourced payment solutions merchants may use. I have not worked with any one of these services:

- Affiliate Speedpay
- AnyPay
- Chexx Inc.
- EntroPay
- ePassporte
- Payoneer
- PayPal Mass Pay
- RevUpCard
- Webmasterchecks

Whether you decide to handle the payments part in-house or outsource it to a third party, make sure you are prompt and accurate. As mentioned, this is a touchy area that must be handled properly at all times.

Friday: Understand the Importance of Cookies

Affiliate sales are normally tracked using *cookies*—small text files set on the visitor's computer. The duration of how long to keep them on the visitor's machine is chosen by the merchant while setting up their affiliate program, and it is most frequently called the *cookie life* or *return days*. In our context, it basically means the time period between the click on the affiliate site and the last day when you are willing to pay that affiliate a percentage of the sale made by "their" visitor. Cookie life may be set for any duration of time that the merchant prefers. Once the cookie life expires, the visitor sent by the affiliate becomes "your" visitor. If, for example, the cookie life is set at 60 days and someone (whom an affiliate referred) makes a purchase from you three months down the road, the affiliate is not paid the commission.

Quite naturally, the question of turned off (or disabled) cookies comes up. What happens if the visitor referred by an affiliate has their cookies disabled (Figure 4.14)? It is important to address this question not only for merchants but also because you may be asked this by your affiliates.

Figure 4.14 How end users block cookies in Internet Explorer

Yes, it is true that some people disable cookies in their browsers, believing it provides them with higher online security through privacy. However, cookies are now such an essential part of the day-to-day Internet use that many websites will simply not function properly for the end user unless they have cookies enabled. Most merchants' shopping carts won't work if the user's cookies are disabled. Cookies also help create a more positive and enjoyable Internet experience by customizing each individual user's utilization of the Internet.

The main question should be, how many online users actually turn cookies off? Commission Junction (CJ) quotes 1 percent. Many online advertising agencies, affiliate networks, and websites stress the harmlessness of cookies and educate the end users to keep those cookies turned on. For example, AllAboutCookies.org, a website of the Interactive Advertising Bureau Europe, emphasizes this:

> *Because cookies are just harmless files, or keys, they cannot look into your computer and find out information about you, your family, or read any material kept on your hard-drive. Cookies simply unlock a computer's memory and allow a website to recognize users when they return to a site by opening doors to different content or services. It is technically impossible for cookies to read personal information.*

Let's return to the statistics, because they are what is most relevant to the problem in question. In an article on Internet privacy, Wikipedia states, "Many users choose to disable cookies in their web browsers." However, it does not give any statistics on how many users *exactly*! As mentioned above CJ states that the number is only 1 percent, and Opentracker.net quotes 3 percent. Some of the other stats floating around claim that 5 percent of Internet users don't have their cookies enabled or run some sort of blocker, while another 5 percent delete them on closing the browser.

According to Nielsen/NetRatings' researches, in the United States alone, more than 200 million people use the Internet, so 1 percent to 3 percent is "many users." It is basically anywhere between 2 and 6 million people in the United States alone. However, it is by far not a considerable number, because 97 percent to 99 percent of users have those cookies turned on. Moreover, we do not know how many of those who disable cookies in their browsers are online shoppers. Not all Internet users shop online. Considering that only about 75 percent to 80 percent of Americans shop online, it is safe to assume that some of those who disable cookies in their browsers may not be online shoppers at all.

Unless you are using an affiliate tracking platform that is not dependent on cookies (I'll talk about these in more detail in the following chapters), the affiliate program will not be able to credit affiliate accounts on the sales made by those users who have disabled their cookies. However, the percentage of users who disable cookies is small enough for your affiliates not to give it too much concern.

We will return to the question of cookies in Chapter 6, "Week 4: Finalize Payment Models and Cookie Life," while talking about optimal cookie life and finalizing your affiliate program setup.

Week 3: Evaluate Program Management Options

5

I can't count the number of times merchants have approached me asking whether I can "just set up and launch an affiliate program" for them. Some actually do believe that once the program is up and running, they will no longer need a consultant's expertise. This is a very dangerous approach. In fact, one of the deadliest mistakes a merchant can make is running their affiliate program in an unmanaged mode. The subject of program management deserves careful attention right from the start. In this chapter, you'll learn the basics of affiliate program management, key terms, responsibilities of managers, your sourcing options, and other important elements you want to know.

Chapter Contents

Monday: Understand the Basics
Tuesday: Set Your Expectations
Wednesday: Outline Qualifications and Certification
Thursday: Weigh In-House vs. Outsourced Solutions
Friday: Determine Compensation and Draft Contact

Monday: Understand the Basics

One of the most commonly committed, and altogether one of the deadliest, merchant mistakes is adopting what I call an autopilot approach to affiliate marketing. In part, this tendency is conditioned by a fallacy that affiliate marketing is so simple that all you have to do is just launch your affiliate program, announce it in your blog and in affiliate forums, insert it into affiliate program directories, and affiliates will come. They indeed *will*. However, unless your affiliate program is closely managed and each affiliate is scrupulously reviewed before approval and monitored after approval, you may run into some serious troubles.

Autopilot vs. Proactive Management

First things first, let's expand our "autopilot" analogy a bit further. Webster's Dictionary defines autopilot as "a device for *automatically* steering ships, aircraft, and spacecraft" (see also Figure 5.1). Such systems of directing vehicles without assistance from human beings are excellent when used in the context for which they were created. Affiliate marketing is *not* one of them. However, numerous merchants run their affiliate programs the "autopilot way," and many are not even aware they do.

Figure 5.1 Autopilot in action

I've found this problem to be more common with programs run on affiliate networks. When a merchant starts a program on a network, they often mistake the affiliate network for a self-adaptive autopilot. An aerospace avionics expert, George Siouris, defines this particular type of autopilot as one that "measures its own performance, compares it to a standard, and adjusts...parameters until its performance meets the standard." Similarly, some merchants believe that once an affiliate program is started on an affiliate network, the network will both measure its performance and ensure that the program keeps developing according to a "standard." However, as outlined in the previous chapter, this is not the primary job of the affiliate network, which is there to provide the merchant with tracking, reporting, and payment solutions. The rest is affiliate program management, and although some affiliate networks do offer program *management* as add-on service, extremely seldomly does a network do this by default.

An affiliate program is your marketing campaign. Launching it on a reliable platform (an affiliate network, for example) is only half the job. The second half entails *proactive* affiliate program management.

It is important to understand that a proactive approach to program management is one of the keys to the success of an affiliate program. How often do you visit a doctor when nothing is going wrong with you (or, rather, when you feel that everything is all right)? I personally seldom do so unless I am concerned about something. The last time I checked my cholesterol levels was three or four years ago when I felt chest pain. (The cholesterol levels needed improvement, but the pain wasn't in any way related to my heart.) Similarly, many merchants do not seek any assistance from an affiliate program manager until something is going wrong with the program. This is typical *reactive* affiliate program management. It is better than no management, but merchants can and should do better than that.

You may also compare affiliate program management to gardening. If you choose to have an "autopilot garden," the only thing it will produce in great abundance will be weeds (a good analogy for rogue affiliates). "Reactive gardening" wouldn't be much better. Yes, you can get rid of the weeds, but unless you take steps to prevent them from coming back (read: practice "proactive gardening"), you won't see really good results. Thanks to Michael Coley, a good friend and this book's technical editor, for an idea on this excellent analogy.

What you really want to practice is a *proactive* approach to affiliate program management. Webster's Dictionary defines *proactive* as "acting in anticipation of future problems, needs, or changes." You do not want to wait for the problem to come. You want to foresee it and deal with its causes before it occurs. A proactive approach is always more constructive than a reactive one.

Key Management Elements

The key elements of affiliate program management are (a) recruiting *new* affiliates, (b) educating and motivating *current* ones, and (c) policing *all* affiliates for compliance with your terms of service (TOS). We will talk about your program's TOS agreement in detail in Chapter 9, "Week 3: Feeds, Coupons, Widgets, and Videos," but at this stage, let me just say that one of the most important sections of it will specify what affiliate behavior is unacceptable. In your TOS agreement, you will specify what affiliate behavior is prohibited and what consequences such behavior will bring about. Examples of the most frequently banned affiliate behaviors include trademark bidding, forcing clicks, cookie overwriting, cookie stuffing, and use of downloadable software.

Besides recruiting affiliate and policing their compliance with the TOS, the affiliate program manager is also responsible for reviewing new applications and maintaining a healthy communication channel with the affiliates. In February 2009,

Econsultancy.com published its U.K. and U.S. affiliate censuses. Among the top reasons for not promoting a merchant, U.S. affiliates (Figure 5.2) pointed to "slow acceptance to program" (17 percent) and "bad follow-up communication" (10 percent).

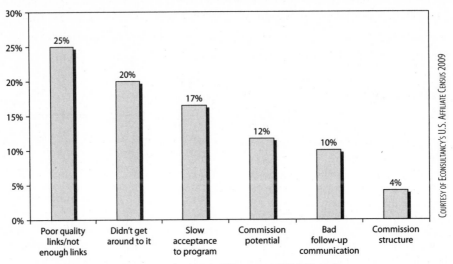

Figure 5.2 Reasons for not promoting merchants; U.S. affiliate census 2009 by Econsultancy.com

Poor communication was mentioned by 12 percent as the reason for dropping affiliate programs. U.K. affiliates (Figure 5.3) have also stated that "merchants do not communicate a variety of issues to them," and whatever communication does exist "ranges from bad or impersonal contact" to "failure to convey important information." U.S. affiliates echoed this observation by underscoring that "merchants do not communicate enough with them," and when they do, it is performed in a generic, mass-mailing style.

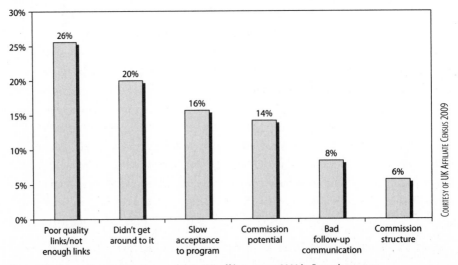

Figure 5.3 Reasons for not promoting merchants; U.K. affiliate census 2009 by Econsultancy.com

None of the previous elements can be effectively attended unless there is an affiliate program manager at the helm of your affiliate program.

The dangers of the "autopilot approach" are numerous and will increase only with the online marketing and promotion techniques getting more and more intricate. If you are serious about your online presence, treat your affiliate program as a serious marketing campaign, and commit to manage it closely. Otherwise, gaining genuine trust and loyalty of affiliates will be an impossible task.

Merchant Naïveté

There is no such thing as successful affiliate marketing on autopilot. In fact, by running an affiliate program in such a manner, merchants open up the program to affiliates, which can hurt the development of the program, hindering the sign-up of new affiliates by their very presence in the program. I call this a phenomenon of merchant naïveté.

I know you didn't expect a goose to be a part of this book, but these geese are quite different from the ones most of us see in our daily life. Living on isolated islands, they exhibit a very interesting, and altogether a very logical, behavior. This biological phenomenon bears the name of island tameness or ecological naïveté. In essence, it is a tendency of animal species living on isolated islands to lose both wariness of potential predators and defensive behaviors to stand against the threats they may impose. By analogy, I use the term *merchant naïveté* to characterize advertisers that start/run their affiliate programs first, without any clearly outlined terms of service (naïvely entrusting the promotion of their brand to whomever decides to join their program), and second, without any affiliate program manager to actually manage the program (naïvely presupposing that it is the affiliate network's responsibility to manage it).

Both of these facts can (and often do) lead to disaster. The affiliate program then becomes vulnerable to an array of affiliates who specifically hunt for such merchants as easy prey.

Manage the Program, Not Affiliates

Something else deserves our attention this Monday. You will often hear the terms *affiliate manager* and *affiliate management* used interchangeably with *affiliate program manager* and *affiliate program management*. Although the industry-accepted terminology will not be changed by one book, it is important to define the terminology at the outset and not let some of these terms have a negative effect on our very approach to managing the affiliate program.

I don't believe it is possible to manage affiliates. The reason for this is the very essence of the relationship at stake. Affiliates are very different from any traditional workforce. Although they all vary in types of marketing methods used, psychological maturity, professional experience, and training, there is one thing that is true about all affiliates, and it is the driving force that moves them. All affiliates are motivated by their love of independence. They are normally not tied by performance contracts and can choose what affiliate programs to promote and what merchants to drop, without notifying the merchants themselves. By the very definition of the term, affiliates are unmanageable. Therefore, merchants who believe that their job is to manage affiliates frequently fail. Management is often associated with a top-down, directing, controlling, perform-or-we'll-terminate-you kind of approach. As I will discuss in the more advanced chapters, affiliates are intolerant of such management techniques and of merchants who practice them. Instead, online businesses that run affiliate programs should understand that their job is to manage the program and not these independent marketers who have chosen to join it. Therefore, even if at times you are called an *affiliate manager*, remember that in reality you are managing an affiliate marketing *program*, *not* the independent *marketers*, who are the driving force of your program but by definition unmanageable.

So, although throughout the industry and this book affiliate program managers are frequently called *affiliate managers*, you should always be mindful of the difference and realize that you should actually be an affiliate *program* manager.

Tuesday: Set Your Expectations

So, what should a merchant expect your affiliate program manager to do for them? I've already listed some of the key elements of affiliate program management in the previous chapters, so now let's take a closer look into the manager's responsibilities.

As the main person in charge of managing and organizing a company's affiliate program, the affiliate program manager should be expected to routinely fulfill the following tasks:

- Identifying and recruiting new affiliates
- Activating new and/or inactive affiliates
- Maintaining stimulating relationships with the current affiliates
- Developing and monitoring affiliate promotions

- Reporting for affiliate marketing promotions and activity
- Maintaining ongoing communication campaigns
- Identifying and implementing other opportunities to enhance the affiliate program
- Keeping affiliates up-to-date on new products and any program enhancements
- Continually motivating affiliates to perform better
- Keeping track of affiliate sales and paying affiliates in a timely manner (for in-house affiliate managers)
- Monitoring and reporting on competitors' affiliate campaigns and promotions
- Representing the interests of the affiliate program within the company

The previous list outlines the fundamental and fairly generic duties and responsibilities of affiliate managers. Such specific tasks as creating and developing an affiliate database, directing the creative development for the program, approving affiliate applications and/or pending transactions (if this is required by the program setup), developing an attractive program description, compiling a FAQ database for current and potential affiliates, developing ongoing communication through newsletters and blog posts, participating in online affiliate forums, and performing many other tasks are all included in the affiliate manager's job description and responsibilities.

Five Pillars of Affiliate Program Management

I like to look at affiliate program management as I would at the façade of a building that rests on five pillars. This is because, in essence, every affiliate program manager should be expected to manage the program on the following five levels: recruitment, activation, policing, communication, and optimization.

Recruitment   An affiliate program manager is responsible for identifying and recruiting new affiliates. Affiliate recruitment normally takes anywhere between 40 percent and 60 percent of the affiliate manager's time and is one of the most important parts of the program manager's work. After all, affiliates are the main driving force of every affiliate program.

Continues

> ### Five Pillars of Affiliate Program Management *(Continued)*
>
> **Activation** Affiliate activation is one of the most frequently overlooked components of affiliate program management. Activation is a step between affiliate recruitment and conversion of the recruited affiliates into producing ones. I believe that activation should be practiced in three phases: the *recruitment phase* (where you motivate affiliates not only to join your program but also to put up your links and refer their first orders/leads), the *welcoming phase* (where you motivate affiliates to get active in the very text of the application approval email), and the *routine phase* (where you run aggressive monthly activation campaigns to move those who are already in your program but not yet active).
>
> **Policing** Next in importance to recruiting and activating affiliates is the policing of inappropriate affiliate behavior. Whatever you prohibit in your affiliate program's terms of service—be it downloadable toolbars that aim to overwrite other affiliates' cookies or paid search bidding on your trademarks, URL, or any variations of misspellings of these—you want your affiliate manager to constantly police affiliates for these behaviors.
>
> **Communication** An affiliate manager should also be expected to support a two-way communication channel with affiliates. I believe this responsibility is threefold: maintaining stimulating relationships with the current affiliates and continually motivating them to perform better, keeping affiliates up-to-date on new products and any affiliate program enhancements, and handling ongoing communication campaigns and all affiliate correspondence.
>
> **Optimization** Continuous affiliate program optimization is the last area of responsibility worth underscoring. Your affiliate manager should be identifying and implementing opportunities to enhance your affiliate program, developing and monitoring affiliate-centered promotions (do not confuse these with promos directed at customers), reporting for affiliate marketing promotions and activity, and monitoring and reporting on competitors' affiliate campaigns and promotions.

Wednesday: Outline Qualifications and Certification

Is there a set of qualifications a manager should be expected to possess? Should they be specially trained or certified? I will answer these two questions in detail in the following sections.

Affiliate Program Manager Qualifications

What qualifications should an affiliate program manager possess? Well, since as an occupation this is still a fairly new one, there is no exact set of qualifications typically required to work as an affiliate program manager. You can take the qualifications in the following list and adapt them to your own industry. The following attributes comprise some basic prerequisites for an affiliate manager.

College Degree Three- to four-year bachelor's degree. The field of the degree depends on your vertical industry, but marketing and advertising, business studies, business administration, ecommerce, psychology, and communications are good general ones to favor.

Experience A minimum of two to four years of work experience, out of which one and a half to two years should be affiliate marketing experience. The longer, the better, but more experienced affiliate managers obviously tend to cost more. Also, when I say "affiliate marketing" experience, I do not mean affiliate manager experience only. Affiliate marketing history is full of examples of how great *affiliates* also became tremendous affiliate managers. Please keep this in mind.

Knowledge Basic HTML, graphics applications (such as Photoshop), basic ecommerce operations.

Skills Excellent verbal and written communication skills, analytical skills, attention to detail, ability to handle multiple tasks simultaneously, organizational and people management skills.

Character Self-motivated, highly initiative, enthusiastic, outgoing, flexible, and responsive.

The following skills, knowledge, and abilities are not compulsory but may be preferable for your business:

Skills Negotiating, research, copywriting.

Knowledge Foreign language(s), specific software applications, specific affiliate network knowledge, connections in the industry, CSS, PHP, JavaScript, database concepts.

Abilities Willingness to travel.

Education and Certification

No certification is necessary to practice affiliate program management, and neither is there a unified certification accepted across the industry. Various companies run seminars on affiliate program management, which last anywhere from one day to a weekend. These are generally very informative and practical. Attending a seminar will undoubtedly enrich one as an affiliate manager, as well as help in the networking aspect of the business. Attending affiliate conferences, networking, and other relevant events helps one grow in the knowledge and increase the list of your contacts in the industry. I always encourage merchants to attend conferences and seminars, even if their affiliate program will be run by a dedicated manager. Although it may not be necessary to know all the ins and outs of the industry, every business owner who runs an affiliate program must understand the basics. Otherwise, how will they be able to make sense of the metrics and what is going on in their affiliate program?

So, although certification is not necessary, educating yourself is a *must*. Those of you working on a tight budget may not be able to afford attending the previously mentioned events right from the start. It is no reason for despair. There are multiple affiliate marketing blogs, message boards, white papers, magazines, broadcasts, and research articles published online. Do not let a day pass without learning something new. Sir Francis Bacon stressed, "Knowledge is power," while Margaret Fuller wrote, "If you have knowledge, let others light their candles at it." When merchants do not heed these wise words, they undoubtedly find themselves and their affiliate program wandering in the dark.

Thursday: Weigh In-House vs. Outsourced Solutions

As mentioned in Chapter 2, "Budget, Payments, and Related Considerations," while looking at your affiliate program management options, you will have a choice to make: Entrust the management of your program to an in-house staff or hire an external agency to handle your affiliate program management. Outsourced affiliate program management services are provided by some affiliate networks, as well as by stand-alone outsourced program manager (OPM) companies (see Figure 5.4 for an example).

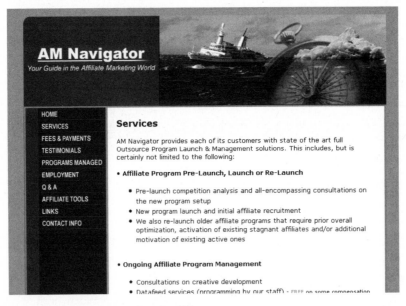

Figure 5.4 AM Navigator—award-winning OPM agency

Your choice between an in-house or an OPM manager will depend on the size of your business and your own capabilities. If your business is not a very large one or you have plenty of time to educate yourself in affiliate program management, I highly recommend managing the program on your own. I myself have gone the route from an online shop owner to an affiliate program manager and, later, to an outsourced program manager.

In school I was especially impressed by accounts of the Russian emperor's (Peter the Great) learning experiences. He was known for striving to learn everything firsthand, from the inside out. Experience is an invaluable asset, especially if this experience is directly related to your particular business. If you have the capability, do try the waters of affiliate program management yourself. If, however, business management is consuming a lot of your time and you have no way of taking on additional responsibility or hiring an extra office worker, I encourage you to look into outsourcing your affiliate program's management to an OPM. An outsourced program manager—when compared to one who is in-house—can save you a lot of money, without compromising the quality of the program's management. Table 5.1 outlines the key benefits of having an affiliate program run each way.

▶ **Table 5.1** Cross-comparison of in-house vs. outsourced affiliate program management options

	In-house manager	OPM agency
Business relationship	Subordinate	Partner
Training	Required	Not required
Experience	Varies	Substantial
Equipment and software	Provided by company	Present
Connections	Varies	Significant
Payment	Dependent on average job rate	Flexible
Payment structure	Salary + benefits + bonuses	Retainer + performance bonus
Accountability	Tight	As defined in contract
Confidentiality	Easy to control	Look at reputation, location + safeguard by contract
Noninterruption of work	Dependent on subjective factors	Present

To summarize, to some degree, your decision on the program management route will be conditioned by the size and structure of your company, as well as its strategic environment. The primary benefits of hiring an OPM include the experience, expertise, and connections that a good OPM brings to the table right away. Among other obvious benefits, you may also mention avoidance of health/401k benefit expenses, office space, computer costs, and training expenses. The ostensible disadvantage is a looser accountability, but with a properly worded contract, you can define the types and frequency of the reports you want to get from your OPM. Generally, however, outsourcing the management of your affiliate program leads to better price-quality inferences.

Also, consider synergetic options: Have both an in-house person responsible for the development of your affiliate program (and who ensures that affiliates have everything they need to do their part effectively) and an experienced OPM with who(m) they work closely.

Friday: Determine Compensation and Draft Contact

Once you have decided what program management solution you want to go with, it's time to look into compensation costs and to work on your contract with the program manager of choice.

Determining Compensation

So, how much should you pay your affiliate manager? It depends on the following three variables: the industry, the experience of the person you are hiring, and whether you are looking for an in-house affiliate manager or have decided to outsource the work.

Speaking of outsourced program managers, prices will vary significantly and will depend on the OPM's experience, expertise, and connections. OPM fees normally represent a combination of a monthly retainer and a performance bonus (see the "OPM's Performance Bonuses" sidebar).

OPM's Performance Bonuses

(This originally appeared as part of the "Affiliate Networks, OPM Companies, Transaction Fees, and Performance Bonuses" blog post at AMNavigator.com.)

A performance bonus is something that an OPM normally charges you. It can be tied either to the affiliate commissions paid out or to the cumulative monetary value of all affiliate-referred orders that occur within a set period of time (normally, one month). Incorporation of a performance bonus into the contractual agreement with the OPM is important for both the merchant and the outsourced program manager. For the merchant, it ensures the affiliate program manager is motivated to keep the program growing, while for the OPM, it essentially provides a "no-cap" arrangement, making the job follow the standard affiliate marketing model: the more you sell, the more you're paid.

To give you an example, let's look at the breakdown of your expenses in an affiliate program that pays 10 percent commissions, is being charged by an affiliate network a 20 percent override (transaction fee), and the agreement with your OPM states that they will work for you on a $500/ retainer + 15 percent performance bonus basis (where the performance bonus is calculated

OPM's Performance Bonuses *(Continued)*

based on the total order value). When in such a program and you have an order for $100, your affiliate marketing expenses will look as follows:

$10 to affiliate (that is, 10 percent commission of the $100 order)

$15 to OPM (that is, 15 percent performance of the $100 order)

$2 to affiliate network (that is, $10 affiliate commission × 20 percent)

That equals $27.

I see your eyebrows raised at that $15 performance bonus already. "That's a rip-off!" you're probably saying. Stay with me for five seconds longer, and I'll explain how it normally works with OPMs. The lower the monthly retainer, the higher the performance bonus. You have to keep them motivated too. They invest a lot of time and energy into getting a program off the ground, and $500 may not be covering much of it (again, this is just an example, so don't take the remuneration figures literally). Along with the "$500/retainer + 15 percent performance bonus" option, any OPM would more than likely offer you options that would follow such patterns as these:

$1,000/retainer + 10 percent performance bonus (in the previous example, it would amount to $10 of each $100 sale)

$1,500 + 5.0 percent performance bonus (or $5 of each $100 order)

$2,000 + 2.5 percent performance bonus (or $2.5 on every $100 affiliate-referred sale)

Discuss the exact compensation model with your outsourced program manager prior to signing a contract; generally OPMs are open to switching between the payment model options on advance notice and, certainly, mutual agreement.

In-house position salaries generally tend to range from $50,000 to around $85,000. The exact figure largely depends on the experience, which carries with it an affiliate manager's education, creativity, popularity, and the number of contacts in the industry (among other affiliate managers and affiliates alike). OPM fee ranges, on the other hand, are not as tight as those of the in-house affiliate managers' fees. By and large, OPM charges fluctuate between $1,000 and $10,000 per month. The lower the fee, the larger the performance bonus attached to it. Very seldom would any OPM work on a "performance compensation–only" pattern. It is erroneous to presuppose that when you are paying them a flat monthly fee, they are no longer interested in performing. If you as a merchant are hesitant to pay a large monthly fee, negotiate a lower one with a larger performance compensation attached. Also, make sure you word your contract in such a way that, on mutual agreement, you could always go up to a larger monthly fee with a smaller performance bonus.

As in any business, you can always find a worker that will fit into the budget you have apportioned for the position to which they are hired. Two hints about paying them too little: ask for recommendations before you sign anything, and beware that a lower quality of service may be reflected in a lower level of pay.

Drafting the Contracting Agreement

What points do you pay attention to while drafting your contract with the affiliate program manager hired to run your affiliate program (especially if it is an OPM that you're hiring)? Because I understand that this question and answer will be read by both merchants and affiliate managers, I have attempted to make my answer as universal as possible, aiming to make it helpful to both sides of the game. It will be natural for both parties to aim at getting the most out of their contract, so reaching a sound balance between the requirements of one party and the commitments of the other will be your main goal. As in any contracting agreement, at the end of the day, both parties have to be comfortable with the conditions of the contract. If you are not comfortable with what the other party is offering you, do not be afraid to negotiate. In the years of my affiliate program management practice, I have negotiated both with parties that were easygoing and with those that were extremely demanding. Although some prefer to forego negotiation, solely trusting your word, others will require a detailed agreement. I personally am in favor of the latter, because in the long run, it helps both parties be clear on their respective responsibilities, and it helps determine the ultimate course the relationship will take.

OPM companies normally have a set agreement they offer their new clients to sign. Individual affiliate managers (in-house or outsourced) may not have such an agreement. I hope that the following guidelines to the affiliate program management agreement will help you create your own contract.

When I sign an outsourced program management contract with a merchant, I include the following elements:

Definition of Services In as much detail as possible, outline the duties, roles, and responsibilities of the affiliate manager who is hired by the merchant. A fair number of them are listed in the "Set Your Expectations" part of this chapter. In this part of the agreement, the merchant may also want to outline the penalty that is entailed (in the form of deductions from the affiliate manager's payment) for failures to carry out any specific imperative responsibilities (weekly/monthly reporting, email affiliate support, newsletter publishing, and so on).

Term of Agreement   This is the time period that the agreement is signed for, as well as the agreement cancellation terms and procedures. Some OPM companies insist on a 60-day termination clause. I am supportive of the termination clause itself. However, the time period that needs to pass between the termination notice and the termination itself does not need to be that long. Neither the merchant nor the affiliate manager should bind themselves for such a long period.

Time   Clearly state what time you expect the affiliate manager to devote to their services, including how many hours per week and the minimum number of hours per month.

Place   The physical location is either on the company's premises for in-house affiliate program management or "at a location of the affiliate manager's discretion" for an outsourced program manager.

Payment Terms   These can vary widely. It is recommended not only to have a set monthly fee but also a performance bonus. A performance bonus is a percentage of all affiliate sales and is collected in addition to the monthly fee. For the merchant, it ensures the AM is motivated to keep the program growing. For the AM, it essentially provides a "no-cap" arrangement, making the job follow the standard affiliate marketing model: the more you sell, the more you're paid. I have had agreements for full 100 percent prepayment, for a 60/40 payment structure (60 percent in advance and 40 percent at the end of the month when the performance bonus is paid), for small monthly fees tied to a large performance bonus, and so on. One of my more shrewd clients put together the following payment model (I am quoting the actual contract, replacing the amounts only):

> For the work performed in accordance with this agreement, the affiliate manager will be paid at the rate of $4,500.00 (four thousand five hundred U.S. dollars) per month or the below-outlined commission structure, whichever is greater for the first six months. After the first six months, the $4,500 minimum guarantee is going to be replaced by a $1,500.00 (one thousand five hundred U.S. dollars) monthly management fee plus the below-outlined commission structure. If the commission is greater than $4,500 during the first six months, then the $1,500 monthly management fee will be added. The affiliate manager will submit an invoice, and the company will pay the affiliate manager one month in advance. The amount due is to be paid by the 10th of each month. In the event of the payment running overdue, the affiliate manager may stop all work until the payment is received. In the event of the payment running 10 business days overdue, the affiliate

manager may cease the relationship, notifying the client in writing, by certified mail, email with reading confirmation, or personal delivery.

Performance Bonus. The consultant will be paid a monthly "performance bonus," specifically defined as a percentage of all affiliate sales and collected in addition to the above fee. The performance bonus rate is going to be calculated as follows:

Monthly Sales	Commission
From $0–$10,000	10% commission with guaranteed minimum of $4,500 per month for first 6 months
From $10,000–$15,000	Calculated at 15% commission
$15,000+	Calculated at 20% commission

The consultant should include the exact amount due in the invoice submitted.

Employment Benefits If you are hiring an in-house worker, you will want to outline employment benefits here. If you are hiring an OPM, stress that no benefits are provided and that "the affiliate manager shall be responsible for payment of all local taxes arising out of the manager's activities in accordance with the contract."

Confidential Information Here you should have your nondisclosure clause regarding the merchant's "trade secrets, processes, data, procedures, know-how, intellectual property, discoveries, developments, designs, improvements, inventions, techniques, marketing plans, business plans and methods of the merchant's operations, strategies, forecasts, software, software documentation, financial statements, budgets, projections, licenses, prices, costs, client and supplier lists, and information pertaining to employee training, compensation, and bonuses."

Conflicting Management It is recommended that in your agreement you have a separate clause regarding the management of the competing affiliate programs, whereby the affiliate manager commits to "not engage in any other employment, occupation, consulting or other business activity related to the business in which the merchant is now involved or becomes involved during the term of the agreement, nor will the affiliate manager engage in any other activities that conflict with the affiliate manager's obligations to the merchant."

Noncompetition Some merchants also add a separate noncompetition clause to their agreement with the affiliate manager, whereby the latter commits to "not either directly or indirectly engage in (whether as an employee, consultant, proprietor, partner, director)... the financing, operation, management, or control of any person, firm, corporation, or business that produces or sells products that directly compete with any of the merchant's products."

The agreement may also contain clauses pertaining to the solicitation of employees, contact with the merchant's suppliers, affiliates that were on board the merchant's affiliate program before the management was taken over by the new affiliate manager, and other additional clauses (such as a payment problems clause to safeguard OPMs, and so on). However, eight of the previously mentioned points cover most of the areas important to both parties in the contract (Figure 5.5).

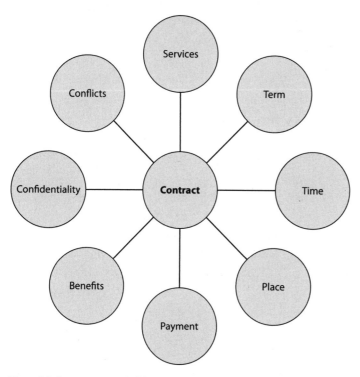

Figure 5.5 Key components of affiliate program management contract

Sample OPM Agreement

Outsourcing affiliate program management to an external agency is a very popular practice. To help you draft your OPM agreement, I am providing you with a sample to use for guidance. Do not treat it as any legal advice but just as a sample. Consult with your lawyer prior to arriving at the final version of any agreement.

Continues

Sample OPM Agreement *(Continued)*

Sample Outsourced Program Management Agreement

This agreement dated _____, is made By and Between _____ of Merchant Company Name, whose address is _____, ("Company"), and _____ of OPM Company Name, whose address is _____ ("Consultant"),

1. Consultation Services. The company hereby employs the consultant to perform the following services in accordance with the terms and conditions set forth in this agreement: The consultant will consult with the officers and employees of the company concerning matters relating to the management and organization of the company's affiliate program and provide full OPM (out-sourced program management) including but not limited to identifying and recruiting new affiliates to the program, maintaining relationships with current affiliates, reporting for affiliate marketing promotions/activity and recommending strategies to improve the performance, monitoring affiliate promotions and promotional placements, identifying and implementing opportunities to enhance affiliate program, new growth opportunities, and optimization of ROI.

2. Terms of Agreement. This agreement will begin _____ and will end _____. Either party may cancel this agreement on sixty (60) days notice and/or request a change of fee pattern on thirty (30) days notice to the other party in writing, by certified mail, email with reading confirmation, or personal delivery.

3. Time Devoted by Consultant. It is anticipated the consultant will spend approximately 12 hours a week in fulfilling his/her obligations under this contract. The exact amount of time may vary from day to day or week to week. However, the consultant shall devote a minimum of 40 hours per month to his/her duties in accordance with this agreement.

4. Place Where Services Will Be Rendered. The consultant will perform most services in accordance with this contract at a location of consultant's discretion. In addition the consultant will perform services on the email, IM and/or telephone and at such other places as necessary to perform these services in accordance with this agreement.

5. Payment to Consultant.

    5.1. General Terms. The consultant will be paid at the rate of $1,000 per month with a 2.5% performance bonus. Every $10,000 increase in monthly sales will qualify the Consultant for an increase of the fixed monthly payment by $200 (i.e., reaching a $16,000 monthly threshold will increase the monthly retainer to $1,200, whereas reaching $26,000 will increase the retainer to $1,400, and so on).

    5.2. Performance Bonus. The above-quoted monthly "performance bonus" is specifically defined as a percentage of all affiliate sales and collected in addition to the monthly fee. The consultant should include the exact amount due in the invoice submitted.

5.3. Invoicing. Late Payments. The consultant will submit an invoice, and the company will pay the consultant within 5 business days of the invoice receipt. In the event of the payment running overdue, the consultant may stop all work until the payment is received. In the event of the payment running 10 business days overdue, the consultant may cease the relationship notifying the client in writing, by certified mail, email with reading confirmation, or personal delivery; and forward the case for collection to a law firm or a collection agency. Should the latter happen, the company will be liable for all legal and/or collection agency fees incurred. Moreover, the company will incur a late payment fee of $20.00 per calendar day starting 5 business days past the receipt of the overdue invoice.

5.4. Initial Deposit. Balance Maintenance. As a step of good will the company shall make an initial $2,000 deposit into the consultant's account, which will count toward the first month's retainer fee, and future payments due.

6. Independent Contractor. Both the company and the consultant agree that the consultant will act as an independent contractor in the performance of his/her duties under this contract. Accordingly, the consultant shall be responsible for payment of all local taxes arising out of the consultant's activities in accordance with this contract.

7. Confidential Information. The consultant agrees that any information received by the consultant during any furtherance of the consultant's obligations in accordance with this contract, which concerns the personal, financial, or other affairs of the company will be treated by the consultant in full confidence and will not be revealed to any other persons, firms or organizations.

8. Conflicting Management. The consultant manager agrees not to engage in any other employment, occupation, consulting, or other business activity related to the business in which the merchant is now involved or becomes involved during the Term of the Agreement, nor will the consultant engage in any other activities that conflict with the consultant's obligations to the company.

9. Employment of Others. The company may from time to time request that the consultant arrange for the services of others. Unless otherwise agreed, all costs to the consultant for those services will be paid by the company but in no event shall the consultant employ others without the prior authorization of the company.

10. This Agreement and the Order constitute the entire agreement of the parties with respect to the subject matter of the Order. This Agreement shall be governed by and construed in accordance with the laws of the State of Virginia, without giving effect to principles of conflicts of law. Any dispute arising out of or relating to this Agreement shall be brought exclusively in the federal or state courts located in the State of Virignia, the jurisdiction and venue of which the parties irrevocably consent to for this purpose.

Week 4: Finalize Payment Models and Cookie Life

Now is the time to make the decisions pertaining to affiliate compensation, which is one of the most important parts of the prelaunch phase.

In an effort to help you choose the best payment model for your case, this chapter will cover real-life examples of how other merchants have set up their programs. It will explore whether a two-tier program is right for you as well as look at the important subject of cookie life. By the end of this week, you should have a good idea of what and how you will be paying your affiliates.

Chapter Contents

Monday: Decide on the Payment Models to Use

In Chapter 2, "Budget, Payments, and Related Considerations," I defined the payment models used in affiliate programs. Now is the time for you to decide which ones you're going to use and how.

Out of the four payment models mentioned—pay-per-click (PPC), pay per lead (PPL), pay per sale (PPS), and pay per call (PPCall)—I strongly discourage merchants (especially those new to affiliate marketing) from using the first one. As mentioned previously, this model makes a merchant particularly vulnerable to click fraud, and unless you have a savvy fraud prevention system in place, it is better to refrain from using it in your affiliate program.

Also, please do not confuse the PPC payment model with pay-per-click marketing (also commonly abbreviated as PPC), which is a viable marketing method used by many affiliates. When I say PPC now, I am referring to a model where merchants decide to pay affiliates for clicks/hits referred to the merchant's site.

Now, let's turn to the remaining three payment models; with the help of real-life examples, I'll illustrate how some merchants are utilizing them (exclusively or combining more than one payment model within one affiliate program).

PPS Model or Paying for Sales

Figure 6.1 shows how Walmart.com uses this classic payment model, remunerating affiliates by sharing a percentage of every sale with them.

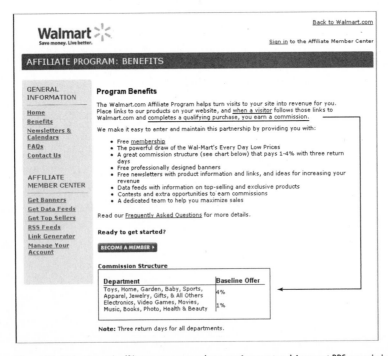

Figure 6.1 Walmart.com's affiliate program pays between 1 percent and 4 percent PPS commission.

It is not unusual for the term *revenue sharing* to be transferred onto this payment model, but it is not exactly the correct term to use here. Unlike it is in traditional business contexts where revenue sharing presupposes the sharing of both profits and losses between business partners, the PPS affiliate payment model implies rewarding affiliates through a commission off the full sale amount.

PPL Model of Paying for Leads

Intuit's Small Business division runs a PPL affiliate program for its website-building software (Figure 6.2).

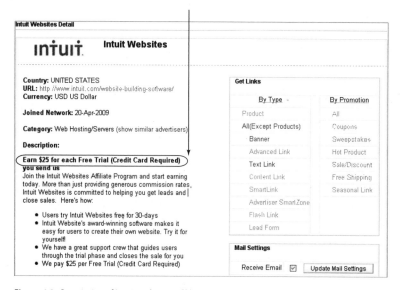

Figure 6.2 Description of Intuit website's affiliate program

Lead is defined by Intuit as a subscription for a 30-day trial with a compulsory provision of credit card. Once these criteria are met, affiliates receive their commissions.

Remember, when deciding to pay for leads, you want to clearly understand both the fraud potential and the low quality of leads that can come from incentive affiliates. That's not to say this is not a good model to use. It is just one that requires additional affiliate screening and scrupulous monitoring of affiliate-referred leads. In certain situations, you'll be better off using the PPS model instead.

PPL and PPS Models Used Conjointly

Figure 6.3 demonstrates how a merchant uses both the pay-per-lead and pay-per-sale models together.

Figure 6.3 The RingCentral affiliate program pays both for leads and for sales.

RingCentral provides exemplary definitions of each qualifying action. *Lead* is defined as a "submitted Free Trial of a RingCentral product," while *sale* is an action whereby the end consumer purchases "a paid subscription," either directly through a Buy Now option or by converting into a paid customer after trying the product for free (that is, while having a lead status).

Besides the above-quoted way of doing it, some merchants choose to combine PPL and PPS by paying commissions on sales (PPS) but also by paying a new customer bounty (PPL) if the order comes from a *new* customer. This turns your affiliate program into a good customer acquisition (and not merely customer retention) tool.

PPCall Model or Paying for Calls

I do not know of any affiliate programs that pay for calls only, even though it is possible to set up a program like that. Most merchants use the PPCall model conjointly with either PPS or PPL models (see the following examples). One of the more popular platforms is RingRevenue (mentioned in Chapter 2), which works with most major affiliate networks. If you accept phone orders or are interested in phone leads, I strongly encourage you to look into utilizing this model in your affiliate program as well.

PPS and PPCall Models Used Conjointly

It isn't unusual for a PPS affiliate program to add a pay-per-call component to it and start compensating affiliates both for sales that close online and for sales that close over the phone. Figure 6.4 shows how one online merchant utilizes this combination.

Figure 6.4 USSatellite.com's HughesNet affiliate program pays for online and over-the-phone sales.

The dedicated toll-free phone numbers mentioned in the description of this particular affiliate program constitute the primary way PPCall transactions are tracked by the PPCall platform.

PPL and PPCall Models Used Conjointly

Figure 6.5 shows how a merchant uses PPCall conjointly with the older PPL compensation model.

The previous examples have illustrated the different options; now you just need to decide which one(s) will work best for you and move on to the next step.

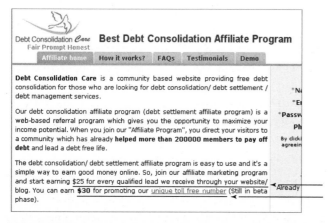

Figure 6.5 DebtConsolidationCare.com remunerates both online and phone leads, paying more for the latter.

Tuesday: Determine Whether You Need a Two-Tier Program

Remember our discussion in Chapter 1, "Understand Affiliate Marketing," about sub-affiliates? Now the time has come to decide whether you want them, and consequently, whether you need a single- or a two-tier affiliate program.

I've already mentioned that merchants should avoid multitier commission structures. My advice is the same for two-tier programs. Unless you are starting your affiliate program to recruit affiliate program directories to find affiliates for you, do not even start thinking about that second tier. Put yourself in the affiliate's shoes. What would you rather do: recruit competitors (other affiliates) to earn the first-tier money while you get your second-tier cuts, or get a larger (and only) first-tier commission from the start?

Speaking with affiliates over the years, I have found that although some do join two-tier affiliate programs, the vast majority would much rather get a higher commission on the first (and only) tier, because most affiliates promote merchants by themselves and have no use for the second tier at all.

If you do decide to have a two-tier affiliate program, you can compensate affiliates for bringing new affiliates into your affiliate program in two ways:

- A flat fee per every sign-up they refer
- A percentage tied either to the commission received by the first-tier affiliate or to the monetary value of sales they refer

Figure 6.6 gives you a sneak peek into how you could easily set up a two-tier program on one of the affiliate networks.

Figure 6.6 Two-tier affiliate program setup interface on ShareASale

A percentage tied to the performance of the first-tier affiliate is obviously preferred by second-tier affiliates, while a bounty per sign-up is often preferable for merchants. The latter model also works well for affiliate program directories, which will then be remunerated for the affiliate recruitment help you will receive from them.

Also, should you decide to go with a percentage, do not be surprised if you start seeing affiliates self-referring themselves (under different accounts)—just to ensure they receive the maximum possible commission from your affiliate program. Be prepared to address such situations in an affiliate-friendly way.

Wednesday: Study Cookie Retention Data and Make Conclusions

Cookies constitute an integral tracking element both for online marketing and analytics in general and for affiliate marketing in particular. In fact, at the time of this writing the *majority* of affiliate marketing platforms rely on cookies for tracking.

As explained in the previous chapters, affiliate cookie life is the time span that starts with a consumer clicking an affiliate link and that ends on the day beyond which you, as a merchant, do not want to remunerate the affiliate for the visitor they sent to you. It is the time period within which you will pay the referring affiliate their commission on the orders placed by the referred customer.

At this stage, you need to decide on the length of cookie life. However, before I make any recommendations on it and you decide what makes sense in your own context, I'll briefly show two research studies on the subject: a study of cookie retention rates and a return days analysis.

Cookie Retention Rates

A study conducted by Paul Strupp and published on his Web Analytics Analyzed blog in mid-2009 revealed some very interesting data. Strupp gathered data on how long cookies are on users' computers before they get deleted and discovered the following numbers (Figure 6.7):

One day: 85 percent

Two days: 75 percent

Three days: 70 percent

Four days: 63 percent

Five days: 55 percent

Past day 5, the drop becomes less sharp, and by day 45, we see that some 50 percent of users have their cookies deleted; 360 days past the initial visit, the rate levels out at around 20 percent.

This data shows that the majority of Internet users who delete cookies do so within the first 30 days since the moment that cookie is set. Starting from day 60, the rate of decay acquires a more gradual character, dropping 45 percent to 40 percent between days 60 and 120, then from 40 percent to 30 percent from day 120 to 210, and from 30 percent to about 20 percent between days 210 and 360.

This study has immediate implications for the context of affiliate marketing. It helps merchants make a more educated decision on the fair affiliate cookie life to set, and it equally makes affiliates better equipped for determining which merchants to partner with based on the cookie life they offer through their affiliate programs.

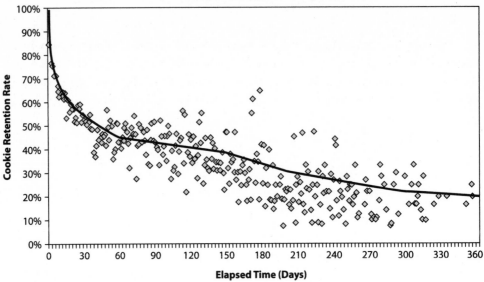

Return Users on Same Computer

Figure 6.7 Cookie retention rate analysis by Paul Strupp

Return Days Analysis

Now let's look at the timing of affiliate-referred purchases. Does the previous data on consumers deleting cookies from their computers mean that affiliates lose some 15 percent of their sales at the end of day 1, 25 percent by the end of day 2, and as many as 45 percent by the end of day 5? No, it doesn't.

Analyzing the data on the purchasing days of affiliate-referred traffic, I looked at the sales in two affiliate programs of merchants in different verticals: one with a 30-day average order value (AOV) of $45.26 and cookie life of 90 days and another one with a 30-day AOV of $95.66 and cookie life of 60 days.

Figure 6.8 shows the data for Merchant A, revealing that the vast majority of orders (82 percent) occurred on the day of click on the affiliate link, 3 percent occurred within one to two days, 3 percent occurred within three to five days, 6 percent occurred within five to fifteen days, and 6 percent of consumers took more than fifteen days to make their purchase decision.

Some may think that higher value orders take longer to put through, and this was generally confirmed by the data under review. Looking at the stats for Merchant A, you can see the following:

Same-day purchases: $45.95

1–2 days: $35.15

3–5 days: $36.85

5–15 days: $55.11

The rest: $57.21

Now let's turn to Merchant B. In Figure 6.9, you can see that 88 percent of customers made their purchase on the day of click on an affiliate link, while 5 percent took one to two days to decide, 2 percent took three to five days, 3 percent took five to fifteen days, and 3 percent took more than fifteen days.

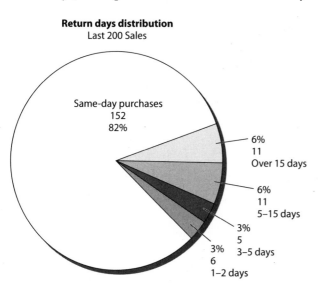

Return days distribution
Last 200 Sales

Same-day purchases
152
82%

6%
11
Over 15 days

6%
11
5–15 days

3%
5
3–5 days

3%
6
1–2 days

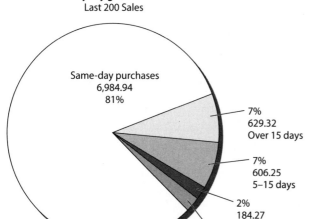

Return days by gross sale amount
Last 200 Sales

Same-day purchases
6,984.94
81%

7%
629.32
Over 15 days

7%
606.25
5–15 days

2%
184.27
3–5 days

2%
210.92
1–2 days

Figure 6.8 Return days distribution for Merchant A

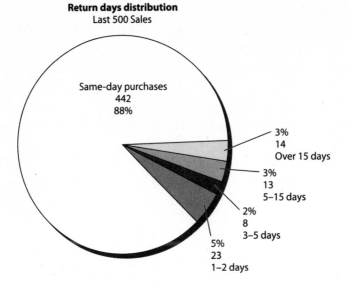

Return days distribution
Last 500 Sales

Same-day purchases
442
88%

3%
14
Over 15 days

3%
13
5–15 days

2%
8
3–5 days

5%
23
1–2 days

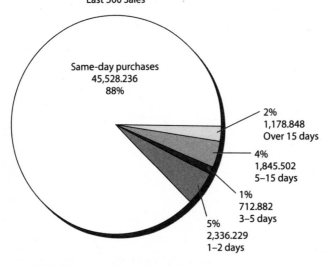

Return days by gross sale amount
Last 500 Sales

Same-day purchases
45,528.236
88%

2%
1,178.848
Over 15 days

4%
1,845.502
5–15 days

1%
712.882
3–5 days

5%
2,336.229
1–2 days

Figure 6.9 Return days distribution for Merchant B

What about the average order amounts? The stats for Merchant B are as follows:

Same-day purchases: $103.01

1–2 days: $101.58

3–5 days: $89.11

5–15 days: $141.96

The rest: $84.20

Conclusion

Although it does take customers somewhat longer to decide on higher-priced items and larger orders, the vast majority of affiliate-referred purchases happens on the day of the user's click on an affiliate link. Based on the previously quoted statistics, why not offer affiliates 365 days of cookies or even lifetime cookies?

I recommend to my clients that they set the default cookie life for their affiliate programs at the 90-day mark and offer affiliates cookie life increases (to 180 and 365/ unlimited days) as a bonus for their activity in your affiliate program. As the previous data has clearly illustrated, there is no reason not to do this. Longer cookie durations certainly have a high perceived value in affiliates' eyes, being of a relatively low "cost" to the merchant.

Thursday: Calculate Commission Budgeting in Incentives

When deciding the level at which to set the default commission rate, you want to calculate what you can afford to pay but also remember to leave room for network fees, commission increase offers, promos, and private offers. Also, it is good to factor in tiered commission increases that would be tied to the affiliate's performance with your program. Figure 6.10 shows how a merchant's performance incentives look on the affiliate end at Commission Junction.

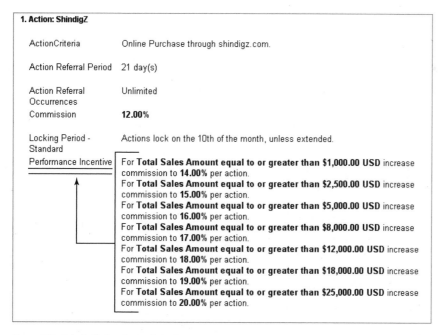

Figure 6.10 ShindigZ's tiered commission increase structure

The goal with these commission increases is to make them enticing and motivating to affiliates to perform better. Therefore, you must set *realistic* goals. Figure 6.11 portrays how a merchant with an average order value of some $450 has their performance incentives set up on Commission Junction.

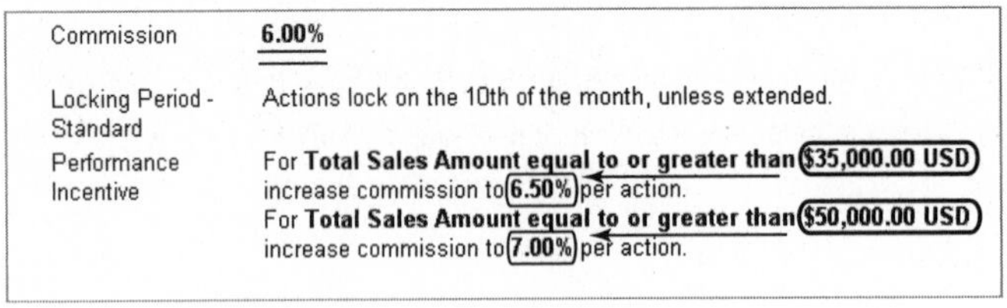

Commission	**6.00%**
Locking Period - Standard	Actions lock on the 10th of the month, unless extended.
Performance Incentive	For **Total Sales Amount equal to or greater than** $35,000.00 USD increase commission to 6.50% per action. For **Total Sales Amount equal to or greater than** $50,000.00 USD increase commission to 7.00% per action.

Figure 6.11 Example of unrealistic goals for commission increases

Simple math shows that to get a 0.5 percent commission increase, an affiliate has to refer some 78 orders for this fairly pricey product. Multiplying $450 by 0.5 percent, you will see that they will then earn $175.50 more than usual (not too big of an incentive, in my opinion). Looking at the next tier, you can see that to get a 1 percent commission instead, an affiliate would have to send more than 111 orders to this merchant. If that's all you can afford, replace these minimal commission increases by cash bonuses instead (for example, $100 with every 45th order referred).

There are various opinions on how to calculate what you can afford to pay your affiliates. Some would say to pay as much of your gross profit margin as possible, and if you can afford to pay out as much as 50 percent of that margin, do so. The idea behind such thinking is to be generous to your affiliates, as you indeed should be. However, do not forget to think three steps ahead and leave a little room for growth. Starting from around 40 to 50 percent of your gross profit margin may be a better idea to determine the *maximum* affiliate commission you want to pay.

If your calculations show that the maximum you can afford to pay your affiliates is 15 percent of each sale they send to you, do not set the base commission at the 15 percent. Leave the largest possible commission for private offers. Private offers are essentially special commission rates offered to a limited number of affiliates—those that already have the traffic you are interested in (or are already promoting your direct competitors) and, hence, are able to send you a considerable amount of traffic and sales. Again, you want to leave the maximum possible commission amount for those private offers.

A word of warning about private offers (and tiered commissions too): you do not want to have too big a disparity between your public offer and your highest tier (or private offer). For example, having a 1 percent base commission with tiers going up to 5 percent (depending on volume) is very unmotivating for affiliates.

> **Note:** As you decide on the affiliate payment model, there is one mistake you want to avoid at all costs. Do not set your default commission/payout level so high that you have to lower it at a later time.
>
> I've seen merchants do this in the past, and it is a really dreadful mistake. It will do a lot of damage to your program and in some cases will even bury it. Put yourself into your affiliate's place, and you will understand why. Respect your affiliates, and let your actions mirror this respect.
>
> If, for some reason, you absolutely have to lower your base commission level, make sure you grandfather all your existing affiliates at the current rate (even if it produces a slight loss on each sale) and have the new lower commission rate apply only to new affiliates.

Incentives and Tiered Commission Increases

Let's now talk about commission increases and promotions in a little more detail. If you are going to be managing your affiliate program the very best way you can, you will be running various promotions (the third part of this book will help you with those), and you will, at times, need some room to raise that commission level or offer various bonuses. I advise my clients to set the default commission rate at least 20 percent lower than the maximum commission they are willing to pay. Some superaffiliates, however, will not consider a 20 percent increase to be substantial and will consider only 50 percent or even 100 percent commission increases. In some situations, it will work for you; in others, it won't. The very first affiliate program I launched had the base commission set at 10 percent, but I was paying nearly all active affiliates 14 to 15 percent and one superaffiliate 18 percent.

Although I believe that monetary, or extrinsic, motivators are not the best motivators to help one achieve optimal performance, there certainly is room for them in affiliate program management. I also recommend being prepared to offer between 30 percent and 40 percent (depending on your niche and what your competitors are doing) of your default commission to stimulate performance (even if for a limited time period or to select affiliates).

Types of Monetary Incentives

Extrinsic affiliate incentives come in three basic forms:

- Cash bonuses (for example, refer 5 leads within 30 days of sign-up; get a $50 bonus on top of commission)
- Commission increases (for example, place our link above the competitor's and get a higher per-sale payout)
- Prizes (for example, electronics such as Kindle devices, iPods, video game systems, and so on; Amazon.com gift certificates; tickets to industry conferences; a year's supply of coffee)

Every extrinsic incentive should always have a definitive and measurable action attached to it. Be it a link placement, a sale, or a certain volume of sales, monetary incentives follow the basics of the "carrot-and-stick" theory—with the only difference being that with affiliates, sticks don't work. I will discuss the subject of motivation at a later point in the book, but now know that monetary incentives may differ in character/frequency. They may be *temporary*, meaning that affiliates are required to perform continuously to qualify for them, or *permanent*, meaning that they are activated for *life* when the affiliate reaches a certain performance threshold (see Figures 6.12 and 6.13).

How Is My Referral Rate Determined?

If you select the Performance structure, your referral rate will be based on your total number of shipped items from both Amazon and third-party sellers. The same rate will apply equally to both Amazon and third-party items, and will apply to all referred items shipped during the month. Please refer to the Referral Rate Tier Chart below for additional detail.

Referral Rate Tier Chart	Glossary
Total Items Shipped	**Referral Rates (All Categories except Consumer Electronics)**
1 - 6	4.00%
7 - 30	6.00%
31 - 110	6.50%
111 - 320	7.00%
321 - 630	7.50%
631 - 1570	8.00%
1571 - 3130	8.25%
3131 +	8.50%

Figure 6.12 Amazon.com compensates affiliates with higher commissions for selling more items, but the commission drops back to 4 percent at the beginning of each month.

Commission Rates

It is our belief that affiliates should be justly remunerated for their marketing efforts. We have therefore created a commission structure where your earnings (and commission levels) are directly connected to your performance with our program.

Our default commission levels are:

12% for "non-card" products
15% for all "card" sales

Once you have referred a cumulative amount of $1,500 worth of sales to DaySpring, we will raise your commissions to:
13% for non-card products
16% for cards

Finally, once you've crossed the $2,000 threshold, your commission levels will be raised to:
14% for non-cards
18% for cards

Once you have reached the next qualifying level, please contact us via e-mail for us to push the new Program Terms your way.

FAQ

Sign Up

Copyright 2009 DaySpring ® Cards. All rights reserved.

Figure 6.13 DaySpring.com's affiliates are rewarded by permanent commission increases.

There is room for both temporary and permanent application of extrinsic incentives. Things are pretty straightforward with the permanent commission increases or regularly paid out bonuses. When it comes to temporary commission increases, however, there is a right and wrong way of doing it. It is OK to set monthly goals (in other words, sales/leads thresholds) and consistently remunerate better performance. It is not

OK to raise the payouts for *all* affiliates in the program (to facilitate post-Christmas sales, for example) but then drop them once the sales pick up again.

Ultimate Affiliate Contest

This is an example of a contest that involved very tangible extrinsic incentives in the form of prizes. The only thing that has been taken out of the wording are the names of participating merchants.

All over the world the countdown to Christmas begins around this time of the year. In the United States, today is, of course, Black Friday.

I am a firm believer that those who work hard deserve to play hard. Today I hope to bring a little more excitement into the pre-Christmas sales by introducing you to this new affiliate contest. Here are the details of the contest:

Contest Type: Performance-based affiliate contest

Dates: November 23, 2007, to November 23, 2007 (contest ends at midnight PST)

Conditions: To qualify for the prizes announced, an affiliate has to generate a set qualifying number of sales either within one of or across the following five affiliate programs we manage:

- *Merchant A*
- *Merchant B*
- *Merchant C*
- *Merchant D*
- *Merchant E*

Prizes:

First Prize 500 or more sales—Cruise around Europe for two (with Holland America Line; round-trip airfare to Europe included)

Second Prize 300 or more sales—Latest MacBook Pro (4 GB 250 GB 17-inch Intel Core 2 Duo 2.4 GHz and much more)

Third Prize 100 or more sales—500 gallons of gas (valid for continental United States only, any state; non–U.S. affiliates will be remunerated with a prize of equal monetary value [approx. $1,500])

Important: There is one first prize, two second prizes, and three third prizes. Prizes will be awarded on the "first-come/first-served" basis (or rather: the first qualified is the first awarded, of course).

Restrictions: Affiliates who bid on trademarks with programs that prohibit doing so will not qualify regardless of how many sales they send.

Looking forward to a hot season of pre-Christmas affiliate sales now!!

Friday: Finalize Overall Payment Terms

The key program terms you should get finalized by the end of this week are all related to governing your affiliate payments. There are six, as covered in the following sections. You will want to document them all—both for yourself and for your affiliates. You will need these notes for the affiliate program agreement, which you will develop prior to having your program go live.

Qualifying Action

Be it buying a product, filling out a lead form, or anything else, define the qualifying action as clearly as possible. There should be no misunderstanding between you and your affiliates on what exactly they will be compensated for.

Also, having reviewed descriptions of several affiliate programs run by established brands, I've noticed that some of them state they will reward affiliates only for "*new* and *unique*" customers. I am strongly against such an approach. These merchants are pushing away thousands of affiliates in the prerecruitment phase just by having this policy in place. In fact, this is just one silly affiliate marketing policy to have. Why? Let's go back to Figure 2.5 in Chapter 2. Close to 72 percent of respondents said that they *will* shop around again before making their next purchase even after receiving satisfactory service from a merchant. Therefore, merchants that run affiliate programs should compensate every sale equally—or even offer an additional bonus for new customers—but by no means should they limit affiliate commissions to new customers only.

Cookie Life

I discussed cookie life at length earlier. My recommendation is to set your default cookie life at a period between 90 and 120 days but offer cookie life increases to 180 and 365 days (or unlimited, if your affiliate platform supports this) on an ongoing basis. One idea is to include a commission increase *and* cookie life increase right in the affiliate application approval email (providing one level of increase for link placements and a higher level for a certain performance). Be generous with those cookies. It is the very least you can do to make your program affiliate-friendly.

Payment Models

Which payment models are you going to employ? Is it going to be just one or more than one model? With the pay-per-call model generating truly impressive results and yielding valuable leads, it seems that the age of one payment model per program is quickly coming to an end. Decide what you're going do in your program, and write it down.

Commission

Define how much you are going to pay affiliates within each supported model. Remember to do your due diligence researching what competing affiliate programs offer, and keep in mind the incentives that you do want to factor into the game as well.

Incentives

Although incentives may come in the form of one-time cash bonuses or permanent or temporary commission increases, may depend on continuous performance, or may be tied to reaching particular performance thresholds, the math always remains the same. I recommend leaving between 30 percent and 60 percent of your default affiliate commission for any additional incentives.

Locking Period

In Chapter 2 I talked about scenarios when reversals of affiliate commissions are possible. These range from fraud to duplicate and canceled orders. The time period within which you may reverse an affiliate transaction is called a *locking* or *lock* period. If you take the ShareASale affiliate network, for example, you will see that for every transaction in its reports, merchants see a lock date (Figure 6.14).

Figure 6.14 Merchant's transaction report on ShareASale

Affiliates, on the other hand, see both the lock date and the transaction status (Figure 6.15).

Date [sort]	Transaction ID [sort]	Sale Amount	Commission [sort]
08/24/2009 12:03:02 PM	[22768756]	6.99	$0.56
OrderID Sale - 100518779 ↕ Defined Sub-Tracking:		Processing Lock Date: 09/20/2009	
		Affiliate Sub-Tracking:	
	IP: Available to Merchant	Port: GET 443	

Figure 6.15 Example of how an affiliate sees the previously quoted transaction

If you look at Commission Junction, you'll notice that affiliates see the same data in the program terms. Figure 6.16 shows how it looks in Overstock.com's affiliate program.

Program Term: Overstock

Special Terms and Conditions

1. Action: Sale

ActionCriteria	Customer must complete an online purchase within our shopping cart.
Action Referral Period	14 day(s)
Action Referral Occurrences	Unlimited
Commission	**7.00%**
	1.00% on Item List: Electronics
	1.00% on Item List: Media
	5.00% on Item List: Apparel
	5.00% on Item List: JewelryWatches
	7.00% on Item List: AutoParts
	7.00% on Item List: Bulk
	7.00% on Item List: Gifts
	7.00% on Item List: GiftCards
	7.00% on Item List: Home
	7.00% on Item List: Office
	7.00% on Item List: Sports
	7.00% on Item List: Warranties
	7.00% on Item List: Worldstock
	$0.00 USD on Item List: Donations
Locking Period - Custom	Actions lock **50** days after event date.

Figure 6.16 Overstock.com affiliate program's locking period

Overstock.com is giving itself 50 days to reverse (or adjust) any affiliate transaction. Once the locking period has passed or the lock date has come, the commission gets permanently locked in the affiliate account, and the merchant can no longer do anything to that transaction (voiding, editing, and so on).

Most affiliate networks allow merchants to choose the length of time within which they want to be able to edit/void affiliate commissions. Merchants base this decision on how quickly they can verify the validity of affiliate-referred sales/leads, on their experience with returns, or on whatever other reasons may influence the commission reversal/adjustment. For example, Commission Junction's default locking period/date is the 10th date of every month (on ShareASale it's the 20th of each month), but as is evident from the previous example, Overstock.com has decided to tie it to the number of days past the order placement.

Affiliates do understand why you want to have the "locking periods" in place. As with anything, however, merchants want to be careful not to abuse this right, and my recommendation is to do all possible not to go beyond the default locking period time suggested by your affiliate network. If you're setting up an in-house affiliate program, do all you can to make the locking period as brief as possible (within your own constraints, of course).

Once all six of the previously quoted payment-related components/terms are finalized, you are ready to proceed to the next step, which is the setup phase.

Month 2: Setting Your Affiliate Program Up

III

Now that you're ready to proceed with the setup of your future affiliate program, you want to diligently work your way through several fundamental areas. These will include your creative inventory, additional tools and functionalities (like data feeds, plug-ins, widgets, video, etc.), a detailed and thorough program agreement, tracking implementation and testing, and so on. By the end of the next four-week period you should have your affiliate program ready for the launch.

Week 1: Develop Creative Inventory

7

You cannot launch an affiliate program without a single creative. Be it a banner or a text link, you want to have something for affiliates to use. However, not all creatives are created equal. Some are just for particular contexts, and others are more universal. Some consistently show higher click-through rates (CTR), while others consistently yield lower volumes of clicks.

This chapter will be devoted to the important subject of affiliate creatives. At the end of this week, you should have a creative arsenal to be proud of. Just pay attention to all of the details, and it will save you a lot of time redoing what could have been done right from the very start.

Chapter Contents

Monday: Review Types of Creatives Used by Affiliates
Tuesday: Understand and Put Together Text Links
Wednesday: Learn About Banner Usage and Popular Sizes
Thursday: Review Banner Creation Mistakes and Work on Banners
Friday: Develop a Dynamic Creative Policy

Monday: Review Types of Creatives Used by Affiliates

Depending on their own marketing strategies and approaches, affiliates use different types of creatives—frequently multiple types at the same time. Types of creatives include the following:

- Text links
- Data feeds
- Banners
- Widgets
- Video
- Flash
- Advanced Form-Based Links

Let's look at each type of creative to understand what it means:

Text Links A text link is a kind of hyperlink. Unlike image or script-based hyperlinks, text links have only text in the "body" of the link. Many affiliates use them, positioning them within the content (Figure 7.1) that is of immediate use to the website visitor.

If you find it hard to resist incredible **deals on Christmas clearance**, do not check out all the adorable stuff at <u>DaySpring</u>.

If you do, you just might find some irresistible prices on gifts, ornaments, decor at up to 75% off. I simply love the "Jesus is the Gift" collection!

Of course, if you prefer to stock up on items like this- after the holidays- then <u>see what is available</u>. The good stuff is going quickly, so don't wait if you see an item you love!

- Use coupon code **NOSHIPCHARGE** on orders of $10 or more to receive free shipping upon checkout!

Share this Post:

Figure 7.1 Blogger using DaySpring.com affiliate text links

Data Feeds Any data feed is essentially a file (CSV, XML, XLS, or any other type) that lists all your product information in a format that the affiliate can interpret and understand, with or without the help of any additional piece of software. By supplying affiliates with data feeds, merchants are aiming to enable them to feature their products right at the affiliate websites (Figure 7.2). I will discuss product feeds in greater detail in the next chapter.

Banners As a linguist, I can't help but appreciate the etymology of the word *banner*, which historically stood for a piece of cloth attached to a staff and used by monarchs and military men, such as knights. In our day and age, the word is more frequently being used to designate a graphic image online advertisement. Banners are still one of the easiest ways to get an affiliate link up and running, and Figure 7.3 shows a very vivid example of an affiliate website running banners of various sizes.

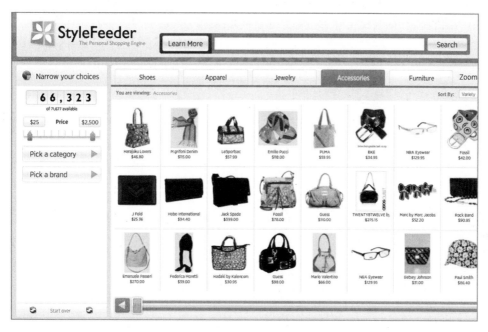

Figure 7.2 Acting as an affiliate, StyleFeeder.com uses hundreds of merchant data feeds.

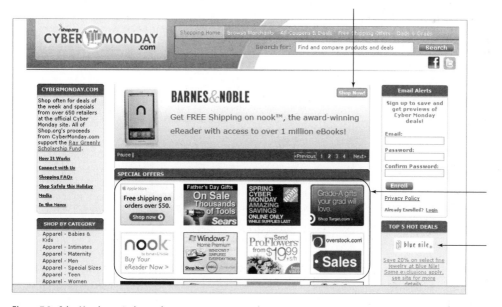

Figure 7.3 CyberMonday actively uses banners to promote merchants.

Widgets A widget normally represents a concise string of code that an affiliate can grab and execute within their web pages. The uniqueness of widgets in comparison with other creatives is that they are dynamic, and even once placed on affiliate sites, the merchant can update the widgets' contents. One of the first affiliate networks to promote affiliate widgets was ShareASale, and Figure 7.4 shows an example of one such widget. As is frequently the case, this example shows a list of merchants' best sellers by category, as well as provides access to each merchant's latest coupons and deals.

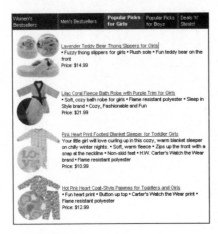

Figure 7.4 Affiliate widget from CrazyForBargains.com

Amazon's exemplary affiliate widgets should definitely be mentioned too. Not only does Amazon have a variety of them—see http://widgets.amazon.com/—but it also provides its affiliates with a capability to build and customize their own widgets (Figure 7.5).

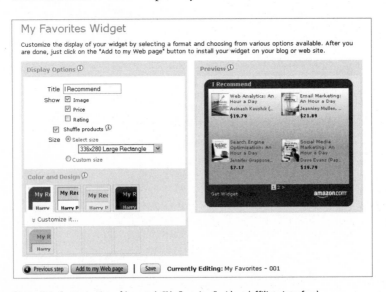

Figure 7.5 Customization of Amazon's "My Favorites" widget (affiliate interface)

Video Online video does not require much introduction. YouTube—which is the world's third most visited website and one of the top three Internet's search engines—is known to everyone, my six-year-old daughter included. The level of viewer engagement that online video makes possible is unparalleled, which often yields a conversion rate that is one of the highest among all other creatives. More and more affiliates are starting to experiment with online video (Figure 7.6).

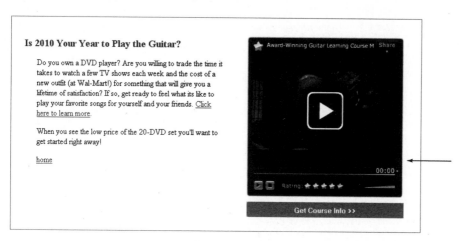

Figure 7.6 Affiliate using a Legacy Learning Systems video creative

Regardless of the fact that online video has already been around for some time, it is still a fairly untapped affiliate marketing resource. We will discuss the topic in further detail in the following chapter.

Flash Flash is a multimedia technology created to make effective interactivity happen on a graphic creative of a relatively small file size. Flash ads are nearly impossible to convey via printed media because with a static look they do not differ from traditional banner JPEG or GIF ads. The dimensions of Flash ads also follow traditional banner size conventions.

Advanced Form-Based Links These types of creatives are a little more advanced and are altogether more technologically beautiful forms of affiliate creatives. They are the solutions that are offered by merchants to affiliates for the latter to act as marketers of merchants' goods/services, plugging an advanced creative into their site but pulling the necessary information from the merchants' server. One example of such a solution is a search box banner (see Figure 7.7).

Other examples of form-based affiliate links include instant online quotes (for example, insurance), domain registration, or any custom services (for example, translation). Figures 7.8 and 7.9 show how the process works from an affiliate website to a merchant website.

Figure 7.7 Priceline.com's affiliate banner with three search options embedded

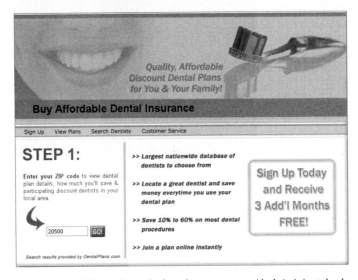

Figure 7.8 This affiliate website asks the end consumer to provide their zip/postal code.

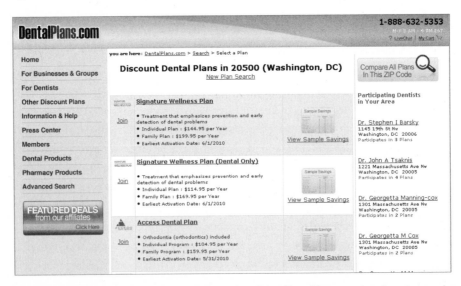

Figure 7.9 Upon hitting the Go button, the user lands on the website of DentalPlans.com where the options may be reviewed.

Deciding Where to Start

Having reviewed the previous definitions and examples, you're probably thinking "But what types of creatives are more important: banners, text links, data feeds...?" This is an understandable question. Do not be overwhelmed by all these choices, but also understand that asking a question like that is akin to asking which type of affiliates is more important: those that use banners, text links, or data feeds? All are important, and your aim is to provide all of these affiliate groups with data, graphics, and links with which to work.

However, I cannot cover all of these in a quality way in a short period of time, and if I were to single out just one type of creative, it would certainly be text links. Interestingly, it isn't unusual to see an affiliate program without any text links at all. That's no good. Historically, text links have had a better click-through rate (CTR) than banners and almost always *convert better.* Why "almost"? In reality, much depends on the type of affiliate program in question and other factors, such as what landing pages the creatives lead to, what type of offers/products you are comparing, how exactly affiliates are using the code (fully or picking up just the tracking part out of it), and so on.

Figures 7.10 and 7.11 show some interesting data that I have collected to review and compare.

ᐱLink type	Clicks	Imps	CTR	CR
Banner	29,347	16,273,959	0.18%	1.71%
Flash Link	335	16,339	2.05%	7.16%
Product Catalog	18,138	217,739	8.33%	1.31%
Text Link	27,775	1,428,495	1.94%	2.80%

Figure 7.10 Performance of different types of affiliate links in a PPS affiliate program (retail merchant)

ᐱLink type	Clicks	Imps	CTR	CR
Banner	2,405	700,902	0.34%	5.28%
Flash Link	0	4	0.00%	0.00%
Text Link	4,060	6,747	60.17%	0.74%

Figure 7.11 Performance of different types of affiliate links in a PPL affiliate program (insurance vertical)

So, in a pay-per-sale affiliate program of one retailer (Figure 7.10), you can see the following:

- *Product links* have the highest CTR (as is often the case with online retailers).
- *Text links* outperform all other links (I will comment separately about Flash in a moment) both in CTR and in conversion rate (CR).
- *Banners* have the lowest CTR of all other creatives in the program.
- *Flash links* show a surprisingly beautiful CTR and an excellent CR of more than 7 percent, but, in all honesty, the sample is too small to make any final conclusions on this one.

In a pay-per-lead affiliate program of one insurance company (Figure 7.11), you can see a very interesting picture (one that is somewhat different from the previously described one):

- On the CTR front, *text links* outperformed banners with a truly impressive lead (60 percent vs. 0.3 percent).

- But on the CR front, *banners* seem to be significantly more effective than text links, improving conversion by more than seven times (5.28 percent vs. 0.74 percent).

This comparison illustrates the importance of practicing an *assortment strategy* when it comes to affiliate creatives. Cover all of these, and beyond, and give affiliates room to experiment with different kinds of links.

In the rest of this chapter you will look at text links and banners, while in the following chapter I will talk about data feeds, online video, and other types of creatives.

Landing Pages

Before we go any further, let's address something that is all too often ignored by merchants with affiliate programs.

Each creative—regardless of type—is connected to a landing page, and the success of every affiliate campaign is always shared between the affiliate's marketing efforts, the quality of the creative, and the excellence of the corresponding landing page. Let's briefly look at the main things to focus on while creating your landing pages, one of the most frequently overlooked components of creative strategies.

Merchants should keep five things in mind while creating landing pages for their affiliate program(s):

Keep It Short but Sweet Whatever content the landing page features, it should be enticing yet laconic and to the point throughout it.

Don't Sound Like a Salesperson Oh yes, your job *is* to sell, but in the process of it, remember that too-good-to-be-true promises, fancy exaggerative adjectives, and anything else of the kind build *mis*trust.

Avoid Visual Distractions In line with keeping it short, you want to avoid anything that would divert your customer's attention from taking the desired route of action.

Provide Clear Call to Action Whatever it is that you want the end user to do upon landing on your web page, reinforce it.

Always Be Testing Never cease split-testing and improving the quality of your landing pages. Use visual attention heatmaps, as well A/B tests, to increase your (and, consequentially, your affiliates') conversion rates.

Most Valuable Creatives

Econsultancy's US Affiliate Census 2009, which asked affiliates to rank linking methods (that is, methods of sending traffic to merchant websites) in order of their relative value, revealed that banners and text links are the two most popular types of creatives (refer to Figure 7.12).

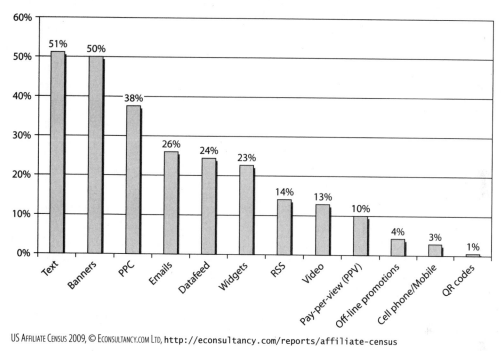

US AFFILIATE CENSUS 2009, © ECONSULTANCY.COM LTD, http://econsultancy.com/reports/affiliate-census

Figure 7.12 Most valuable affiliate linking methods

Therefore, in the remainder of this chapter, you'll learn about text links and banners, and you'll be provided with detailed recommendations on how to best handle their creation.

Tuesday: Understand and Put Together Text Links

Text links are extremely effective. They are nearly always ranked as the number-one affiliate-preferred type of link; and according to various surveys, between 35 percent and 51 percent of affiliates use them.

Properly created by the merchant and positioned by the affiliate, text links yield strong click-to-sale conversion rates. Therefore, while setting up your affiliate program, you want to provide your affiliates with a substantial array of text links leading to as many specific sections of your website as possible.

The mention of proper creation of text links wasn't accidental. There is really just one type of text link that converts best: one that is narrowly deep-linked. Nielsen Norman Group's studies of ecommerce usability show that getting from the home page of the website to the correct product page accounts for more than a quarter of all failures. NNG also measured that improved linking—and by extension, an enhanced ecommerce site's usability—can *double* an online merchant's sales! To me, this also explains why generic affiliate links seldom convert as successfully as the deep links. A merchant's home page is just one of the ways to enter the website, and its content may not fit the individual needs of any given affiliate. The one mantra that you want your affiliate text links to associate with is this: "Deep-link, deep-link, and deep-link again!"

Treat deep-linking as one of your main responsibilities. Remember two things: Text links convert eight times times better than banner links, and deeply linked text links convert two times better than those that are generic.

Another way to underscore this point is to look at the very phrase *text link*. It consists of two semantic components: "text" and "link."

Affiliates may always improve the quality of the first one (the "text"), but they may not always be able to improve the quality of the second (the "link"). Provide them with as vast a selection of deeply linked text links as possible, covering as much ground as possible. If you have a website with a total of 10 sections and 49 subsections, you should have at least 70 text links: 1 for each section, 1 for each subsection, 1 for the home page, and 10 for each of your best sellers (leading to specific product pages). Also, whenever possible, provide your affiliates with a way/tool to build their own deep links. In fact, as Gary Marcoccia, CMO of AvantLink affiliate network, says, "A deep linking tool is probably the single most important (and simple) tool to provide for affiliates." However, seldom would a merchant be able to provide affiliates with deep-linked creatives for every single page of their website. This is why a custom/deep-link tool is a must-have, and some networks (see Figures 7.13 and 7.14 for examples) do a really good job on this one.

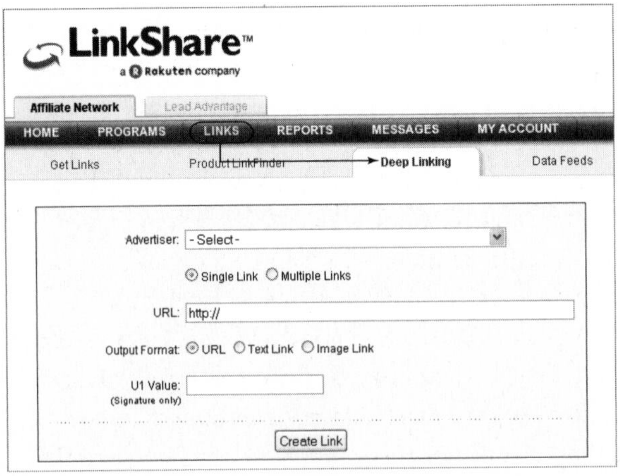

Figure 7.13 LinkShare's "deep linking" tool

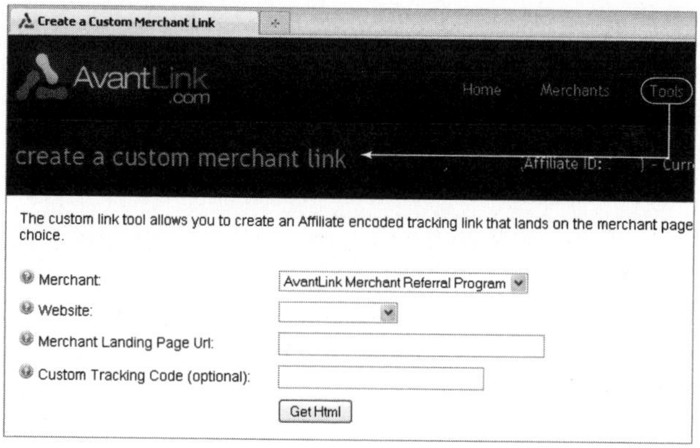

Figure 7.14 AvantLink's "create a custom merchant link" tool

Wednesday: Learn About Banner Usage and Popular Sizes

Now let's turn to affiliate banners, so you can learn how to put together a good set of them, ensuring they are also 100 percent affiliate-friendly.

Banner Sizes

The banner size (and quantity, I should add) issue is an extremely important one. I cannot understate it by saying that an affiliate manager/merchant should be prepared to put together as many banners as affiliates they recruit. Yes, there is a concrete set of banner sizes that I recommend every affiliate program to have. However, you have to be prepared that some affiliates will ask you for custom-sized banners, and you'll either want to possess basic graphics-editing skills or have access to a banner designer to readily accommodate such requests. That is one of the reasons why I recommend that merchants recognize that graphic design skills are definitely an advantage when they are hiring an affiliate program manager.

In Table 7.1, you will find the banner sizes that I recommend you eventually have for your program (they are arranged in the order of importance and affiliate demand). Some of these recommendations come from my personal observations of the sizes that affiliates prefer (for example, 88×31 pixel buttons, the importance of which you should never underestimate). The choice of some other sizes rests directly on my assumption that some of the webmasters, who will be recruited into your affiliate program, are already monetizing their traffic using Google AdSense (which consequentially translates into the importance of providing them with a banner to upload in place of an AdSense unit—for example, 120×600 pixel and 160×600 pixel skyscrapers) or display advertising networks (hence, traditional banner sizes like 468×60 pixels are a must).

Keep in mind that these sizes also apply to Flash ads, should you want to put any together. The reason for this is that, as mentioned earlier, Flash ads adhere to the same sizing conventions as traditional banners.

▶ Table 7.1 Recommended banner sizes

Size	Quantity (min–max)
468×60 pixel	7 to 10+ (target different demographics, website categories, specials, and promos)
125×125 pixel	4 to 6
120×600 pixel	4 to 6
120×90 pixel	4 to 6
120×60 pixel	4 to 6
88×31 pixel button	3 to 4
728×90 pixel	3 to 4
160×600 pixel	2 to 3
120×240 pixel	2 to 3
234×60 pixel	2 to 3
250×250 pixel	2 to 3
254×331 pixel	2 to 3
100×100 pixel	1 to 2
720×300 pixel	1 to 2
300×250 pixel	1 to 2

Do not underestimate the importance of well-designed 88×31 pixel buttons. Many affiliates love them because they can fit them in just about any place on their websites. They do convert, and they are also excellent for creating lists of merchants. However, many affiliate managers ignore these little pieces of creative. They may deem it hard to create a nice aggressive banner of that size, and for this reason they may simply skip it. Your affiliates will not appreciate this. Please let them decide what will fit their websites and what won't. Yes, you are there to advise and guide, but not offering that little button (or preferably, a *few* buttons in a variety of colors, mostly nonanimated) in the selection of your creative, or not agreeing to create one when they specifically ask you to, will not build your affiliate program a good affiliate support reputation.

Another point that needs to be made pertains to monitoring the tendencies and statistics in the graphical ads sphere throughout the Internet. Such statistics are not only viable for the company's overall advertising campaigns but can also be powerfully utilized in offering affiliate creatives that will enhance your program, putting you one step ahead of your competitors in the affiliate support arena.

NielsenOnline AdRelevance Data Glance reports are great for such monitoring. As I write this book, for example, the most popular standard ad sizes are as follows:

- Medium: 300×250 pixel rectangle (28 percent)
- Tall: 728×90 pixel leaderboard (25 percent)
- Wide: 160×600 pixel skyscraper (13 percent)

Nielsen refreshes this data on a weekly basis, so I encourage you to check the most current data as soon as you've finished this chapter. If you see some of the irregular creative sizes being used widely, ask your affiliates if they could be of use to them. They will appreciate your care in asking and will recognize your willingness to go out of your way for them.

File Size

The file size is another important area to address. Surprisingly, at the time of this book's writing, most major affiliate networks make *no recommendations* on the maximum suggested banner file size. The only network that I have seen make such a recommendation is LinkConnector. It advises that merchants' banner sizes never exceed 30 kilobytes. This particular network has actually gone as far as turning this "recommendation" into a restriction. You wouldn't be able to upload a banner that is larger than 30 KB while setting up your affiliate program with them. Although imposing such restrictions may not be a very good idea (30 KB is not much for larger skyscrapers and leaderboards, especially if you want them to be of high quality), advising merchants on the file size is actually a very good idea. It helps everyone who is involved in the affiliate marketing channel: affiliates who are using the banners, networks that are hosting them, and merchants who risk being promoted less when/if their files are too bulky.

Having polled affiliate marketers on the subject of banner file size, I have found that the 30 KB limit is right around the comfort level mark for affiliates as well (Figure 7.15).

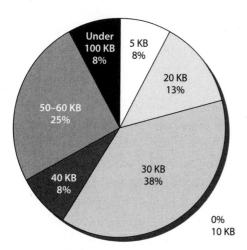

Figure 7.15 Affiliate-preferred maximum banner file size

Banner file size is not a small issue. Knowing what's preferred by affiliates helps you build more affiliate-friendly programs. So, by all means, do everything possible to prevent most of your banners from exceeding 30 KB each. If one does have to be larger than that, 60 KB is the next threshold that you want to keep in mind. It is easy to remember: $30 \times 2 = 60$.

Thursday: Review Banner Creation Mistakes and Work on Banners

Today you will concentrate on banners. You will look at the most frequently committed mistakes, examples of well-put-together banners, and also the role that competitive intelligence can serve in your task of creating a good affiliate banner inventory. By the end of the day, you will be well-equipped so that your creative team can start working on your banners.

10 Mistakes to Avoid

In this section, you will find the 10 guidelines I have put together for you to keep in mind while creating your affiliate banners. All of these are important and can make the difference between an affiliate choosing to use your banner or a banner of your competitor. So, study these thoroughly, and also let your banner designer read through them prior to starting work on your affiliate banners.

Mistake 1: Poor Graphics Many merchants use poor, pixelized graphic on their banners, and not necessarily because they do not have good graphics in their possession. Most of them are just not paying enough attention to the way the final saved version looks. This often results in an affiliate program having banners that affiliates do not want to use.

Mistake 2: Unreadable Font Make sure that the inscription (or any part of the inscription) on your banner is not too small to read. Blurry, unreadable font is neither doing your brand any good nor helping your conversion. Taglines under logos may not read well on banners of smaller sizes (like 88×31 pixel buttons). So, just take them out!

Mistake 3: Including a Phone Number Yes, some merchants actually put a toll-free phone number on their affiliate banners! If the word for the untrackable route the end user can take is a *leak*, this is an example of one super-leak, because the end consumer doesn't even need to click the banner on the affiliate site. All they have to do is just call the merchant directly, and the affiliate can forget about their commission.

Mistake 4: Including a URL No banner should have your URL spelled out on it. Affiliates do not like it because, just as in the example with the phone number, it leaves the option for the end user to bypass the click and type the URL into the address bar directly. If your domain name extension (.com, .net, .co, .uk, and so on) is part of your logo, use everything but the extension on the banner.

Mistake 5: Excessive Animation By all means, avoid excessive animation. Especially flee from short time intervals between frame changes in GIF files, which make the text on the banners too hard (if not impossible) to read. Some of the merchant's banners can make your eyes hurt. This is just one of the reasons why affiliates generally prefer banners with no animation at all. There is no need to make it flash or blink and hurt the online consumer's eyes, even when you want to emphasize something or attract attention. Play with different fonts and different colors. You can attract attention in a much more effective way if your banners do not blink.

Mistake 6: Missing Call to Action It is extremely important that each banner has a clear call to action on it (animation is acceptable, but avoid being too intrusive). Do not assume that the end user realizes that your banner is on the affiliate website to click. Less savvy users could think it merely shows the website's affiliation with you, and nothing more. So, some consumers will not even think of clicking your banners unless you explicitly ask them to. "Shop now," "Click here," "Claim/redeem now" (for coupons), and other calls to action are a must for all marketing banners, and affiliate ones are no exception.

Mistake 7: Poor Contrast It isn't unusual for an affiliate banner to have poor contrast between the inscription and the background of the banner. This makes the font very difficult to read and considerably decreases both the aesthetics and, by extension, the marketing effectiveness of the banner.

Mistake 8: Grammar Mistakes Some are bad, and others are not terrible, but a merchant has no right to make grammatical mistakes (in spelling, syntax, punctuation, anything!) on an ad. Period! Your banner on an affiliate website creates the first impression of you as a merchant. It is also providing you with branding that better be good.

Mistake 9: No Border However small this detail may seem, this is a very substantial yet widespread mistake. As a result, banners with white backgrounds literally blend into white backgrounds of affiliate websites, looking considerably less effective than the other banners an affiliate uses. Aim to stand out, not blur in!

Mistake 10: No Brand I have actually seen merchants use banners with extremely beautiful graphics but that are completely devoid of their brand names. Why? No, seriously! Do not leave your brand name out.

To conclude, the affiliate banners should attractively display your products/ offers, emphasize your selling points, and include a call to action. Their design should spell out your respect both for the end consumer and for your affiliates. For more real-life examples of all these previously quoted mistakes, you can go to `http://opmit.com/ banner-mistakes`.

Examples of Good Affiliate Banners

Russians say that "It's better to see once than hear 100 times." So, to illustrate what good affiliate program banners should look like, a few good examples are shown in Figures 7.16 through 7.24.

Figure 7.16 88×31 pixel Apple button

Figure 7.17 120×90 pixel Expedia banner

Figure 7.18 125×125 pixel JCPenney banner

Figure 7.19 180×150 pixel Expedia banner

Figure 7.20 250×250 pixel Adobe banner

Figure 7.21 468×60 pixel Priceline Europe banner

Figure 7.22 468×60 pixel Hanes banner

Figure 7.23 300×250 pixel Home Depot banner

Figure 7.24 500×200 pixel LendingTree banner

These examples should give you a few ideas and illustrate my earlier points on what to do and what not to do.

Check What's Working for Your Competition

In Chapter 3, "Week 1: Perform Competitive Marketing Analysis," I talked about the importance of ongoing competitive intelligence. It becomes extremely handy in the research phase prior to creating your affiliate banners.

Many affiliate networks allow affiliates to sort affiliate programs' links by EPC (which normally stands for average affiliate earnings on 100 clicks on a link). Look through the creatives your competitors are using, and analyze the wording and the design of their best-performing links. Once you've gotten a clear idea of what works well for them, write down the text and design ideas you want to experiment with. This should give you some great information to start with. However, remember to never stop experimenting (read: split-testing) and improving the quality of your affiliate creatives even after the launch of your affiliate program. See what's working, and replicate successes. This will benefit both you as an advertiser and your individual affiliates.

Friday: Develop a Dynamic Creative Policy

The idea behind dynamic creatives is simple—create a hassle-free solution whereby an affiliate website would always display the most updated and relevant merchant's creative. So, a creative becomes "dynamic" when it self-updates on the affiliate site every time an affiliate program manager updates it on the merchant's end. The code that the affiliate uses remains the same, but the image is swapped on the merchant's side.

Let's look at two examples of how this works: deals and seasonal banners.

In the first example, you can decide to offer time-limited deals through your affiliate program. These can refresh with whatever frequency you want: hourly, daily, weekly, biweekly, and so on. Every time your offer changes, you replace your existing "dynamic deal banner" (reflecting the most up-to-date information on what's on sale) and a new landing page link. Affiliate websites that use your dynamic "deals" creative instantly reflect the change and start serving the new banner to their visitors and landing them on the new appropriate web page.

The Global Market

If you ship/sell globally, remember to focus your dynamic creatives on the global market as well. You may know that Thanksgiving Day is celebrated on different days in Canada and the United States (second Monday in October and fourth Thursday in November, respectively), but did you know that Mother's Day is celebrated on two completely different dates (almost two months apart!) in the United States and the United Kingdom? Yes, it is. While Father's Day (in the United States and the United Kingdom) always falls on the third Sunday of June, Mother's Day is different. In United Kingdom and Ireland, they celebrate Mother's Day (also known as Mothering Sunday) on the fourth Sunday of Lent. The United States and Canada, on the other hand, celebrates Mother's Day on the second Sunday in May. Should you care to know, most of Eastern Europe, which doesn't have Mother's Day as such, congratulates mothers (with flowers and gifts) on March 8, as part of the International Women's Day. Merchants working in gifts-related and flower delivery verticals should take advantage of this—just as sports-related merchants must keep a close eye on calendars of various competitions and championships and keep their affiliates equipped with the tools to market them effectively.

With seasonal banners, you can decide to update your creatives (and corresponding offers) either with the approach of every new holiday (Christmas, New Year's, Mother's Day, Father's Day, Halloween, Thanksgiving, and so on), with every new shopping season (Graduation and Prom, Back to School, Black Friday and Cyber Monday, Christmas Shopping, and so on), or even with something specific to your industry (seasonal gardening, sports championships, different types of fishing, and so on). The idea here is exactly as with any other dynamic creatives: Keep the offers and the look of your affiliate banners fresh and relevant to what's happening in the consumer's world and your own business.

Figure 7.25 illustrates how DaySpring is handling this right after Christmas, before Valentine's Day, Mother's Day, and graduations too.

Figure 7.25 Four DaySpring holiday-specific skyscraper banner ads

To develop your dynamic creative strategy, follow these steps:

1. Decide on what pattern you're going to follow (deals, seasons, both, anything else).
2. Put together a plan.
3. Create your banners.
4. Get ready to start implementing your plan.

Also, do not forget to announce that you do have dynamic creatives in your inventory, and mark them accordingly. Not many merchants stick to such policies (or even have them in place). So, if you decide you *will*, it'll certainly create a good competitive advantage of your affiliate program over what your direct rivals in the market are doing.

Week 2: Data Feeds, Coupons, and Plug-Ins

8

Now that you've created your banners and text links, it's time to turn to the rest of your affiliate program's creative inventory and discuss data feeds (their purpose and structure, as well as tools for their creation and import into affiliate sites), coupons, widgets, and video. This is how you will spend this week. By Friday, you'll be one more step closer to the launch of your affiliate program.

Chapter Contents

Monday: Learn About Data Feeds
Tuesday: Study and Avoid Common Data Feed Mistakes
Wednesday: Discover Data Feed–Importing Options
Thursday: Develop Your Coupon Strategy
Friday: Pay Attention to Add-Ons and Plug-Ins

Monday: Learn About Data Feeds

Any data feed is essentially a convenient compilation of data on product inventory. It comes in the form of a file (CSV, XML, XLS, or any other type) that lists all the product information (such as product ID, product name, description, price, stock availability, and so on) that you want to make available to your affiliates. The format of the affiliate data feed is normally such that the affiliate can interpret and understand it, be it with or without the help of any additional piece of software.

By supplying affiliates with data feeds, merchants are making it easy for the affiliates to feature the merchants' products on the affiliate websites. For this purpose, they also include URL paths to thumbnail and larger product images, URLs leading to the pages where the individual products are featured, product categorization, and, often, even product-specific keywords.

Affiliates can import merchant data feeds into their websites with the help of a software application (I'll discuss them in detail tomorrow) or by possessing the relevant programming skills themselves. The final goal is to present either a merchant's entire product line or a certain part of it on the affiliate website (Figure 8.1), giving the visitors of the latter a chance to browse, search, and view the products right on the website. Customers get transferred to the merchant website *only* when they click a Buy, More Info, Purchase, or a similar button or link on the affiliate website. Therefore, merchant data feeds have a powerful potential to enhance almost any affiliate website.

Figure 8.1 Shopzilla is one of the world's top data feed–driven websites that among other models also employs a performance-based (or affiliate) model.

How Do You Create a Data Feed?

If your own webmaster is of no assistance, there are three basic options for creating a data feed:

- Hiring a coder to put together a feed-generating script
- Purchasing a ready-made script/tool
- Going with an external agency/service that specializes in feed generation and maintenance

Hiring a Coder

Hiring a PHP programmer is one of the ways to handle this. The task itself is not at all complicated, and the whole project will cost you anywhere from $20 to $150, depending on the geographic location of the programmer and the complexity of the task. The programmer would have to write a script that pulls all the necessary data from your site's database. A data feed file is then created in the requested format that you could pick up from your server (if the feed-generating script resides on your server) and upload it to the affiliate network; have it self-upload to your affiliate network or in-house-based program; or offer it to your affiliates directly.

Purchasing a Script/Tool

For merchants whose online stores are run on popular platforms (such as Yahoo! Store or osCommerce, for example), there are ready-made scripts out there. They basically allow you to convert your CSV or XML feed from your platform's standard output to whatever is required by your *affiliate marketing* platform (affiliate network, for example). I won't endorse any given coder (or script creator), but these should be easy to find through your affiliate network or affiliate marketing forums.

Outsourcing Feed Maintenance

A number of companies specialize in the compilation and ongoing maintenance of merchant data feeds for affiliates. The following are just a couple of examples of such agencies:

GoDataFeed.com This is a full-service data feed optimization and automation company that also supports generation and maintenance (automatic FTP uploads) of affiliate data feeds for merchants. You can find more at `http://godatafeed.com/`.

FusePump This examines the structure of your website and database(s) and creates "a set of agents for automating the navigation and data extraction steps required to populate your feed." It supports static and dynamic feeds, allowing output format to be customized depending on the needs of the affiliates. You can find more at www.fusepump.com.

Your Store Wizards Previously known as Y Store Tools, this service creates customized feeds tailored specifically toward the requirements of the affiliate platform your program operates on and helps you maintain them. You can find out more at www.yourstorewizards.com.

Data Feed Standard

Although each affiliate network has its own requirements for data feed specifications, affiliates want to see a number of items in your feed. Some of them are absolutely crucial to have, while others are preferable but not mandatory. Table 8.1 shows the product data to include in your feed: mandatory data, recommended additional data, and optional data.

▶ **Table 8.1** Product data to include in your feed

Mandatory	Recommended	Optional
Merchant name	Product description (full)	Additional images
Product name	Price	Currency
SKU	Search terms	Last updated
Product description (brief)		Brand/manufacturer UPC, ISBN, or any other industry-specific product identifier
Thumbnail image URL		
Product URL		
Sale price		
Medium-size image URL		
Large image URL		
Category		
Subcategory		
Stock availability		

Properly using all the important data feed categories is instrumental to the success of individual product marketing. A good example of one of the most important (yet most inconsistent) fields is the category. Oftentimes, merchants do not categorize their products in the feed. This, in turn, makes it virtually impossible for affiliates to display the merchant's products in a way that's convenient to the end user. In the process, everyone loses, especially the merchant.

A tool worth mentioning in this regard is ShareASale's Feature Utilization Indicators tool (Figure 8.2), which helps affiliates get a snapshot of how well the merchant's data feed is organized, as well as how many of the optional features are being used by the merchant.

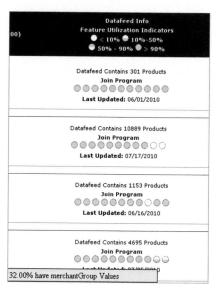

Figure 8.2 Feature Utilization Indicators tool by ShareASale

At the time of this book's writing, ShareASale is the only network (that I know of) with a tool like this.

Tuesday: Study and Avoid Common Data Feed Mistakes

You should be aware of a number of common data feed-related mistakes right at the outset. This will make life easier for your affiliates, thereby maximizing your own success with feed-employing affiliate marketers.

The following are these mistakes:

Strange Characters in Data Feed Keep these away from your data feed. Characters such as &, ", >, %, !, #, @, ~, |, &nsbp;, other HTML-code symbols, and anything that is not your regular text should be kept out of data feeds.

Data Feeds with No Categories It is OK to have one or even no categories if all you are selling is, let's say, eight camera bags. But if your data feed contains hundreds or even dozens of products from different categories and you have put that data feed together for affiliates to use it, have those categories in place. Most affiliates will not even work with a no-category data feed.

Data Feed Product Images of One Size Some merchants would presuppose that affiliates should have a way of converting the large files they supply in their data feed to thumbnails. Trust me, affiliates do not appreciate this. Neither do they appreciate having only thumbnails in their data feed. Do not presume. Just give them large images for the close-ups and small images for thumbnails. A good size for thumbnail images is around 100×100 or 150×150 pixels.

Data Feeds with Direct URLs Since some of your website's structure may include cross-references between product pages within the same website, you want to remember that those will not track and therefore must be avoided from your data feed.

Identical Product Descriptions There are some merchants who have identical product descriptions (at least in the first 250 characters) for each product in their data feed. This is sometimes because this data is pulled from the merchant's database, which really has each product description start in the same way and then lists the differences later in the text. Keep in mind that affiliates may not have more than 200 to 250 character spaces for each product description! List such important parameters as dimensions, color, material that the product is made of, and other product-specific characteristics in the very beginning of the description you are providing to your affiliates.

Major Data Feed Changes If you are going to make any major change in your data feed, talk to your affiliates before you start. Ask them for feedback. Find out what other things they would want to see changed and/or added to it. After you implement the changes, alert your affiliates that you are about to upload the new feed, upload it, and notify them that the new feed is available. Do not apply any major changes to your data feed too frequently. Adding new products, deleting the ones that went out of stock, refining product descriptions, and adding product-specific keywords into a custom field are all fine. What I mean by major changes are mainly changes in category and subcategory names and groupings.

Data Feeds with Out-of-Stock Items That Are Not Expected to Return If a product is sold out and is not expected to come back, delete it from the data feed. Make sure you keep the thumbnail image of the product or have it replaced with a "sold out" image of the thumbnail size, but do not keep the product information in the data feed if there is no hope for it returning. Otherwise, you will end up with a lot of sold-out products in your data feed, affiliates will keep featuring them on their websites, and the end result will be disappointed prospective customers.

Data Feeds with Outdated Prices Some merchants choose not to have the prices in their data feeds, and others are required to have them there by their affiliate network. If you do mention prices in your data feed, make sure you update them in that feed as frequently as you update them on the website, and notify your affiliates of the availability of new prices in a timely manner. If this is not done, sooner or later you will run into problems with customers that will tell you of your product being featured on the Internet at much lower prices and asking you to honor those prices. Merchants with data feeds should also remember to recommend to their data feed affiliates that they either automatically update their data feeds/websites or do not display prices.

Data Feeds with Useless Data Ensure that yours does not contain any information that is not directly related to the way your affiliate is going to use a product. You do not have to include all possible information in it—just what will be useful for your affiliates and required by the data feed specifications.

Microcategorized Data Feeds In trying to do their best with the categorization of products, select merchants may microcategorize them to such an extent that some of the categories end up having only one or two products in them, with no way to unite them into larger, more embracing categories. It may help your affiliates if you only have categories and subcategories, and limit the number of larger categories to a quantity that gives affiliates a chance to choose for themselves. They may then choose to go with a larger category that has an assortment of products from narrower subcategories or else use your finer categorization. Another solution to consider is using a hierarchy (such as Electronics > TVs > LCD TVs > 42² LCD TVs). Then, the affiliate can split it apart and use the level of detail *they* want.

Product IDs or SKUs Missing from Data Feeds Many affiliates do need these to match up the products of different merchants within one website. It isn't that hard to include them in your data feed. Do not presume they are unnecessary pieces of information.

Changing Product IDs or SKUs This point is directed specifically at affiliate networks, but you as a merchant should also remember to keep the same product ID or SKU for each product from data feed to data feed, regardless of the time of the year.

Uploading Old Data Feeds Do not play with the idea of uploading your same old data feed to the network just to get that "last updated" date refreshed and replaced by a newer one. Affiliates who have their notifications or software fetches set up to catch all data feed updates will be extremely disappointed to find out that nothing has changed and that they just spent their time on what they already uploaded.

Lack of Deep Links Having all data feed product links point to the *same* web page of the merchant's website is another big mistake. The very purpose of the feed is to make deep product-specific linking possible. I've seen merchants who do not have dedicated product-specific web pages, listing all products on the same page. This is not the way to do it, and not only because of the affiliate program. You're killing your own organic search opportunities. Each product should have a page of its own.

Lack of Individual Product or Category Links If you are selling multiple products, try your best to make a data feed available to your affiliates. If, however, for some reason you cannot make one available to them, either provide them with a way to create product links or make yourself available to create these for them. The same applies to category links. Some affiliates may only be interested in either linking to specific products or specific product categories. Do not assume that linking to your home page will suffice. Not giving them a chance to get the links they need will eventually deprive you of the traffic and sales they may send you.

Landing Page Problems I've seen data feeds with product links leading to entirely different products when the link is actually clicked. Just like everything else in your affiliate marketing, test how your data feed works before you offer it to affiliates.

Wednesday: Discover Feed Importing Options

Compiling a good data feed is only the first part of a two-step process. The second part is making it easy for affiliates to import your full feed or parts of it into their websites. A number of applications assist affiliates in this task, and today we are going to look into them. Not all affiliates are technically savvy to create their own custom data feed–importing solutions. Therefore, I believe it to be the merchant's responsibility to make the task of creating storefronts on affiliate sites easy and fun.

I like to split the available feed-importing solutions into five groups:

- Computer programs
- Online-based solutions
- On-server scripts and applications
- Private-label solutions
- Network-based options

Let's now look at each of these in more detail.

Computer Programs

This type of feed-processing software requires an installation onto an affiliate's computer where it may be executed thereafter.

WebMerge (Figure 8.3) is one of the industry's oldest, tried-and-true data feed–processing solutions. Created by Richard Gaskin of Fourth World Media Corporation, it basically allows affiliates to publish data feeds "with templates from any HTML editor on any web server and then automate it." It lets you work with databases and spreadsheets in multiple formats including Excel, Microsoft Access, FileMaker Pro, and AppleWorks, and host-generated HTML pages on any web server without needing to set up MySQL databases. It takes some time to learn how to operate this software and requires basic HTML knowledge as well, but once you get comfortable with it, you can be really productive, working with virtually any data feed. You can find more at www.fourthworld.com.

Online-Based Solutions

These solutions do not require an installation but reside on the supplier's website and can be utilized via a subscription to the service, which grants an affiliate access to the online tool.

GoldenCAN This company (Figure 8.4) offers a number of easy cut-and-paste integration solutions including one for affiliate data feeds of multiple merchants. See the sidebar "GoldenCAN vs. PopShops" for more information, and go to www.goldencan.com.

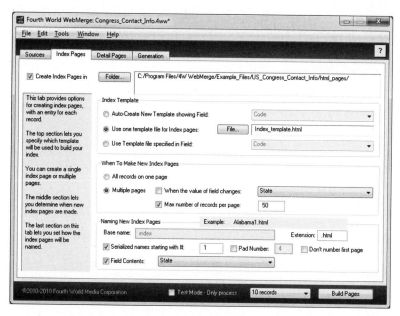

Figure 8.3 From the WebMerge interface: the way affiliates see things when they are setting things up

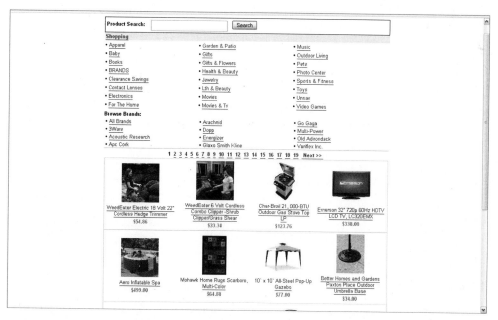

Figure 8.4 Sample data feed–driven store put together with the help of GoldenCAN, one of the oldest online-based data feed–importing solutions for affiliates

DataFeedFile This company borrowed GoldenCAN's concept and created a similar tool, adding a price comparison shopping functionality. Supports HTML, XML, CSV, and other formats. You can find more at www.datafeedfile.com.

Datafeedr This company positions itself as "a system that enables you to create and embed an affiliate store into your WordPress blog without touching any clunky data feed files, learning a programming language, or hiring expensive programmers." It does not have a free option for affiliates but is known for being a robust and easy-to-use solution. The official website is www.datafeedr.com.

PopShops.com This is one of my personal favorites (Figure 8.5). It has an extremely easy-to-use API solution with a web interface that allows affiliates to create storefronts, mixing and matching products from different merchants on different networks. While I am writing this book, it supports more than 3,000 merchants and a total of more than 60 million products. You can find more at http://popshops.com/.

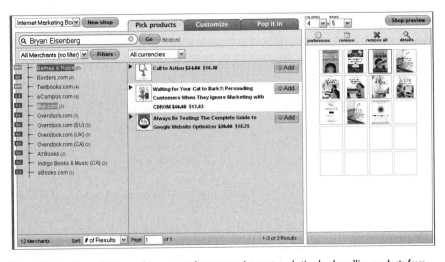

Figure 8.5 PopShops affiliate working on a product page on Internet marketing books pulling products from data feeds of different merchants

easycontentunits.com This is a U.K. equivalent of PopShops, with a price comparison option. You can find more at www.easycontentunits.com.

Store Burst UK This is a solution that works as a subaffiliate "network," allowing its users to create and run affiliate shops (by picking merchants and product categories to feature) without having affiliate accounts of their own. You can find more at www.storeburst.co.uk.

Biz Zites This is a site-building solution with a data feed integration option, as well as a content management system embedded in it. It is integrated to work with a number of major affiliate networks. You can find more at www.trafficgenesis.net.

Many of these solutions offer affiliates convenient WordPress plug-ins as well.

GoldenCAN vs. PopShops

(This was adapted from my article originally published in Website Magazine in the fall of 2008.)

Affiliates are in this business to generate revenue. But the road to this goal is often bumpy and difficult to navigate. Selecting and participating in some of the thousands of affiliate programs can be overwhelming. Attempting to integrate several programs into a single website and maintain a consistent, quality web presence can cause many to look for another path.

But some tools aim to ease integration woes and increase profits for one of the hardest working group of web professionals—affiliate marketers.

PopShops and GoldenCAN fit no mold. These data feed–integrating tools facilitate populating a website with valuable offers from merchants and give affiliates an opportunity to differentiate their websites from the competition, while earning some extra revenue. Both are extremely powerful for merchants running affiliate programs and for affiliates wanting to quickly import merchant data feeds into their websites. After a thorough examination, you might ultimately find that the two services work well together, so let's look and the similarities and differences to get you started.

Perhaps the most significant challenge for web marketers in the affiliate space is success with search engines. Fortunately, both GoldenCAN and PopShops have several search engine–friendly options available, straight out of the box. With Pro and Enterprise plans from PopShops, server-side snippets of PHP will render shop contents (including product names and descriptions) to the search engines, while data feeds under the Enterprise plan can be customized to include keywords. GoldenCAN openly touts its own SEO features. As an end-to-end point-and-click storefront, the service enables affiliates to develop strong internal linking structures that carry the ability to potentially influence search rankings.

Couple these SEO features with a search function (available at both providers), and by all accounts you have the framework of a full-fledged website catering to consumers seeking niche products. Additionally, in regard to the end user shopping experience, GoldenCAN, with the help of its Coupon Integration tool, allows affiliates to serve coupons to their visitors. GoldenCAN affiliates are able to display thousands of specific promotions and recent price drops for the products of their selected merchant with a single line of code.

Although it might serve you best to utilize both services, for the sake of simplicity you will probably want to select one solution over the other. And although both are highly effective, there are some differences.

GoldenCAN gives affiliates one-click storefronts. PopShops has stayed away from this model to allow affiliates to create their own completely unique storefronts. Affiliates can pick products, change descriptions, and, in short, develop custom shops across different affiliate networks

Continues

GoldenCAN vs. PopShops *(Continued)*

(to the point of including products from merchants on Commission Junction, LinkShare, Google Affiliate Network, ShareASale, and even an independent program on the same page) and have it all appear seamlessly as a stand-alone site.

Pricing is a mixed bag with these services. GoldenCAN (the more obtuse pricing model of the two) has two types of merchants from which affiliates can choose. The first is "fourth-click merchants," or those that pay via a fourth-click ID swap; this essentially means that GoldenCAN takes any revenue from every fourth click from an affiliate's listing. The second is "free merchants," or those that are free of the fourth-click commission share. The latter merchant pays GoldenCAN a fee so that affiliates can use merchant fees completely free and not share revenue from any click.

PopShops is free for merchants. Affiliates bear the cost of business but can choose from several different plans—from a free option to a $30-per-month Enterprise version, which includes enhancements such as RSS and XML product feeds, SEO features, unlimited shops, product search, and more. The good part is that affiliates keep 100 percent of commissions at all times, and the straightforward pricing means less confusion on what will generate the most revenue.

Either one of these tools will help your offerings stand out from the competition, while carrying the potential of extra revenue. In time, you might decide to use a combination of both. In the end, it still boils down to old-fashioned elbow grease to get the job done in such an aggressive marketplace. PopShops and GoldenCAN can help get the wheels turning.

On-Server Applications

These are ready-made scripts (generally in PHP) and applications installable on the affiliate's server in order to easily process, import, and display affiliate data feeds. Generally, they support data feed formats of multiple different affiliate networks.

Here are just a few examples of such scripts:

Datafeed Studio This is a classic web application (Figure 8.6) installable on the affiliate's server to upload merchant data feeds, turning them into different types of websites and web pages (for example, niche online store, price comparison website, or niche landing page). The official website is at www.datafeedstudio.com.

CSV to WordPress Post Script This is a script that helps affiliates upload CSV merchant data feeds to their WordPress-based sites, creating online stores of their own. You can find more at www.matboo.co.uk/2009/04/02/csv-to-wordpress-post-v2-released/.

Cusimano Scripts These are CGI-bin Perl affiliate scripts put together by Cusimano Corporation to allow affiliates to either integrate them into their existing websites or use them "to create stand-alone websites." You can find more at www.c3scripts.com.

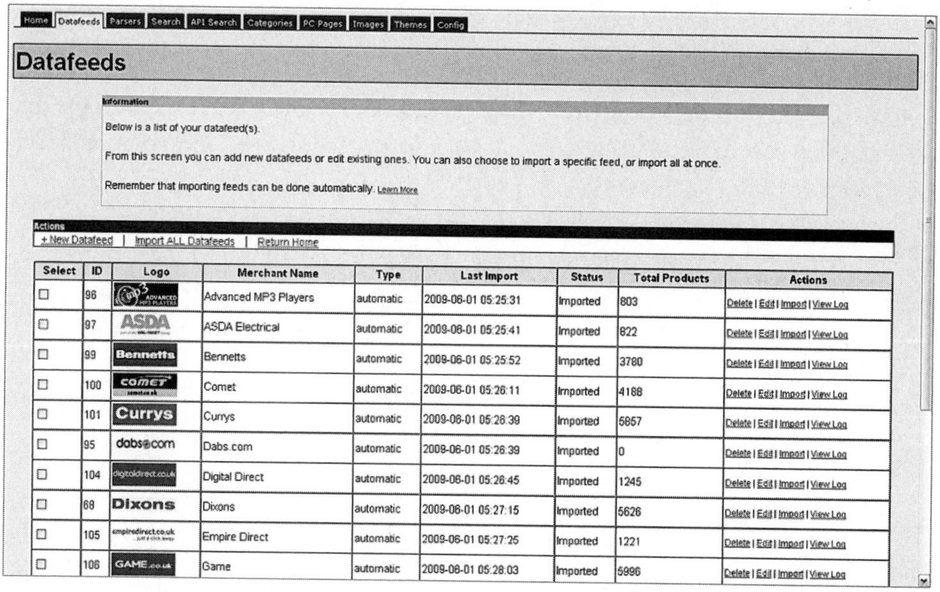

Figure 8.6 Datafeed Studio user interface as an example of interface where affiliates may work with various data feeds

MySQL Product Feed Website Creator This is a PHP script that allows an affiliate to create a website "from almost any CSV product feed." You can find more about it at www .affiliatescript.co.uk/mysql_productfeed_script_creator/.

Price Tapestry This is a PHP and MySQL price comparison engine based on Magic Parser, a PHP library designed for working with affiliate product feeds and for automatically recognizing and parsing any data feed file format. The script includes a simple but effective frontend that is designed to be very easy for you to customize using only HTML and CSS. You can find more at www.pricetapestry.com.

Private-Label Solutions

These are essentially data feed–importing solutions built to suit the merchant's own requirements and offered by the merchant for its affiliates to use.

These can be built to create either static storefronts that do not automatically remove out-of-stock or inactive products or dynamic storefronts that do. If you do decide to work on such a data feed–importing solution for your affiliates, make sure it is a dynamic one.

A basic example to look at is the AffSolutions' Product Showcase Creator, which is one of the older solutions on the market, created by Akiva Bergstrom in 2003 and meant to offer merchants a way to help affiliates create basic product showcases based on the merchant's affiliate data feed. Regardless of this being a fairly basic solution, it may give you ideas on what components to include in your own. You can find more at `http://www.affsolutions.com/solutions/product_showcase_creator/product_showcase_creator.html`.

With a bit of a budget and access to a programming talent (easy with all the outsourcing options available nowadays), you can get a robust private-label solution built from scratch.

Network-Based Solutions

Finally, in addition to all of the previous options, some affiliate networks (see the sidebar "AvantLink's Data Feed Manager" as an example) offer convenient data feed–processing tools for the merchants on their network. Contrary to European affiliate networks, not many U.S.-based networks do it, and I hope that with time this will change and more people will follow the AvantLink example.

Here are some of the world's affiliate networks that offer their affiliates convenient data feed–processing tools:

Affiliate Window's Create-a-Feed This is part of a robust ShopWindow Toolset, which allows affiliates to work with a database of several million products offered by merchants with affiliate programs on this network. You can find details at `http://wiki.affiliatewindow.com/`.

Buy.at's ContentEngine and ShopCentral Both of these tools allow affiliates to create dynamic online stores via Buy.at's APIs. You can find more information at `http://buyat.wordpress.com/` and `http://labs.buy.at/shopcentral.php`.

LinkShare Web Services This is an option "for more technically savvy" affiliates, which gives them access to LinkShare merchant's data "over the Web, without logging into the Publisher Dashboard." The information is returned in a cacheable XML file with such information as the number of products, page number, merchant ID, ability to sort by price, and so on. Read about it at `http://blog.linkshare.com/2008/11/21/linkshare-web-services-explained/`.

PaidOnResults.com's Content Units This is a dynamic solution that allows affiliates to cut and paste a code into their site, resting assured that "the Content Unit will remain current, with the latest products from the Merchant continuously added and updated without any additional work required." You can find more at `www.contentunits.com`.

ShareASale's Make-A-Page This is a feature that helps affiliates search and select products sold by merchants they promote and, with the help of an online interface, create precoded pages that they can thereafter cut and paste the HTML code from into their own website.

Webgains iSense Ad Creator This is a tool that allows affiliates to automatically display relevant products (or contextual ads of a kind) depending on the web page's context.

AvantLink's Data Feed Manager

AvantLink is an affiliate network known for being the "data feed people"—precisely for its focus on merchants with data feeds and continuous efforts to make data feed import hassle-free for affiliates.

Every merchant in this network has three data feed options to offer to their affiliates at no charge:

- Raw data feed

- Dynamic, fully customizable, SEO-friendly, PHP-based, crawlable output content version

- JavaScript plug-in version

This is a sample affiliate store put together with the use of Backcountry.com's affiliate data feed via this tool:

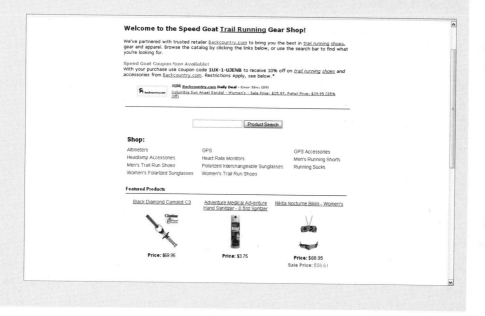

Thursday: Develop Your Coupon Strategy

In Chapter 1, "Understanding Affiliate Marketing," I mentioned *coupon affiliates* as one of the types of affiliates. Coupons are actually used by online marketers of various types and not those with coupon-oriented websites only. The reason is that coupons are excellent conversion catalysts.

Does every affiliate program need coupons? You do not need to have them, but I recommend you do. Various estimates show that anywhere between 20 percent and 50 percent of all online affiliate sales come from coupon sites. So, unless there are really substantial reasons for you to abstain from coupons, I recommend you seriously consider this channel of distribution.

I have heard merchants saying "Our deals are better than those of our competitors. Our prices are more attractive, our orders get processed faster...we are just better. Why do affiliates constantly ask us about coupons?" It's because, as already mentioned, this is what some affiliates bank on: They play on the simple human psychology of trying to get a deal before they buy, and those merchants that offer their prospective customers these deals (in the form of affiliate coupons) normally win. Not every online shopper searches for coupons, but those who do should be able to find them. I know some merchants would not agree with me, but coming from the same background (for more than six years I ran an online business, selling thousands of collectibles online), I think it all comes down to the question of whether you want those 20 percent to 50 percent of coupon sales.

Solution to Possible Conflict with Coupon Affiliates

Macy's, just like some other online merchants, was concerned with overpaying coupon affiliates in instances where orders weren't *originally* referred by coupon websites. So, it came up with a solution that allowed them to keep all coupon affiliates aboard their affiliate program but stop paying twice. *Internet Retailer* magazine featured the Macy's solution in March 2010 in the article entitled "Tougher Customers." The magazine's story opened with a reiteration of the problem:

> *Staffers at Macys.com detected a new pattern in customer behavior last spring: consumers would add items to shopping carts, leave the site, and then return with discount codes they had found on the web sites of Macy's affiliates. Only then would they complete their purchases.*

> *"We said maybe we should just do this ourselves," says Kent Anderson, president of Macys.com.*

And they did—by adding a Find One Now link next to the customary promo code box that many online merchants have on their shopping cart (or checkout) pages (Figure 8.7).

This find-a-coupon link allows shoppers to search for any available coupons but do so right at Macys.com (as opposed to searching the Web for any possible savings), completing the checkout without leaving the merchant's website.

Having tested this solution for affiliate cookie overwriting, I wasn't able to register any. In other words, when landing on Macy's website through an affiliate link (I purposefully went through a link on a coupon affiliate's website), adding a product to my shopping cart, and then searching for any available coupons via the Find One Now link and applying them, I see that Macy's will still pay the affiliate their commission.

This seems like a very good solution to me. It allows you room to partner with coupon affiliates yet safeguard yourself from overpaying on orders that resulted from other marketing activity of yours (for example, with a paid search campaign of your own).

Figure 8.7 Macy's offers its customers to find a coupon without leaving their website.

What Coupons Should Merchants Offer?

Just as is true with banners, you will explore new options for coupons as you go, but I recommend at least six coupon types for merchants to use in their coupon strategy:

One or Two Coupons That Are Good from the First Through the Last of the Year It should aim at getting the customer to spend more money than an average customer would. Examples of such coupons may include "Free Shipping on $99+ Orders" or "$15 Off Each $120+ Order." If you do not limit the use of these coupons to an either/or setup, more than likely they will be published side-by-side at coupon and noncoupon websites alike.

Two or Three New Coupons for Each Month They should preferably target price points different from the ones quoted earlier. For example, you may run such coupons as "$5 Off $45 Order" and "$17 Off $100 Order" during the first month of the year, "$7 Off $60 Order" and "$20 Off $120 Order" during the second month, and so on. If possible, create and support dynamic links (texts or banners) that always show the current monthly coupons. This will show your affiliate that you care about their time and are willing to provide them with such support.

Short-Term Coupons They may be valid for a time as short as a weekend and as long as a week. To get your affiliates interested in these, you want to make them look more attractive than your regular yearly or monthly coupons. For example, you may offer a 25 percent discount on all orders received during a particular weekend (post-Christmas time is a good time to run something like this). Alternatively, you may choose a particular product on which your markup is high enough to offer something as attractive as several coupons I ran for Russian Legacy. Two of them read like this: "$200.00 Off a Black Women's Mink Hat with Ear-Flaps" and "$300.00 Off a Large Authentic Soviet Banner/Flag." Coupon sites are always on the lookout for such coupons.

Holiday-Specific Coupons These may reward "early bird" purchases or offer more attractive deals than those of your competitors. A good example of the latter is something a gourmet food client of ours offered—free shipping with an option to choose the exact delivery date at the same time as the order placement.

Deal of the Day Promos These may be limited to a week, or, if your technical and time resources allow, you can run them for as long as a month or even longer. Deal of the day promos should really provide incredible bargains and, if possible, be automatically dynamically updated on the affiliate sites. Such campaigns may have a tremendous impact on your sales.

Coupons Exclusive to Select Affiliates Make sure that those affiliates whom you value most are aware of your ability to do this. There will be some affiliates that will not want to put up the coupons that all other affiliates (remember, there is competition here!) are using. Exclusive coupons will get such affiliates attracted and motivated to activate their accounts by putting these coupons up at their sites.

Types of Deals That Convert Best

I know that as you're reading this section of the book, you could really use some experience-based advice on the types of deals to offer through your affiliate marketing program. Whether through the affiliate channel or any other online marketing initiative of yours, you want to offer what really converts best. The more popular and better-converting deals are as follows:

- Dollar or percentage off coupons
- Free shipping deals
- Discounts tied either to the number of items purchased (73 percent of customers go for the "Buy 2, Get 1 Free" deal offered by an ink merchant whose program we manage) or to the sale amount that qualifies the customer for a deal.

What Makes a "Killer Coupon"?

I'm glad you asked this one! The following are the recommendations that will help you put together coupons that will convert:

- Word it eloquently and attractively.
- Have a short and simple coupon code.

- Make sure the coupon is *really* offering a deal (and not something available at your website by default such as free shipping on all $70 orders, for example).

- If possible, try to offer a coupon not available through your own website or your own marketing endeavors. Coupons that are truly exclusive to affiliates are always more highly appreciated. It is OK to let your affiliates promote the same coupons you already advance on your website, but let them also have access to a set of coupons not available anywhere else but through your affiliate channel.

- Make a coupon landing page (instead of directing the traffic to your home page).

- If possible, make a precoded affiliate link that would automatically apply the coupon to the shopping cart when clicked.

- Make the coupon banner available in all sizes, displaying the coupon code on each banner.

- Let your affiliates choose between a set of banners and/or a coupon code.

- Treat every holiday as a reason for a good coupon.

With time, you will be getting suggestions on coupons from your affiliates. Listen to them, and make use of the most valuable ideas to make your coupons more effective. Unless there are really strong reasons against it, marketing through coupon websites should be part of your affiliate strategy, occupying not less than 10 percent of your time.

Landing Pages for Coupons

As mentioned, it's preferable that each coupon has its own landing page. However, this point is being all too frequently ignored by merchants.

Your coupon-specific landing page should do the following:

- Reinforce the details of the promo/campaign

- Provide instructions on how to redeem the coupon

- Spell out any restrictions the customer should be aware of

- Contain a clear call to action

More than 95 percent of the merchants whose coupon landing pages I have reviewed—and my sample contained more than 100 coupon campaigns of different merchants—either have only one or none of the previously mentioned points covered. Very few merchants do it the right way, but those that do register higher conversion rates. This makes both the merchant and the affiliate happy and builds up an affiliate program.

Figures 8.8 and 8.9 contain exemplary landing pages—created by merchants specifically for their affiliate coupon campaigns—which either cover all of the previously mentioned points or apply the coupon/discount automatically.

Remember to have accompanying landing pages for each affiliate coupon you offer.

Figure 8.8 Buy.com supplies a detailed landing page for each coupon. Upon clicking the Redeem Coupon button, the coupon automatically applies to shopping cart.

Figure 8.9 Sierra Trading Post effectively reinforces the deals providing full disclosure of restrictions to be aware of.

Friday: Understand Add-Ons and Plug-Ins

Add-ons and plug-ins are essentially software extensions that enable a browser, blogging platform, or other type of software to handle additional tasks or perform new functions.

If your resources allow for it, it is certainly good to offer affiliates add-ons and plug-ins to easily market you (see Figure 8.10 for an example), but since most individual merchants do not have the resources for putting these together, it is imperative that you at least know which publically available plug-ins exist.

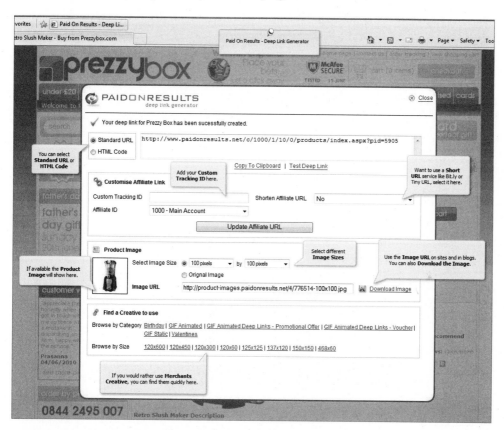

Figure 8.10 U.K. affiliate network PaidOnResults' Deep Link Generator Firefox plug-in in action

Although the PaidOnResults' deep-linking plug-in shown in Figure 8.10 is currently one of the most sophisticated on the market, similar tools are also offered by a few other affiliate networks on both sides of the Atlantic. AvantLink, for example, has had its Affiliate Link Encoder in the United States for as long as PaidOnResults has been offering the Deep Link Generator in the United Kingdom, since 2005. LinkShare has a similar tool called LinkGenerator Bookmarklet (works with both Firefox and Internet Explorer). Affiliate Window and Buy.at in the United Kingdom also offer similar Firefox plug-ins, and new ones are being created by affiliate networks constantly.

WordPress Tools and Plug-Ins for Affiliates

Moving away from network-specific plug-ins, it seems appropriate to cover some blogging platform-specific plug-ins now. Since many affiliates run their websites on WordPress, I have compiled a list of plug-ins and tools that WordPress-employing affiliates use and rate highly. The order is merely topical (network-offered plug-ins, plug-ins related to the import of data feeds, and so on) and does not represent any sort of ranking.

Network-Offered Tools

- Affiliate Link Encoder from AvantLink: Detects and changes direct links into affiliate tracking links for the merchants that are in the AvantLink network
- Commission Junction Product Search: Creates Commission Junction product listings within blog posts and pages
- ClickBank Widget: Adds targeted ads for Clickbank products to your blog's sidebar
- LinkShare RSS DealFeed: Automatically populates your WordPress blog with deals and other promotional content
- LinkShare AdMix: Helps integrate RSS content ads from LinkShare advertisers with your blog posts

Plug-Ins for Data Feeds

- PopShops Affiliate Store Plug-in: Helps add products to your WordPress blog from any of the major affiliate networks (LinkShare, Commission Junction, ShareASale, Buy.at, Google Affiliate Network, LinkConnector, Webgains, and even in-house based programs such as at Amazon).
- Datafeedr: This is a "factory where you build, modify and download your stores, as well as customer support, community forums, and video tutorials."
- Affiliate Wizard: This offers a number of data feed–based WordPress plug-ins including the CompariPress Price Comparison plug-in and network-specific WordPress "affiliate product plug-ins" (for example, CJ Wizard, phpOStock, LS Wizard, AP Wizard). You can find more at www.wizardplug-ins.com.
- DataFeedFile.com Featured Product Plug-in: Helps you add a product of your choice or allows your blog's visitors to compare prices across different merchants without leaving your blog.

- Easy CSV Importer: Good plug-in to use with any CSV file (affiliate data feeds, in particular) to make 500 or 1 million posts or pages. It has such options as manual or automatic updating, importing "at once or spread it out over days or weeks," and much more.
- CSV 2 POST: CSV file and affiliate data feed import plug-in for WordPress, which allows you to import a CSV data file and inject up to 1 million blog posts.

Plug-ins for Linking
- Skimlinks Affiliate Marketing Tool: Allows you to "instantly monetize untapped links on your blog."
- 123Linkit Affiliate Marketing Tool: Transforms keywords into affiliate links.
- Pretty Link: Allows you to "shrink, track, and share any URL on the Internet from your WordPress website," creating shortlinks "coming from your own domain." Each hit is tracked with details "of where the hit came from, the browser, OS, and host."
- Affiliate Link: Another tool to shorten your affiliate links using your own domain name (and not any of the URL-shortening services). Tracking is also provided.

Ad Management Plug-Ins
- Ad Squares Widget: Helps you display and manage 125×125 ad banners (and other sizes). It works "with standard affiliate ads, or even with ad network codes."
- WP125: A robust and popular ad management plug-in for WordPress.

Plug-ins for Amazon.com's Associates
- Amazon Autoposter: Allows users to post products from Amazon.com in their own blogs (automatically, based on keyword match)
- Amazon Product in a Post Plug-in: Helps you "quickly add a formatted Amazon Product/Item to a post or page by using just the Amazon product ASIN (also known as the ISBN-10)"
- Amazon Affiliate Link Localizer: "Automatically changes any Amazon link on your site to use your affiliate ID" and "also changes the link to point to the user's local (that is, country-specific) Amazon store"
- Amazon Store: Helps you quickly create your own Amazon affiliate store
- Amazon Post Purchase: Based on the Product in a Post Plug-in but works with sidebars "in themes that support dynamic sidebars"
- Amazon Product Link Widget: Another sidebar widget for Amazon product links/ads

Week 3: Research and Develop Program Policies

There is hardly anything more foundational to your affiliate program than the program agreement that you are going to work on this week. It will be made up of both general considerations and very specific policies such as the use of trademarks, necessity of disclosures, specific types of marketing employed to promote your brand and your product(s), and other things.

By the end of this week, you should have a comprehensive affiliate program agreement.

Chapter Contents

Monday: Work on Your Coupon and Discounts Policy
Tuesday: Develop Your Trademark Policy
Wednesday: Formulate Policies Regarding Loyalty and Rebates Affiliates
Thursday: Word Your Recommendations on Affiliate Disclosures
Friday: Finalize Your Affiliate Program Agreement

Monday: Work on Your Coupon and Discounts Policy

The previous chapter discussed your coupon strategy. Now that you have one (even if it says "I will have no coupons"), it is time to craft a corresponding policy to go along with it. You'll want to pay attention to several issues while working on your coupon and discounts policy, and the following list of questions should help you address the most vital points:

- Do you accept coupon affiliates into your program? (Even if you do not have coupons, by their very nature, coupon affiliates will rank high on *trademark + coupon*, *trademark + discount*, and other similar search queries).

- Are affiliates permitted to bid in their paid search campaigns on *trademark + coupon*, *trademark + discount*, and similar key phrases?

- If the response to the previous question is yes, can they link to your website directly (also displaying your website as the "display URL"), or should they land such PPC traffic on a website of their own first?

- Do you allow coupon affiliates to feature links not related to your coupons or discounts?

- What penalties (for example, lowering of commission rate, banning from the program, and so on) will you impose on violators of your coupon and discounts policy?

- If you will be offering exclusive coupon codes to some affiliates, you probably need a policy prohibiting affiliates from promoting coupon codes that are exclusive to other affiliates.

- If you are running coupon codes in other channels, you might want to clarify whether affiliates are allowed to promote coupon codes that aren't specifically intended for the affiliate channel.

- Some coupon sites use questionable or deceptive practices to get clicks, such as asking visitors to click to reveal a coupon code and having that click reveal the coupon code and at the same time go to the merchant's site (setting an affiliate cookie) or such as saying to click for coupons when there are no coupons and it's just an affiliate link. If these practices aren't acceptable to you, you should prohibit them. More detail in the following section.

Pseudo-couponing

Besides the obvious ways of promoting merchants on coupon websites, in this section I will discuss one technique that illustrates the need for a comprehensive coupon policy.

One day while searching the Web to see whether a particular merchant offers coupons, I came across numerous affiliate sites that by optimizing their web pages accordingly make it look as if that merchant may have coupons when, in reality, they do not. It got me thinking about two questions:

- How ethical is such a marketing technique in comparison to what other affiliates may be investing their time, energy, and money into (paid search, comparison shopping sites, content projects, and so on)?

- How much value are such affiliates bringing to the merchant?

I christened the technique *pseudo-couponing*, and I believe the term provides my opinion on both of the previous questions. Both answers are negative here. This is neither an ethical competition nor a value-added service. In addition, it isn't unusual for the end user to be led to believe that although it isn't a coupon they are viewing, there may be some discounts beyond the page they are seeing in front of them, and all they have to do to get them is click the link. Figure 9.1 shows examples of such links.

Figure 9.1 Coupon affiliate, whose page is optimized to rank high for coupon-related keywords, that employs a pseudo-couponing technique using blanket wording for merchants without coupons

Upon clicking any of the Activate Coupon buttons, the end user lands on the home page of the merchant they are already familiar with, but there is no sign of any coupon/discount (because there *aren't* any, and the pseudo-couponer knew this from the outset). In meantime, the pseudo-couponer's cookie gets set, and should the customer decide to proceed with their order anyway, it is this affiliate that will receive the commission for the customer referral.

If you, as a merchant, believe that such an affiliate behavior is of no benefit to your business, you should prohibit it in your affiliate program's terms and conditions, spell out the penalties, and actively enforce the policy.

Examples of Coupon Policies

As mentioned, some merchants choose not to work with coupon affiliates altogether. Others have more open policies but prohibit certain behaviors. I haven't seen one that explicitly prohibits pseudo-couponing, which was surprising (most affiliate networks do prohibit deceptive clicks, and as a merchant, I would reiterate the point in the context of coupons too). Nevertheless, I will show a few examples of coupon policies that you may use as starting points for formulating your own policy.

Closed Coupon Affiliates Policy

CustomInk, a merchant specializing in custom T-shirts and other design-it-yourself products, has a closed policy. Here is the wording of the clause that talks about coupon affiliates:

> *CustomInk.com does not accept Coupon Affiliate websites: A "Coupon Affiliate" is an affiliate whose business model substantially consists of making coupons available. Whether an affiliate is classified as a Coupon Affiliate shall be determined by CustomInk.com in its sole discretion. Factors that may lead to classification as "Coupon Affiliate" include, but are not limited to (i) the presence of coupon offerings, especially from many different merchants, on the affiliate's website, especially if such coupons represent many different merchants and/or are indexed or are organized in a directory; (ii) the presence of certain words (or variations or misspellings thereof) in the website's URL or prominently featured in the website's content, such as "coupons," "deals" or "savings"; (iii) a website that is focused on other merchants and the discounts or promotions offered by them, rather than on products, and that features little original, human-generated content.*

Zappos.com has a similar policy (Figure 9.2).

Coupons and Promotional Codes Can publishers use coupons and promotional codes?	Publishers are not allowed to use coupons or promotional codes

Figure 9.2 Zappos.com isn't working with coupon affiliates, as its Commission Junction restrictions clearly spell out.

Open Coupon Affiliates Policy

Having studied more than 100 affiliate program agreements for programs run by major brands, I could not find one with a clause fully dedicated to the dos and don'ts of coupon marketing. In the vast majority of cases, when merchants have restrictions related to coupons, they spell out just those restrictions.

Overstock.com, for example, points out the following in its program agreement:

Publisher may only advertise or promote advertisements which state the actual discount that a visitor may derive by clicking on a Link. Publisher shall not advertise Company's products by taking into account a coupon price without prominently noting that a coupon is being applied to achieve a lower product price. For example, if Company has a product for sale off the Destination Site for $100, but there is an active Company 10% off coupon for such product, Publisher may only advertise the product for $90 by stating in the advertisement that the $90 price is only available when the coupon is applied—i.e., "get this [product] when you use this 10% off coupon."

In addition, it is noteworthy that while prohibiting paid search bidding on "any word, keyword or term...that contains Company's registered or unregistered trademark," Overstock.com allows affiliate PPC bidding "on keyword strings" explicitly including "overstock coupons" in the examples of permitted keyword strings.

PETCO's affiliate program—like multiple other merchants as well—has the following clause in the Prohibitions section of its affiliate program agreement:

Use of unauthorized links or coupon codes (those links or codes not specifically provided to you through The Commission Junction Network) by us in the Program is prohibited, and will result in the forfeiture of all commissions earned hereunder by Partner for the month(s) the unauthorized links or coupon codes appear on your site. Unauthorized coupon codes shall include, but not be limited to those coupon codes unrelated to the Program that are distributed through our stores, consumer email newsletters, retail cards or direct mail promotions. Violation of the foregoing prohibitions may result in, among other things, the immediate termination of this Agreement and/or the commencement of an action by PETCO against you seeking, without limitation, injunctive relief and/or recovery of actual, statutory and/or punitive damages.

Whether you want to have just a brief coupons subclause in the Restrictions clause of your program or put together a detailed section dedicated to coupon marketing is up to you. Whichever way you go, make sure you both safeguard yourself and are clear on your rules and intentions.

The question of transparency in affiliate policies (this one as well as any of the ones I discuss later in the chapter) is so important that I want to pause on it for a few more seconds. Whatever your rules will be, spell them out clearly from the outset. Nobody loves unpleasant surprises, and should you do something that wasn't originally spelled out in your agreement and it comes to light, it's not going to do your affiliate program any good. For example, some merchants choose to pay coupon affiliates lower commissions than their default level. Although I do not support this practice, should you decide to go this route, you must mention it both in your program agreement and in your affiliate program description.

AllPosters.com, for example, is at least being up front with its affiliates by including the following clause in its agreement:

> *For all affiliates other than Coupon Affiliates and Sub-Affiliates (see below), the commission rate is 20% of Qualifying Revenues.*

Coupon Affiliate Commission Credit Rate

> *For Coupon Affiliates, the commission rate is 2.5% of Qualifying Revenues. A "Coupon Affiliate" is an affiliate whose business model substantially consists of making coupons available. Whether an affiliate is classified as a Coupon Affiliate shall be determined by AllPosters.com in its sole discretion. Factors that may lead to classification as "Coupon Affiliate" include, but are not limited to (i) the presence of coupon offerings, especially from many different merchants, on the affiliate's website, especially if such coupons represent many different merchants and/or are indexed or are organized in a directory; (ii) the presence of certain words (or variations or misspellings thereof) in the website's URL or prominently featured in the website's content, such as "coupons," "deals" or "savings"; (iii) a website that is focused on other merchants and the discounts or promotions offered by them, rather than on products, and that features little original, human-generated content.*

Remember that any unpleasant surprise for an affiliate may easily turn into unpleasant consequences for your affiliate program; therefore, give your coupon policy the attention it deserves.

Tuesday: Develop Your Trademark Policy

Trademarks are among your most important assets. Today you will look into the question of protecting them while running an affiliate program. The following sections talk about paid search, domains with trademarks, and more.

Trademarks and Paid Search

Every merchant should be aware of one kind of paid search affiliates, sometimes called *trademark poachers* or *trademark bidders*.

Trademark poachers, or trademark bidders, are affiliates that either exclusively or along with other keywords bid in their paid search campaigns on merchants' trademarks and URLs, as well as variations and misspellings of them. The sole purpose of such activity is to *divert* the trademark traffic to go through affiliate links/ads first. This sets an affiliate cookie on the end user's machine, and should the user place a sale/lead within the cookie life duration, the trademark bidding affiliate will earn the commission on that sale/lead.

Although there can be exceptions (for example, merchants with unknown brands or those whose names consist of generic terms like *calendars*), it is normally in the merchant's best interest to restrict trademark bidding and police it. In the case of *calendars*, Calendars.com may not have any legal grounds for restrictions of affiliate bidding on key phrases involving the word *calendars*; however, it should by all means prohibit bidding on its URL (as well as variations and misspelling of it) as a paid search keyword.

Many merchants are not doing this. As a result, they are paying for something that naturally belongs to them in the first place.

In April 2008, *Revenue Performance* magazine wrote this:

> Trademark poaching is attractive because of the low barrier to entry. For just the price of a PPC ad, publishers can quickly generate handsome commissions without the usual affiliate administration overhead, and reducing the steps from click to purchase increases the likelihood of a purchase.
>
> One PPC affiliate, who asked not to be named, says there is a "pack of about 30 PPC affiliates that closely monitor the list of new merchants at every network and 'crank up campaigns on them all' in order to profit from this behavior."

This is absolutely true. It takes seconds to put together a paid search campaign, and multiple rogue affiliates are continuously taking advantage of merchants' naïveté (in keeping an open PPC policy) or merchants' lack of education on the topic altogether, centering these campaigns on merchants' trademarked terms and URLs only.

I will discuss the tools for policing compliance with your paid search policy in further chapters, but now let's turn to another area you should be aware of as far as trademark use and abuse goes—affiliate domain names.

Trademarks and Domain Names

Domain names are another important area you want to tackle in your affiliate program's agreement. There are essentially two phenomena you want to address: cybersquatting and typosquatting.

Lawyer Kelly M. Slavitt—in her "Protecting Your Intellectual Property from Domain Name Typosquatters" article originally published in the Spring 2004 edition (Vol. 4, No. 1) of Thelen Reid's *Intellectual Property and Trade Regulation Journal*—defines the terms:

> *Cybersquatters register domain names based on a company's trademarks and then attempt to extort payment from the actual trademark owner in exchange for returning use of the domain name...*
>
> *Typosquatters are a variation on cybersquatters, but the motive of both is the same: to profit by trading off of the goodwill of intellectual property assets established by rightful owners. Typosquatters register intentionally misspelled domain name variations of the actual company's trademark. The typosquatter profits by directing traffic away from the actual Web site to the typosquatter's rogue site.*

In the affiliate marketing, there is a fairly wide consensus on the unacceptability of cybersquatting, but this cannot be said about typosquatting. Some stand by the explanation that unless the traffic is being redirected to the trademark owner's competitors, the affiliate is actually adding value to the merchant by registering URLs with misspellings of the merchant's trademarks. They argue that the commissions paid to the affiliates in such instances should be looked at as "a fee" charged to drive the users to the right website.

There is no doubt that the market for misspelled domains is huge. Network Solutions has reported that error traffic makes up 20 percent of total network traffic, and of that, *nonexistent domain* (NXD) errors account for as much as 15 percent. Google indicates that 404 HTTP errors (which are the same as NXD errors) account for 6.9 percent of published pages, or some 11.5 billion web pages on the Web.

Because overwhelming demand always breeds supply, there is a lot of interest among a particular type of affiliate—those that go after this "otherwise lost" traffic. One of the most well-known affiliates operating in this space is Barefruit Ltd., which is currently accepted by many major affiliate networks and affiliate programs.

It is up to you to decide on the value of cybersquatting and typosquatting types of traffic, but whichever way you decide, you want to formulate it into a policy.

How to Word the Agreement

You can find a good example of a comprehensive trademark policy in the operating agreement for Walmart.com's affiliate program. Besides mentioning the use of trademarks in the General Prohibitions clause (and a few other clauses) of the agreement that affiliates get bound by, Wal-Mart also provides an extensive "exhibit" (which is also part of the agreement) where it spells out what exactly what the company is against. Here it is:

Walmart.com Operating Agreement for Affiliate Network

Exhibit A – Trademark Requirements

These requirements apply to your use of Walmart.com and other trademarks and service marks belonging to Wal-Mart.com USA, LLC, Wal-Mart Stores, Inc. or other related entities (the "Trademarks") in content that has been approved by us.

1. You may use the Trademarks only for purposes expressly authorized by us.

2. You may not modify the Trademarks in any manner. For example, you may not change the proportion, color, or font of the Trademarks.

3. You may not display the Trademarks in any manner that implies endorsement of your website or business by Walmart.com outside of your involvement in the Program.

4. You may not use the Trademarks to disparage Walmart.com, its products or services, or in a manner which, in our reasonable judgment, may diminish or otherwise damage our good will in the Trademarks.

5. Each Trademark must appear by itself, with reasonable spacing (at least the height of the Trademark) between each side of the Trademark and any other graphic or textual image. You may place the Walmart .com name or logo adjacent to competitive brands, subject to the requirements of this Agreement, including prohibitions against objectionable material and websites.

6. You must use the TM symbol next to the trademarks. You must use the SM symbol next to the service marks.

7. You must include the following statement in your materials that include the Trademarks: "WALMART.COM SM is a service mark of Wal-Mart.com USA, LLC and Wal-Mart Stores, Inc." You must include similar statements for any other Trademarks used on an ongoing basis in your materials.

8. You acknowledge that all rights to the Trademarks are our exclusive property and all goodwill generated through your use of the Trademarks will inure to our benefit.

9.   *YOU MAY NOT USE THE TRADEMARKED NAMES, WAL-MART, WALMART.COM, WAL-MART STORES, OR ANY VARIATIONS OR MISSPELLINGS THEREOF, IN ANY MANNER INCLUDING KEYWORD BIDDING ON SEARCH ENGINES; YOU MAY NOT USE WAL-MART, WALMART.COM, OR ANY VARIATION OR MISSPELLINGS THEREOF, IN METATAGS OR TO DIRECT TRAFFIC TO ANY WEBSITE OTHER THAN OUR SITE; YOU MAY NOT USE WAL-MART, WALMART.COM, OR ANY VARIATIONS OR MISSPELLINGS THEREOF, IN HIDDEN TEXT OR SOURCE CODE ; YOU MAY NOT USE WAL-MART, WALMART.COM, OR ANY VARIATIONS OR MISPELLINGS THEREOF, IN YOUR DOMAIN NAME OR ANY OTHER PART OF YOUR UNIVERSAL RECORD LOCATOR.*

10. *You may not bid on any keyword or keywords string on any Pay per Click Search Engines (PPCSEs) where such keyword or keywords string is, or includes, one of our Trademarks or any variation or misspelling of one of our Trademarks (see the non-exclusive list of examples set forth below in Section 15). Further, you may not bid on any word or term that is confusingly similar to any of our Trademarks standing alone. You may not bid on keywords strings that contain the terms "Rollbacks" or "Advertised Values".*

11. *You may not employ any "fat finger" domains or typosquatters redirecting web traffic to your website. A typosquatter for "fat finger" domain is any domain that amounts to misspellings of any registered or unregistered Trademarks.*

12. *You may not bid on any keyword or on any PPCSEs that is one of our competitors' trademarks (or a derivation of a competitor's trademark), or any other word or term that is likely to cause confusion regarding its affiliation with the competitor. Examples of these keywords include, but are not limited to: "Target", "Kmart", "Sears", "JC Penney","Toys R Us", "Amazon", "Circuit City", "eToys", and "KB Kids".*

13. *You may not bid on restricted manufacturer brand terms, including but not limited to "MagicJack", or any derivatives thereof that are likely to cause confusion regarding its affiliation with Walmart.com, its affiliates or you, in any paid search.*

14. *You may not use the Trademarks alongside or in conjunction with the following terms: "percent (%) off", "sale", or "coupons".*

15. Walmart.com may, in its sole discretion, terminate you or withhold payment of your Referral Fees for the days that we determine that you were bidding in violation of the keyword bidding requirements above.

16. The list below sets forth examples of impermissible keywords, "fat-finger" domains, and variations of Trademarks that you may not bid on. The list is for example purposes only and is not a complete list of prohibited words which infringe a Trademark, and therefore violate a term of this Agreement.

walmart	*walmart.com*	*wal-mart*	*wal mart*	*www .walmart.com*
wallmart	*wal-mart.com*	*wall mart*	*wallmart .com*	*www .wallmart.com*
wal mart	*Walmart .com*	*Walmart.c*	*www .wal-mart .com*	*www.walmart .com*
walmart stores	*wal-mart store*	*walmarts*	*www .wal mart .com*	*wal mart stores*
wall-mart	*walmart supercenter*	*site:www .walmart .com walmart*	*wal-mart supercenter*	*super Walmart*
walmart stores	*super wal mart*	*walmart.com.*	*walmart store*	*walt mart*
walmart ,com	*wall mart .com*	*walmart online*	*wal mart .com*	*www .wal-mart*
Walmart .c_om	*Walmart.c*	*site: walmart.com*	*-*	*-*

We reserve the right in our sole discretion to modify these requirements at any time.

Your own trademark policy may look different, depending on your own context, but, as I hope I have clearly illustrated, having one is a *must*.

Wednesday: Formulate Policies Regarding Loyalty and Rebates Affiliates

In Chapter 1, "Understanding Affiliate Marketing," you spent a good amount of time looking into the business model employed by loyalty and rebates affiliates and the scenarios in which that model works well and those in which it does not work at all. In many instances, an incentivized website visitor is not a bad thing at all. In fact, a study by CMO Council entitled "Leading Loyalty: Feeling the Love from the Loyalty Clubs" (the findings of which were published and circulated by eMarketer.com in January 2010), indicated that many Internet users love online loyalty programs, especially when they are custom-tailored toward personal relevance or provide financial inducements or savings (Figure 9.3).

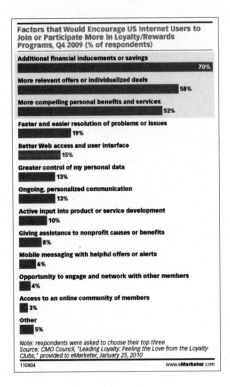

Figure 9.3 Factors that encourage web users to join or participate in loyalty/rewards programs

Many superaffiliates that operate in the loyalty marketing sector provide their members and site visitors with both savings and personalization, and partnership with them works well for some types of affiliate programs (for example, those of retail-oriented merchants).

There are, however, situations when an affiliate program cannot have loyalty affiliates aboard, and you may both refer to Chapter 1 to refresh the different scenarios in your mind.

The Rotten Apple

In addition to the good loyalty affiliates, you need to be aware of a particular type of "affiliate" (which to me is more of con artist than a marketing type). It is the type that encourages their website visitors to fill out surveys, submit application forms, and order samples and then pays them for it (by cash, points, gifts, access to "exclusive" coupon offers, and so on). I like to call this type of affiliates *kekaliménoi kléftes* (from the Greek "thieves in disguise"). These affiliates frequently sell the idea to their website visitors using such wording as "key to financial freedom," unique "work-at-home" idea, "fast and free" money, and other get-rich-quick type verbiage. It is also interesting to point out that many of these affiliates are actually earning good money on this approach—predominantly with the help of two factors: the help of the network that is running the merchant's "offer" and the merchant's cluelessness on the origin of traffic and "leads."

So, the affiliate is making money "selling" free stuff, and the website visitors do all the work (of filling out forms, requesting free trials, and ordering samples) and get paid for it, but what about the merchants featured on such websites? Is this kind of traffic/audience (incentivized to do what they do by cash) even right for the majority of them?

Figure 9.4 shows a website of such an affiliate.

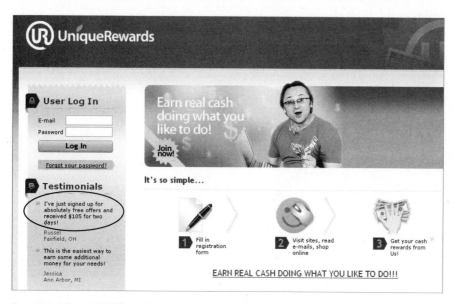

Figure 9.4 A "rewards" affiliate offers people cash for reading emails and signing up for free offers.

Let's take the testimonial circled in Figure 9.4 as an example. Russel from Ohio took his time signing up "for absolutely free offers," and this earned him not only the free samples/trials but also $105 of cash on top of it! Wow. If he keeps at this speed, his house will be full of various samples, plus he'll have close to $1,600 of extra cash in his bank account every month.

While getting into the details of how some of the "free offers" will hit the end users' credit cards past the free trial period unless they cancel their subscription, let's briefly look at the value of such leads for the merchants:

Example 1

- Type of business: health-related etailer
- Qualifying action: order of free sample

- Affiliate commission: $45 per sample
- Incentivized visitor gets $30 to submit their name, contact, and credit card information

Question: What are the chances that they are really interested in *the product*?

Example 2

- Type of business: auto insurance agent
- Qualifying action: fill out name and contact information
- Affiliate commission: $20 per lead
- Incentivized visitor gets $15 to perform the action

Question: Are they really *interested* in the auto insurance or in the $15?

It should be obvious, but to ensure my point gets across, I will emphasize that "customers/prospects" who are motivated to try your product or fill out a subscription/lead application by anything other than a *genuine interest* in your product or service are of *no value* to you. If someone is paying them cash to fill out an insurance quote form, get a free trial of a software application, or get a free sample of a product, that's their motivator—immediate cash, not your product/service.

Due Diligence Prevents Damage

After I blogged about "affiliates" who make money on clueless merchants, generating pseudo-leads and earning money in the process, Kellie Stevens of AffiliateFairPlay.com posted an insightful comment. With her permission, I am republishing it here:

"I remember talking with a merchant who 'got taken' (as they put it) to the tune of over $16k when their offer was promoted via incentive sites on a CPA network. They pulled the offer quickly (within a couple of weeks), but the financial damage had been done. On top of the direct marketing costs in network fees and commissions, something like 90% of the referred customers ended up canceling their subscription to the service after getting their 'free' sample. So the total cost was significantly higher for them. I remember doing a lot of education with the merchant about how this particular model wasn't reflective of all of affiliate marketing.

"There are several very large 'work at home' forums out there that are devoted solely to end users discussing how to make money off of these types of offers (i.e., which offers require credit cards, which ones actually pay out the incentive, which merchants provide an easy cancel process before the cc is billed, etc. Basically, how to work the system. Interestingly, I've seen representatives of some CPA networks participating at some of them.

Now that we've looked at the different types of loyalty affiliates, you can ana-lyze your own business model against theirs and make an educated decision on the policy to have for them. Whatever your decision is—however inclusive or exclusive—write it down now so that you have it for the pinnacle of this week's work, which will be your complete affiliate program agreement.

Thursday: Word Your Recommendations on Affiliate Disclosures

As I am writing this book, the following considerations are a must-read for all U.S.-based merchants and affiliates. I understand that with time the need for affiliate disclosures may expand well beyond the United States. Therefore, I highly encourage everyone to study this section of the chapter regardless of their current geographical location.

Requirement to Disclose Relationships

On December 1, 2009, the Federal Trade Commission's "Guides Concerning the Use of Endorsements and Testimonials in Advertising" (Endorsement Guides) came into force. With these guides, the FTC sought to patch the gaps in the Federal Trade Commission Act that was too general for the realities of new media. The FTC Act originally pro-hibited deceptive and unfair acts and practices in commerce, as well as misleading advertising. According to the FTC, the Endorsement Guides "really intended to provide additional guidance on how these prohibitions apply to online marketers, bloggers, and, in some cases, affiliates." Although officially the guides are not regulations but interpretations of the FTC Act, all businesses are expected to "voluntarily comply" with them (source: Richard Cleland's interview to Jim Edwards, http://jimedwards .s3.amazonaws.com/ftc-advertising-interview/index.html).Therefore, it is imperative that we look at them in a bit more detail.

You can download the full 81-page Endorsement Guides at www.ftc.gov/os/2009/ 10/091005endorsementguidesfnnotice.pdf.

Here I am quoting just a few of the excerpts that affiliates and affiliate program managers should pay attention to:

Imposing liability…hinges on the determination that the advertiser chose to sponsor the consumer-generated content such that it has established an endorser-sponsor relationship. It is foreseeable that an endorser may exaggerate the benefits of a free product or fail to disclose a material relationship where one exists. (p. 15)

This section is on responsibility:

When the Commission adopted the Guides in 1980, endorsements were disseminated by advertisers… through such traditional media as television, commercials and print advertisements. With such media, the duty to disclose material connections between the advertiser and the endorser naturally fell on the advertiser.

The recent creation of consumer-generated media means that in many instances, endorsements are not disseminated by the endorser, rather than by the sponsoring advertiser. In these contexts, the Commission believes that the endorser is the party primarily responsible for disclosing material connections with the advertiser. However, advertisers who sponsor these endorsers (either by providing free products — directly or through a middleman — or otherwise) in order to generate positive word of mouth and spur sales should establish procedures to advise endorsers that they should make the necessary disclosures and to monitor the conduct of those endorsers. (pp. 38–39)

Merchants are also expected to both have a policy for endorsers to follow and have policing procedures in place:

The Commission does not believe, however, that it needs to spell out the procedures that companies should put in place to monitor compliance with the principles set forth in the Guides; these are appropriate subjects for advertisers to determine for themselves, because they have the best knowledge of their business practices, and thus of the processes that would best fulfill their responsibilities. (p. 49)

It is also important to understand the following:

Advertisers are subject to liability for false or unsubstantiated statements made through endorsements, or for failing to disclose material connections between themselves and their endorsers. Endorsers also may be liable for statements made in the course of their endorsements. (p. 61)

Connections must be clearly disclosed:

When there exists a connection between the endorser and the seller of the advertised product that might materially affect the weight or credibility of the endorsement ... such connection must be fully disclosed. (p. 75)

Here's a helpful example:

A college student who has earned a reputation as a video game expert maintains a personal weblog or "blog" where he posts entries about his gaming experiences. Readers of his blog frequently seek his opinions about video game hardware and software. As it has done in the past, the manufacturer of a newly released video game system sends the student a free copy of the system and asks him to write about it on his blog. He tests the new gaming system and writes a favorable review. Because his review is disseminated via a form of consumer-generated media in which his relationship to the advertiser is not inherently obvious, readers are unlikely to know that he has received the video game system free of charge in exchange for his review of the product, and given the value of the video game system, this fact likely would materially affect the credibility they attach to his endorsement. Accordingly, the blogger should clearly and conspicuously disclose that he received the gaming system free of charge. The manufacturer should advise him at the time it provides the gaming system that this connection should be disclosed, and that it should have procedures in place to try to monitor his postings for compliance. (pp. 79–80)

The whole document is chock full of examples, and although it is not a quick read, it is a document every affiliate and affiliate program manager should study to arrive at their further course of action.

It is also helpful to review FTC's video responses to related questions at www.ftc .gov/multimedia/video/business/endorsement-guides.shtm and also link to both of these URLs from your affiliate program's support website/web page.

Implications for Affiliate Marketers

I personally view the FTC's Endorsement Guides as a positive development, and most digital marketers would agree with me. First, the Endorsement Guides helped some (and forced others) to move into the light, making online marketing more transparent—which is better both for the industry and for the end consumer. Second, unless an affiliate/endorser really has something to hide, there should be no fear here. Transparency and honesty build *trust*, which is ultimately better for all parties affected by the introduction of the guides: merchants, affiliates, and online customers. Existence of material connection does not discredit an affiliate website when the latter has been built as an authentic, objective, and customer-oriented resource. Anything else doesn't benefit the market and hence shouldn't be cherished.

Everyone Is Accountable

Although initially the Federal Trade Commission sounded like it was going to chase bloggers (read *affiliates* who endorse merchant products for any kind of remuneration), two days after the announcement of the new rules, an FTC's representative stated that bloggers should not be afraid of any penalty fines because they would first receive a warning, and then, if they refuse to comply, the FTC "would institute a proceeding with a cease-and-desist order and mandate compliance with the law." We were also told that it was in reality *advertisers* that the FTC was going to focus on—on the education that they provide their publishers/affiliates with and on the monitoring and policing mechanisms they put into place.

Regardless of whether some believe that the FTC's expectations (such as effective policing of publishers' compliance with the new rules) are realistic, I think approaching the subject as one affecting both affiliates/publishers *and* merchants/advertisers—where both parties are responsible and accountable—is good.

The fall 2009 issue of the *Online Strategies* magazine had an interesting article by two lawyers, Jeffrey Knowles and Thomas Cohen. It is believed that they were given advanced notice of impending changes and therefore were able to write the article (that came out before the new Endorsement Guidelines came into power) that educated both affiliates and merchants on how to stay compliant with the FTC's rules. Their advice was split into two sections—one for affiliates and another one for merchants:

Affiliates

- Ensure that you're marketing in a "truthful, substantiated, and not deceptive or unfair" manner.

- Stay away from publishing false content or offering "incentives to consumers in return for their response to any ad, unless the offer's terms and conditions of the offer are clearly and conspicuously disclosed."

- Stay away from "fake news articles," and always clearly disclose when "the content is an advertisement."

- Do not post "false or unsubstantiated endorsements, and be sure" you always "disclose any material connections with the merchant."

- Do not infringe trademarks, copyrights, patent rights, "or any other intellectual property right."

Merchants

- When entering into an agreement with an affiliate marketer, make it mandatory for the affiliate to agree that all content used to drive traffic to your site will "abide by all state and federal consumer protection laws and regulations including the FTC Act and the CAN-SPAM Act."

- Make it explicit that affiliates are also agreeing "to comply with the FTC's Endorsement Guides."

- Ensure that affiliates are also agreeing to stay away from intellectual property rights infringements.

- Ensure that your affiliate program agreement requires "that affiliates clearly and conspicuously disclose the terms and conditions of any incentives, points, rewards, cash, or prizes promised to consumers in return for their response to any advertisement."

- Finally, the agreement "must provide that any affiliates who violate these laws, regulations, and guides shall be terminated by the merchant or network and shall forfeit any commissions earned in the course of committing such violations."

You can find the full text of the Knowles and Cohn's article at http://amnavigator .com/book/Knowles-Cohn.pdf. The advice is easy to follow, and with the recommendations provided later in this chapter, you should have no problem complying.

How to Word Disclosures and Agreements

As a merchant and/or an affiliate program manager, you want to know the answers to two questions:

- How should affiliates word their disclosures?

- What addendum/clause will cover you as a merchant in your affiliate program's agreement?

Affiliate Disclosures

Several good examples of affiliate disclosure policies have been posted online by affiliates and nonaffiliates alike. Here I am listing the three I have found to be especially well put together. They should provide you with good examples of how an affiliate disclosure should look:

- Scott Jangro's blog—www.jangro.com/disclosure/

- Tim Carter's website—www.askthebuilder.com/Disclosure_Policy.shtml

- Matt Cutts's blog—www.mattcutts.com/blog/disclosure/

Additionally, DisclosurePolicy.org provides affiliates with a great starting point for crafting a disclosure policy. The tool is free to use, and I highly recommend it.

According to the Federal Trade Commission, affiliates are not expected to include the disclosure on every page of their websites. "Whether you make it outside of the text but in proximity to the blog, or incorporate it into the blog discussion itself;

those are the issues that bloggers will have discretion about" (see their interview in *Fast Company* dated October 7, 2009, for details). So, a dedicated Disclosure Policy page visible from every page of the website should suffice.

Merchant's Agreement

For merchants, I recommend putting together a subclause of an Affiliate Obligations clause in their programs' terms of service. Here is a sample of how it may look:

> *We strongly advise affiliates to stay compliant with the Federal Trade Commission (FTC) guidelines on testimonials and endorsements. All endorsements, reviews, testimonials on CompanyName.com's products and services, as well as relationships, between other types of content websites (forums, blogs, microblogs, and other Social Media channels) and CompanyName must be clearly disclosed in a separate policy on the affiliate sites. The FTC points out that "when there exists a connection between the endorser and the seller of the advertised product" it is imperative that such a connection is "fully disclosed." The FTC deems the relationship in an endorser-sponsor light and believes that the end user has the right to understand that one exists [full text here]. We share the undergirding idea of this approach and strongly encourage our affiliates to adhere to the FTC's rules. We also reserve the right to terminate our relationship with any non-compliant affiliates.*

The [full text here] link should be pointing to the full text of the Endorsement Guidelines on the FTC's website.

Do not take any of this as a legal advice, and by all means, consult with your lawyer whenever possible.

Friday: Finalize Your Affiliate Program Agreement

The affiliate program agreement is without a doubt the *most important document* in your affiliate program. It will serve as a guide both for the manager of your program and for your affiliates. It will safeguard you when disputes or violations arise. I cannot emphasize this enough—this is the *backbone* of your affiliate marketing campaign. Today you will put it together, interweaving all of the previously discussed policies into it and also covering a few other important areas.

I recommend you structure your affiliate program agreement as follows: foreword, summary, and agreement. The summary is extremely important. Facts speak for themselves: The majority of affiliates do not have the time to read the full agreement (see Figures 9.5 and 9.6). So, the key points should be highlighted in a "Summary" section.

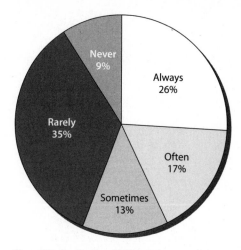

Figure 9.5 Results of my "Affiliates, do you read program agreements prior to applying?" poll

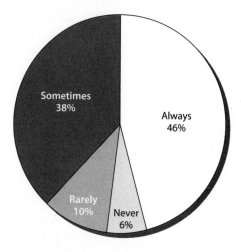

Figure 9.6 AffStat Report 2009 findings on whether affiliates read program agreements

Additionally, it is good to reinforce the key agreement points in the program description and in the affiliate approval email and put the full agreement on your affiliate program website/web page so that affiliates can always go back to it.

Sample Affiliate Program Agreement

Here is a very general sample affiliate program agreement (with Merchant.com chosen as a sample merchant name and ShareASale chosen as the affiliate platform for the affiliate program). Feel free to take this text and modify it to suit your own affiliate program, interweaving all the previously mentioned policies into it.

FOREWORD

Our affiliates are very important to us. We do our best to treat you with the fairness and respect you deserve. We simply ask the same consideration from you. We have written the following affiliate agreement with you in mind, as well as to protect our company's good name. Please bear with us as we take you through this legal formality.

If you have any questions, please don't hesitate to let us know. We are strong believers in straightforward and honest communication. For the quickest results, please email us at affiliates@merchant.com. You can also reach us via phone, toll-free: 1-800-XXX-XXXX.

Best regards,
Geno Prussakov
Merchant.com Affiliate Program Manager

SUMMARY

1. Do not apply if your website promotes sexually explicit materials, violence, discrimination, and/or illegal activities.
2. We do not work with distributors of downloadable software, toolbars, browser helper objects, shopping assistance applications, etc.
3. You must comply with FTC's Endorsement Guidelines.
4. Fraud will be policed and penalized.
5. Spamming is prohibited.
6. Paid search campaigns containing our trademarks are prohibited.
7. Cybersquatting and typosquatting are prohibited.

AFFILIATE AGREEMENT

PLEASE READ THE ENTIRE AGREEMENT.

YOU MAY PRINT THIS PAGE FOR YOUR RECORDS.

THIS IS A LEGAL AGREEMENT BETWEEN YOU AND MERCHANT, INC. (DBA MERCHANT.COM).

BY SUBMITTING THE ONLINE APPLICATION YOU ARE AGREEING THAT YOU HAVE READ AND UNDERSTAND THE TERMS AND CONDITIONS OF THIS AGREEMENT AND THAT YOU AGREE TO BE LEGALLY RESPONSIBLE FOR EACH AND EVERY TERM AND CONDITION.

Sample Affiliate Program Agreement *(Continued)*

1. Overview

This Agreement contains the complete terms and conditions that apply to you becoming an affiliate in Merchant.com's Affiliate Program. The purpose of this Agreement is to allow HTML linking between your website and the Merchant.com website. Please note that throughout this Agreement, "we," "us," and "our" refer to Merchant.com, and "you," "your," and "yours" refer to the affiliate.

2. Affiliate Obligations

2.1. To begin the enrollment process, you will complete and submit the online application at the ShareASale.com server. The fact that we autoapprove applications does not imply that we may not reevaluate your application at a later time. We may reject your application at our sole discretion. We may cancel your application if we determine that your site is unsuitable for our Program, including if it:

2.1.1. Promotes sexually explicit materials

2.1.2. Promotes violence

2.1.3. Promotes discrimination based on race, sex, religion, nationality, disability, sexual orientation, or age

2.1.4. Promotes illegal activities

2.1.5. Incorporates any materials which infringe or assist others to infringe on any copyright, trademark, or other intellectual property rights or to violate the law

2.1.6. Includes "Merchant" or variations or misspellings thereof in its domain name

2.1.7. Is otherwise in any way unlawful, harmful, threatening, defamatory, obscene, harassing, or racially, ethnically, or otherwise objectionable to us in our sole discretion.

2.1.8. Contains software downloads that potentially enable diversions of commission from other affiliates in our program.

2.1.9. You may not create or design your website or any other website that you operate, explicitly or implied in a manner that resembles our website nor design your website in a manner that leads customers to believe you are Merchant.com or any other affiliated business.

2.2. As a member of Merchant.com's Affiliate Program, you will have access to Affiliate Account Manager. Here you will be able to review our Program's details and previously-published affiliate newsletters, download HTML code (that provides for links to web pages within the Merchant.com website) and banner creatives, browse and get tracking codes for our coupons and deals. In order

Continues

for us to accurately keep track of all guest visits from your site to ours, you must use the HTML code that we provide for each banner, text link, or other affiliate link we provide you with.

2.3. Merchant.com reserves the right, at any time, to review your placement and approve the use of Your Links and require that you change the placement or use to comply with the guidelines provided to you.

2.4. The maintenance and the updating of your site will be your responsibility. We may monitor your site as we feel necessary to make sure that it is up-to-date and to notify you of any changes that we feel should enhance your performance.

2.5. It is entirely your responsibility to follow all applicable intellectual property and other laws that pertain to your site. You must have express permission to use any person's copyrighted material, whether it be a writing, an image, or any other copyrightable work. We will not be responsible (and you will be solely responsible) if you use another person's copyrighted material or other intellectual property in violation of the law or any third party rights.

2.6. We strongly advise affiliates to stay compliant with the Federal Trade Commission (FTC) guidelines on testimonials and endorsements. All endorsements, reviews, testimonials on Merchant.com's products and services, as well as relationships between other types of content websites (forums, blogs, microblogs, and other Social Media channels) and Merchant.com must be clearly disclosed in a separate policy on the affiliate sites. FTC points out that "when there exists a connection between the endorser and the seller of the advertised product," it is imperative that such a connection is "fully disclosed." FTC deems the relationship in an endorser-sponsor light and believes that the end user has the right to understand that one exists [full text here]. We share the underlying idea of this approach and strongly encourage our affiliates to adhere to the FTC's rules. We also reserve the right to terminate our relationship with any noncompliant affiliates.

3. Merchant.com Rights and Obligations

3.1. We have the right to monitor your site at any time to determine if you are following the terms and conditions of this Agreement. We may notify you of any changes to your site that we feel should be made or to make sure that your links to our website are appropriate and to notify you further of any changes that we feel should be made. If you do not make the changes to your site that we feel are necessary, we reserve the right to terminate your participation in the Merchant.com Affiliate Program.

3.2. Merchant.com reserves the right to terminate this Agreement and your participation in the Merchant.com Affiliate Program immediately and without notice to you should you commit fraud in your use of the Merchant.com Affiliate Program or should you abuse this program in any way. If such fraud or abuse is detected, Merchant.com shall not be liable to you for any commissions for such fraudulent sales.

Sample Affiliate Program Agreement *(Continued)*

3.3. This Agreement will begin upon our acceptance of your Affiliate application and will continue unless terminated hereunder.

4. Termination

Either you or we may end this Agreement AT ANY TIME, with or without cause, by giving the other party written notice. Written notice can be in the form of mail, email, or fax. In addition, this Agreement will terminate immediately upon any breach of this Agreement by you.

5. Modification

We may modify any of the terms and conditions in this Agreement at any time at our sole discretion. In such an event, you will be notified by email. Modifications may include, but are not limited to, changes in the payment procedures and Merchant.com's Affiliate Program rules. If any modification is unacceptable to you, your only option is to end this Agreement. Your continued participation in Merchant.com's Affiliate Program following the posting of the change notice or new Agreement on our site will indicate your agreement to the changes.

6. Payment

Merchant.com uses a third party to handle all of the tracking and payment. The third party is the ShareASale.com affiliate network. Kindly review the network's payment terms and conditions.

7. Access to Affiliate Account Interface

You will create a password so that you may enter ShareASale's secure affiliate account interface. From their site you will be able to receive your reports that will describe our calculation of the commissions due to you.

8. Promotion Restrictions

8.1. You are free to promote your own websites, but naturally any promotion that mentions Merchant .com could be perceived by the public or the press as a joint effort. You should know that certain forms of advertising are always prohibited by Merchant.com. For example, advertising commonly referred to as "spamming" is unacceptable to us and could cause damage to our name. Other generally prohibited forms of advertising include the use of unsolicited commercial email (UCE), postings to non-commercial newsgroups, and cross-posting to multiple newsgroups at once. In addition, you may not advertise in any way that effectively conceals or misrepresents your identity, your domain name, or your return email address. You may use mailings to customers to promote Merchant.com so long as the recipient is already a customer or subscriber of your services or website, and recipients have the option to remove themselves from future mailings. Also, you may post to newsgroups to promote Merchant.com so long as the news group specifically welcomes

Continues

Sample Affiliate Program Agreement *(Continued)*

commercial messages. At all times, you must clearly represent yourself and your websites as independent from Merchant.com. If it comes to our attention that you are spamming, we will consider that cause for immediate termination of this Agreement and your participation in the Merchant.com Affiliate Program. Any pending balances owed to you will not be paid if your account is terminated due to such unacceptable advertising or solicitation.

8.2. Affiliates that exclusively bid in their Pay-Per-Click campaigns on keywords such as merchant.com, merchant, www.merchant, www.merchant.com, and/or any misspellings or similar alterations of these—be it separately or in combination with other keywords—and do not direct the traffic from such campaigns to their own website prior to redirecting it to ours, will be considered trademark violators and will be banned from Merchant's Affiliate Program. We will do everything possible to contact the affiliate prior to the ban. However, we reserve the right to expel any trademark violator from our affiliate program without prior notice and on the first occurrence of such PPC bidding behavior.

8.3. Affiliates are not prohibited from keying in prospect's information into the lead form as long as the prospects' information is real and true and these are valid leads (i.e., sincerely interested in Merchant's service).

8.4. Affiliate shall not transmit any so-called "interstitials," "Parasiteware™," "Parasitic Marketing," "Shopping Assistance Application," "Toolbar Installations and/or Add-ons," "Shopping Wallets," or "deceptive pop-ups and/or pop-unders" to consumers from the time the consumer clicks a qualifying link until such time as the consumer has fully exited Merchant's site (i.e., no page from our site or any Merchant.com's content or branding is visible on the end user's screen). As used herein "Parasiteware™" and "Parasitic Marketing" shall mean an application that (a) through accidental or direct intent causes the overwriting of affiliate and non affiliate commission tracking cookies through any other means than a customer-initiated click on a qualifying link on a web page or email; (b) intercepts searches to redirect traffic through an installed software, thereby causing pop ups, commission tracking cookies to be put in place, or other commission tracking cookies to be overwritten where a user would under normal circumstances have arrived at the same destination through the results given by the search (search engines being, but not limited to, Google, MSN, Yahoo, Overture, AltaVista, Hotbot and similar search or directory engines); (c) set commission tracking cookies through loading of Merchant site in IFrames, hidden links, and automatic pop ups that open Merchant.com's site; (d) targets text on websites, other than those websites 100 percent owned by the application owner, for the purpose of contextual marketing; (e) removes, replaces or blocks the visibility of Affiliate banners with any other banners, other than those that are on websites 100 percent owned by the owner of the application.

Sample Affiliate Program Agreement *(Continued)*

8.5. Affiliates that are found to be cybersquatting or typosquatting on trademark-related domains will be banned from the program with all their commissions reversed.

9. Grant of Licenses

9.1. We grant to you a nonexclusive, nontransferable, revocable right to (i) access our site through HTML links solely in accordance with the terms of this Agreement, and (ii) solely in connection with such links, to use our logos, trade names, trademarks, and similar identifying material (collectively, the "Licensed Materials") that we provide to you or authorize for such purpose. You are only entitled to use the Licensed Materials to the extent that you are a member in good standing of Merchant.com's Affiliate Program. You agree that all uses of the Licensed Materials will be on behalf of Merchant.com and the goodwill associated therewith will inure to the sole benefit of Merchant.com.

9.2. Each party agrees not to use the other's proprietary materials in any manner that is disparaging, misleading, obscene, or otherwise portrays the party in a negative light. Each party reserves all of its respective rights in the proprietary materials covered by this license. Other than the license granted in this Agreement, each party retains all right, title, and interest to its respective rights and no right, title, or interest is transferred to the other.

10. Disclaimer

MERCHANT.COM MAKES NO EXPRESS OR IMPLIED REPRESENTATIONS OR WARRANTIES REGARDING MERCHANT.COM SERVICE AND WEBSITE OR THE PRODUCTS OR SERVICES PROVIDED THEREIN, ANY IMPLIED WARRANTIES OF MERCHANT.COM ABILITY, FITNESS FOR A PARTICULAR PURPOSE, AND NONINFRINGEMENT ARE EXPRESSLY DISCLAIMED AND EXCLUDED. IN ADDITION, WE MAKE NO REPRESENTATION THAT THE OPERATION OF OUR SITE WILL BE UNINTERRUPTED OR ERROR FREE, AND WE WILL NOT BE LIABLE FOR THE CONSEQUENCES OF ANY INTERRUPTIONS OR ERRORS.

11. Representations and Warranties

You represent and warrant that:

11.1. This Agreement has been duly and validly executed and delivered by you and constitutes your legal, valid, and binding obligation, enforceable against you in accordance with its terms.

11.2. You have the full right, power, and authority to enter into and be bound by the terms and conditions of this Agreement and to perform your obligations under this Agreement, without the approval or consent of any other party.

Continues

Sample Affiliate Program Agreement *(Continued)*

11.3. You have sufficient right, title, and interest in and to the rights granted to us in this Agreement.

12. Limitations of Liability

WE WILL NOT BE LIABLE TO YOU WITH RESPECT TO ANY SUBJECT MATTER OF THIS AGREEMENT UNDER ANY CONTRACT, NEGLIGENCE, TORT, STRICT LIABILITY OR OTHER LEGAL OR EQUITABLE THEORY FOR ANY INDIRECT, INCIDENTAL, CONSEQUENTIAL, SPECIAL OR EXEMPLARY DAMAGES (INCLUDING, WITHOUT LIMITATION, LOSS OF REVENUE OR GOODWILL OR ANTICIPATED PROFITS OR LOST BUSINESS), EVEN IF WE HAVE BEEN ADVISED OF THE POSSIBILITY OF SUCH DAMAGES. FURTHER, NOTWITHSTANDING ANYTHING TO THE CONTRARY CONTAINED IN THIS AGREEMENT, IN NO EVENT SHALL MERCHANT.COM'S CUMULATIVE LIABILITY TO YOU ARISING OUT OF OR RELATED TO THIS AGREEMENT, WHETHER BASED IN CONTRACT, NEGLIGENCE, STRICT LIABILITY, TORT OR OTHER LEGAL OR EQUITABLE THEORY, EXCEED THE TOTAL COMMISSION FEES PAID TO YOU UNDER THIS AGREEMENT.

13. Indemnification

You hereby agree to indemnify and hold harmless Merchant.com and its subsidiaries and affiliates, and their directors, officers, employees, agents, shareholders, partners, members, and other owners, against any and all claims, actions, demands, liabilities, losses, damages, judgments, settlements, costs, and expenses (including reasonable attorneys' fees) (any or all of the foregoing hereinafter referred to as "Losses") insofar as such Losses (or actions in respect thereof) arise out of or are based on (i) any claim that our use of the affiliate trademarks infringes on any trademark, trade name, service mark, copyright, license, intellectual property, or other proprietary right of any third party, (ii) any misrepresentation of a representation or warranty or breach of a covenant and agreement made by you herein, or (iii) any claim related to your site, including, without limitation, content therein not attributable to us.

14. Confidentiality

All confidential information, including, but not limited to, any business, technical, financial, and customer information, disclosed by one party to the other during negotiation or the effective term of this Agreement, which is marked "Confidential," will remain the sole property of the disclosing party, and each party will keep in confidence and not use or disclose such proprietary information of the other party without express written permission of the disclosing party.

15. Miscellaneous

15.1. You agree that you are an independent contractor and nothing in this Agreement will create any partnership, joint venture, agency, franchise, sales representative, or employment relationship between you and Merchant.com. You will have no authority to make or accept any offers

Sample Affiliate Program Agreement *(Continued)*

or representations on our behalf. You will not make any statement, whether on Your Site or any other of Your Site or otherwise, that reasonably would contradict anything in this Section.

15.2. Neither party may assign its rights or obligations under this Agreement to any party, except to a party who obtains all or substantially all of the business or assets of a third party.

15.3. This Agreement shall be governed by and interpreted in accordance with the laws of the State of New York without regard to the conflicts of laws and principles thereof.

15.4. You may not amend or waive any provision of this Agreement unless in writing and signed by both parties.

15.5. This Agreement represents the entire agreement between us and you and shall supersede all prior agreements and communications of the parties, oral or written.

15.6. The headings and titles contained in this Agreement are included for convenience only and shall not limit or otherwise affect the terms of this Agreement.

15.7. If any provision of this Agreement is held to be invalid or unenforceable, that provision shall be eliminated or limited to the minimum extent necessary such that the intent of the parties is effectuated, and the remainder of this agreement shall have full force and effect.

Week 4: Final Brushstrokes

10

The time has come for you to work on the final brushstrokes; by the end of this week, you should be ready to launch your affiliate program.

In this chapter, you will look at such things as your pixel implementation and testing, email templates, program description page, text of the announcement email, and more. At the end of the week, you should be good to go and ready to have your program go live.

Chapter Contents

Monday: Implement Tracking and Test the System
Tuesday: Prepare the Text for Three Email Templates
Wednesday: Set Up Your Affiliate Program Support Base
Thursday: Prepare Announcement Text
Friday: Compile Lists of Keywords and Best Sellers

Monday: Implement Tracking and Test the System

The essence of affiliate tracking can be very simplistically split into two types of actions: clicks/hits and qualified actions (sales, leads, subscriptions, or anything else that the merchant decided to remunerate affiliates for). Clicks, or the number of visitors that an affiliate refers to the merchant, get tracked through the link placed on the *affiliate* side (website, paid search campaign, email link, and so on). Sales, leads, and other qualified actions, on the other hand, get tracked by a string of code (sometimes also referred to as the *tracking pixel*) placed by the *merchant* on their confirmation page. So, as soon as the end user, referred by an affiliate, lands on the "thank you" page on the merchant's website (Figure 10.1), the tracking is triggered, and both the merchant and the affiliate know that the desired action has occurred.

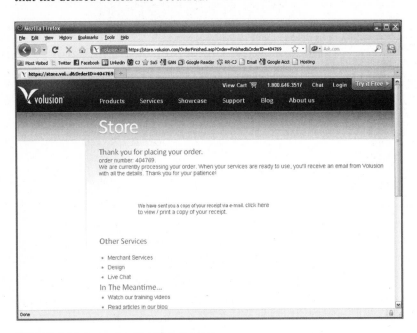

Figure 10.1 Volusion.com's order confirmation page

It is important to ensure that your tracking is implemented properly and works well. For this reason, the majority of affiliate networks will provide you with detailed technical assistance (Figure 10.2) and double-check that your tracking works before allowing you to activate your affiliate program.

Since the tracking pixels differ from affiliate network to affiliate network and from solution to solution, there isn't much more that can be said about the tracking implementation and testing. Just make sure it is done thoroughly and works in all browsers (provided cookies are enabled, of course) before having your program go live. Although affiliate networks do help you test this, in cases with in-house affiliate programs, the burden of proper tracking implementation and testing is fully on the merchant's shoulders.

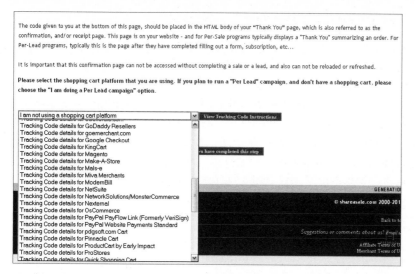

The code given to you at the bottom of this page, should be placed in the HTML body of your "Thank You" page, which is also referred to as the confirmation, and/or receipt page. This page is on your website - and for Per-Sale programs typically displays a "Thank You" summarizing an order. For Per-Lead programs, typically this is the page after they have completed filling out a form, subscription, etc...

It is important that this confirmation page can not be accessed without completing a sale or a lead, and also can not be reloaded or refreshed.

Please select the shopping cart platform that you are using. If you plan to run a "Per Lead" campaign, and don't have a shopping cart, please choose the "I am doing a Per Lead campaign" option.

Figure 10.2 During affiliate program setup, ShareASale offers merchants various integration methods that are tied to the shopping cart used by the merchant.

Also, if in addition to your own merchant account you're using alternate checkout options (such as PayPal or Google Checkout, for example), make sure that the tracking of affiliate-referred transactions functions properly when the end user chooses to use these options. At the time of this book's writing, a high percentage of such alternate checkout options *do not track* in multiple affiliate programs.

In addition, everyone who has access to modify the confirmation page of your website *must* be informed of the importance of the small string of code that supports your affiliate program's tracking. More than once I have witnessed situations when the tracking pixel was removed (either by a web designer, by an SEO consultant, or by an analytics guy), messing up the tracking of the whole affiliate program. That small string of code is *extremely* important, and its importance should be conveyed to everyone who has access to your "thank you" page at any time before or after the launch of the program.

Tuesday: Prepare the Text for Three Email Templates

I can see your eyebrow raised at the mention of that *template* word. In my articles and presentations, I preach personalization as a number-one thing in communication with affiliates. That *template* word is actually in no contradiction to my preaching. It is just that in many cases your affiliate network (or affiliate program software) will allow you to send automated messages to affiliates. Normally, these templates can be configured to go out in three cases:

- To confirm application receipt
- To welcome an affiliate into the program
- To notify an affiliate of an application decline

In the following sections, you will look at the best practices for each of these three scenarios.

Application Receipt

This is the email that each of your affiliates will receive upon applying to your affiliate program. In cases when affiliate networks (or the software you're using for your affiliate program) allow you to customize this email, by all means do so! Do not leave the default message or a blank message.

The text of this email should tell applicants the following:

- Acknowledge the receipt of the application.
- Notify them how soon their application will be reviewed.
- Explain how they can reach you in the meantime.

A word of warning is in order regarding the time frame within which you want to respond to the applicant. According to a poll I have conducted, most affiliates (38 percent) expect to receive your decision on their application within 24 hours. A quarter (25 percent) is willing to wait up to 48 hours, and almost a quarter more (21 percent to be exact) is willing to wait up to three days (Figure 10.3).

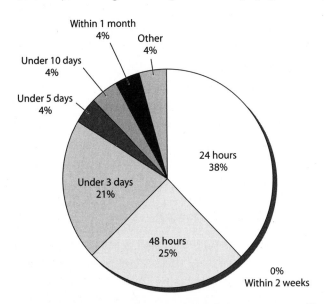

Figure 10.3 Distribution of affiliate votes on "What's the maximum acceptable affiliate program application response time?" poll

Based on this data, I highly recommend you do everything possible to review and make your decision on affiliate applications within 24 hours of application submission. Also, whatever you put into your application receipt email, stick to it!

I know you could use a sample of a good application receipt email. Here's the text I used while managing Roni Deutch's affiliate program:

> *Thank you for your application into the Roni Deutch affiliate program! Your application has been submitted for approval and we will get back with you on it within 24 hours.*
>
> *Should, in the meantime, any questions arise, you may always reach me at 1-888-123-4567 (toll free within the United States and Canada) or by email at [email address here].*
>
> *Sincerely yours,*
>
> *Geno Prussakov*
>
> *Roni Deutch affiliate program manager*

Approval Email

Affiliate approval email can be a terrific tool when used to the max.

Recruiting an affiliate into your program is only half the job done. You need to motivate them to get *active*. And one of the main places to call them to activation is the affiliate program's approval email (sometimes also called a *welcome email* or acceptance email). In addition to the call to activation (the motivational piece), you want your approval email to contain useful/practical information about your affiliate program.

Here's the pattern I recommend following:

1. Remind them of your program details (oftentimes affiliates apply to a number of programs at once, so it's worth reminding them) and of your company (short but sweet and motivating enough for them to start pushing you right away).

2. Include an activation promo (a commission increase opportunity, cookie life increase, and so on). Activation, as used here, should be understood as putting up your links on their site(s).

3. Include also a performance-based incentive (for example, cash for a certain number of sales referred by the end of the first 45 days since signup, or the like).

4. Enclose precoded affiliate links in your email. Make it easy for them to get active with your program, in other words, as easy as a simple cut-and-paste job. If you have coupons that they can start using right away, include details of two to three of those as well. If you provide affiliates with access to your product feed, supply them with the details on how they may access one.

5. In conclusion, assure them that you are there for them, and provide them with your detailed contact information. If you are capable of putting together custom coupons and/or creatives, do mention this too.

Figure 10.4 is a sample approval email for UpscaleLighting.com's affiliate program that I used to manage on ShareASale in the past. The program had the default commission set at 5 percent and cookie life at 45 days.

In addition to all of these mentioned points, it is also a good idea to include brief demographic data in your approval email. It will help your affiliates focus their marketing campaigns in a way that effectively targets the right markets, yielding faster results. While managing HealthCompare.com's affiliate program, I included the following section in the affiliate approval email:

Helpful Information:

Basic Demographics/Target Audience:

- *Employed/Self Employed*
- *Recently Unemployed or QE (Qualified Event)*
- *Long Term Unemployed*

Our Online Customers:

- *On average, our customers are anxious about their current health insurance plan. They are not aware that there are alternatives to COBRA or that their group plan offered by their employer may be overinflated with coverage that does not apply to them. We need to educate them, let them know there are options that may save them hundreds of dollars a year.*
- *They are seeking information to explain the current healthcare reform bills. HealthCompare is a trusted advisor, offering unbiased information at their time of need.*
- *Overwhelming majority rate us as "excellent" on usability, convenience, and customer service.*

Links to any other helpful information (such as lists of keywords and best sellers that I'll talk about in a little bit) are also good to provide.

Basically, the two fundamental tasks behind your approval email are motivating affiliates to get going with the program and equipping them to do so quickly and effectively.

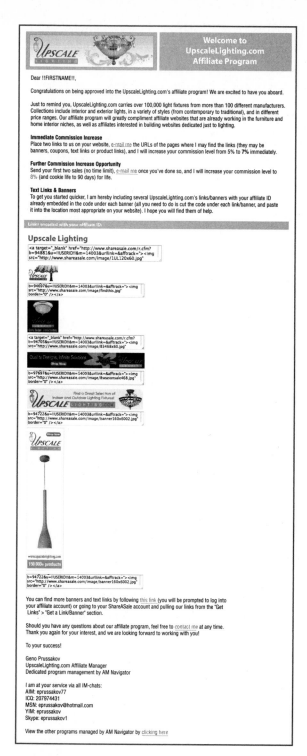

Figure 10.4 Approval email for UpscaleLighting.com's affiliate program

Calls to Action

The activation promo, which is an integral part of your affiliate approval email, is essentially a type of a call to action. I call this particular type a *call to activation*. The following article on calls to activation originally appeared in the April 2009 issue of *FeedFront Magazine*, the official magazine of the Affiliate Summit:

One of the keys to running a fruitful affiliate program lies in understanding that not only should there be a robust affiliate recruitment strategy in place but also a continuous activation of the recruited affiliates into becoming producing affiliates.

Affiliate activation is one of the most frequently overlooked components of affiliate program management, especially by newly launched programs.

Sooner or later, every merchant realizes that success is not measured by the numbers of recruited affiliates but rather by the numbers of those whom are truly active.

Over the years of experimenting with different ways of motivating affiliates, I have realized that the best way to activate affiliates is to expose them to activation offers in each step of their interaction with the affiliate program.

Just as banners with a clear call to action outperform those that do not, affiliate programs with a compelling call to activation outshine other affiliate programs.

There are three phases of affiliate engagement: the recruitment phase, welcoming phase, and routine phase.

Recruitment Phase

Here you want to motivate affiliates to not only join your program but also to put up your links and refer their first orders/leads. This can be done by remunerating the desired actions with a tangible bonus or a commission increase.

This should be practiced throughout the recruitment process—from the outgoing emails soliciting affiliates to join the affiliate program to the very text of the program description on the merchant's website.

Welcoming Phase

Stop your reading here, and take a new look at the application approval email that you are currently sending. Do you sound motivating enough for them to set aside their other projects and put up a few links for you? Does it inspire them to start a few new paid search campaigns to generate a couple of orders for your program within an X number of days after signing up?

Convincing calls to activation in the text of the welcome emails are like seeds falling on fertile soil. It is evident just from their application that they have intentions of promoting you. They applied, and you approved their application.

Calls to Action *(Continued)*

Don't just send them a "welcome-aboard-you'll-love-working-with-us" message. Offer them a reason to jump right on it, or you may well be put at the very end of that endless merchants-to-develop queue.

Routine Phase

It is the routine that has "an unbelievable power to waste and destroy" (source Henri de Lubac). Do not waste your affiliates' time with predictable monthly newsletters. Turn this part of your routine into fun for them. Run especially aggressive monthly activation campaigns for the affiliates that are already in your program but are not yet performing.

The market of affiliate programs will only continue to grow more and more competitive. If you want your program to succeed, make it stand out, and weave the calls to activation into the very structure of it.

Additional Approval Emails

Whether there is a data feed that affiliates have to apply for separately or any other functionality (for example, an API/passport solution) access that goes through a separate application, you want to remember to have a separate approval text template for that email as well.

The text of these emails has to be concise, and I suggest you follow this pattern:

- Approval announcement
- Activation promo (to encourage them to start using the tool/function)
- Performance promo

In addition to the previous information, it may be a good idea to provide them with instructions (or a link to such) on how to use the tool/function, data feed, and so on.

During the time that I managed HalloweenMart.com's affiliate program on ShareASale with every permission to access the affiliate data feed via FTP, I was sending out the following email:

Dear [Firstname Here]

Congratulations! You have just been approved for FTP access to the HalloweenMart.com's affiliate data feed.

PROMOS:

(1) Import our data feed (or at least one-third of it) into your website, email me, and I will pay you a $5 cash bonus and increase your cookie life to 180 days.

(2) Send $799 in sales by [Date Here], and I will deposit a $50 cash bonus into your ShareASale acount. With an average 30-day sale currently being $50+, reaching this goal is not hard, and we are looking forward to your participation!

Looking forward to hearing from you soon.

And if you need any help do not hesitate to email me at any time.

[Affiliate Program Manager's Name]

[Full Contact Information]

Very few affiliate program managers are doing this. I highly encourage you to be different here.

Denial Email

This is probably one of the most frequently misworded emails. In the vast majority of cases, denials are worded like death sentences—rigidly and without an option to appeal.

Lester B. Pearson, a Canadian prime minister who is often acknowledged as the greatest Canadian of all time, once said that "The chief distinction of a diplomat is that he can say *no* in such a way that it sounds like a *yes*." This is exactly what affiliate program managers should learn to do when dealing with affiliate applications that may not seem to fit the affiliate programs they manage (note the choice of the verb *seem* in this sentence). Never assume that you can be 100 percent right in your decision to decline an affiliate application. Even when saying "no," give them the benefit of the doubt. Phrase the text of the email you send to the declined affiliates in such a way that gives them another chance, if they want it. Here is a sample based text to start from:

Unfortunately, your application to the [MerchantURL.com] affiliate program has been declined. If you feel that it has been done in error, please contact me, the [MerchantName] affiliate program manager, directly at [EmailAddressHere] and I will be happy to discuss this with you. I do not want my company to miss out on opportunities to collaborate with promising partners, and will reply to your email within 24 hours of its receipt.

Do not burn bridges. You can never know for certain what exactly the affiliate who applied to your program had in mind. Give them an opportunity to communicate it to you prior to deciding to decline, and if they don't, decline their application, but don't burn the bridge.

Additionally, whenever possible, the program manager should give the affiliate the exact reason for the decline. You can dedicate a space in your template to customize this part every time you decline an application. If an affiliate program manager chooses to decline an affiliate application for reasons related to the quality of the website or another factor the manager believes the affiliate can improve, this should definitely be communicated as well. A famous Harvard professor, James L. Heskett, wrote that effective motivation always "starts not with compensation but with effective communication." Don't send out demotivating denial emails. It is possible to make them effective and actually help your affiliate recruitment and/or development.

Bad Denial Emails Can Hinder Recruitment

Do you know that the text of your affiliate denial email can actually hurt your recruitment efforts?

Here is a scenario:

You are running a blog for your affiliate program, which attracts good targeted traffic (affiliates interested in promoting your product/service) and lands affiliate sign-ups. You are reviewing applications manually (good for you!), and when finding affiliates whose websites do not suit your vertical/audience, you decline their applications. When an affiliate application is declined, you are sending them a blanket email, which tells them that unfortunately their application was denied on any of the included reasons.

The previously described case is a situation where your denial email hurts your own affiliate recruitment. How? You are not giving them a chance to explain why they have applied to your program in the first place!

Give the applying affiliates the benefit of the doubt. Even when declining their applications, keep the two-way communication channel open. Here is some brief text you can use to show them that you're open to communicating with them, learning more, and reevaluating your decision:

We are sorry, but the website(s) listed on your profile do(es) not meet our approval criteria. We have therefore declined your affiliate application.

If, however, you feel that we have overlooked your potential, we would like to hear from you. Just email us a brief explanation of how you were planning on marketing our product/service, and we will gladly reconsider your application.

You never know which of them will become the next superaffiliate. Do not assume you do.

Wednesday: Set Up Your Affiliate Program Support Base

Today I'll talk about your affiliate program support base. It starts with things as basic as a sign-up link, a program description page, and a dedicated email address. We will also spend time discussing the importance of mini-sites created for program support, and I will help you put your very own one together as well.

Sign-up Link

The easiest way to recruit affiliates into your program is to place a link to your affiliate program sign-up page on your website (Figure 10.5). This should be the very first thing you do as soon as your affiliate program is launched. Simple, and very natural, isn't it? Yet this could possibly be the most underutilized method of affiliate recruitment! Some merchants do have it, but you'd be surprised how many do not.

Figure 10.5 Home Depot recognizes the importance of highlighting its affiliate program on its website.

In March 2009, as I was looking through websites of merchants across various verticals, I was shocked to see how many of the established brands ignore this easy and effective recruitment tool. More than 60 percent of websites I looked at (my sample contained some 40 of them) lacked that affiliate program signup link. The following were the most common problems registered:

Nonexistent Link

- Apartments.com
- Equifax.com
- GameHouse.com
- Allstate.com
- Cars.com
- TradeMonster.com
- ...and many others

Broken Link

- Real.com—problem with internal linking landed every prospective affiliate on a "Sorry, we can't find the page you were looking for" page.

No Real Info

- TradeKing—not a word about payout, cookie life, platform used, or anything else that could attract me as an affiliate.

- Automotive.com—this link was to a cobranded Commission Junction page that contained no information on commission. Inviting affiliates "along for the ride earning high commissions" was not very motivating without the actual commission information.

Vague Verbiage

- LowerMyBills.com—at the time of my experiment, its page said they had "two different commission structures": a "traditional" one "with multiple ways to earn huge commissions," and a "geo-targeting solution" with "bounties of up to $70 per lead" and "minimum volume requirements" to be eligible for it; but no further details were provided.

So, the *first* thing you want to do is add an easy-to-locate Affiliate Program link or Become an Affiliate link to your website's navigation/menu.

Program Bio

The merchant's affiliate program description page (see Figure 10.6 for an example) is frequently the first place from which a prospective affiliate learns about the program. It is also one of the first places an affiliate turns to when they are looking for affiliate program details and conditions.

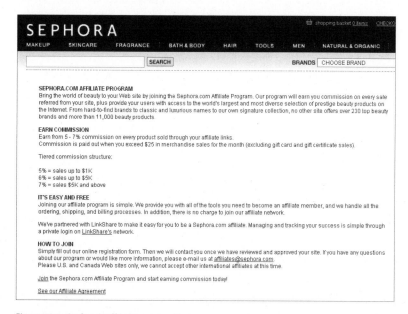

Figure 10.6 Sephora's affiliate program bio page

There are different ways to word the text and lay out the page, but the structure of every affiliate program description should always cover the main elements/data that affiliates care about. I believe that we can boil these elements down to seven pillars:

1. Merchant description with link to main website.

2. Commission structure and a clear breakdown into tiers/levels if any exist.

3. Information on cookie life.

4. Precise statistical data—vague verbiage like "impressive conversion" and "industry-leading payouts" — not only sounds tasteless but also brings the credibility of your affiliate program down. When quoting conversion rates, EPC, and AOV, either be exact or quote ranges.

5. Availability of data feed for etailers and/or multiple landing pages for lead-pursuing affiliate programs.

6. Information on tools or any other competitive advantages (for example, anti-parasite policy, tracking of affiliate-referred phone orders, custom on-demand creatives and/or landing pages, easy-to-import data feed solutions, widgets, performance bonuses, award-winning manager, and so on).

7. Any restrictions and/or special terms that affiliates should know about from the very outset (for example, "trademark bidding and/or usage of trademarks in domain names is prohibited," "coupon sales receive lower commission," and so on).

I also recommend staying within a 250-word limit for your main affiliate program description page. If you have more than that to say (which I certainly hope you do, because there is simply no way to squeeze everything into such a brief program description), break the information down into separate sections, and build a mini-site.

Mini-Sites

If you're serious about affiliate marketing, your affiliate program needs its own mini-site. Why? Let's turn to some stats now. In Figure 10.7, you can see a pie chart from the 2010 AffStat report. I like to call this chart "Effective Affiliate Recruitment Through Affiliates' Own Eyes." The question posed in front of affiliates was "How do you most often find out about an affiliate program and then join?"

If we add the Google (18 percent) piece of the pie to Personal Research (5.7 percent), which inevitably encompasses browsing the Web, and then add the Affiliate Manager Blogs (5.7 percent) piece to these two, we will almost hit a 30 percent mark.

On one hand, the previous data underscores the importance of having the dedicated affiliate program page I just talked about. One the other hand, however, it tells you that for lasting and constantly improving results, you should go beyond a one-page program description. Creating and maintaining an affiliate program mini-site, with a blog embedded into it, is what I recommend that every merchant do. This will help you improve the organic rankings of web pages that talk about your affiliate program, consequently positively affecting your passive affiliate recruitment (one done by your very website).

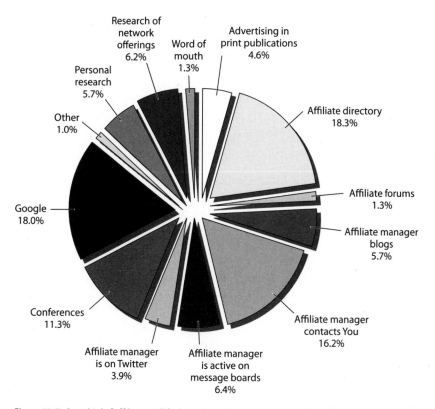

Figure 10.7 One-third of affiliates will find you through their online research of affiliate programs.

The affiliate program support mini-site, preferably hosted at the `http://affiliates.[merchantURL]` subdomain, may be started with as few as three pages:

- Program details (with sign-up link/form)
- Program agreement
- Blog

Ideally, however, you want your affiliate program support site to contain the following pages:

Program Details The text of this page will be similar to the text of your program bio page discussed earlier. Ideally, you want it to be more detailed than the brief bio I discussed. Include more details on your company and why it'll be a good partner for webmasters with the right traffic. Elaborate on the commission tiers (if there any), bonuses, and so on. If the text becomes lengthy, add an index of subtitles with anchor links to specific sections of the page.

Program Agreement Paste the full text of your affiliate program agreement (with preface, summary of key points, and the main text of the agreement as discussed before) here.

Frequently Asked Questions Start with basic questions like "What is affiliate marketing?" and "How will I get paid?" and go as deep as you want. Figure 10.8 shows a sample FAQ page. The important thing about the FAQ section is to constantly expand it based on questions asked by affiliates and answered by you via email, phone, and other means of communication. Document them all (removing any sensitive details) in this section, thereby continuously expanding it.

Figure 10.8 The Fabric.com affiliate FAQ page starts with an index of all questions.

Tips and Ideas Tell them of the types of affiliates that exist or the channels of marketing others are employing (caution: avoid mentioning affiliate sites, because this is both sensitive information and "leaks" from your site to affiliate websites); include links to video and text tutorials (your own or ones based on YouTube or other sites). See Figure 10.9 for a good example of such a section.

Creatives Show them the banners, text links, Flash links, and examples of other types of creatives (for example, widgets) that they will be able to use once they join your affiliate program.

Blog This one will require discipline. A blog (Figure 10.10) cannot be just put together. It has to be continuously maintained and updated. With time, your affiliate program blog will become one of the most important elements of your affiliate program support, helping you build up your mini-site, increasing your chances for ranking high on search engines for phrases important to your affiliate recruitment, and, after all, showing that you're actively managing your program and care about your affiliates. Not many affiliate programs do this, but I'd make program-specific blogging part of the job description for every affiliate program manager.

Contact Us List all possible contact information (phone, email, instant messengers, Twitter account, and so on) for the manager of your affiliate program.

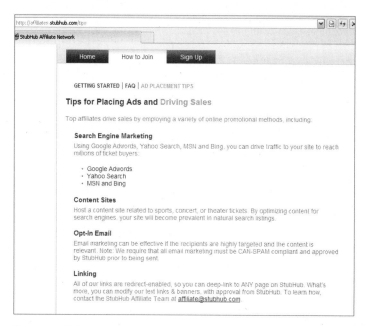

Figure 10.9 StubHub's generic Ad Placement Tips page, which is part of its affiliate program support mini-site

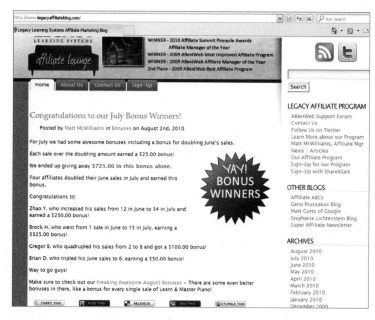

Figure 10.10 Legacy Learning Systems' affiliate program blog

Five Common Problems with Text

Back in April 2009, as I was doing a competitive analysis of vertical-specific affiliate programs for a client, I had to read through more than 25 affiliate program descriptions and program support mini-sites. Here are the five common problems that I noticed being repeated by different merchants (large and small):

Missing Information Many merchants leave out important information, such as the following:

- Cookie duration (we all know these can range from only a couple hours to "unlimited," so it is extremely important information for affiliates to know from the outset)
- How exactly performance-based commission increases will be applied (do not just mention a "payout of $20 to $50 per lead"; instead, state what you're going to pay $20 for and what affiliates need to do to get the $50)
- Qualification information (what exactly constitutes a valid sale/lead)
- Reversal policy/procedures
- Contact information (how will they be able to contact you with questions regarding your affiliate program if they want to do so prior to joining it?)

Vague Verbiage I already alluded to this when asking you to be concrete about your affiliate program performance when describing it on the program bio page. The most commonly abused quotes are "excellent payouts," "industry leading" [affiliate program], "most competitive" [commission], "guaranteed," and "highest conversion rates." Avoid being vague! Such verbiage can be a major turn-off. Affiliates want *concrete* information (exact payout details, exact conversion rates, and so on), not just a collection of beautiful words that convey no meaning.

Unnecessary Phrases Phrases like "there is no limit to how much you can make with our program" or "our affiliate program will provide for an unlimited income" are just too amateur. Every affiliate knows that the sky is the limit. That's the essence and the main beauty of the performance marketing industry. By putting things in such an amateur way, I personally believe that merchants are bringing their affiliate program's credibility down. Be not only concrete but also *eloquent*.

Spelling Mistakes C'mon, folks...*payouts* is one word (not *pay outs*), and so is *throughout* (not *through out*). And it's not *defenitely* but *definitely*. Also, there's a world of difference between *their* and *they're* (or *your* and *you're*). The list of the spelling mistakes I continuously see in the text of the program sign-up pages could certainly go on, but the point is clear. Spelling (and grammar) mistakes hurt credibility. Period.

Missing Sign-up Link Out of more than 25 affiliate program descriptions that I've looked at, two had the most important part—the sign-up link—missing. And these were programs with fairly good descriptions. Don't leave the most important part out! And, of course, don't charge for sign-ups.

Email Address

Finally, last but not least, put together a dedicated affiliate program support email address. The most common way to have it—and also the more frequently expected by affiliates themselves—is `affiliates@[merchantURL]`. Flee from `AffiliateMgr@[merchantURL]` and other nonconventional ways to word this email address, as well as from using `[Merchant]Affiliates@[FreeEmailService]` types of email addresses. The former are confusing, while the latter don't add credibility. Finally, it's a good idea to put together an `affiliate@[merchantURL]` (singular form) email address, forwarding it to your main (plural form) `affiliates@[merchantURL]` inbox.

Thursday: Prepare Announcement Text

When your program goes live, you'll want to announce it through various affiliate marketing message boards, affiliate program directories, and other platforms. Today you will work on the text of your announcement.

The Checklist

For the most part, the text of your program announcement will resemble your affiliate program bio, with a few minor adjustments meant to address the differences in readership. Realize that the announcement will be seen by multiple eyes that may not be really interested in your program unless you interest them in it.

Here is a five-point checklist for you to use while putting together the text of your affiliate program announcement:

- Brief merchant description (remember to link to the main website affiliates are called to promote)
- Program details such as commission, cookie life, and bonuses (you want to be attractive)
- Statistical data (on average order value, conversion rates, and so on), if available
- Primary call to action (CTA) to join the program backed up by a sign-up and/or activation promo
- Secondary call to action (read more in the following section)

Three Types of Calls to Action

There are three types of calls to action that affiliate program managers and merchants should be using with affiliates: primary, secondary, and post-primary.

The vast majority of affiliate program managers and merchants use only one type (the first one), and this hurts the development of their affiliate program in at least the areas that the other two types cover.

Primary These are calls to the action you want them to take in response to an outgoing recruitment email or when they visit your affiliate program bio page. This may be contacting you about your affiliate program or, most typically, submitting their application to join your affiliate program.

Secondary Secondary calls to action provide an alternative route of action for your prospective affiliates or those who may not be ready to take the primary action. Are you going to be inviting them to contact you anyway, providing them with enough of contact information *and* motivators to get back with you? You could also include an offer to at least exchange links or a hint at the fact that you may be open to other partnerships (for example, a synergy of a placement fee + a CPA model).

Post-primary This is the call to activation you should have in the approval email you send to the affiliate who has just been accepted into the program (I covered this earlier, not classifying the CTA as such). Examples of motivators on the level of post-primary calls to action would be a commission bump, a cookie life increase, or a monetary bonus in exchange for them putting your links on their websites.

As an affiliate program manager, you want to be using *all* three types. It won't take more than 15 minutes of your time to put the secondary and post-primary CTAs in places where they belong, and you'll be pleasantly surprised with the results.

Sample Announcement

It is hard to find a good program announcement, but one did catch my eye. It was the program launch announcement made by Mighty Leaf Canada:

> *Montreal, QC. July 21, 2010—Mighty Leaf Canada* [comment: brand name linked, as recommended*], a gourmet tea manufacturer best known for its handcrafted, silken and award-winning biodegradable tea pouches, has now launched its affiliate program exclusively on the Share Results affiliate network.*
>
> *Mighty Leaf Canada is offering affiliates who join their program* [comment: CTA link #1] *a 10 percent commission per sale, and a launch promotion that features a Performance Bonus and a Banner Contest, that is in effect until September 30, 2010.*
>
> *The Performance Bonus rewards affiliates with the following pay structure: affiliates who refer 10–19 sales will earn a $25 bonus; 20–29 sales will earn a $50 bonus; over 30 sales will garner a $100 bonus. With the Banner/Text link contest, affiliates who send Mighty Leaf Canada a page or link where they are promoting its tea products, in addition to their affiliate ID, will be entered into a draw to win a $50 cash prize.*
>
> *"We're very excited about launching our affiliate program* [comment: CTA link #2] *with Share Results, and we're confident that our unique tea products will be particularly interesting for Retail, Coupon and PPC*

affiliates, who target a Canadian audience," said Nick Martin, Affiliate Manager at Mighty Leaf Canada. "With the Share Results affiliate marketing software, affiliates have access to a powerful suite of reports that focus on accuracy, reliability and security, plus the communication and marketing tools they need to succeed."

Mighty Leaf tea is served in the finest hotels and restaurants, and is recognized for its unparalleled quality. A gourmet food product, Mighty Leaf retails principally in specialty food stores and natural food stores, and 70 percent of its customers are women. Affiliates can promote this program through direct and deep linking, paid search, email and incentivized traffic. Cookie duration for the program is 45 days.

"Mighty Leaf offers a strong niche product to an in-demand audience, while providing affiliates with the commission structure and promotions to ensure they maximise their earning potential," said Le Michelle Nguyen from Share Results. "This is an exciting opportunity for affiliates targeting a Canadian, female audience."

The average order size at Mighty Leaf Canada is $100+, free samples are provided with each order and free shipping is available on all orders $99 and over. Only Canadian traffic/customers are accepted.

About Mighty Leaf

Mighty Leaf Canada was born for the sole purpose of infusing life into an ancient indulgence by creating tea products that reach new heights of quality and innovation.

The genesis of Mighty Leaf Teas came in 1996 as a result of a shared passion and dream envisioned by husband-and-wife team Gary Shinner and Jill Portman when they founded their teahouse on Fillmore St. in San Francisco. Their passion is for creating the most incredible handcrafted tea blends found anywhere, globally sourcing the finest ingredients available. Paralleling the highest standards of quality at Mighty Leaf Tea is ongoing creative innovation.

Our specially created handcrafted tea pouches are designed to unleash the essence of the quality that is Mighty Leaf teas. Supporting our quality and innovation is our promise to deliver the highest level of customer service excellence in serving you the finest tea products available.

CONTACT INFORMATION
Nick M...
Affiliate Manager
nick@[URLhere]

I have only two minor criticisms to make about the Mighty Leaf announcement text:

- It isn't too easy to follow. I always highly recommend using bullet points (or other easy-to-follow formatting) and being more eloquent.
- It lacks a secondary call to action (as many program announcements do).

Having said this, it is a very solid announcement—which I don't see often these days—and there is a lot to learn from this example.

Friday: Compile Lists of Keywords and Best Sellers

Finally, I'll talk about two basic lists you want to prepare for your affiliates. These will be a list of keywords and a list of your best sellers.

Keyword Lists

When you hear the word *keyword*, more than likely the first thing that comes to your mind is paid search or pay-per-click (PPC) marketing. This is certainly one of the types of affiliates that will be able to use your keyword lists. However, that's not the only reason you'll want to compile your list of keywords. There are at least three areas in which affiliates can use your keyword help:

- Search engine optimization (SEO)
- PPC
- Domain name choice

PPC and SEO

Keywords are the common ground between paid search and search engine optimization. Although the ways of applying keywords in each of these two contexts differ, affiliates of *both* types will find your keyword lists helpful. Of course, the more thorough those lists are, the better.

As mentioned by John Jerkovic in his 2009 *SEO Warrior* volume, "When it comes to choosing keywords, you should generally be interested in high-volume, low-competition keywords." The exact lists will differ drastically depending on the industry you're in. So, there is not much else I can add here. I will, however, suggest two further considerations specific to paid search: a list of negative keywords and basic advice for affiliates who are just starting out with PPC.

Negative Keywords

Negative keywords are essentially words (and phrases) for which you do *not* want your ad to show in paid search results, because they are unlikely to convert into the desirable action.

Table 10.1 lists 90 negative keywords to help all kinds of paid search affiliates. Let me stress that this is a basic list to start with. You can use it as a basis for the list you'll offer to your affiliates.

▶ **Table 10.1** Negative keywords

about	Amazon	bargain
bargains	blog	blogs
book	books	cheap
clearance	close out	close outs
closeout	closeouts	community
comparison	comparisons	complaint
complaints	complimentary	contest
costless	deal	deals
define	definition	discount
discounted	DIY	example
examples	forum	free
freebie	giveaway	gratis
gratuity	help	how to
how-to	illegal	info
information	journal	journals
liquidation	learn	magazine
magazines	manual	model
news	no charge	no cost
offers	photo	photos
picture	pictures	price
pricing	problem	problems
project	reclamation	reclamations
research	retail	retailer
retailers	returns	review
reviews	sample	samples
scam	stats	suck
sucks	support	tip
tips	training	tutorial
tutorials	user manual	video
warranty	what are	what is

Again, this is a very basic list. It isn't unusual for a thorough negative keyword list to consist of hundreds of keywords. You can start from this one, as well as play with WordStream's negative keywords tool (Figure 10.11), to compile your own list.

As it is with *any* keyword list, do not let its length alert you. The more the merrier. Keep expanding and refining your keyword lists on a regular basis.

Although not all merchants may be willing to share their keyword inventories with affiliates, I believe that sharing the list of the negative keywords is a *must*. After all, if they burn themselves (and lose cash, with low or no conversion), it is the merchant, who they will eventually stop promoting, that will lose too. So, take the time to compile your own list of negative keywords (the previous one will help you get started quickly) and offer it to your affiliates.

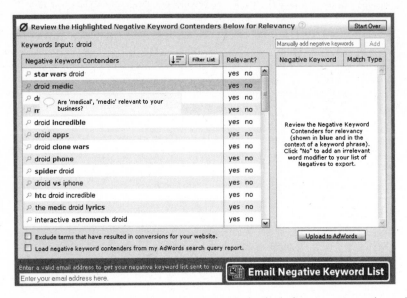

Figure 10.11 WordStream's online negative keywords tool is free for the first 10 negatives per keyword but shows you more comprehensive lists with the paid version.

Paid Search Advice

The following are five tips for affiliates who are just starting with paid search:

- Educate yourself thoroughly; a good place to start is Marshall and Todd's book *Ultimate Guide to Google AdWords* (Enterpreneur Press, 2006).

- Remember to constantly test (watch your CTR as well as your conversion ratio and work on improving them on an ongoing basis).

- Don't rush. You can burn a lot of money overnight. Take small steps until you really know what you're doing.

- Develop inventories of long-tail keywords, looking at things through the end user's eyes and employing tools such as Wordtracker, Google AdWords Keyword Tool, and so on).

- Use negative keywords.

Idea for Your Affiliates: Peel-the-Inventory Method

Originally published in the AMNavigator.com blog on 06/12/2009:

If you are running out of ideas of how to promote a merchant, here's something you can do: Peel their inventory to arrive at long-tail key phrases to target.

Say you are promoting a footwear merchant that has an extensive inventory of different brands and kinds of shoes. Let's take Zappos, for example, and suppose we decided to narrow our focus to just loafers.

Now let's go to Google AdWords Keyword Tool and narrow our focus even further—by color. I've searched for red, black, white, and tan loafers, and black is by far the most popular color among these four. Here's the data:

Keywords	Advertiser Competition ⑦	Local Search Volume: April ⑦	▼ Global Monthly Search Volume ⑦
Keywords related to term(s) entered - sort by relevance ⑦			
black loafers		27,100	12,100
black loafer		14,800	5,400
shoes black loafers		Not enough data	3,600
black leather loafers		4,400	2,900
women's black loafers		1,600	2,900
mens black loafers		5,400	1,900
black patent loafers		1,900	1,900
men's black loafers		Not enough data	1,600
black patent leather loafers		1,300	1,000
black suede loafers		1,300	1,000
womens black loafers		3,600	1,000

How can you use this information now?

Continues

Idea for Your Affiliates: Peel-the-Inventory Method *(Continued)*

1. Paid Search Campaigns

The most obvious way is to start bidding on *shoes black loafers, black leather loafers, women's black loafers,* and other long-tail key phrases.

The less frequently used techniques that I myself have found to be of great effectiveness (while promoting Langbridge.com) are the following.

2. Keyword-Rich Domains

While someone is sitting on the BlackLoafers.com domain not monetizing it in any way (unfortunate but very common), BlackLoafer.com is still free and so are longer tail key phrases that you can use right in the domain names. If you then use your keyword-rich domain to build a website centered around the very keywords that appear in the domain name, you will soon start getting some good organic traffic. For obvious reasons, I will not give you the exact domain names, but some of the three-word domains I registered and developed for Langbridge are now in the top 10 rankings (out of *more than 2 million* other web pages) on Google, Yahoo, MSN, and other search engines.

3. Long-Tail Blogging

Another technique that affiliates can use is blogging about the frequently searched-for products (or services) or putting together web pages that are optimized for ranking well on these key phrases. It is a common technique used by bloggers in general, and more affiliates should be taking advantage of it.

So, peel those inventories, and monetize the knowledge.

Domain Names

Another area where keyword knowledge becomes extremely handy is in domain name selection. I mentioned keyword-rich domains as part of the peel-the-inventory method, but the idea is worth emphasizing.

In a 2009 SearchEngineJournal.com blog post, a fellow digital marketer, Ann Smarty, wrote that "search engines are reported (or rather expected) to be putting less and less emphasis on keywords in domain names" to exclude spammer abuse of the long-tail domains technique. She also points out that "today it is almost impossible to get hold of any 'exact match' domains that wouldn't be too long or pointless." However, after conducting her little experiment, she has noticed that, in reality, search engines love keyword-rich domains (see also the results of her poll on the topic in Figure 10.12). Additionally, with a bit of extra research, it is still possible to find good long-tail domains. Based on my experience, I highly recommend affiliates start experimenting with this idea.

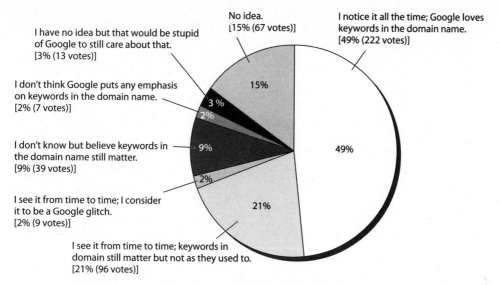

I have no idea but that would be stupid
of Google to still care about that.
[3% (13 votes)]

No idea.
[15% (67 votes)]

I notice it all the time; Google loves
keywords in the domain name.
[49% (222 votes)]

I don't think Google puts any emphasis
on keywords in the domain name.
[2% (7 votes)]

I don't know but believe keywords in
the domain name still matter.
[9% (39 votes)]

I see it from time to time; I consider
it to be a Google glitch.
[2% (9 votes)]

I see it from time to time; keywords in
domain still matter but not as they used to.
[21% (96 votes)]

Figure 10.12 Distribution of votes on "How much weight do keywords in domain name still have?" poll.
The vast majority of digital marketers believe that keyword-rich domains do carry ranking weight.

Best-Seller Lists

The reasoning behind this list is simple—what sells well for you will more than likely sell well for affiliates with relevant traffic.

Obviously, this primarily applies to etailers, or merchants with online retail storefronts. If you're selling services packaged into different types of packages, providing affiliates with information on what sells best, and corresponding text links, is also important.

If you are an etailer, here are the three types of best-seller lists that you can create for your affiliates:

- Generic all-time best-seller lists—top 5, top 10, top 20 products across your inventory
- Holiday/seasonal lists—what people buy during particular periods of time (Christmas for gifts-related merchants, specific times of the year for gardening- and outdoors-related merchants, and so on)
- Section-specific best-seller lists—top products in specific product categories

In some cases—for example, if you're running your affiliate program on ShareASale—you will have a chance to go beyond text links only and create best-seller widgets for your affiliates. Anything of this kind—things that are done above and beyond the standard practices of deep-linked text links—is certainly encouraged and appreciated by affiliates.

Month 3: Program Launch and Affiliate Program Management

IV

In this part we will look at various crucial aspects of affiliate program management. I will walk you through everything you need to know about effective management of your affiliate program. Starting with the program launch, announcements, and initial recruitment, all the way through such vital subjects as building a healthy affiliate communication channel, motivating affiliates, and managing the program driven by an independent (and therefore unmanageable) "workforce," I'll prepare you to be an effective affiliate program manager.

Week 1: Launch the Affiliate Program and Recruit

The day has finally come. Your affiliate program is all set up and ready to go live. You've reached a landmark that's altogether exciting and critical. It's a starting point, and this week you want to concentrate on very specific things: the announcement of your program to the affiliate marketing world, as well as the development and rollout of your affiliate recruitment campaigns. In addition to these, we will also chart the guidelines of the social-media strategy for your program, as well as look at various conferences and shows you want to plan on attending.

11

Chapter Contents

Monday: Announce Program Launch
Tuesday: Study Affiliate Recruitment Tools and Techniques
Wednesday: Develop a Direct-Contact Recruitment Strategy
Thursday: Formulate Your Social-Media Approach
Friday: Plan to Attend Conferences and Shows

Monday: Announce Program Launch

The very first thing you want to do once your program goes live is announce this fact as loudly and as widely as possible. You should already have your program announcement text ready from the previous week. Now, let's talk about the options you have as far as the platforms for the announcement of your freshly baked affiliate program. There are five options to be aware of here:

- Press release websites
- Affiliate marketing websites
- Affiliate program directories
- Social media channels
- Affiliate networks

Press Release Websites

I am not a big fan of press release distribution websites, but if you have a good relationship with a press release distribution agency that you're using for other marketing purposes, you might as well announce your program through a press release too.

I'm not going to pause on this point any further. I have seen merchants (large and small) announcing their programs this way, but since the main goal of this announcement is to reach the ear of your prospective affiliate, I believe this particular method to be one of the weakest out of the five.

Affiliate Marketing Websites

This type represents the most effective avenue for affiliate program announcements. By affiliate marketing websites, I mean forums like ABestWeb.com and 5StarAffiliatePrograms.com, blogs that cover industry-related news and happenings, and, last but not least, industry-leading resources such as AffiliateSummit.com, ReveNews.com, GeekCast.fm, and the like.

Forums

With forums, things are very straightforward. Most have a dedicated program announcement section (Figure 11.1) where your program will be announced. Don't post your announcement just anywhere. It may be deemed as spamming the message board, and the consequences will be diametrically opposite from what you'd expect from a proper forum announcement.

Some forums and affiliate program directories, which I'll discuss in the next section, charge you a fee for announcing your program. Is it really wise to pay to announce/list your affiliate program? In some cases, such an announcement may be extremely effective, while in others it may not. Things always boil down to what you are going to get in return. Before you pay anyone to list your affiliate program, ask them the same questions you would ask a website if you were a merchant buying banner or any other ad space. Ask them about their traffic, about the demographics of the visitors, and for references. Those who are more serious would have these listed right at their website, and you could contact the references directly. Less reliable one will not even reply to your emails. Do your homework and then make an educated decision. Beware of con artists, because they are very much present in the affiliate marketing industry. In the early days of my affiliate marketing education, I got stuck with one paid "affiliate directory" so deeply that neither requests to unsubscribe nor chargeback filings worked. I had to close the credit card account and get an entirely new credit card to fully "unsubscribe" from them.

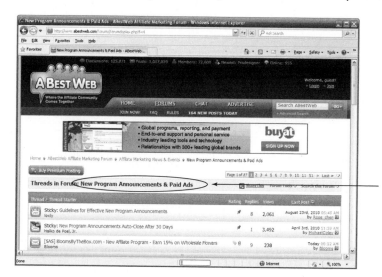

Figure 11.1 ABestWeb.com's New Program Announcements section

Blogs

With blogs, especially the most popular of them, and other industry-leading websites, the situation is very different from forums. Being an affiliate marketing blogger myself, I can tell you that most publishers of valuable (and hence highly demanded and trusted) content will not publish just a program announcement. Unlike press release websites, these sites can be attracted only by something that is really worth writing about. Examples of such content would include breakthrough ideas and technologies, case studies, and other things worth announcing. I like to split content publishers (affiliate marketing ones included) into three types: reporters, theoreticians, and coaches (Figure 11.2).

Some of the first type may agree to announce your program (especially if it is a program long awaited in the affiliate community). The latter two won't be interested unless you provide them with some unique and quality content like the examples I've mentioned. Even the reporter types generally like to have a bit more than just your standard press release. So, keep this in mind if you approach bloggers or other content producers.

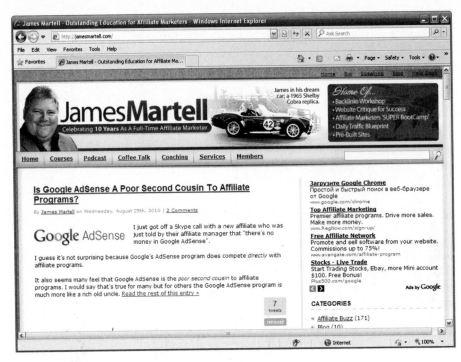

Figure 11.2 James Martell is a classic example of a coach-type blogger.

Affiliate Program Directories

I recommend listing your program in affiliate directories. They are the references affiliates go to (Figure 11.3) when they are searching for affiliate programs, and they are normally very well positioned in search engines.

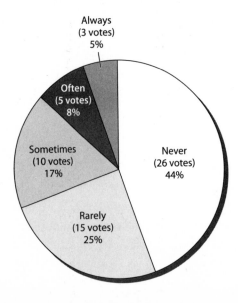

Figure 11.3 Results of my "Do you use affiliate program directories to find programs to join?" affiliate poll

Based on various polls and surveys (see also Figure 11.4), I can confidently state that around *one-fifth* of affiliates are using affiliate program directories to find programs to join.

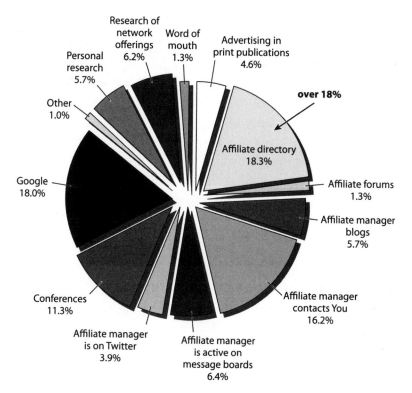

Figure 11.4 Per a AffStat report in 2010, 18.3 percent of affiliates find out about affiliate programs from affiliate directories.

The only logical question to follow this data is, "What are the affiliate program directories to submit my program information to?"

There are many directories out there, but I suggest adding your programs to the following:

AffiliateFirst.com

AffiliatePrograms.com

AffiliateRanker.com

AffiliateScout.com

AffiliatesDirectory.com

AffiliateSeeking.com

AllAffiliatePrograms.com

AssociatePrograms.com

JamAffiliates.com

Top-Affiliate.com

(The previous list is a merely alphabetical one and should not be considered as a ranking or an endorsement of any kind.)

Although it might be tempting to focus entirely on affiliate directories, keep in mind that this particular recruiting avenue accounts for only some 20 percent of affiliates. Many affiliates never use directories, and you'll miss out on 80 percent of the market if you neglect the other avenues.

Social-Media Channels

Social media will become an integral part of your affiliate program support efforts. There are a number of channels to utilize, and I will discuss them on Thursday of this week. You may now flip through right to the "Formulate Your Social Media Approach" section of this chapter, review the various media, and plan on starting to use the ones you'll begin with right from the announcement of your program. This will be a good start. Between the Thursday of last week (when I talked about the five-point checklist for your affiliate program announcement) and the Thursday of this week, you'll have some good information to begin using social media to promote your affiliate program.

Affiliate Networks

Many merchants don't know this and consequently aren't taking full advantage of the opportunity, but when a program goes live on an affiliate network, it almost always gets a free listing in a "new programs" category (see Figure 11.5 for a LinkShare example) in addition to the main category you choose during the setup phase.

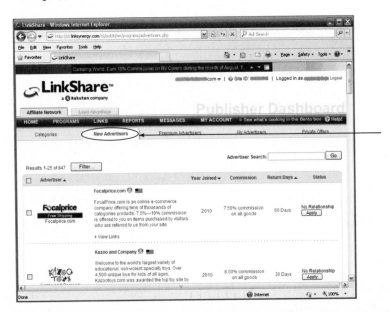

Figure 11.5 LinkShare's New Advertisers section as seen through its affiliate/publisher dashboard

This is why having a great program description with a time-sensitive join-and-activate program launch promo is a must. Affiliates do look through the lists of the newly launched programs, and this is your chance to stand out and attract them. Since you will have no (or little) performance statistics reported for your program, your program description is your main weapon now. Make sure that it *not only* rests on the seven pillars discussed during the previous week but also that it has an additional bonus incorporated into it: a commission increase or a monetary bonus you will apply to all affiliates that join your program and put up links to you within a certain number of days (I recommend setting it at something between 30 and 45 days) since the launch of your program.

Tuesday: Study Affiliate Recruitment Tools and Techniques

Affiliate recruitment is probably the most important duty of every affiliate program manager. After all, if there are no affiliates in the program, there is no point having/maintaining the program itself. Affiliates are your main sales force, and the more quality affiliates you partner with, the more successful an affiliate program you will be able to build.

As soon as you have started your affiliate program, one of the industry's most frequently asked questions becomes your main concern. The question comes in many forms: "Where do I find affiliates? What websites do affiliates hang around? Are there any good conferences at which I may recruit affiliates? Are there any tools to automatize affiliate recruitment?" But the essence is this: "How can a merchant effectively recruit affiliates?" This is the subject you're going to tackle today.

Common Misconceptions

One of the common misconceptions of merchants starting new affiliate programs is a belief that once they have invested in the start-up of their program, no other investments are required; the rest will "take care of itself." I have heard merchants telling me "We have tried affiliate marketing, and it hasn't worked for us." When investigating deeper, I would find out that in 95 percent of the cases their "trying of affiliate marketing" consisted of starting an affiliate program and posting the information about it in several affiliate program directories throughout the Internet. To this I would say, is that it?! Are you telling me you have "tried it"? This may come as a shock, but if that's all you've done, you have not even taken a tiny bite out of it! It's no wonder you have never seen any worthwhile sales volume. When you start an affiliate program, you have to be ready to invest. You may invest money or time, depending on which of these you, the merchant, have in greater supply. Affiliate recruitment can be done on your own, or you can hire someone to do the job for you.

Free Recruitment Tools

I'll start with smaller merchants or those that work on tight budgets (and do not have much room for investment into affiliate recruitment tools) and list a few good tools that can be used for affiliate recruitment virtually without any initial investment.

Merchants on limited or nonexisting budgets can start with the following five tools:

- Search engines: Search them to find potential affiliate partners.
- Twitter.com: Follow relevant hash tags, use the search function, and maintain a dedicated Twitter account for your affiliate program.
- Internet Success Spider: See www.grabthespider.com.
- Your affiliate program's blog: See the previous chapter.
- Affiliate program directories: This was discussed earlier.

Carefully crafting and implementing your recruitment strategy while incorporating these five tools will help you cover as much as 63 percent of the avenues that affiliates routinely use for finding and joining affiliate programs.

The *key rule* to remember throughout using these five tools is thou shall not spam. Seriously. Respect your potential partners, and they will respect you in return.

Seven Avenues of Affiliate Recruitment

Now, let's turn to the tools and techniques you can use when your budget is better than $0.

The key to building a successful affiliate recruitment campaign is in a thorough and well-organized strategy. All tools and techniques that you can employ to serve the purpose of affiliate recruitment can be divided into seven categories. Trying to make things easier to remember, I have made each group's name start with the letter *S* (just like *seven*, the total of all points, does).

The seven *S*-factors list includes the following:

1. Software
2. Social media
3. Search engines
4. Second-tier affiliates
5. Summits and symposiums
6. Symbiotic methods
7. Structure-based recruitment

1. Software

Software applications can help you find prospective affiliates that either already work with competing affiliate programs or run websites that target the traffic you're after.

I have personally used IBP's Arelis Link Manager (Figure 11.6) and have heard of other affiliate program managers successfully working with LinkCapture (and other link-building solutions) on the same objective. Both of these applications can be great when used wisely. They help you quickly search the Internet, pulling websites that may be good affiliate partners (either because they are working in the niche you're working in or because they link/write about your competitors or maybe even are already working as affiliates of your competitors) together with information on their website and their contact information. Improper use of such applications can also ruin your affiliate recruitment campaign. That is if you end up spamming those who should be treated as potential business partners.

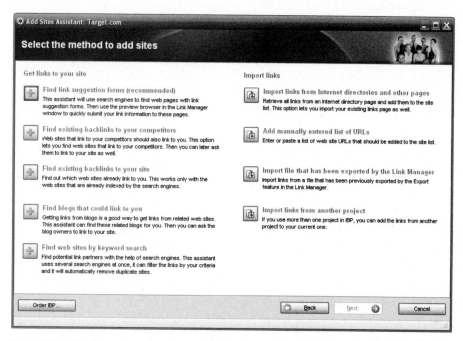

Figure 11.6 Arelis offers a variety of options to search for potential affiliates (by links to competitors, keywords, blogs that could link to you, and so on).

Once you have obtained the contact information of the prospective affiliates, do not rush to send out the same email to thousands of them. Unsolicited email is still called spam. First, do a careful prescreening of all webmasters the software finds for you. Make sure you do not contact those who you do not want to contact. Second, take your time to personalize your emails or even try to approach them via snail mail. Innovation pays off. Finally, remember to have a working "unsubscribe" mechanism in place. I will discuss these elements in more detail on Wednesday, when I cover the subject of affiliate recruitment by email.

In addition to link exchange and website promotion software, and if your budget allows it, you may also want to have a look into an application called Syntryx (Figure 11.7). It's a robust platform that claims to contain close to 2 million affiliate contacts in it, and I have heard of other outsourced program managers using it quite successfully.

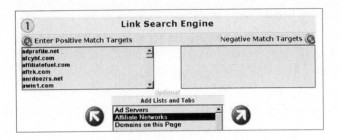

Figure 11.7 Unlike many link-building tools, Syntryx allows you to find actual affiliates by searching for websites with affiliate links.

2. Social Media

In addition to software, you should also dive into the social media of affiliate marketing. There are numerous blogs and forums, Facebook and LinkedIn groups, and other online communities where affiliates "hang out."

Forums deserve a special mention. In Ancient Roman times, "forums" were places of meetings for judicial or public business activity. Nowadays, this concept has transferred onto online communities or "message boards," where each member is free to discuss or voice their ideas, interacting with the other members of the forum. The Roman concept remained but adjusted to the current-day reality of the nearly omnipresent Internet, which changed the way people interact.

Any merchant/affiliate manager should focus on two types of forums: those for affiliates and those that are industry-specific. These can be found easily with the help of any major search engine. For example, if you are selling digital cameras and you have an affiliate program, you would want to make sure you're registered with the major online affiliate marketing forums, as well as photography forums and, more specifically, digital photography forums. These forums offer you multiple options for affiliate recruitment, starting from affiliate program announcement and inclusion of your sign-up URL in your signature to running your own affiliate support forums.

Professional forums may also offer you some options to push your affiliate program. However, please abide by the forum's rules by not blatantly promoting your own affiliate program. This may be a violation of the forum's regulations, and your account could be suspended for such behavior. It is always best to register with the forum and start posting information that is helpful to others, getting to know the people at the forum, and building your own reputation. A little down the line you may consider announcing your affiliate program, but only after getting the approval of the forum's administrator. By first building credibility as a participant in the forum, your promotional/advertising efforts will be much more effective.

Another tool worth mentioning is Twitter (Figure 11.8). It can also be excellent for affiliate recruitment.

There are two rules to remember while marketing your affiliate program through social media: Thou shalt not spam, and thou shalt not take more than thee have given. The first rule is pretty self-explanatory. If you're on a forum, play by the forum's rules. Do not start off by blatantly promoting your affiliate program. Most forums will ban you. Similarly, your comments can be banned and removed from blogs and social-network groups. The second rule is also the secret of successful social-media usage; you cannot take more than you have contributed in the first place. If and when you are of genuine help to the community, blog, or forum, you will be warmly accepted and collaborated with.

Figure 11.8 Merchants on both sides of the Atlantic (Amazon, eBay, Argos, and so on) are maintaining affiliates-oriented Twitter accounts, both for program support and recruitment.

3. Search Engines

Although you certainly want to automate as much of the affiliate recruitment process as possible, do not forget about the good ol' search engine ranking analysis. If you run across websites that rank high for relevant keywords, approach them. Coupon affiliates may be easily discovered by such keywords as *coupon, coupons, rebates,* and so on. Data feed affiliates may be found by typing in the name of any other merchant that also has an affiliate program, and so on.

There will also be a plethora of potential affiliates who are already monetizing their traffic by running Google AdSense units on their sites but not through affiliate links yet. AdSense on a website is a good sign. This tells you they are familiar with at least one model for monetizing sites. Since they are familiar with cost per click (CPC), it will make it easier for you to explain your cost-per-lead (CPL) or cost-per-sale (CPS) models (whichever your affiliate program is based on) to them.

4. Second-Tier Affiliates

Although I normally do not recommend having a second-tier commission and recommend paying as much as possible on the first tier, it makes sense to pay a bounty on new affiliate referrals. In fact, some "affiliates" are making this their main business. I am talking about affiliate program directories. These directories are the references that affiliates go to when searching for affiliate programs, and they are normally very well positioned in search engines. Most of them do not charge you anything for listing an affiliate program, but, for obvious reasons, they generally prefer listing affiliate programs that pay a bounty on every new affiliate sign-up. There are also quite a few mainstream affiliates that are interested in similar relationships with merchants.

5. Summits and Symposiums

Any type of conference or convention attended by affiliates is a great place to recruit. Affiliate Summit is a must; and when you go, make sure you get at least a table at the Meet Market that is held on the first day of the summit. In the United States, the Affiliate Summit is held biannually: in Las Vegas during the winter and on the East Coast during the summer (Figure 11.9).

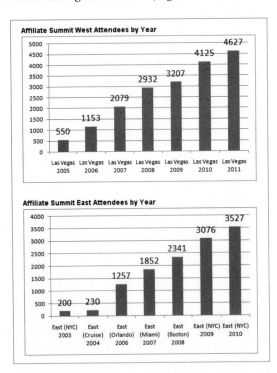

Figure 11.9 Charts that break out Affiliate Summit registration growth by location

Many affiliate networks (particularly LinkShare, Commission Junction, Google Affiliate Network, and ShareASale) have their own affiliate conferences. If your affiliate network has one, this is another great place to make contact with affiliates.

Besides the Affiliate Summit, I have personally found the following conferences to be good for making connections with affiliates: ad:tech, PubCon, Search Marketing Expo (SMX), Internet Marketing Conference, eMetrics Summit, and Search Engine Strategies (SES).

6. Symbiotic Methods

Webster's Dictionary defines *symbiosis* as a "cooperative relationship (as between two persons or groups)." What I am referring to is promoting your affiliate program on a cross-program basis. You can form short- or long-term cross-program recruitment relationships with affiliate programs run by merchants that sell related (but not competing) products or services. You announce their affiliate program to your pool of affiliates, while they do the same for you in the circular sent out to their affiliates. If you go with cross-program promotions, remember to respect your affiliates' privacy and not abuse their trust. When they agree to receive your affiliate newsletter, they agree to receive the information that will help them succeed with your program and may consider your aggressive pushing of some other affiliate program a spam. So, if you do a cross-program promo with another affiliate program, make sure to handle it gently.

Additionally, while getting involved in cross-program promotions, you want to beware that if you are on an affiliate network, such promotions may be in violation of the network's terms and conditions. Check them carefully beforehand.

7. Structure-Based Recruitment

In addition to the previous six, most affiliate networks offer their merchants an array of internal affiliate recruitment options. Some of them are actually free if you have something truly interesting to offer to your affiliates. In the past, for example, I've had buy.at affiliate network in the United Kingdom agree to include unusual promotional offers in the weekly network newsletter that goes out to *all* affiliates in the network. ShareASale in the United States has included seasonal promos of some of my merchants in their newsletters too. Talk to the network reps to find out more about the recruitment opportunities that they may offer you.

Many affiliate networks also have an array of paid recruitment options (see Figure 11.10 for a Commission Junction example, and see the "ShareASale Affiliate Recruitment Opportunities" sidebar for ShareASale examples). Normally, these can be utilized right from within your merchant interface and are quite self-explanatory.

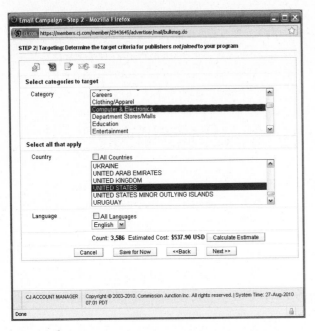

Figure 11.10 For a fee you can create a category-based email recruitment campaign to approach the CJ affiliates who are not yet working with you.

Finally, whichever method(s) of affiliate recruitment you're utilizing, make sure you continuously work on building your own affiliate list by cataloging contact information of affiliates (both current and prospective ones) and hosting a "subscribe to affiliate newsletter" form on your website. Even if an affiliate isn't ready to work with you just yet, they may be open to staying updated on the life of your affiliate program. So, it doesn't hurt to ask.

ShareASale Affiliate Recruitment Opportunities

The ways to recruit affiliates within an affiliate network will differ drastically depending on the affiliate network, but let's take ShareASale for an example.

At first look, on this particular network a merchant will notice an inability to contact any affiliate directly (unlike at AvantLink or Google Affiliate Network, for example) or even search the network's affiliates by the verticals they are working in (like at Commission Junction, for instance). ShareASale has its solid reasons for this policy. Affiliates generally prefer not to be contacted by the merchants they haven't signed up with, and ShareASale is protecting their privacy.

ShareASale does provide merchants with a few excellent tools and opportunities for affiliate recruitment. The first one worth mentioning is a free listing of a newly launched program in the New Programs section. After that, there are several paid options to choose from. They can be located under the Tools menu in your merchant account. Out of all of them, I have personally found the "Featured Program of the Week" and the "Holiday Center" inclusions to yield the highest click-to-sign-up conversion (more than 25 percent and more than 50 percent, respectively).

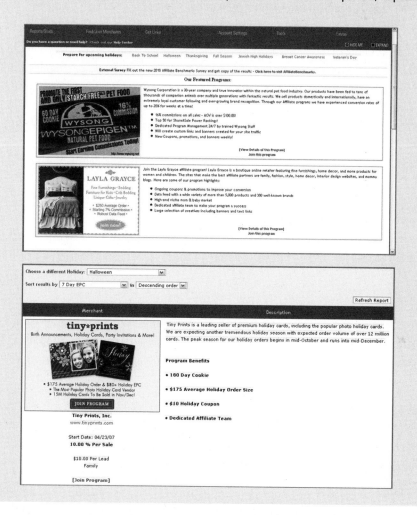

Wednesday: Develop a Direct-Contact Recruitment Strategy

Today I'll talk about affiliate recruitment in more detail, focusing on a highly effective approach to it—contacting prospective affiliates directly.

A friend and fellow affiliate marketer, Mark Welch, once wrote that "The single most important source of successful affiliates is a direct invitation from the program manager to the site owner or advertising manager" ("Affiliate Recruitment Strategies and Practices," MarkWelchBlog.com). I fully concur with Mark.

Three Forms of Direct Contact

The direct-contact method may take place in the following ways:

- Electronic message
- Regular mail (postcard or similar invitation)
- Face-to-face contact (at a conference or other meeting)

Out of all of these, *electronic messages* are by far the most widely used method of a merchant's/manager's coming into direct contact with a prospective affiliate (with the purpose of inviting them into an affiliate program). In this category, I include both traditional *emails* and *direct messages* sent via an instant messenger, affiliate network, social-media platform, or other messaging options. The latter basically represents a condensed form of email invitation. Being the most popular method among affiliate program managers, it is email recruitment that I will spend most of this day on.

Regular mail as a direct-contact method of affiliate recruitment is without a doubt the most underused method, which gives it the edge most prospective affiliates will appreciate. Most of my following recommendations about email recruitment can also be applied in postal invitations.

Finally, suggestions about industry-specific conferences for *face-to-face contact* will be made on Friday.

Email Company Uses Regular Mail with Affiliates

One of the few merchants who is using direct mail as a communication channel with affiliates is AWeber. In a way, it is symbolic, because AWeber is an email marketing software vendor. Yet, it understands the power of the good ol' snail mail enough to complement its own email correspondence with postcards sent via regular mail.

AWeber sends a direct-mail piece to welcome every affiliate into their affiliate program, which is rare and definitely makes them stand out. It tells the affiliate that the merchant has gone out of their way and done something others don't do. Besides the information about the program, the welcome-into-the-program postcard also has a credit-card-sized card in it, and the latter includes the affiliate's information and all the necessary contact details for them to get a hold of the affiliate manager and get going with the program.

More companies should be doing the same, not only to welcome new affiliates into the program but also for *affiliate recruitment*.

At the time of managing the AWeber's affiliate program, Ron Givens made numerous valuable comments in my blog at AMNavigator.com; one of them read as follows:

As the Affiliate Manager for AWeber Communications, I always make sure I can be reached directly by any of our affiliates.

Not only do I make sure I listen to our affiliates' needs, but I also go out of my way to see to it that they get the best possible solutions to their problems, or they are provided with the best possible resources available.

It's great to be very personable and take the approach that we are all in this together. Let's work hard and have fun doing it!

…We actually send snail mail welcome letters to all of our customers and affiliates with their login details and details on how to contact us if they need help. . . .I always like to communicate with our affiliates, just so they know I am a live person, am always reachable and will respond directly to their needs.

What an excellent example to follow!

How Not to Do It

Let's start with a real-life example. Back in May 2009 I received an email from an affiliate manager who had found my www.amnavigator.com website and decided to invite me to join their affiliate program.

Here's the text of that email (with sensitive information removed):

Date: Thu May 21 09:17:53 CDT 2009

Sender: "Drop S… A…" <support@URLhere>

To: <info@amnavigator.com>

Subject: Become a DSA Affiliate

Hello,

I was looking at your website, and I thought it might be a good candidate for our affiliate program. We pay you [commission details here]. You also receive a 5 dollar commission on sales made by any affiliates you've referred through you link. You can learn more about our service on [link to their website here].

Click here to see the details of our affiliate program [linked].

If you don't think this is a good fit, just click here [linked] and I won't contact you again.

Best regards,

[Name]

Affiliate Manager

There are at least five mistakes that you can commit when putting together an affiliate recruitment message, and the previous example made them all.

Mistake #1: Impersonal The Sender field contains no name (just the company name and some generic email address). Additionally, it is easy to tell that they haven't looked at my website, which does have my name that they could have used to make the previous piece of correspondence really attract my attention.

Mistake #2: Unenticing That Subject line doesn't make them stand out. Imagine how many recruitment emails an affiliate receives every day. Make yours special. Yes, it is a good idea to "brand" your subject line with the company name, but in my experience "become an affiliate" is not the most enticing phrase to use. Use phrases like "partnership," "business proposal" (after all, it is one), and "private offer" (if you're making one, of course). You want your email to stand out among the hundreds of others they receive.

Mistake #3: In-Concrete How exactly is my website a good fit for this affiliate program? The www.amnavigator.com address is simply *not*. They did not do their homework. It is apparent that I was sent a blanket email, impersonal and in-concrete.

Mistake #4: Intrusive So, now I have to opt out for you to understand that I am not "a good candidate" and stop sending this to me? This may make things right from the CAN-SPAM Act perspective, but if you are an "affiliate manager" seeking to recruit me as your affiliate, it's not only the "requirements for commercial emailers" that you should rely on. You should want to approach your prospects with respect, a personal message, and something to really catch their attention.

Mistake #5: Incentive-Free This mistake may well be added to mistake #2, but I have decided to make it into a separate one. The previous text is not offering an affiliate anything on top of the default commission structure. There is neither an urgency nor any additional attractiveness that would make an affiliate click that "details of our affiliate program" link, join it, and start sending the traffic their way.

So, the formula for failure is: Impersonal + Unenticing + Incentive-free + In-concrete + Intrusive = *Ineffective*.

How do you want to do it then?

How to Make It Shine

Affiliates are receiving multiple solicitation emails from merchants; the bigger the affiliate, the more emails they receive. Obviously, you want *your* recruitment email to stand out from the rest. Besides doing the opposite of the previously quoted five mistakes, the following tips should help you achieve your goal (and keep you out of trouble too):

Don't Be Anonymous Use that dedicated email address I discussed in the previous chapter and also have your full name attached to it. For example, while I was managing Forbes .com's affiliate program, the From field of my emails looked like "Geno Prussakov <affiliates@forbes.com>." As shown in Figure 11.11, Medicus Golf is doing just this.

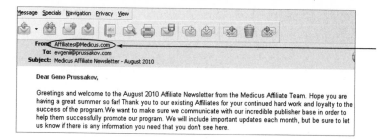

Figure 11.11 Medicus.com has a dedicated email address for its affiliate program.

Stay Compliant with the CAN-SPAM Act You can review the requirements at www.ftc.gov. Additionally, reviewing what SpamCop.net says about emails that cannot be reported as spam would be helpful. SpamCop.net says the following:

> *Unsubscribing*
>
> *On January 1, 2004, the CAN-SPAM Act became law in the US. (CAN-SPAM is an acronym for Controlling the Assault of Non-Solicited Pornography And Marketing). CAN-SPAM requires that all unsolicited commercial email contain a label of unsolicited commercial email (although it doesn't require a particular method or label), a working unsubscribe mechanism and a physical address for the sender. It also prohibits the use of forged or falsified headers and misleading or deceptive subject lines. Many legitimate senders are complying with some or all of the provisions of the CAN-SPAM act, but so are many spammers. CAN-SPAM compliance is not necessarily a reliable way to distinguish solicited from unsolicited email. Be aware that CAN-SPAM requires that an individual be removed from a list upon request.*

Having said all of that, no one is 100 percent guaranteed not to be reported for spam. Since such complaints (however unjustified they may be at times) may result in your host taking your full website down (a risk no serious merchant can afford to take), it is a good idea to register a separate domain name, just for your affiliate program support site and email addresses. For example, when managing HealthCompare.com's affiliate program, I had a separate HealthCompareAffiliates.com domain name for a dedicated support site. All recruitment emails were also sent from the affiliates@healthcompare-affiliates.com email address.

Develop an Effective Subject Line Your subject line should be attractive, nonspammy, and rightly portraying the intent for your contact. A bad example is "Make Millions Overnight with [MerchantName]." A good example is "Partnership Proposal from [MerchantName]." Also, "[AffiliateSite] and [MerchantName]" has worked well for me.

Introduce Yourself and Your Company Because this introduction, as everything in this email text, should be eloquent, it must include names, a link to the company's website, and an effective description of your business.

Explain *Why* Exactly You Have Decided to Contact Them For example, use "Your website caters to the traffic that is also immediately relevant to us, yet we are not in direct competition with your site" or "I see that you're already monetizing your traffic through affiliate links." Also, be specific about what it is precisely that you have in mind (for example, "an opportunity for us to partner together, whereby you'd be earning commission on...").

Personalize Your Email Include the details that truly tell them you have taken the time to look through their website, to read their content, and to seriously analyze how your partnership could be *mutually* beneficial.

Flee from Blanket Texts for Your Recruitment Emails They are not only detrimental to your recruitment efforts but can also get you in trouble (for example, webmasters reporting you for spamming, affiliates mocking you in blogs and forums, and so on).

Include Concrete Data on Your Affiliate Program Include the data that makes the prospective affiliate's decision easier to make (for example, conversion rates, EPC, AOV, and other details I discussed in the previous chapter while talking about your affiliate program description page).

Include Both *Primary* and *Secondary* Calls to Action This was discussed in the previous chapter (primary CTA: sign-up link to join the program; secondary CTA: one showing you're open to discussing alternative collaboration opportunities or at least a link exchange). I normally include two primary CTAs (one in the middle and one closer to the end of the affiliate recruitment email) and one secondary CTA.

Watch Your Grammar (Lexis, Syntax, and Punctuation) I've talked about this in the previous chapter, but it's worth reiterating here. You want to understand that you'll never have a second chance to make that first impression. Upon an analysis of some 40 different affiliate recruitment emails, I have found out that the majority of them are so full of clichés, it isn't even funny. Flee from using words and phrases like "instantly," "ultimate," "perfect match," "X money in X days/months," "make $X every day/month," "highest payouts," "best affiliate program," "number-one affiliate program online," and so on. Also, avoid spelling words in uppercase, and drop those exclamation marks.

Keep Records Always record the full prospect's information (where the basic "set" includes their URL, name, and email address, while a larger record may also include data on traffic, phone, address, and so on), the date of contact, and their response (interested, not interested, bounced email, and so on).

Remember to Follow Up If the reply has been positive or no reply has been received, I recommend sending your first follow-up email seven to ten days after the first one (I've witnessed cases where this first follow-up email doubled the affiliate sign-ups received upon the initial contact). The second follow-up email should be sent out some three weeks after the initial contact (and not sooner than two weeks after the first follow-up email). Finally, it's a good idea to work through your list of previously contacted prospects four to five months after the initial contact. It isn't unusual for this third follow-up email to yield additional affiliate sign-ups.

Remember Regular Mail and Phone Follow up via these means with the most promising prospects.

When neither the application you're using nor WhoIs query help you find out the prospective affiliate's email address, fill out a Contact Us form (Figure 11.12) on their site or even post a comment in their blog, clearly indicating your intent and following the previously described principles.

Figure 11.12 Typical Contact Us form (screenshot from BryanEisenberg.com), which many website publishers prefer to listing an email address, because it makes them less susceptible to spam

If they are interested, they *will* write back. I have indeed had success in reaching prospective affiliates this way when no other method was available.

Sample Texts for Affiliate Recruitment

In this section, you will find several samples of text (with opening greetings and signatures removed) that I have used for affiliate recruitment via email. Feel free to reword them to suit your needs and use them in your recruitment campaigns. The underlining you'll see in each sample indicates hyperlinked words and phrases. Since eloquence is one of the main guidelines for affiliate recruitment by email, you want to include links to web pages with further information, should the prospect decide to learn more about this or that part of your proposition.

Email to Prospect Familiar with Affiliate Marketing (LCIPaper.com example)

My name is Geno Prussakov and I manage the <u>LCI Paper</u> affiliate program on ShareASale. We provide fine stationery for weddings, community, and corporate events.

Since it appears that your website caters to the traffic we're very much interested in, I wanted to take a moment to reach out regarding an opportunity for us to partner together, whereby you'd be earning commission on all sales referred through an affiliate link in your website. The commission earnings start from 11 percent and go up to 14 percent per sale (depending on your performance with our affiliate program).

Special offer: if you <u>join our affiliate program</u>, and put up our two links by [date here], I will increase your default commission level from 11 percent to 12.5 percent.

If, for some reason, you are not quite ready to sign up with our affiliate program, I will also be glad to answer any questions you may have, or see how our two websites could still work together.

Many thanks in advance for your reply.

Email to Prospect Not Using Affiliate Links (HealthCompare.com example)

My name is Geno Prussakov and I manage the HealthCompare.com affiliate program on Commission Junction, which already shows some amazing results ([exact data here]).

<u>HealthCompare</u> is an innovative, consumer focused company that helps individuals and families compare and apply for health insurance plans online. Founded by Word & Brown Companies, HealthCompare.com enables anyone to receive free health insurance quotes from most major carriers in their state, compare alternative plans, and finally, apply and purchase health insurance.

Since your [ProspectURL] website obviously caters to the traffic that is also immediately relevant to HealthCompare.com, I wanted to take a moment to reach out regarding an opportunity for us to partner together, whereby you'd be earning commission on all leads (applications submitted) referred through an affiliate link in your website. Our payouts range from $5.00 to $6.50 per lead, but we want to offer you a private commission of $10/lead right off the bat (as soon as you add our affiliate link to your site).

To join (or learn more about) our program you may _fill out the application here._

If you're not ready to join the affiliate program right away, I would still love to hear back from you: to see how/if we can still work together.

I'm very much looking forward to your reply.

Blog Comment or Contact Form (Volusion.com example)

I have just read your recent [URL here] blog post on shopping cart(s) and would like to offer you a collaboration.

I run Volusion's affiliate program and would love to get you aboard as our affiliate, helping you to monetize your blog beyond the methods you're already using (like AdSense units and banners).

Volusion's program is run through Commission Junction, and you may read more about it at [URL to program description here].

We pay for every purchase made by the traffic you refer, and I want to get you up on a private commission level right off the bat:

1. $50/100 per sale as soon as you've added 2 affiliate links to your site

2. $60/120 per sale (less on cheaper packages, more on the more expensive ones) as soon as you've referred 3 sales to us

For your information, the default commission levels in this program also depend on performance and represent a $30–45 range for less expensive subscriptions and a $60–90 range for the more expensive ones. Therefore, what I'm proposing now is actually higher than the top levels ($45/90) offered through the default program settings.

Let me know if you're interested.

I am very much looking forward to working with you.

Follow-up Email to Interested Prospects (DaySpring.com example)

Hi and thanks for getting back to us!

Our affiliate program is a great tool for bloggers and is very easy and flexible to work with.

Basically, you earn a commission between 12–18 percent every time someone purchases from _the DaySpring Online Store_ after clicking on a link on your blog, website, Facebook page, or tweets, etc.

You can use text links, specific product images, buttons, or banners. And we provide a large selection of <u>banners and buttons</u> to help you out.

There are no requirements or restrictions about how often or how much you talk about DaySpring. But obviously you will earn more income from the program the more you promote it.

We offer a 90-day "life of a click," which basically means that if anyone buys something from us within 90 days after clicking on your link, we will pay you a commission (unless they've clicked on someone else's affiliate link in between yours and the sale). It's a pretty sweet deal!

Many bloggers love to use giveaways or product reviews to promote DaySpring and that works great too.

Really, any way you choose to do it, you can! (but we are here to help if you need us...)

It's free and easy to <u>sign up</u> for the program through either <u>Commission Junction</u> or <u>ShareASale</u>. If you don't know which to choose, read <u>this blog post</u> of ours for a quick comparison.

You can learn all the details about the program <u>here at our website</u> or get tips and updates here <u>on our blog</u>.

And, of course, we are here to answer any questions that you may have about affiliate marketing, <u>our program</u>, or <u>DaySpring</u>.

We are really looking forward to partnering with you! Please don't hesitate to contact us with questions.

As for the follow-ups emails to those prospects that haven't expressed interest, they should pretty much mirror the initial email to them with a preface specifying the exact date of your original attempt to contact them and emphasizing that you are looking forward to hearing from them and discussing this opportunity.

Thursday: Formulate Your Social Media Approach

Social media is a reality no business can ignore, especially a business that runs an affiliate program. Today you will look at the different types of social media that exist, as well as learn how to effectively take advantage of them.

Types of Social Media and Where to Start

There are 17 types of social media that marketers can successfully use nowadays:

- Blogging
- Content aggregation (for example, Netvibes)

- Crowdsourcing (outsourcing tasks to a large group of people—great as a source of content/ideas; just remember to give everyone the credit they deserve)
- Forums (for example, ABestWeb.com in the affiliate marketing space)
- Livecasting (for example, Ustream, LiveStream, and even Skype)
- Microblogging (for example, Twitter)
- Photosharing (for example, Flickr and Picasa)
- Podcasting (recording digital media files, often in the form of seminars or other educational forms, for regular distribution via the Internet)
- Presentation sharing (for example, Scribd)
- Reviews and opinion sites (for example, Epinions.com and Yelp)
- Social bookmarking (for example, Delicious and StumbleUpon)
- Social networking (for example, Facebook)
- Social news (for example, Digg and Reddit)
- Video sharing (for example, YouTube and Viddler)
- Virtual worlds (for example, Second Life)
- Widgets
- Wikis (for example, Wikimedia)

Obviously, when you're starting to promote your affiliate program from scratch, you can't start with all 17 at once. So, to begin with, start with a blog, actively using social bookmarking and social news buttons/plug-ins for easy social sharing and further distribution of your content by your readers. That will be the integral part of your affiliate program support mini-site. Additionally, as discussed earlier, you want to register at various affiliate marketing forums, open a Twitter account, start a Facebook fan page, and start interacting with other affiliate marketers. It is also good to participate in discussions sharing your thoughts under blog posts of other digital and affiliate marketers. This will get you known in the affiliate marketing industry and help you make valuable connections. With time, you will also want to start video sharing (recording both instructional and announcement-type videos) and podcasting or participating in podcasts of others (see GeekCast.fm).

Essential Points to Remember

It is essential to remember the principal difference between "traditional" and social media. The former has been a broadcasting/monologue type (there was no effective way to communicate to your TV or newspaper), while the latter is a dialogue/interaction type. Instead of pushing your proposition at potential customers, you want them to notice you and come to your blog, follow you on Twitter, friend you on Facebook, subscribe to your YouTube channel, and so on.

It is the same when you are using social media for your affiliate program. You want to provide your affiliate readers, friends, followers, and listeners with engaging content. You want to interact with them on an individual basis, thereby building relationships with current and prospective affiliates—the relationships that so much in affiliate marketing is based on (Figure 11.13).

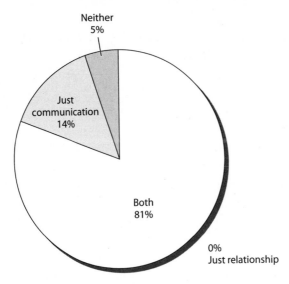

Figure 11.13 A poll created to discover whether affiliates want relationships or just communication discovered that most want *both*.

Blogging Tips

Since your blog will more than likely be one of the first social-media channels you'll employ, I'll share with you a few tips I have learned from my own blogging on topics related to affiliate marketing.

On January 1, 2009, I made *daily* blogging one of my New Year's resolutions. Ever since then, between my own AMNavigator.com blog and my guest blogging efforts, I have already put together well over 800 blog posts. Learning from the successes and failures, I will now bring you three lists: a list of essential components of good blogging, a list of the types of blog posts that tend to become popular, and a list of new meanings for old abbreviations.

Components of Blogging Strategy

Throughout my own blogging experience (as well as by watching other blogs grow in their success), I have pinpointed the following factors that may contribute to a blog's success:

- Posting valuable content
- Putting together meaningful titles

- Replying to comments on your blog in a timely fashion
- Creating communities around blogs
- Leaving comments on other blogs
- Posting regularly
- Being SEO-friendly
- Utilizing social bookmarks
- Providing outbound links
- Submitting to blog directories
- Using plug-ins and widgets

I've also noticed that on the road to success some of the previously quoted components carry more value than others. To find out whether this has been only my experience or whether other bloggers share the same belief, I conducted a poll asking bloggers to rank the previous factors by their importance. The top three criteria I arrived at were value-added content, regularity in posting, and meaningful titles. The fourth place was occupied by timely responses to comments. I hope this helps you craft your own approach to blogging.

Five Types of Popular Blog Posts

Having put together hundreds of blog posts, I have found it especially interesting to monitor which of my posts get the most readers' attention.

It appears that certain types of blog posts are destined to become more popular than others, even though the content in those "others" can at times be significantly more profound and original. I've arrived at five types of blog posts that consistently get a lot more attention than others. The following are all five, with titles of examples listed for each type. You can find these examples by searching my blog at www.amnavigator.com/blog.

Lists This, in my opinion, is by far the most popular type. The main reason for this is that lists are easy to follow and digest. This is precisely why this very section comes in the form of a list as well.

Examples: Digital Marketer's Twitter 100+ Master List, 20 Affiliate Plugins for WordPress

How-Tos How-tos have always been popular, and blogging (be it text-, video-, or both types of blogging together) is an excellent way to explain how things work or how to do something.

Example: Online Guide to Affiliate Marketing

Breaking News This is especially popular in your blog post when you're not merely bringing the news to your readership but you're drawing fresh conclusions and providing new perspectives.

Example: 6pm.com Loses $1.6 Million in 6 Hours, Handling It Gorgeously

Contests These always draw a lot of attention, and some bloggers make a living off contests. I do them for the fun of it and always get a lot of response.

Example: 400th Day Contest: Computer & Internet Jokes

Interviews Interviews are great and provide value to all three parties involved: the interviewee, the interviewer, and the readers.

Example: Interview with John Ferber, Founder of Video Affiliate Network

What CCCP Stands For

I know, CCCP may not bring up good memories in most minds, but today I'd like to give the old abbreviation a new meaning: one that comes from my personal experience and understanding of what makes a good blog post and a good blogger.

There are four adjectives to remember:

C: Consistent (a-post-a-day keeps search engines awake)

C: Concise (most blog readers appreciate eloquence)

C: Clear (most blog readers don't want rocket science)

P: Practical (and, of course, be as pragmatic as possible)

Most of my blog posts that have become popular reflected all of these.

Get Ready to Rock 'n' Roll!

Now that you have finished reading this section, break your approach to social media into three steps:

1. Create a plan that includes which social-media channels to start with and when/how to add the other others.

2. Recall the essentials of successful social-media marketing in general and successful blogging in particular.

3. Be ready to get going with it (more in the next chapter), and don't be afraid to make mistakes! As Orlando A. Battista put it, "An error isn't a mistake until you refuse to correct it." Just remember to correct yours.

Friday: Plan to Attend Conferences and Shows

Every year there are some 20 affiliate marketing conferences going on around the globe, half of which generally happen in North America. There are also a number of other beneficial conferences, and therefore, I will bring you two lists now: a list of affiliate marketing conferences and events and a list of other conferences.

Affiliate Marketing Conferences and Events

The following are the events that took place during 2010 (with corresponding websites). Many of them happen more than once a year (in different locations), so be sure to check the conference's official website to find out the future dates and places.

- a4uexpo: www.a4uexpo.com
- Affiliate Summit: www.affiliatesummit.com
- Affili@Syd: www.affiliatsyd.com
- Affiliate Convention: www.affiliateconvention.com
- Affilicon: www.affilicon.com
- Commission Junction University: http://cj.com/news/event_cju.html
- eComXpo: http://wbresearch.com/ecomxpo/
- LeadsCon: www.leadscon.com
- LinkShare Symposium: www.linkshare.com/events/
- London Affiliate Conference: http://londonaffiliateconference.com/
- Performance Marketing Expo: www.performancemarketingexpo.com

The previous list is in alphabetical order, apart from the first two conferences listed. The reason for singling them out is that if I were to pick one affiliate marketing conference to attend in the United States, I'd stick with Affiliate Summit (see its attendance data in the "Affiliate Recruitment Tools" section, while the pie-chart splitting attendees by type is in Figure 11.14). For Europe, the one conference I would go to is a4uexpo.

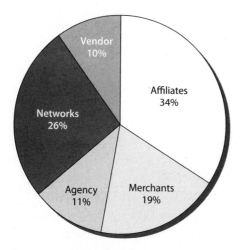

Figure 11.14 Split of Affiliate Summit attendees by type

Other Conferences on Online Marketing

Besides the previously listed affiliate marketing conferences, attending other ones related to online marketing can be helpful. Out of all others that are regularly being held throughout the world, I personally recommend the following:

- ad:tech: www.ad-tech.com
- eMetrics Marketing Optimization Summit: www.emetrics.org
- Internet Retailer Conference & Exhibition: http://irce.internetretailer.com/
- Internet Marketing Conference (IMC): http://internetmarketingconference.com/
- PubCon: www.pubcon.com
- Search Engine Strategies (SES): www.searchenginestrategies.com
- Search Marketing Expo (SMX): www.searchmarketingexpo.com

Of course, there are many other helpful conferences, meetings, and seminars to choose from, and new ones spring up nearly every year. Keep your finger on the pulse of the industry, and compile your own list of shows that will benefit your particular case.

Week 2: Plan Your Affiliate Communication

Webster's dictionary defines communication *as "a process by which information is exchanged between individuals through a common system of symbols, signs, or behavior." Unfortunately, in the context of affiliate program management, both the process and the system are frequently impaired. During this week, you will learn the best practices of communication with affiliates so you are equipped to handle this important component of program management in the way it should be handled.*

12

Chapter Contents

Monday: Study Affiliate-Preferred Channels of Communication
Tuesday: Decide on Frequency of Newsletters and Approach
Wednesday: Learn How to Put Together Affiliate Newsletters
Thursday: Launch Social-Media Efforts
Friday: Start Writing Your Affiliate Program's Blog, Developing FAQs and Tutorials

Monday: Study Affiliate-Preferred Channels of Communication

If there is one area of affiliate industry relationships that cries for improvement, it is the communication channel. The problem of communication in affiliate marketing is *huge*. Between the attention deficit on the affiliate network level and unanswered/ignored affiliate messages to merchants, everyone who is involved (affiliates, advertisers, networks, OPMs) is losing real money. In late 2009, Genesys released the report "The Cost of Poor Customer Service: The Economic Impact of the Customer Experience and Engagement in 16 Key Economies," which attributed as much as $338.5 billion in lost business to flawed customer service. That no one has tracked such data for the affiliate marketing industry specifically does not mean it isn't happening the same way in affiliate marketing. Day in and day out disappointed affiliates just pull merchants' links and terminate relationships with unresponsive affiliate networks and merchants.

Global Problem

Econsultancy's 2009 Affiliate Census reports revealed the universality of the problem. The vast majority of affiliates on both sides of the Atlantic (64 percent in the United States and 70 percent in the United Kingdom) stated they had limited communication, indirect communication, or no communication with merchants. You can find the exact breakdowns in Figures 12.1 and 12.2.

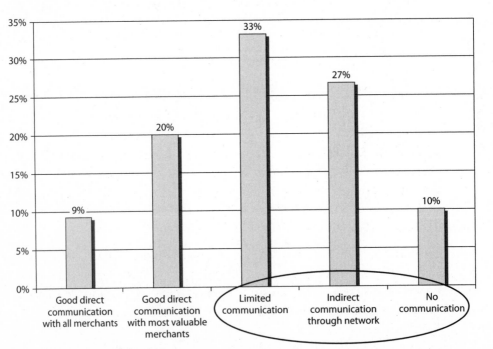

Figure 12.1 How British affiliates describe their level of communication with merchants

US AFFILIATE CENSUS 2009, © ECONSULTANCY.COM LTD, http://econsultancy.com/reports/affiliate-census

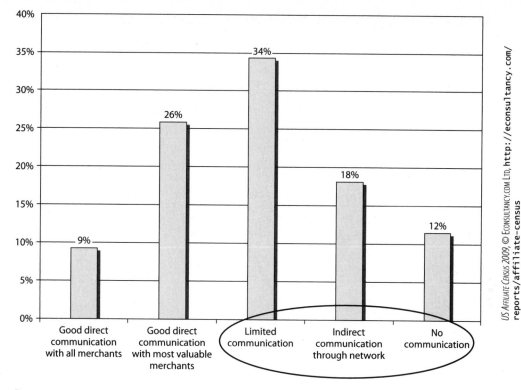

Figure 12.2 How American affiliates view their level of communication with merchants

US AFFILIATE CENSUS 2009, © ECONSULTANCY.COM LTD, http://econsultancy.com/reports/affiliate-census

Many complained about the lack of personal attention, irregularity of communication, and other related problems. The U.K. Affiliate Census emphasized the following:

> *A lack of communication is clearly holding back the industry. In this research, the need for greater communication between affiliates and merchant was frequently cited, either as something for networks and merchants to improve upon, or as an example of a change that would positively impact the affiliate marketing sector.*

Preferred Communication Channels

By turning to another benchmark industry report published annually, you can learn about the affiliate-preferred methods of communication. Affiliate Summit's 2010 AffStat Report—based on a survey conducted among 1,150 affiliates worldwide—had affiliates answer this important communication question for merchants. Figure 12.3 illustrates its findings.

Email (more than 62 percent) is by far the most popular method, because regular email contact was mentioned by 41 percent of surveyed affiliate marketers, and 21.4 percent chose network internal email. The second avenue you want to be actively utilizing is your own *company's website*, because almost 22 percent of respondents chose it next (company site 13.8 percent; affiliate program's blog 8.1 percent). Interestingly, Twitter (2.4 percent), instant messaging (2.4 percent), social networks (1 percent), and forums (0.5 percent) were chosen as the least preferred methods of communication; but as the popularity of social media grows, this is expected to change. Note also that *phone* was mentioned only by 1.4 percent of affiliates, and my experience tells me that in the vast majority of cases this would mean that affiliates want a way to get a hold of the program's manager via phone, not the other way around (in other words, not managers calling affiliates about joining their programs).

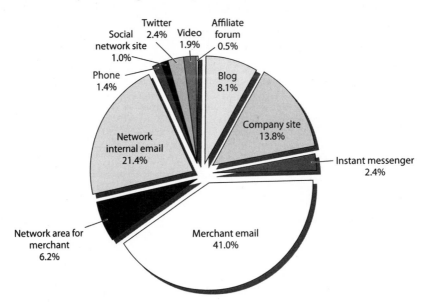

Figure 12.3 Methods of communication preferred by affiliates

Two-Way Symmetric Communication

As Everett M. Rogers, a famous communication scholar, wrote in his renowned work, *Diffusion of Innovations* (the fifth edition of which was published in 2002), some view the overall communication channel as "the means by which messages get from one individual to another." To me, such a definition allows for a "one-way street" scenario— where the messages do get announced but an element of feedback/cooperation is lacking. I personally believe that effective communication should not only involve an announcement part but also a feedback part and a response part. In the context of the affiliate program management, it means not only communicating to/at your affiliates but also encouraging their input, listening to their proposals/comments/ideas, and responding to them.

Another important aspect to emphasize is the need for symmetric communication. From research in public relations, we know that communication can either be asymmetric (where the company's final goal is having the public come to the company's way of thinking rather than changing anything in the organization itself) or symmetric (where the organization is willing to learn *from* the public and change *for* the public). In his *Effective Public Relations and Media Strategy* volume published by PHI Learning in 2009, C.V. Narasimha Reddi pointed out that the difference between the way of handling public relations in the 20th century vs. the 21st century is that the last century practiced primarily "the one-way asymmetric" model, while "the 21st century will witness a two-way symmetric public relations model with a balanced flow of information from organisation to the target public and from the public to the organisation." In the course of this information flow, both parties "will have an equal say and importance to both feed-forward and feedback information." I've been noticing how this shift is facilitated by the social media, but even before Facebook and Twitter, affiliate program managers understood the importance of two-way symmetric communication while managing their affiliate programs. Unless your program management rests on a two-way symmetric communication model, it will never reach the heights that it could have reached had it been undergirded by such a model.

Types of Communication

When looking at the methods of communicating with the affiliates, I find it helpful to divide my communication-related considerations into three groups:

Open Communication Channel Provide for a channel of communication that affiliates can always turn to, and be confident that they will find you there. I am taking about phone, email, instant messengers, your blog, affiliate marketing forums, and any internal system of communication that your affiliate network may be providing.

Regular (Expected) Communication Here I am talking about your affiliate newsletters, seasonal greeting cards/gifts in the mail, and other types of keeping in touch with your affiliates on a regular/recurring basis.

Publications Yes, publishing articles in magazines and on various online platforms will both help you recruit new affiliates and help your current partners achieve newer heights. Therefore, there is no reason to ignore these.

In what follows, we will dig deeper into the specifics of communicating with affiliates, but throughout the rest of the chapter I encourage you to keep all of what you've studied today in mind, especially the importance of keeping an open two-way channel of communication.

Tuesday: Decide on Frequency of Newsletters and Approach

Now that you know which methods of communication affiliates prefer most and understand that email constitutes the most popular means of communication, the only logical continuation is to look at the frequency with which affiliates would like to hear from affiliate program managers.

Communication Frequency and Response Time

The 2010 AffStat Report mentioned earlier also has information on this question (Figure 12.4).

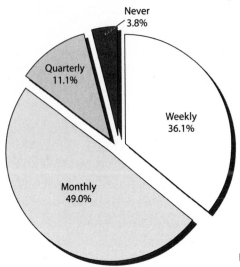

Figure 12.4 Communication frequency preferred by affiliates

As the pie chart reveals, most affiliates (more than 85 percent) want to hear from managers *monthly* (49 percent) or *weekly* (36.1 percent). Based on this data, I recommend contacting your affiliates at least once a month but also experimenting with bimonthly newsletters.

Additionally, it must be emphasized that the majority of your affiliates will want to be contacted every time there is something significant to report, regardless of the newsletter schedule. As Michael Coley, the technical editor of this volume, puts it: "A monthly newsletter is too often if there's nothing new or significant in it. A weekly newsletter isn't often enough if there's something significant that comes up mid-week." So, an alternative approach to scheduled newsletters would be sending them out every time there is something important to share with your affiliates (either all affiliates or just one type—for example, coupon affiliates).

It is important to underscore that all the previous data should be used as guidance only for cases when it is the manager who is trying to contact an affiliate. When, however, it is the affiliate who is reaching out to an affiliate program manager, the latter should be significantly faster than that. Figure 12.5 shows the results of my own poll among affiliates, which asked how long affiliates are willing to wait for a merchant's reply before they give up and pull merchant's links from their website, replacing them with competitor's links.

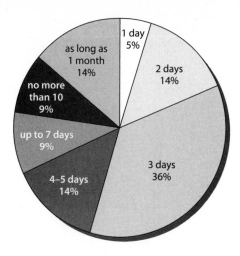

Figure 12.5 Results of a poll on a maximum acceptable period of time affiliates are willing to wait for a reply to their message

The majority of affiliates (55 percent to be exact) want to get a reply within three business days, and although the more patient ones are willing to wait for as long as a month, 86 percent of affiliates want to hear from you within 10 business days or less.

In the days of managing HalloweenMart.com's affiliate program, I remember getting an email with a question from an affiliate who was seriously considering replacing a data feed of another Halloween-related merchant with HalloweenMart's data feed. I replied to them as soon as I received their query and received the following reply: "Your quick reply is impressive. I appreciate ease of contact with our merchants and affiliate program managers, and look forward to working with you." It is still easy to stand out as an affiliate program manager if you address affiliate concerns/questions promptly. Make it your rule.

Formulate Your Approach and Stick to It

I talked about this when discussing the fundamental rules of successful social-media usage: "give, do not take" and "communicate, do not broadcast."

A 2010 Affiliate Summit panel comes to mind. It was dedicated to creating lasting affiliate-merchant relationships and had three affiliates and two affiliate program managers on it. The managers were from Target.com and Overstock.com. Ryan Sorensen, the affiliate program manager from Overstock.com, stressed the importance of understanding that the manager-affiliate relationship is a two-way channel. Jillian McGary, the affiliate manager at Target.com, on the other hand, provided a great real-life illustration of the importance of communicating with every affiliate (however new or inexperienced). She told a story of a newbie affiliate who joined their affiliate program without any knowledge of the affiliate marketing industry, but with proper attention and training, grew into *one of the top* Target.com affiliates within 2.5 years.

So, first, remember that broadcasting (be it through newsletters, Twitter, forums, or any other channels) does not work with affiliates.

Second, remember a three p's approach, and make sure that every communication piece (from a 140-character-long tweet to a full affiliate newsletter) mirrors the following three elements:

Personalization Use all available means to make it a personal and personally relevant communication piece.

Preciseness Flee from vagueness, and be concrete (for example, not "our affiliates enjoy some of the best conversion rates in the industry" but "during the month May our affiliates' average conversion rate was 2.3 percent, while our top three performers have enjoyed 0.8 percent, 2.45 percent, and 5.71 percent conversion, respectively").

Practicality This one flows right out the previous point. Examples of practicality would include lists of best sellers, best-performing links, affiliate tools, new coupons, and so on. It is also important to point out that just including the information on these in your affiliate newsletter is not enough. In our context, only *actionable* information is worth including. So, you want to also give your affiliates an easy way to act based on this information. For instance, I once received an affiliate newsletter where a merchant listed their best-performing links but did it in an extremely inconvenient manner. Instead of including the code for each link in plain text (or a separate box), they linked text within the newsletter through my affiliate URLs. So, to grab the actual code for each link mentioned, I had to view the HTML code of their newsletter as opposed to simply cutting and pasting. You want to make sure your practical advice is also convenient to implement.

These points will also work well in contexts other than affiliate program management, and you may successfully use them in multiple areas including email marketing, blogging, social-media marketing, and other directions.

Wednesday: Learn How to Put Together Affiliate Newsletters

Today you're going to get real practical and both look at the format recommendations and review samples of affiliate newsletters. In addition to this, I will also touch on the subject of affiliate motivation through newsletters.

Affiliate Newsletter Format and Characteristics

I know you could use a quick guide to how exactly to layout your affiliate newsletters, and in this section I'll give you one.

There are many ways you can lay out your affiliate newsletter, but most of the time I stick to the following format:

- Introduction (with reiteration of how much you appreciate the work your affiliates are doing for you)
- Affiliate program and/or website news
- Statistics of top performers and/or announcement of contest winners for the previous month (make sure you keep any sensitive information out!)

- Bonuses, contests, and affiliate-geared promos for the current month
- Ready-made links (with cut-and-paste code included under each) or clear instructions on where they may be picked up
- Tool/technique of the month (that is, an idea for them to grab and start using right away)
- Conclusion (reinforce any key information, as well as that you are there for your affiliates, reminding them how exactly you can be contacted)

Additionally, you may borrow some of the rules on how to make your email recruitment effective and make every newsletter of yours personal, enticing, concrete, containing an incentive (or several) to make their partnership with you worth their while, and grammatically correct.

In every one of the previous newsletter elements, you want to show your affiliates that you value them and genuinely care. This will greatly multiply your newsletter's chances of broader success. I still remember an August 2009 affiliate newsletter I sent out for DaySpring.com's affiliate program on Commission Junction. That newsletter covered six of the previously mentioned seven elements. Several affiliates emailed back almost immediately (they *didn't have to* do it, but they did) just to say "thank you." One of them, in particular, wrote, "I have been with Commission Junction for almost a year, and you are the first advertiser to send out such a personal, intriguing, well-written newsletter."

Emotions aside, to me—and to any affiliate program manager—that response should illustrate two things: that it's realistic to know what affiliates want to see in your newsletter and that it is still easy to stand out, because very few merchants are doing their newsletters the right away. Affiliates want your newsletters to be the following:

- Personal(ized)
- Motivating (and here you want to remember that effective change always starts from creating a sense of urgency)
- Helpful

Also, let's quickly look at the three must-pay-attention-to p's that you want to remember while focusing on the previous three characteristics.

Three p's to Remember Before Hitting Send

Whether it's an affiliate newsletter, a recruitment email, or any other piece of correspondence you are sending to your affiliates, you want to remember the following three p's, which will save you a lot of headaches:

Proofread Nothing brings a piece of marketing text to a faster death than typos and outright mistakes. They discredit brands and bury relationships without even giving them a chance to start. I've learned it the hard way. Proofreading is a must.

Preview Before sending off the text, make sure you test it on yourself first! Email it to your own address, see how it looks, and see whether it can use improvements. Just as you never get a second chance to make a first impression, so do you never get a second chance to correct a sent piece of email. Of course, you can re-send it with apologies, but you know how it will make you look.

Provide Options When possible, provide your affiliates with an option to choose the format in which they prefer to receive your messages. Some like HTML, others plain text. If you cannot customize things in such a way that every affiliate receives the message in their preferred format, provide both an HTML version and a plain-text version, and they will choose the one they want.

All of these points also apply to affiliate program descriptions and any other online correspondence of yours.

Ignoring just one of the three p's can drastically influence the look of your affiliate newsletter. The sidebar "Preview Before Hitting Send" illustrates this.

Preview Before Hitting Send

A solid online retailer, voted one of Internet Retailer's Hot 100 Companies of 2009 and visited by more than a million unique visitors every month, sent out their affiliate newsletter. It was written well, but some of the things could certainly use some improvement. Here is a screenshot of part of that newsletter.

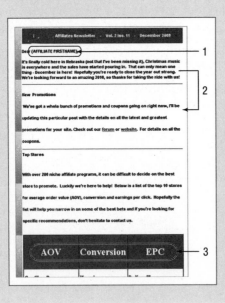

Preview Before Hitting Send *(Continued)*

It has good style, but the formatting of your affiliate newsletters deserves much closer attention! Here are a few points to keep in mind:

- The short code for the affiliate's first name never translated into the first name but stayed in the short-code form (the affiliate program manager must have made a mistake in the code).

- The paragraph line spacing suddenly jumps from single to double (starting from the second paragraph) and never returns to the single form again.

- The font type and size choice hasn't been great at all. The whole newsletter is typed up in bold font, and I could count as many as three different types of fonts and three different sizes (often within the same type of font).

I know I've mentioned it before, but it's worth repeating. Prior to sending out your affiliate newsletter, by all means preview it and, whenever possible, send yourself a test email with it (to ensure it will look nice and clean on the affiliate end). Otherwise, regardless of how well you write, it'll quickly show that you haven't put enough time/effort into it.

Sample Affiliate Newsletter

Here's a sample affiliate newsletter. Note that all short codes were automatically replaced by relevant info or banners with HTML codes.

Dear {RECIPIENT_NAME},

August is here, and we are sending out our monthly newsletter to thank our affiliate partners for being aboard our program and promoting DaySpring through your online marketing campaigns.

There are four things that I would like to bring to your attention in this newsletter: July bonus winners and their impressive statistics, our special August 2009 promo for inactive affiliates, our new banners, and our participation in the upcoming Affiliate Summit East 2009.

July Winners

Every affiliate who activated their account (by starting to send in sales) by the end of July has just received a $20 cash bonus in their accounts. Congratulations to the five winners!

Continues

Sample Affiliate Newsletter *(Continued)*

Here are their July stats:

	COMMISS.	SALE AMT.	SALES	CR	EPC
Affiliate A	$49.48	$412.35	7	24.14 percent	$170.63
Affiliate B	$23.22	$191.56	3	5.26 percent	$40.74
Affiliate C	$16.65	$136.14	2	50.00 percent	$416.30
Affiliate D	$7.97	$64.73	3	20.00 percent	$53.14
Affiliate E	$7.61	$63.45	3	42.86 percent	$108.77

August 2009 Promo

If by July 31 you have not referred any sales to DaySpring, get active within the 30 days starting August 5 (in other words, between 08/05/09 and 09/03/09), and the first three orders you refer to us will qualify you for a $20 cash bonus (money deposited into your account on top of your regular commission) + a $15 gift certificate from DaySpring. The offer is limited to the first 20 affiliates to claim their bonuses. Just drop me an email once you have generated your first three sales, and I will take care of the rest for you.

Creatives

In addition to our full data feed (which is also available through PopShops), we have an extensive selection of banners and text links (51 banners, 20 text links, and 11 Flash banners), and I am hereby including just a few of them to get you started more quickly:

{LINK_10676651}
{LINK_10676663}
{LINK_10676166}
{LINK_10676642}
{LINK_10676650}
{LINK_10676677}

To view a complete set of our banners, log into your affiliate account at CJ.com.

Meet Us at Affiliate Summit East 2009

Affiliate Summit is coming to New York in less than a week, and if you're attending, we would like to meet you in person. You can meet me at Table #67 where I will be representing only one affiliate program—that of DaySpring.com. The first 10 people to come to the table and say the passphrase "It's all about looking at things through consumers' eyes" will get an autographed copy my *Online Shopping Through Consumers' Eyes* book. In addition to the books, there will also be hundreds of giveaway items from DaySpring (as well as a special coupon code to help you promote this merchant) for you to pick up.

Motivating Through Newsletters

Every affiliate newsletter should motivate your affiliates to do more for your affiliate program.

I remember how in spring 2010 I received a newsletter geared at CSN Stores' affiliates that generated some traffic for their affiliate program but no sales. The opening text of the newsletter read as follows:

> *Congratulations! You have been chosen as a* CSN Stores Affiliate Program Rising Star. *All the members of this group have been able to bring in a significant amount of traffic to our sites over the last few month. We want to help you make sure those visits lead to sales and commissions! For the next month, April 1st–May 1st, the CSN Stores Affiliate program will be offering an exclusive promotion to the members of this Rising Stars group.*
>
> *If in the month of April you can convert just 10 sales you will receive an additional $150 bonus on top of your commissions!*

I had generated 14 clicks for them (some by myself, and some with the help of my friends) and not one sale. So although the "significant amount of traffic" part constituted quite a bit of an exaggeration, I couldn't help but love the "Rising Stars" hyperbole. This beautiful technique, and the whole text of this affiliate newsletter, reminded me of Bronwyn Fryer's "Moving Mountains" article (which can be found in

June 2003 *Harvard Business Review on Motivating People* compilation of articles on the topic) where the author wrote that to motivate others effectively, managers must have "a clear, unbiased understanding of the situation at hand, deep insights into the vagaries of human nature, the establishment of appropriate and reasonable expectations and goals, and the constructions of a balance set of...incentives." Fryer also proposed several practical techniques to make one a better motivator. Out of the ones she listed, the immediately relevant ones for affiliate program managers are as follows:

- Start with the truth.
- Appeal to greatness.
- Make them proud.
- Stick to your values.
- Provide a constant and consistent communication channel.
- Build trust.
- Care for the little guy.
- Set different incentive levels.

I will be returning to some of these principles in the following chapters but would like to emphasize that caring for the little guy and setting different (and *reachable*) incentive levels are extremely important. I'll discuss these more in Chapters 14, "Week 4: Affiliate Motivation," and 17, "Deadliest Mistakes to Avoid."

It seems that the CSN Stores' affiliate program manager hit at least half of these nails right on the head and did it beautifully. Make sure *your* affiliate newsletters are as motivating too.

Thursday: Launch Social-Media Efforts

In the previous chapter, while discussing types of social media, I covered quite a number of ways you can use it but recommended starting with a few. I believe that an affiliate program support blog and participation on affiliate marketing forums should be among your first steps. As I pointed out on Monday of this week, the blog is so important that I will set it aside to discuss on a separate day (tomorrow), but today let's look at three other social-media channels you want to plug your affiliate program into: affiliate forums, microblogging platforms, and social networks.

Affiliate Forums

There are at least 10 active affiliate marketing forums at the time I'm writing this book. A number of them have been around for a decade or so, and more than likely they will stick around for many years to come.

Here are 10 forums you should be aware of:

ABestWeb: www.abestweb.com/forums/

Affiliates4u: www.affiliates4u.com/forums/

5 Star Affiliate Programs: http://affiliate-marketing-forums.5staraffiliateprograms.com/

Affiliate Summit: http://forum.affiliatesummit.com

Associate Programs: http://associateprograms.com/discus/index.php

Affiliate Trust: http://at.affiliatetrust.org/

eWealth: www.ewealth.com/

ABCsPlus: http://abcsplus.com/forum

AffSpot: www.affspot.com/

WebmasterWorld Affiliate Section: http://webmasterworld.com/advertising/

Obviously, you will not be able to actively use *all* of these. Out of all of these, the first, an online affiliate marketing forum, is a must for U.S.-based affiliate program managers, while the second (Figure 12.6) is a must for U.K.-based managers of affiliate programmes (British spelling intentional). On a separate note, the extensive section of ABestWeb devoted specifically to affiliate managers deserves a mention. You can find it at www.abestweb.com/ams.

Figure 12.6 Forums within Affiliates4u, the United Kingdom's largest online affiliate community

The golden rule of social-media usage is that one cannot take more than they have given to the community, and this is especially true when you're talking about online forums. Most of them are fairly close-knit communities of people—not devoid of their intricate relationships and attitudes but worth all the diplomacy and consideration you may put into building your reputation in such places. Take it easy, be helpful and easy-going, and you will be able to build good relationships that will help you advance both in your overall growth as an affiliate marketing professional and in the growth of your affiliate program in particular.

Microblogging

There are a number of microblogging platforms (tumblr, Jaiku, mySay, and so on), but none of them can compare in popularity to Twitter. When you look at this platform's year-over-year growth and measure the latter by the number of tweets (short text messages posted/microblogged through your account), you can see that by mid-September 2010 Twitter's users were sending 90 million tweets on a daily basis (which works out to be 33 billion tweets a year), up 450 percent compared to the year before. Figure 12.7 shows Twitter's spectacular growth annotated by BusinessInsider.com, which speaks louder than any words, making the point—you *must* be on Twitter.

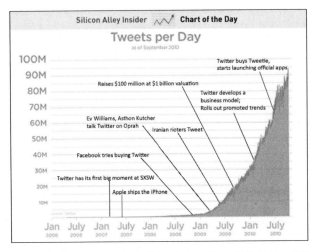

Figure 12.7 Twitter's tweets' growth from its inception until September 2010, graph created by Business Insider Inc.

When using Twitter for communication, remember to stay away from pure broadcasting but react to affiliate comments and tweets to you. Only if such an approach is taken will Twitter be really useful for you. Not many affiliate program managers are doing an exemplary job utilizing Twitter, but those who understand its potential are already microblogging actively, and the following is a list of Twitter accounts to review for ideas on how to run your own Twitter account. The order is merely alphabetical, and the descriptions were copied directly from each account (some of them will give you ideas for what you may include there; just flee from sounding cheesy).

- Amazon (http://twitter.com/AmazonAssociate): "Official twitter of Amazon's affiliate program, launched in 1996. Earn up to 15 percent by advertising Amazon products!"
- eBay (http://twitter.com/eBay_Affiliates): This one had no description.
- Legacy Learning Systems (http://twitter.com/LegacyAffiliate): "Commissions start at 20 percent, and bonuses are frequent for our top affiliates. Our affiliate program is managed by award-winning Affiliate Manager, Matt McWilliams."
- MacMall (http://twitter.com/MacMall_Aff): "Official MacMall.com Affiliate Advantage Network Account."
- New York Times Store (http://twitter.com/NYT_Affiliate): Earn $$ while selling special gifts, fine art, classic photos, sports collectibles, memorabilia, and New York Times themed keepsakes."
- Target (http://twitter.com/AffiliateTarget): "The Target.com Affiliate Program. Stay tuned for program updates, offers, and news."
- TicketNetwork (http://twitter.com/tnaffiliates): "We represent the TicketNetwork Affiliate Program—offering 12.5 percent commission, 45-day cookie life, and a huge inventory."

A little hint as far as your Twitter handle goes: When a combination of your brand name and the word *affiliates* or *affiliate* ends up being longer than the permissible handle name, you can use words like *partners* or *partner* instead.

Social Networking

Here the situation is very similar to that of the previously described Twitter dominance in the microblogging sphere. If there is one social network that you want to be on, it is Facebook with more than 500 million active users (July 2010 data).

With time, you may want to experiment with Facebook ads for affiliate recruitment, but as far as day-to-day communication with affiliates goes, you want to create a fan page for your affiliate program (Figure 12.8), link to it from your affiliate program support blog, and use it to keep affiliates up-to-date on what's going on in your affiliate program (from contests and bonuses to sales and consumer-oriented promos). You may also plug your Twitter RSS feed to stream on your fan page. This will help you automate part of the process. But by no means let it be the only thing you do there. Be active (not only on the wall but also in the discussions), be engaging, and remember the three r's of successful communication with affiliates (you want to be reachable, responsive, and real/authentic), and you will inevitably build a loyal following on Facebook.

Figure 12.8 Las Vegas' famous Blue Man Group has a Facebook page for its affiliate program.

Friday: Start Writing Your Affiliate Program's Blog, Developing FAQs and Tutorials

On Monday I noted the importance of offering affiliates information on your program right on your website. The 2010 AffStat Report revealed merchant's website to be the second most popular way of "finding out information from an affiliate manager." Twenty-two percent of affiliates chose either the company site or the affiliate program's blog as the places they'll go to while looking for the details of your affiliate campaigns. Today you want to start working on your blog and the development of FAQs and tutorials. As mentioned earlier, you can start just with the very basic questions and move on to a more detailed and developed FAQ section with time (turning each blog post into an answer to a popular question or a mini-tutorial).

Basic Questions

To begin with, you can start with these basic questions:

- What is affiliate marketing?
- What is the [merchant's name here] affiliate program?
- How do I get started? Or how do I join [merchant's name] affiliate program?
- Does it cost me anything to become a [merchant's] affiliate?
- What are cookies, and why are they important?
- What is an affiliate disclosure, and how should it be worded?
- Whom should I contact if I have questions about the [merchant's] affiliate program?

Put together a section where all of these questions will be answered—eloquently and enthusiastically (but not cheesily)—and then make it your routine to work on the further development of the FAQ/instructional section.

Figure 12.9 contains an example of a basic affiliate FAQ page.

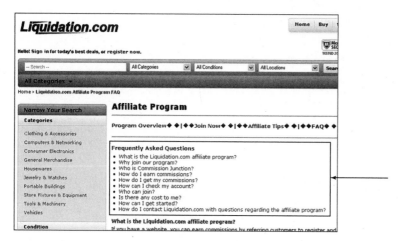

Figure 12.9 Liquidation.com answers basic affiliate questions.

Detailed Instructional Section

A detailed section should eventually cover a number of topics: from the basic information to more advanced tools and techniques. As the number of questions and answers grows, it is helpful to break it into sections, listing all categorized questions in the very beginning, in turn anchor-linking each to its respective answer.

Here you'll find a general sample list of questions to answer in your more detailed instructional/FAQ section:

General Program Information

- What is affiliate marketing?

- What is the [merchant's name here] affiliate program?

- What is an affiliate network (with specifics of your own choice, if you're on a network)?

- How do I get started? Or how do I join [merchant's name] affiliate program?

- Does it cost me anything to become a [merchant's] affiliate?

- How does the [merchant's] affiliate program work?

- What are cookies, and why are they important?

- What is an affiliate disclosure, and how should it be worded?
- Are websites outside the United States eligible for the affiliate program?
- I operate more than one website. Can I still join this affiliate program?
- Is my website or blog eligible for the affiliate program?
- What are my responsibilities as a [merchant's] affiliate?
- Whom should I contact if I have questions about the [merchant's] affiliate program?
- How do I manage my account information?
- Do I earn commission on the tax and shipping costs of a product?

Setting Up Links

- After I join the affiliate program, how do I get the ads and links to put onto my site?
- How do I build links for specific products?
- Where may I place these affiliate links on my site?
- How often should I update my links?
- What are the benefits of using video creatives?

Sales and Commission

- How much can I earn?
- How do I know how much commission I've earned?
- When will I receive my commission payment?
- Can I earn commissions on my own purchases?
- What about product returns?
- How can I monitor my sales?
- Who processes orders and handles customer service?
- How will the merchant know that the orders came from my site?

Instructional and "How-to" Posts

- How do I find links to specific products?
- How can I work with your data feed?
- How do my sales and commissions reports work?
- Can I set coupon links and banners to renew automatically?

Figure 12.10 contains a good example of a fairly detailed affiliate FAQ page.

Figure 12.10 Art.com's affiliate FAQ page

As time allows, plan for and start incorporating "how to" video tutorials (Figure 12.11) into your blog. Make sure you also upload these to YouTube (optimizing video titles and descriptions to rank well for important keywords) to get additional exposure.

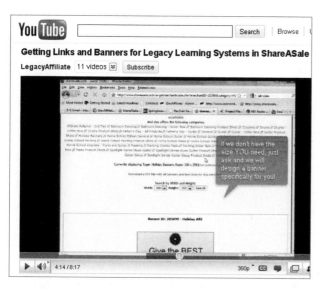

Figure 12.11 Legacy Learning Systems tutorial on how to navigate around links and banners on ShareASale

Week 3: Program Management

13

You have finally come to the management component of things. In this chapter, you will learn where to start, what to look out for, how exactly to manage your program, and what kind of affiliate manager it takes to succeed in the uneasy task ahead of you.

Chapter Contents

Monday: Categorize Affiliates

Affiliate categorization is something you want to start doing right from the outset or before you have too many affiliates. It will help you custom-tailor your approach to each group, thereby maximizing the effectiveness of your management. You can categorize affiliates in several ways. Here are five examples:

- By level of activity (for example, stagnant, traffic-referring, sales/leads-producing)
- By primary promotion method (for example, content, paid search, comparison shopping, coupons, and so on)
- By vertical of focus (for example, shoes, apparel, electronics, and so on)
- By size (for example, newbies, small, medium, superaffiliates)
- By their primary geographic target market or other narrower criteria

Out of all of these, I highly recommend starting with the first—level of activity. In this regard, I find one of Michael Coley's tips of great help. He recommends that affiliate managers look at things like how you visualize a sales funnel and designate milestones to get affiliates to sign up, post links, refer traffic, generate sales, increase performance, and so on. Every affiliate program will have affiliates present at all of these stages at any given point of time. Therefore, the key to developing their potential is in a custom approach to different affiliates, based on the milestone they have already achieved and the one they have yet to reach.

You will also want to add categorization by methods of promotion used by your affiliates. This will help you become even more targeted in your communication with different affiliates.

Back at the dawn of affiliate marketing, in their *Successful Affiliate Marketing for Merchants* published by Que in April 2001, Collins and Fiore wrote this:

> *Most affiliate programs see their affiliates as one big undifferentiated group of Web sites, but that's not true. Each Web site is different and will have a different approach to promoting your offers. ...if you look at your network hard enough and analyze the different sites that it contains, you may be able to find similarities among them from which you can create different affiliate groupings and offer different linking methods.*

Even though this was written more than 10 years ago, most of it holds true today. If not "most," then definitely "many" program managers still do not group affiliates by website type, which results in an identical approach to all affiliates in the program (read: an untargeted and not-as-effective-as-it-could-be approach to affiliates). So, let that method of promotion be your first criteria. Refer to Chapter 1, "Understanding Affiliate Marketing," for help in this categorization.

Returning to the subject of various levels of affiliate activity, it seems appropriate to mention an Objectives-Performance matrix, put together by Goldschmidt, Junghagen, and Harris, in the conclusion of this section.

In their 2003 volume *Strategic Affiliate Marketing*, the three Danish marketers wrote this:

> *The marketer active in affiliate marketing holds some objectives, which we have broken into four prioritized levels: exposure, recognition, attitude, and exchange. Performance is considered by the responses of the end-user, which we also broke into four prioritized levels: attention, interest, desire, and action.*

Matching objectives and performance, they arrived at a comparative matrix (Figure 13.1), which demonstrated "correspondence between objectives and performance" as "measured by four variables: impression, click, lead, and sale." In the same way, you as an affiliate program manager can group (or subgroup) your affiliates, depending on whether their activity yields only link *impressions*, just *hits*, hits and *leads*, or all of the above and *sales*. If your affiliate program does not remunerate leads but sales only, skip the leads. If you compensate affiliates for both, analyze performance on both of these levels.

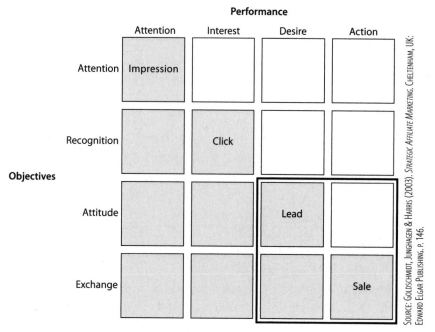

Figure 13.1 Objectives and performance in affiliate marketing

SOURCE: GOLDSCHMIDT, JUNGHAGEN & HARRIS (2003). *STRATEGIC AFFILIATE MARKETING*. CHELTENHAM, UK: EDWARD ELGAR PUBLISHING. P. 146.

Most affiliate networks and in-house affiliate program software solutions make affiliate categorization easy (see Figure 13.2 for an example), and I highly encourage you to start categorizing as soon as you have started approving affiliate applications. This will help you be more targeted in your work with affiliates (be it connected with their performance, the most suitable promos to push through them, or anything else).

Figure 13.2 Sample grouping of affiliates on Commission Junction

Tuesday: Develop Fraud Prevention Policy and Enforcement Rules

I'll discuss the various types of affiliate fraud in detail in Chapter 15, "Week 1: Study and Learn to Deal with Parasitism and Problematic Affiliates," but today you will develop your overall approach to preventing affiliate fraud and violations—be it in brand representation, trademark violations, or any other breaches of affiliate program's terms of service discussed in Chapter 9, "Week 3: Research and Develop Program Policies"—as well as formulate how exactly you are going to enforce your rules.

Fraud Prevention

I'll start by briefly clarifying the terms I'm using. Although some believe that *fraud* is too strong of a word to use for affiliate violations—however unethical at times they may be—I will stick to this word in my book. Just because certain types of unethical activity are not prosecuted by law enforcement agencies as criminal, it doesn't mean they are not fraud in terms of being "deceiving" or "misrepresenting" (the words Webster's dictionary uses in its definition of *fraud*).

Automatic Approval of Affiliates Is Always Dangerous

Automatic approval of affiliate applications (AAAA) is a mistake commonly made among new and seasoned affiliate program managers alike. If automatic declines of affiliate applications can be destructive to the development of your affiliate program, automatic approvals may end up costing you significantly more than an automatically declined application.

The main reason for the danger of the AAAA approach actually matches the reason why automatic declines are a bad idea, and it is the *immediacy of consequences*. These consequences can be more deadly in cases of AAAA because the open-door approval policy can let unwanted affiliates into your program, and an approval of an unwanted affiliate is naturally significantly worse than a nonapproval of a decent affiliate.

I know of affiliate program managers who practice autoapproval but diligently monitor all autoapproved applications on an ongoing basis. The thinking behind practicing a monitored AAAA approach is this: If an affiliate who has the right traffic finds my program and decides to give it a try, it is best to get their application approved immediately (so that they can start promoting the merchant right away). Although there is logic behind such an approach, I would argue that even monitored AAAA is dangerous. Since no affiliate program manager is on duty 24/7, if a rogue affiliate is autoapproved into a program, they will have their time to cause damage to your brand while you're sleeping. Yes, you will be able to reverse any unwanted transactions, but the brand damage is seldom fully reversible. Therefore, in my opinion, the negatives that even monitored AAAA may cause always outweigh the positives (because the immediacy of negative consequences is always more critical than the immediacy of positive consequences).

From spamming to squatting and from cookie stuffing to trademark poaching, hundreds of affiliates are making affiliate program managers' daily tasks similar to that of online detectives.

Merchants and program managers can do the following things to prevent affiliate fraud:

- As mentioned, your affiliate program agreement should clearly spell out what constitutes a valid/commissionable affiliate action (sale, lead, subscription, and so on).

- Flee from automatic approvals (see the "Automatic Approval of Affiliates Is Always Dangerous" sidebar), and always research on a new affiliate (or a marketing method they use) before approving them into the program. (Do they have an active website? What traffic-generating methods are they planning on employing? Are their methods complementary or clearly contradictory/detrimental to what you are doing?)

- Watch out for sudden traffic surges.

- Watch out for quick increases in affiliate-referred transactions (again, sales, leads, and so on).

- Keep an eye on fraudulent transactions (stolen credit card numbers, fake leads, cancellations of self-referred transactions when the commission has already locked, and so on). Two such transactions from the same affiliate should raise a red flag, and three should result in a ban from the program.

- Analyze referral URLs to catch any cyber- or typo-squatters.

- Monitor your brand online (see the "Twelve Free Tools for Online Brand Monitoring" sidebar) to see what customers are saying about it and to catch any spamming affiliates.

- Educate yourself on parasitic and cookie-stuffing affiliates (to keep them out of your program). When in doubt, consult with people like Kellie Stevens of AffiliateFairPlay.com (Figure 13.3) and Ben Edelman of BenEdelman.org.

- Join affiliate marketing forums where fellow managers share information on new developments "on the dark side" of things in general and on specific fraudulent affiliates in particular.

- Diligently police and enforce any other restrictions you may have in your program's agreement (for example, trademark PPC bidding).

Figure 13.3 AffiliateFairPlay.com—resources for fair affiliate marketing practices by Kellie Stevens

Twelve Free Tools for Online Brand Monitoring

Believe it or not, you can use quite a number of free online tools both for brand monitoring *and* for affiliate recruitment. These tools will monitor all the online space for the keywords and key phrases you want to use them for and alert you every time these keywords are mentioned. Here is the list:

- Google Alerts
- Social Media Firehose (by Yahoo!)
- TweetBeep
- BuzzMonitor
- Collecta.com
- BackType
- Omgili
- boardreader
- BoardTracker
- WhosTalkin.com
- Social Mention
- BlogPulse

As mentioned, you can use these tools not only to monitor your own brand but also to monitor a brand of your competitor (for intelligence purposes) or even general key phrases (for affiliate recruitment purposes). In the latter case, if, for example, you are an advertiser in the Auto Insurance vertical, monitoring mentions of such key phrases as *auto insurance* and *car insurance* will help you keep your finger on the pulse of the industry and assist you in identifying new prospective affiliates.

Enforcement Policy

I favor a three-strike approach, which the ShareASale affiliate network uses to support merchants in their fight of affiliate PPC fraud, when affiliates violate merchants' paid search policies/restrictions. In essence, at ShareASale each merchant may report affiliate violations of an affiliate program's PPC policy (by submitting the form shown in Figure 13.4), and once an affiliate is caught three times, ShareASale removes that affiliate from the network.

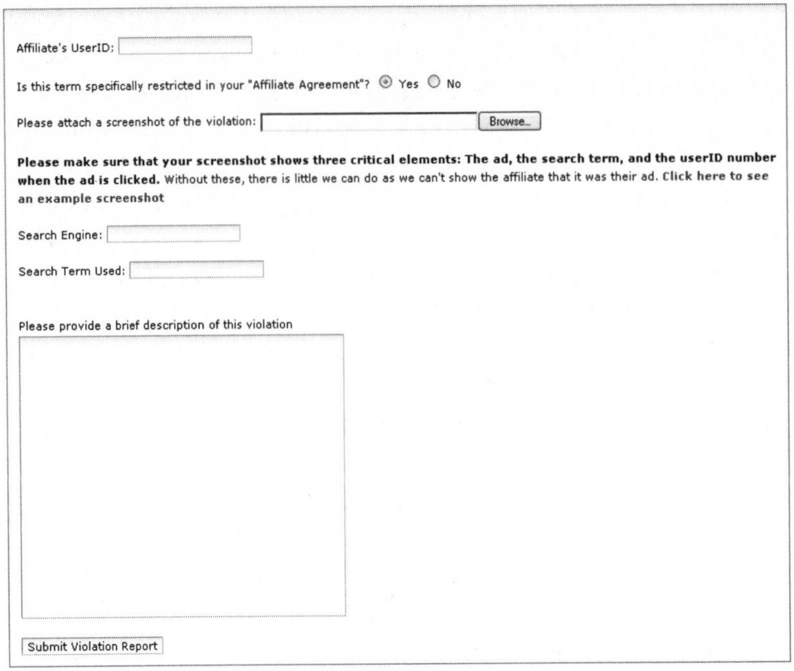

Affiliate's UserID: [   ]

Is this term specifically restricted in your "Affiliate Agreement"? ⊙ Yes ○ No

Please attach a screenshot of the violation: [   ] [Browse...]

Please make sure that your screenshot shows three critical elements: The ad, the search term, and the userID number when the ad is clicked. Without these, there is little we can do as we can't show the affiliate that it was their ad. Click here to see an example screenshot

Search Engine: [   ]

Search Term Used: [   ]

Please provide a brief description of this violation

[   ]

[Submit Violation Report]

Figure 13.4 ShareASale works hand in hand with merchants to fight affiliate PPC violations.

For the majority of the situations described earlier, this is a very good method to adapt. Two violations should raise a red flag, and the third one should result in a ban from your affiliate program, with all unjustly "earned" commissions voided. Of course, there will be exceptions where you will have to address an issue as soon as the first violation appears (for example, bursts of fraudulent "referrals," cybersquatting, parasitic behavior, and so on), but you will be able to identify those right away.

Wednesday: Start Profiling Affiliates

Much has been written about customer profiling, and the technique has been widely used for precision targeting in both online and offline marketing.

Affiliate profiling is something I haven't seen explicitly mentioned anywhere, but I am positive that many affiliate program managers use this technique, simply because it's effective. Just as customer profiling is defined as "a systematic way of documenting customer interests, preferences, future needs, and buying cycles" (*Customer Chemistry*, McGraw-Hill Companies, 2002), so should affiliate profiling be understood in terms of "a systematic way of documenting." However, affiliate profiling is not so much about the interests, needs, and preferences of affiliates as it is about understanding what makes them productive and using their "profile" to steer your recruitment campaigns.

Let me give you an example. Say you've been running an affiliate program for a month or two and have noticed that a product review affiliate website has been performing well for you. That's a profile (with time, it will be one of many) that a successful affiliate in your program fits. That is also, obviously, the channel through which your target consumer is happy to be presold. Now that you know this, go after other websites that do product reviews, and try to get them aboard your affiliate program as well.

Additionally, when I talk of profiling, I do not necessarily mean going into compiling detailed profiles of individual affiliates. This is a voluminous and not necessary task. What I suggest is taking note of what types of websites/affiliates produce especially well for your program and targeting similar types in your affiliate recruitment campaigns. Also take note of the types of promotion they are engaged in and the niches in which their target audiences are. For instance, not all content websites will produce equally great results for your affiliate program. In fact, the majority of them won't. You want to understand which types of affiliates, marketing methods, and audiences match up with what you're trying to achieve through your affiliate program. Some of the data you will already have from the demographic analysis of your own customer database (Figure 13.5). Other pieces of the puzzle will fall in their places as you analyze successes of your affiliates. Be careful with the information you discover, though, and *make sure it is never used against* any of your *affiliates* (read: Never disclose any sensitive information to the public).

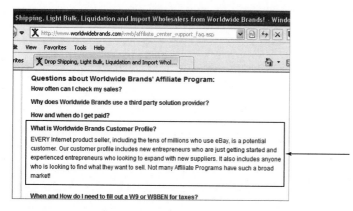

Figure 13.5 In its Affiliate Center, Worldwide Brands defines its target audience as *every* Internet product seller.

When profiling affiliates, it is helpful to pay attention to the five categories outlined in Figure 13.6.

Figure 13.6 Five principal variables to pay attention to while profiling affiliates

To elaborate a bit further, the main variables you want to pay attention to are as follows:

Website What type of websites does the affiliate operate?

Target Audience What type of visitor does the affiliate predominantly cater to?

Promotional Methods Which promotional methods work best for the affiliate (couponing, contests and giveaways, cashback, product reviews, and so on)?

Marketing Focus Does the affiliate rely solely on SEO, paid search, social-media marketing, mobile, or a combination of these and/or other marketing methods?

Competitors Promoted Which competitors of yours does your successful affiliate promote in addition to you? This will both give you room for competitive intelligence observations and tell you which affiliates of competitors to target in your recruitment efforts.

In some cases, it will be just one of these variables that makes an affiliate especially successful with your program. In other instances, a bouquet of factors will predetermine success. Either way, you want to clearly understand what types of affiliates your affiliate program really works well with and, conversely, which types of affiliates are not a good fit for your program.

Thursday: Forget About Managing, and Start Leading!

I am a soccer (well, actually, being from Europe I personally prefer the word *football*) fan, but I also greatly enjoy watching other team sports (ice hockey, volleyball, basketball), especially when you're talking about the national team playing. Being Russian, in international tournaments I root for Russian national teams.

Russian ice hockey is always a treat to watch in action. As I am writing this book, the 2008 and 2009 world champions (and silver medal winners in 2010) are being coached by a legend of both Soviet and Russian ice hockey, Vyacheslav "Slava" Bykov.

I love reading biographies and watching biographical documentaries. During the Winter Olympics in 2010, I watched one on Slava Bykov. With this coach, one thing especially hit the nail on the head for me—his style of coaching. Bykov first played in Switzerland, and he coached a local team there. Apparently, upon returning to Russia, he stood out in his very different approach to dealing with team players. In contrast with the widely accepted dictatorial style of Soviet school coaches, he practiced an approach based on *mutual respect* between the coach and team players. Later, when he headed up the national team of Russia, it was this approach that proved more effective than the ones used by previous coaches of the national team. This is because when Russian players returned from their NHL teams to play on the national team, Russian coaches simply did not know how to communicate with them. After being exposed to a very different approach in the West, these hockey players would not respond to dictatorship and tyranny in coaching.

This illustrates a very important point. Coach Bykov is a true leader. He understands that although some players do benefit from the yelling and harsher style, many do not. The key to the hearts of most is in practicing respect—building a mutual respect as a result.

In affiliate program management (which many still mistakenly believe to be a task of "affiliate management"), it is precisely the same—the managers who practice sensitive coaching and mutual respect are the ones who achieve more. Affiliates respect them in return and want to do more for them.

An effective manager is always a *leader* first. To better understand the differences, let's start by comparing management to leadership.

Twenty Differences Between Management and Leadership

When comparing leadership with management, it is essential to understand that they are *not* mutually exclusive. In his *Leadership: Theory and Practice* (Sage Publications, 2006), Peter Northouse pointed out that they are similar in many ways. Both leadership and management involve influence, working with people, concern about effective goal accomplishment, other shared characteristics, and so on. Additionally, as Richard Daft wrote, "Leadership cannot replace management" but rather is something that is to be practiced "in addition to management" (see *The Leadership Experience*, South-Western College, 2007).

According to Daft, the main difference between leadership and management is that in the classical managerial context, "managers are thinkers and workers are doers," while in a leadership context both leaders and workers/followers think, do, lead, and "expand their minds and abilities to assume responsibility" for their decisions and actions.

Another researcher who wrote about management as opposed to leadership was Warren Bennis. In the *On Becoming a Leader* (Basic Books, 2009), Bennis listed the following differences:

1. *The manager administers; the leader innovates.*
2. *The manager is a copy; the leader is an original.*
3. *The manager maintains; the leader develops.*
4. *The manager focuses on systems and structure; the leader focuses on people.*
5. *The manager relies on control; the leader inspires trust.*
6. *The manager has a short-range view; the leader has a long-range perspective.*
7. *The manager asks how and when; the leader asks what and why.*
8. *The manager has his or her eye always on the bottom line; the leader's eye is on the horizon.*
9. *The manager imitates; the leader originates.*
10. *The manager accepts the status quo; the leader challenges it.*
11. *The manager is the classic good soldier; the leader is his or her own person.*
12. *The manager does things right; the leader does the right thing.*

Richard Daft looked at the differences between management and leadership from five different angles: direction, alignment, relationships, personal qualities, and outcomes. Based on Daft's work, we can add these characteristics to Bennis' list:

13. *The manager plans and budgets; the leader creates vision and strategy [direction].*
14. *The manager is generally directing and controlling; the leader allows room for others to grow and change him/her in the process [alignment].*
15. *The manager creates boundaries; the leader reduces them [alignment].*
16. *The manager's relationship with people is based on position power; the leader's relationship and influence are based on personal power [relationships].*
17. *The manager acts as boss; the leader acts as coach, facilitator, and servant [relationships].*
18. *The manager exhibits and focuses on emotional distance, having an expert mind, talking, conformity, and insight into an organization; the leader focuses on emotional connectedness, having an open mind, listening, nonconformity, and insight into self [personal qualities].*

19. *The manager maintains stability; the leader creates change [outcome].*

20. *The manager creates a culture of efficiency; the leader creates a culture of integrity [outcome].*

The area of affiliate program management provides one of the most vivid illustrations of the differences between management and leadership. You cannot manage affiliates. Hence, you have to lead them. In fact, leadership is *the only* way—sensitive, respectful, open-minded leadership. Making personal connections and allowing affiliate experts to steer their way to success (as opposed to an intruding, controlling, and directing management) will help you succeed in building a successful affiliate program.

The Four Most Valued Characteristics of a Leader

Have you ever wondered what makes an excellent affiliate program manager? What characteristics should one strive to possess in order to succeed in this capacity?

In the course of more than 25 years, two luminaries of organizational leadership, James Kouzes and Berry Posner, have been studying the characteristics of admired leaders. One of the methods they used was a survey with an open-ended question: "What values, personal traits, or characteristics do you look for and admire in a leader?" Several hundred different traits and characteristics were gathered, analyzed, and documented. The striking part was that over the course of decades, some of the same characteristics were consistently brought up regardless of the countries and continents where the survey participants lived. The researchers identified the top four characteristics people look for in a leader. People want their leaders to be the following:

- Honest
- Forward-looking
- Inspiring
- Competent

It is obvious from the table in Figure 13.7 that these four characteristics scored significantly higher than the other ones mentioned.

What can you learn from the previous data? I believe the top four characteristics to also be the cornerstones of successful affiliate program management. *Forward-looking* implies a "well-defined orientation toward the future" and vision; *inspiring* is about enthusiasm, drive, and motivation; *competent* reflects a well of knowledge that never goes dry; but it is *honesty* that is the greatest and the most valued characteristic.

Characteristic	2007 edition	2002 edition	1995 edition	1987 edition
Honest	89%	88%	88%	83%
Forward-looking	71%	71%	75%	62%
Inspiring	69%	65%	68%	58%
Competent	68%	66%	63%	67%
Intelligent	48%	47%	40%	43%
Fair-minded	39%	42%	49%	40%
Straightforward	36%	34%	33%	34%
Broad-minded	35%	40%	40%	37%
Supportive	35%	35%	41%	32%
Dependable	34%	33%	32%	33%
Cooperative	25%	28%	28%	25%
Courageous	25%	20%	29%	27%
Determined	25%	24%	17%	17%
Caring	22%	20%	23%	26%
Imaginative	17%	23%	28%	34%

Figure 13.7 Top 15 characteristics of admired leaders

No matter whether it is a military leader, a president of a country, a CEO of a corporation, or an affiliate program manager, people want to be confident in their leaders, and confidence is always dependent on the leader's integrity. Most frequently integrity gets challenged when an affiliate program manager commits a mistake. You need to remember that it is OK to commit mistakes. It is how you deal with them that shows who you really are. One of my favorite quotes about mistakes comes from Dr. Dale E. Turner who said that "the highest form of self-respect" is "to admit our errors and mistakes and make amends for them. To make a mistake is only an error in judgment, but to adhere to it when it is discovered shows infirmity of character." Admitting mistakes only builds up one's integrity and shows an individual as one possessing a strong and solid character.

Another element that is extremely important to remember is that one's honesty is always tied to values and ethics. Know your principles and stand up for them. This is especially important in an industry as vulnerable to unethical behavior—of both affiliates *and* affiliate program managers—as affiliate marketing.

SOURCE: KOUZES & POSNER. THE LEADERSHIP CHALLENGE (4TH ED.), PP. 28-31

Theorizing Vaynerchuk and Learning from Trait Approach

This originally appeared as an article in my AM Navigator blog.

You know who Gary Vaynerchuk of the Wine Library TV—aka GaryVee on Twitter—is, don't you? He's the guy who is one day predicted to become "bigger than Oprah," mostly because of his passion, drive, and authenticity. To me, Gary is living proof that the trait approach has the right to live (in a slightly modified form, but it still does).

The trait approach, which dominated the scene up to the late 1940s, was one of the earlier approaches to leadership that attempted to study various leadership traits in order to determine what made certain people great leaders. A number of scholars assumed that the Y chromosome was indispensable for "born leaders" and that it was through this chromosome that leadership qualities were inherited. Several scholars who worked separately from one another arrived at sets of traits and characteristics, some of which echoed one another. Among the common characteristics, there were intelligence and cognitive ability, initiative, persistence, (self-)confidence, integrity, and responsibility. Most of these can be found both in the great historical leaders and in prominent business leaders of our time. However, the trait approach "suffers from the difficulties of specifying the traits that constitute effective leadership and of explaining how much of each trait one needs in order to cope best in different situations" (source: *Leadership in Times of Change* by W.G. Christ [New Jersey, 1999]).

So, the approach was abandoned for several decades to be resurrected in 1991 by Kirkpatrick and Locke who, believing that individual characteristics *can* predict leadership behavior, developed a variation of the trait approach in their assessment center technique. Their technique is based on a belief that there are six core traits on which leaders differ from nonleaders:

- Drive
- Desire to lead
- Honesty/integrity
- Self-confidence
- Cognitive ability
- Knowledge of the business

It is also important to mention that the developers of the assessment center technique went away from the deterministic undertone of the trait approach and used the six traits as *positive preconditions* of becoming a successful leader, leaving room for personal initiative to condition the rest.

Continues

Theorizing Vaynerchuk and Learning from Trait Approach *(Continued)*

Back to Gary Vaynerchuk, who we started with. In his blog, Jason Keath—the founder of the social-media education company Social Fresh and the guy who predicted Gary to become "bigger than Oprah"—summarized the essence of Vaynerchuk's success in the following six (very action-able) principles:

- Be genuine—be true to yourself.
- Hustle—put in more work than the other guy.
- Pursue your passion—if you are not working on what you love, you won't make it.
- Delegate—learn how to partner and connect with others to get it done.
- Watch the tools—always pay attention to the nerds, when the nerds talk I listen—the tech scene is the future.
- Be the expert—learn everything you can about your industry, and know more than the other guy.

Do they correspond to the six positive preconditions that Kirkpatrick and Locke talked about? Not word for word, but the essence is definitely there. Gary is all about the drive, desire to lead, integrity, self-confidence, cognitive ability, and knowledge of the business. His personal initia-tive has turned these in the right direction, shaping him into the man that he is now. To me, it's a good modern-day example of how, while not necessarily being deterministic, certain personal characteristics help an individual become an excellent leader *and* influencer.

It's All About Emergent Leadership

Leadership always comes in one of two forms: *assigned leadership* and *emergent leadership.*

Assigned leadership is based on being appointed to a position within the organi-zational structure. Say you have been in charge of an SEO or web design team within your organization. With time, your company decided to launch an affiliate program, and since the higher management deemed you to be the most fit for the job (be it based on your experience with ecommerce, your familiarity with the current marketing cam-paigns the company ran online, or anything else), you were assigned the position of an affiliate program manager. This is a tough situation to be in, but it's not hopeless if you are willing to learn from others and grow in the process.

Emergent leadership, on the other hand, is very different in nature. Northouse points out that "the person assigned to a leadership position does not always become the real leader in a particular setting." It is emergent leaders who are most respected and most followed. Northouse carries on to clarify that "this type of leadership is not assigned by position" but, rather, "it emerges over a period of time through communication" [see *Leadership: Theory and Practice* for more details]. The key elements here are *persistence* (it "emerges over a period of time") and *communication*. Additionally, *personality* plays an important role too (refer to the "Theorizing Vaynerchuk and Learning from Trait Approach" sidebar for a real-life example) but is certainly not deterministic.

The point I'm trying to get across is that in a setting as different from any traditional management context as affiliate program management—or any leadership that involves influencing independent minds—emergent leadership is *the only path to follow*. Bill Gates, Sergey Brin, and Mark Zuckerberg are just a few examples of self-emerged leaders, and their stories are certainly encouraging. Armed with persistence and such communication essentials as getting involved firsthand, always staying informed, initiating new ideas, and seeking others' opinions, you have a significantly better chance of really succeeding than by merely relying on your formal position of leadership. The days when real influence came with the position of authority are long gone, especially in settings where people are free to choose their leaders—affiliate program management is certainly one of the most vivid of such settings.

Friday: Become a Transformational Leader

Having studied multiple theories of leadership and having always looked at them through the angle of affiliate program management, I've found that there is definitely a lot you can learn from each. However, although many of these theories—if adjusted and adopted to the context—do fit, it is the *transformational leadership* that, in my opinion, is best suited for affiliate program managers (new and seasoned!) to keep in mind.

Just as the name implies, transformational leadership is one that provides for a process of change and transformation. This transformation happens not only with those who are lead but also with the leaders themselves under the influence of their followers.

Bernard M. Bass, famous scholar in the area of organizational behavior and distinguished professor emeritus in the School of Management at Binghamton University (NY), singled out the role of the leader's charisma as one of the key elements of transformational leadership. Not all researchers share his view, and in looking into ways in which the transformational leadership can be applied in the context of affiliate program management, I believe you should actually exclude the element of charisma. The main reason for the exclusion is that charismatic leadership is not something that can be learned but rests heavily on the leader's individual traits, whereas all other elements of the transformational approach exist and function irrespectively of whether the leader is capable of, and followers are accepting of, the practice of idealized influence (also known as *charisma*).

The other three elements of transformational leadership can greatly improve the work of affiliate program managers in a way that would facilitate productive transformation in both affiliates and the manager. They are what I like to call "the three i's of effective leadership":

- Inspirational motivation
- Intellectual stimulation
- Individualized consideration

The essence of *inspirational motivation* is both in communicating high expectations to followers and in "inspiring them through motivation" to become continuously inspired and committed. This can be done through appealing to affiliates' emotions, and communicating the "integral role they play in the future" of the affiliate marketing campaign (*Leadership Theory and Practice*, Northouse). Appealing to emotions, affiliate program managers can demonstrate successes of other affiliates (keeping names and other sensitive information discrete), as well as underscore the role affiliates play in building up the industry as a whole (tax legislation bills not passing in Minnesota, Maryland, and Hawaii because of affiliates' efforts is a good illustration) and the particular affiliate program. The question of motivation deserves greater attention than a one-paragraph write-up, and you will look at it in significantly greater detail in the next chapter.

The second transformational leadership technique that affiliate program managers should employ is that of *intellectual stimulation*. In traditional leadership contexts (read: in traditional workplaces), this approach "consists of encouraging employees to think for themselves, to challenge cherished assumptions about the way in which work takes place, and to think about old problems in new ways" (from Snyder and Lopez's *Handbook of Positive Psychology*). In an affiliate program management context, managers should shape this method in light of the situational variables (more on this in the next chapter), stimulating affiliates intellectually respective of the level on which each affiliate currently is. Affiliates who are just starting with affiliate marketing will require more instructional and educational participation from the affiliate manager, whereas more professionally and psychologically mature affiliates can have higher and more complex tasks discussed with them.

Finally, *individualized consideration*—or when special attention is paid "to each individual's needs for achievement and growth" and the leader acts "as coach or mentor"—is truly one of the cornerstones of effective affiliate program management. In their *Improving Organizational Effectiveness Through Transformational Leadership* (California, 1993), Bass and Avolio listed the following key elements of this technique:

- Creating new learning opportunities in a "supportive climate"
- Recognizing "individual differences in terms of needs and desires" and accepting these individual differences

- Providing for a "two-way exchange in communication" and managing "by walking around"
- Personalizing interactions with affiliates
- Practicing effective listening
- Delegating tasks when the follower's level allows for it
- Closely monitoring "to see if the followers need additional direction or support"

Just as I mentioned while describing the previous transformational leadership factor, the key is in intertwining situational leadership with the practice of individualized consideration.

Make it your goal to turn into a transformational affiliate program manager, and keep all of the previous recommendations in mind while performing your daily management tasks.

Week 4: Affiliate Motivation

There are multiple ways to define motivation, but with affiliates, the first place to start is agreeing on the goal. This part is actually fairly easy. Although you want them to put up your links, increase exposure, integrate a data feed, increase average order size, bring in new customers, and run specific consumer promotions, the main thing you want to see happening are referrals of sales or leads. Here your goals are fully aligned, because affiliates also want to see those leads. The hard part is motivating those who are not interested, not capable, or have burned themselves in the past.

In this chapter, I'll lay the foundation with some introductory remarks on motivation in the affiliate marketing context and then move on to the "meat" of things.

14

Chapter Contents

Monday: Learn About Motivation in General and Marketing to Marketers in Particular
Tuesday: Study Contingency Theory
Wednesday: Understand How Extrinsic Motivation Works
Thursday: Learn More About Intrinsic Motivation
Friday: Arrive at Your Own Optimal Approach

Monday: Learn About Motivation in General and Marketing to Marketers in Particular

Today you'll look at motivation in general and the peculiarities of motivating affiliate marketers in particular. Most of the general principles I will discuss apply to affiliates, but throughout the rest of the chapter it is important to remember the specifics of context. Affiliates are independent professionals who have chosen to partner with you and may choose to leave at any time. They are not (and in the vast majority of cases cannot be) bound by performance requirements, so they are free to plan their marketing efforts independently of the merchant's say (provided they comply with the merchant's terms of service, of course). This makes the context all the more challenging yet truly interesting. You are dealing with a fairly unique situation of *marketing to marketers* and should fully appreciate specifics of the context to be effective in the uneasy task of motivating affiliates.

Motivation Is Always Multifaceted

In the summer of 2009, AdAge interviewed a world-famous marketer and author of more than a dozen marketing books, Seth Godin (available at `http://adage.com/brightcove/lineup.php?lineup=1182767334`). In that interview, while discussing the future of philanthropy, Godin pointed out that for a proper understanding of the subject, it is important to realize "there isn't just one reason why people are doing something." He used an example where he compared Starbucks with Dunkin' Donuts, saying that with Starbucks, people go to the coffee shop not just to get the caffeine that they can get at home for much cheaper, but they do so for a whole number reasons "that don't match" what the competitor is doing for people. (The main one, of course, is having a whole different experience of coffee drinking than you have at home.)

As often is the case, Godin went right to the heart of the problem. His statement goes hand in hand with what Fyodor Dostoyevsky pointed out more than a century earlier. Dostoyevsky wrote that "man *never* acts from a single motive," and it is important to appreciate this.

There is a common misconception among affiliate program managers that the main need affiliates have is money. Such thinking leads to a one-sided approach to motivating affiliates (through cash bonuses, tiered commission increases, gifts, and other cash-based motivators). It is true of every individual—we do need money to buy food and provide for a comfortable living for our families—but it is a generalization that makes us forget that people have other needs (for example, the need for self-realization, the need for job satisfaction, and the need to feel secure, to compete, to have status, and so on). These needs become our drives and motives, and it is essential for affiliate program managers (and other types of managers too!) to understand that only a complex approach to every individual's needs will result in a truly motivating approach. Few people get motivated by cash *only*.

Keys to Moving Mountains

In 2003, *Harvard Business Review* published a fascinating article by Bronwyn Fryer, a former senior editor of the magazine and famous business writer. The article was called "Moving Mountains," and it was always reprinted in a highly recommended *Harvard Business Review on Motivating People* edition.

In her article, Fryer wrote this:

> *There's no trick to motivating others. It requires a clear, unbiased understanding of the situation at hand, deep insight into the vagaries of human nature at both individual and the group levels, the establishment of appropriate and reasonable expectations and goals, and the construction of a balanced set of tangible and intangible incentives.*

So, as an affiliate manager, you want to have a clear and truly unbiased understanding of the situation and deep insight into what your affiliates want/need individually and cooperatively as an industry. Additionally, you want to set realistic goals and continuously motivate by both tangible and intangible incentives.

Fryer continued, "It requires, in other words, hard thinking and hard work." Add restless self-education and relationship building, and you'll have a complete bouquet of characteristics of every successful affiliate program manager.

Furthermore, Fryer proposed several practical techniques on how to make yourself a better motivator. Most of them hit the affiliate program management nail right on the head! Here are the ones that I picked out as immediately relevant for the context of motivation of affiliate marketers:

- Start with the truth.
- Appeal to greatness (once-in-a-lifetime opportunities, and so on).
- Make them proud.
- Stick to your values.
- Provide a constant and consistent communication channel.
- Build trust.
- Care for the little guy.
- Set different incentive levels.

All of Fryer's recommendations are good to keep in mind as you continue to study the question of effective affiliate motivation.

Focus on Personal Advancement, Needs, and Goals

In his *Psychology in Organizations: The Social Identity Approach* (Sage Publications, 2004), S. Alexander Haslam wrote that "despite the plethora of seemingly distinct theoretical approaches to motivation, a unity of process" can be traced throughout all of them, and this unity "arises from the fact that the nature of work motivation is bound up" with the followers' "sense of who they are." Every manager should understand that motivation has two main dimensions: the personal one and the organizational one. Figure 14.1 has a helpful chart from Haslam's book.

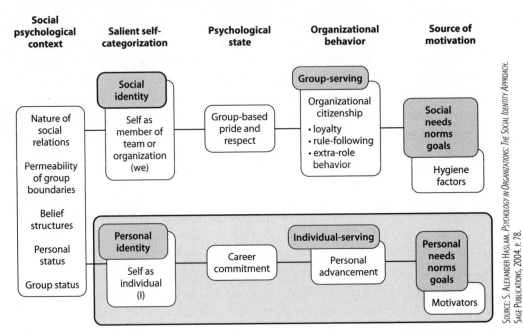

Figure 14.1 Two dimensions of motivation or relationship between levels of self-categorization, organizational behavior, and different classes of motivators

SOURCE: S. ALEXANDER HASLAM. *PSYCHOLOGY IN ORGANIZATIONS: THE SOCIAL IDENTITY APPROACH.* SAGE PUBLICATIONS, 2004. P. 78.

I have highlighted the focus on personal identity (self as individual); commitment to career and personal advancement; and motivation by personal needs, norms, and goals. This is what affiliate program managers should be focused on while seeking to motivate affiliates. Affiliate marketers are highly motivated by *personal* advancement. Therefore, affiliate program managers should motivate by underscoring the affiliate's personal benefit and focusing on their individual objectives. Much tailoring should take place, but remember this dimension, and communicate it to the management of your company. Countless affiliate program management mistakes stem from misunderstanding the context and treating affiliates as employees and members of a team (when, in reality, the majority of affiliates can be justly called "teams of one"). Focus on individual advancement of every affiliate and on personal needs and goals.

Forget About "Motivation" by Threat

Since I have touched upon a common mistake of treating affiliates like employees, now is a good time to address a common motivation mistake that stems from such an approach.

Not a month passes by without an affiliate getting an email message from a merchant who is threatening to remove them from their affiliate programs if the affiliate does not become "active." Here is the text of just one of such messages:

Please become an ACTIVE member of our program and send sales our way by January 31, 2009. Otherwise, we will be removing you from our program.

Without getting too emotional about the verbiage, let's answer one question: What is the main motive behind such removal threats sent to affiliates when they show little or no activity in an affiliate program? Of course, it is motivation! And in certain circumstances, you could indeed motivate by fear. However, because of the very nature of the merchant–affiliate relationship, motivation by threat is nothing but a dead-end strategy. Back at the dawn of affiliate marketing, Alexander Hiam wrote about this in his *Streetwise Motivating & Rewarding Employees: New & Better Ways to Inspire Your People* (Adams Media Corporation, 1999). No, he did not touch on the affiliate marketing context in it but discussed motivation and reward in traditional management. Still, his ideas are directly applicable to the situation in question. Hiam wrote that "high motivation is commonplace where there is either great opportunity or great threat. People rise to either occasion but are typically less motivated between these extremes" (see Figure 14.2).

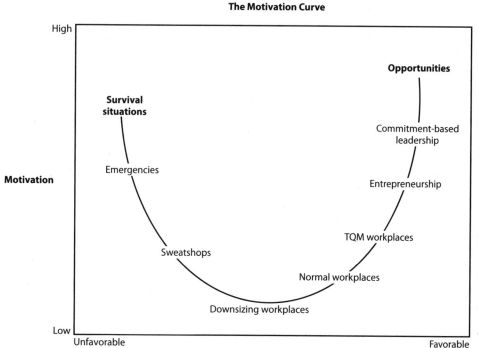

The Motivation Curve

Source: *Streetwise Motivating & Rewarding Employees: New & Better Ways to Inspire Your People.* Adams Media Corporation, 1999. p. 8.

Figure 14.2 Alexander Hiam's Motivation Curve

As mentioned, the affiliate marketing context is very different from any traditional management situation—mainly because affiliates differ from your traditional workforce. They love their independence and aren't accountable for performance; they are the ones who choose which affiliate programs to promote and which merchants to drop, without notifying the merchants themselves. In light of this, threats that could work in some of the traditional contexts (Soviet Union or North Korea regimes inevitably come to mind) are absolutely out of place in the affiliate program management context. Haim emphasized that even in traditional management "threats are generally counterproductive" and "always demotivating." In 1999 he arrived at a theory that "we can motivate people to their highest levels of potential by presenting them with opportunities to succeed instead of telling them what to do." Yet, almost a decade later, in an industry where the workforce does not tolerate any expression of a directing, controlling, top-down management, I see the deadly mistake repeated time and again—"get-active-or-I'll-remove-you" emails are sent to those who should be presented with *opportunities*, not threats.

Tuesday: Study Contingency Theory

If there is one leadership theory that every affiliate program manager *must* know about, it is the contingency theory. Its principles, without a doubt, make up one of the most widely used models in leadership training in both the public and private sectors. More than 350 of Fortune 500 companies report using it, including IMP, Bank of America, Mobil Oil, and Xerox. It is also commonly employed in training in the U.S. military and by organizational development specialists at the state and local governmental levels.

This theory bases its guidelines for successful management on the characteristics of individual followers, and there is nothing more important in affiliate program management than an individualized approach to each affiliate.

Contingency Approach

The idea behind this approach is that particular management styles and behaviors, while effective in some settings and situations, might be completely ineffective in others. *Contingent* means "dependent on" or "conditioned by something else." As Montana and Charnov (2000) put it, "The contingency approach stresses that there is no one universal solution to management problems but that the correct solution will depend on the unique needs of the situation."

The main contingencies to consider in the affiliate marketing setting are the situation, the affiliates, and the affiliate manager or merchant (Figure 14.3). The latter can vary and may include one of the two or both, depending on whether the affiliate manager shares the opinion and position of the merchant.

An affiliate manager corresponds to the classical "leader" contingency, while affiliates correspond to "followers." Daft also emphasizes that the nature of followers has been classified by researchers as one of the key variables, and this is very true about our context as well.

Figure 14.3 Three contingencies and corresponding variables to take into account

The Nature of Affiliates

As I have already mentioned repeatedly, affiliates are very different from any traditional workforce. They do vary in maturity and training, but one thing that is true about all affiliates is that they are driven by the same force—love of independence. Affiliates are generally not tied by contracts. They can choose which affiliate programs to promote and which merchants to drop, without notifying the merchants themselves. They are the born-to-be-free types and do not tolerate any expression of a directing, controlling, top-down management. This peculiarity of affiliate nature naturally influences affiliate manager behavior, but you should also keep in mind such variables as individual needs of affiliates, maturity, training/education, and experience.

Applications of Contingency Models to Affiliate Program Management

Over the years, I have seen a number of situational leadership models develop. For affiliate program managers, it is especially important to focus on two. One of them is Yukl, Gordon, and Taber's hierarchical taxonomy of leadership behavior, while the other one is Hersey and Blanchard's situational theory. I will cover both as applicable to affiliate program management.

In essence, all contingency approaches seek to discover the best matches between a leadership/management style and organizational situations. Most researchers have been differentiating between task-oriented leaders (those who are primarily concerned about task accomplishment) and relationship-oriented leaders (those prioritizing relationships with the team). The nature of affiliates described makes it clear that affiliate managers who don't develop relationships with their affiliates stand little chance of motivating them.

The best affiliate managers, recognizing the importance of personal affiliate–affiliate manager relationships, develop unique individualized connections with nearly every affiliate. Those who are not afraid of making genuine emotional connections are rewarded by affiliates aggressively promoting their affiliate programs. It is because of these observations that I believe that out of the four metacategories of leader behavior proposed by Yukl, Gordon, and Taber in their "A Hierarchical Taxonomy of Leadership Behavior: Integrating a Half Century of Behavior Research" article (in *Journal of Leadership & Organizational Studies*, Summer 2002, vol. 9, no. 1), only two are applicable to affiliate program management. They are the high task–high relationship category and the high relationship–low task category. In *The Leadership Experience* (Thomson/South-Western, 2007), Richard Daft clarifies that "high task behaviors include planning short-term activities, clarifying tasks, objectives, and role expectations, and monitoring operations and performance," whereas "high relationship behaviors include providing support and recognition, developing followers' skills and confidence, and consulting and empowering followers when making decisions and solving problems."

Yukl, Gordon, and Taber wrote that high task–high relationship situations call for leaders to practice coaching toward achievement style and combining task and relationship behaviors. The high relationship–low task situations, on the other hand, can be best managed by practicing participative and supportive styles, providing support and encouragement, developing followers' skills and confidence, and consulting followers when making decisions and solving problems. In my experience, most situations faced by affiliate managers are specifically of the latter nature. Therefore, practicing a participative or supporting leadership style, with all of these elements, is the key to successful affiliate management.

Now let's look into the principles of Hersey and Blanchard's situational theory, one that I believe to be among the most applicable to affiliate program management. Their theory is heavily based on the contingency approach, and as I have already mentioned, its guidelines are based on characteristics of individual followers—specifically, on their readiness or maturity level. In their *Work in the 21st Century: An Introduction to Industrial and Organizational Psychology* (Wiley, 2009), Landy and Conte elucidate that "maturity has two different facets to it." On the one hand, it is job maturity, or the "job-related ability, skills, and knowledge"; and on the other hand, it is psychological maturity or "self-confidence and self-respect" of the employee or follower. Hersey and Blanchard argued that depending on their maturity level, different followers should be lead/managed differently. In affiliate program management, this should be translated into a highly individual approach to working with affiliates.

Hersey and Blanchard "developed a grid that they have divided into four leadership styles—telling, selling, participating, and delegating—according to task and relationship" (Stroh, Northcraft, and Neale, *Organizational Behavior: A Management Challenge*, Taylor and Francis, 3rd Ed, 2001). The bell-shaped curve in Figure 14.4 is "called prescriptive curve because it shows the appropriate leadership style" corresponding to the predetermining "level of followers' maturity" (Dwivedi, *Organizational Culture and Performance*, 1995, p. 114).

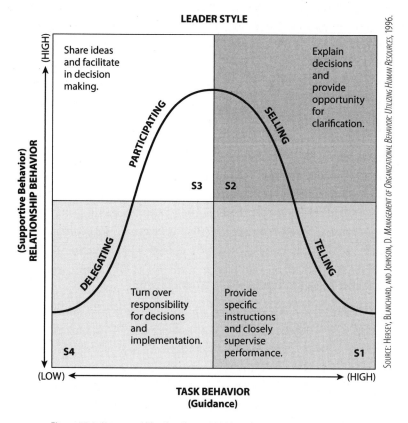

Figure 14.4 Hersey and Blanchard's prescriptive curve

When affiliates exhibit very low levels of maturity, the affiliate manager should not be hesitant to practice the telling style. In this case, the affiliates want to be told exactly what to do—where to best place your links, how to best promote your product/service, what audiences to target, and so on.

If affiliates are confident in their capabilities to promote your affiliate program but lack either education (in other words, job maturity) or self-confidence (in other words, psychological maturity), you want to practice a selling leadership style. Share the exact conversion rates with your affiliates; help them with the lists of best sellers and relevant keywords; and provide them with free data feeds, graphics, and/or any other tools and creatives that will facilitate their progress.

Should you, as an affiliate manager, see that your affiliates are skilled and experienced enough to make a difference but feel insecure or unwilling for whatever reasons, it is your time to practice a participating style. Remember that affiliates normally do not have a deficit of merchant offers. Hence, to help them choose your affiliate program to be the next one to concentrate on, you want to get them interested. Use activation bonuses, commission increases (whether tiered and dependent on the levels of sales they drive in, seasonal, or permanent), exclusive coupons, and other methods to get them interested in promoting your service/product.

Finally, when you start recruiting those who are known as superaffiliates—affiliates capable of generating a significant volume of sales for your affiliate program—be prepared to use the delegating affiliate management style. These affiliates are both confident and equipped to take your affiliate program to the top. Make sure they also have reasons to be confident in your trustworthiness and ongoing support, and give them the space they need for deciding and implementing their own ideas and campaigns.

Finally, I discourage merchants from running autopiloted affiliate marketing campaigns. Such affiliate programs are doomed to mediocrity. If you want your salespeople to bring in sales, you need to support them by proactively managing your affiliate program, and using an individually tailored approach is key to achieving success in your leadership.

Wednesday: Understand How Extrinsic Motivation Works

Now, it is time to understand that there are essentially two types of motivators that stimulate people to sit at their computer and market your product. One type encompasses *external* rewards (such as cash bonuses, tangible prizes, and praise), while the other consists of *internal* motivators (autonomy, prestige, sense of enjoyment, self-fulfillment, mastery, and so on). Today you will mainly focus on the former.

When it comes to affiliate program management, extrinsic rewards are by far the most widely used motivators. In fact, most affiliate program managers never go beyond the extrinsic rewards; I'll discuss the pitfalls of such an approach later. Now I'll discuss how you can successfully motivate affiliates through awards and cash incentives.

Five Golden Rules of Successful Extrinsic Motivation

In September of 2010, Owen Hewitson of Affiliate Window/Buy.at published a good article at Econsultancy.com. Entitled "The Art of Affiliate Incentives" (http://econsultancy.com/us/blog/6522-the-art-of-affiliate-incentives), the article sought to define, describe, and prescribe successful affiliate incentives. Hewitson believes that there are three golden rules you should remember while creating affiliate incentives:

> *Know what you want to achieve. Very often this might not be a simple increase in sales. Recruiting more affiliates, reactivating existing ones, or gaining better placement on affiliates' sites could also be objectives that you choose to design your incentive around.*

> *Make it as simple as possible. Affiliates will be deluged with communication about incentives in the run-up to Christmas. If they have to read more than a few lines to understand what you are offering or what they have to do to be successful, it is likely to be ignored.*

> *Make your incentive as inclusive as possible. The best-designed incentives are those that have the lowest barrier to entry so that as many affiliates as possible feel they can participate. Hewitson also recommends avoiding "winner-takes-all" prize draws and incentives.*

All of these are excellent tips to keep in mind, and I'll add two more pieces of advice:

Notify Them Well in Advance You want to provide your affiliates with enough time to prepare their campaigns in response to your incentive. Sending out Black Friday/Cyber Monday promo details on the Friday morning and expecting a wide reception is naïve, to say the least.

Clearly Spell Out Any Restrictions If you're targeting only stagnant affiliates, clarify that your promo applies only to affiliates who have generated "one sale or less," "zero conversions," or however else you want to word it. Better yet, make your target group the only recipients of the campaign details.

Examples of Incentive Campaigns

You will find many such campaigns in Chapter 18, "Affiliate Program Promotion Ideas," but here I'll share a few well-designed promos from merchants whose programs have not been managed by my agency.

LexingtonLaw.com: First Sale Bonus and More

> *$25 bonus for first sale and $50 bonus for 10 sales (in addition to the $10 CPA increase at 10 sales).*

The LexingtonLaw.com affiliate program's default payout level is set at $30 per filled-out application.

LifeLock: Tiered Payouts

…We've just implemented a very generous sales incentive promo for LifeLock for the months of March and April, just for ShareASale affiliates.

Currently, you earn $32 for every transaction you send to LifeLock. Now, if you hit 10 sales in a month, you'll start earning $50 on all subsequent sales. And, if you hit 25 sales, you'll start earning $80 for each subsequent sale! This commission structure has been coded straight into our system, so you'll instantly see your tiered earnings reflected in your account in real time.

This tiered bonus applies to all valid LifeLock sales, which are defined as legitimate, non-fraudulent sales that are not cancelled in the Lifelock system. Also, all sales and marketing efforts used are subject to our program terms, so please, no trademark bidding.

Legacy Learning Systems: Cash Bonuses

As June is winding down, I know that a couple of you are VERY close to hitting some of our special bonuses this month. As usual, a bunch of you made the 50 sales/month bonus, including some first time members of that club!

The $750.00 bonus for 25 drums course sales and the $2000.00 bonus for 100 sales of our piano course are still for the taking, but as I said, a few of you are looking really close to those bonuses. Keep up the good work!

July has some more awesome bonuses and promotions as well, including one that will last through September.

For the month of July, if you double June's sales (NO MINIMUM), you will earn $25.00 for each extra sale you make. So, if you made 5 sales in June and make 20 in July, you will earn a $375.00 bonus ($25.00 × 15).

If you make 25 sales of our Bass Guitar Spotlight course, you will earn a $250.00 bonus.

20 Sales of Learn & Master Ballroom Dance earns a $500.00 bonus!

Motivation by Money vs. Autonomy, Mastery, and Purpose

One of the YouTube's most popular videos on workplace motivation is that based on Daniel H. Pink's speech given at one of the conferences of the Royal Society for the Encouragement of Arts, Manufactures, and Commerce (RSA). Pink is a *New York Times* best-selling author of several provocative books on changing the world of work, who also served as chief speechwriter to a U.S. vice president. His speech was animated by the talented folks at Cognitive Media and uploaded to YouTube in April 2010 (it is called "Drive: The Surprising Truth About What Motivates Us"). Since then, it has already received more than 3 million views and a storm of accolades from marketing and management professionals around the world. It's no wonder why. Pink talks about one of the most fascinating subjects in the world—human motivation. In his speech, he points out that the popular carrot-and-stick method generally works for simple, straightforward tasks. However, "when a task gets more complicated" and "requires some conceptual, creative thinking, those kind of motivators don't work" (Figure 14.5). He doesn't talk about it, but monetary bonuses, which so many of us managers are using as the main motivators, stop being motivating when used repetitively, and you cannot motivate a worker by the same amount of bonus indefinitely (larger amounts start being expected, and at one point, the whole model stops making economic sense to the employer/manager).

Figure 14.5 Performance at tasks requiring conceptual/creative thinking isn't stimulated by extrinsic rewards.

Pink emphasizes that with tasks that involve purely mechanical skills, monetary (read: extrinsic) motivators work well, but when the task calls for rudimentary skills, larger rewards have actually been registered to lead to poorer performance. The experiment has been replicated in hundreds of settings, and in all contexts experimenters saw that "higher incentives led to worse performance."

Three motivators lead to better performance and personal satisfaction:

- Autonomy—the desire to be self-directed

- Mastery—the urge to get better at stuff

- Purpose—that transcendent something that really makes you race to work in the morning

If this is true about traditional management contexts, what about affiliate marketing—an industry that has autonomous marketers at its very foundation? All three of the motivators described here are called *intrinsic* (in other words, stemming from within the individual) rewards, and they've been proven to create the most lasting motivation, regardless of the context (Figure 14.6). I'll discuss them in more detail next.

Source: "Drive: The Surprising Truth About What Motivates Us. RSA Animate. Available at www.youtube.com/watch?v=u6XAPnuFjJcv.

Figure 14.6 Intrinsic motivators vs. extrinsic rewards

Thursday: Learn More About Intrinsic Motivation

As mentioned yesterday, extrinsic motivation is by far the most widely used approach in affiliate program management. However, as you have already discovered, the secret sauce of true motivation should also include another important ingredient— one made up of a blend of intrinsic rewards. Today you'll look at intrinsic motivation in more detail.

Intrinsic Motivation—The Ultimate Goal

Anyone who is serious about studying motivation must read Frederick Herzberg's article "One More Time: How Do You Motivate Employees" published in the January 2003 issue of *Harvard Business Review*. When I first read it, it struck me that, in reality, making all things go right within your affiliate program—having a 100 percent affiliate-friendly website (without "leaks," with well-converting and wisely formatted landing pages, and so on), running ongoing bonus campaigns, providing performance-based commission increases, satisfying every possible creative need affiliates may have, providing a well-categorized detailed product data feed, and so on—has little to do with the real motivation of affiliates to perform for your affiliate program. Speaking of people management, Herzberg pointed out the following:

> ...*Things that make people satisfied and motivated on the job are different in kind from the things that make them dissatisfied. ...Even if managed brilliantly [environmental factors] don't motivate anybody to work much harder or smarter. People are motivated, instead, by interesting work, challenge and increasing responsibility. These* intrinsic *factors answer people's deep-seated need for growth and achievement. [emphasis mine]*

In our context, however surprising it may sound, ensuring that nothing is wrong with your affiliate program and providing an overall affiliate-friendly environment is no recipe for motivation. Herzberg stresses that "compensation and incentive packages" are not motivating enough for people. He says that a manager "can charge a person's battery, and then recharge it, and recharge it again," but "it is only when one has a *generator of one's own* that we can talk about motivation." [italics mine] And again, superaffiliates come to mind. They do not need much outside stimulation. They are concerned with growth, learning, continuous advancement, and internal recognition. In fact, I have never met a superaffiliate who would choose an affiliate program based on prizes and promos, temporary commission increases, or bonuses. They aren't joining programs to get that $5 sign-up or $10 activation bonus. They always do it because they have a much larger plan in mind.

With other types of affiliates—at least, before they grow into superaffiliates—you do want to be a "battery charger," but even in such cases you want to do everything possible to cultivate these types of motivators within your affiliates and lead them to a point where they are mainly motivated intrinsically (by interesting opportunities with the affiliate campaigns you run and grow to greater achievements).

Exemplary Case of Intrinsic Motivation

(This was adapted from an AMNavigator blog post.)

A Russian math genius, and arguably the smartest man on Earth, who in 2006 declined to collect the mathematical world's equivalent of a Nobel prize, has done it again in 2010. After solving a problem that could not be solved in the past 1,000 years, on the afternoon of June 8, 2010, Grigory Perelman "did not appear in Paris to collect his $1 million prize for solving" the Poincaré conjecture (source: RIA Novosti).

At http://rt.com/news/sci-tech/russian-recluse-mathematician-awarded/, you can find a very interesting video by Russia Today on Grigory Perelman. It was shot prior to the news of him declining the $1 million Clay Mathematics Institute prize but sheds some light on the type of individual he is.

Everyone was, of course, wondering *why in the world* was he declining awards and money?

Besides obviously being a very sensitive person (with the feeling of being "alienated from the mathematical community"), I actually believe there are also other reasons for his puzzling behavior.

What may be of tremendous prestige for you and me doesn't have to feel that honorable for a genius of Perelman's caliber. On the other hand, it is apparent that he didn't do any of his work for the prizes or the money, and this is the part I find to be most fascinating. I believe that Perelman makes an exemplary case for the whole subject of intrinsic motivation that I often blog about. He has reached the highest pinnacle of his profession but not for the money or honors. We definitely have a lot to learn from the world's math genius of the century.

Nicholson's Method and Affiliate Context

As you can imagine, not everyone is ready and willing to jump aboard your affiliate program and start promoting you with the vigor you'd love to see. In this regard, Professor Nigel Nicholson's studies of motivating "problem people" is extremely helpful. Nicholson teaches organizational behavior at London Business School, and in his article "How to motivate your problem people" published by the *Harvard Business Review* 81 (1) in 2003, he looked at manager–employee relationships through the prism of the traditional management context and also described his recipe for working with employees who are neither showing progress nor benefiting the organization/team. According to Nicholson, "problem people" cannot be effectively motivated by extrinsic methods. Rather, managers should look at it as the motivation *from within*. This is achieved by creating circumstances in which the followers' "inherent motivation—the natural commitment and drive that most people have—is freed and channeled toward achievement goals."

Nicholson recommends starting with a dramatic change in a leader's own mind-set: going away from "prodding or coaxing" and focusing on methods and techniques that would aim at "removing barriers" that obstruct the employee's progress "including, quite possibly, your own demotivational management style." This is very good advice for many affiliate program managers, especially those who are working in corporate environments themselves and those who apply the "motivation" methods used for them to the affiliates in the program they manage.

Among the common mistakes that managers in traditional contexts make, Nicholson pointed to managers' beliefs that "people have the same thought process as we do," ignoring individual needs, approaching all employees the same way, and failing to realize that we can't change people's character with external motivation because the profound change always comes from within. All of these mistakes are frequently seen by affiliates with "corporate mind-set" affiliate managers. To facilitate real change, a new approach to motivation should be adapted. Nicholson said it should encompass an understanding that every follower does have a motivational energy, yet this energy is often blocked in the workplace, and removing blockages happens when leaders abandon the technique of pushing solutions on people, but rather pull solutions out of them.

Nicholson's recommendations have several implications for affiliate program managers. As mentioned, the main peculiarity of affiliates is that they are an independent workforce. Affiliates simply do not join programs run by managers who don't motivate them. It is important for affiliate managers to keep perfecting their communication skills, introspection and self-criticism, sincere empathy and open-mindedness and continue to develop more personal relationships with affiliates in informal contexts.

Although employee termination is an option in traditional management contexts, it is not an option in affiliate marketing. In fact, it predominantly happens the opposite way—affiliates are the ones who terminate relationships with nonempathetic and unresponsive merchants or those who believe in motivation by fear or exercise a top-down management approach. Nicholson says that "all available evidence suggests that external incentives—be they pep talks, wads of cash, or even the threat of unpleasant consequences—have limited impact." In fact, such inducements are most frequently effective with people who are all ready and running, while the other folks should be approached through a highly individualized approach that aims at discovering the motivation energy that they already have, and directing it toward achievable goals. This insight—without any adjustments needed—is directly and immediately applicable in the area of affiliate program management.

Motivating Culturally Diverse Affiliates

As stated earlier, the ultimate goal of every affiliate program manager should be making affiliates intrinsically motivated. But what about motivating people in culturally diverse contexts? Affiliate marketing and the relationship between the manager and affiliates is certainly a good example of a truly cross-cultural context. Upon studying this from different angles, I've concluded that every affiliate program manager (just as any marketer, for that matter) should also take time to study country-specific observations pertaining to the general needs and motives that people are seeking to satisfy with their work activity.

One study that is directly applicable is a 1987 study by the Meaning of Working (MOW) International Research Team. This research explored how such variables as work centrality (or "value of working in one's life"), entitlements (the "right to meaningful and interesting work"), and obligations (the "duty to contribute to society by working") manifest themselves in different countries. Although this particular study concentrated on only eight countries, it is a good place for an affiliate manager to start in order to develop an understanding of cultural priorities and the best motivational strategies to use with affiliates that come from different cultural contexts. The two observations that were made in the MOW study that are directly applicable in the area of affiliate program management are as follows:

- 86 percent of all subjects indicated they would continue to work even if they had sufficient money to live in comfort for the rest of their lives.

- Working was second in importance among different life roles, and only family rated higher.

The former observation supports my previously expressed belief that affiliate managers should aim at cultivating intrinsic motivation in affiliates. The fact that these people are involved in the affiliate marketing business coupled with the previously mentioned observations implies that affiliates are naturally predisposed to being strongly motivated *from within*. Hence, it is the affiliate program manager's task to facilitate the development of this type of motivation to the highest levels. The latter observation, in my opinion, supports the peculiarity of affiliates to place a high value on their personal freedom, family life, hobbies, personal goals, and independence from any form of higher management. It appears that these two observations are cross-cultural and should be used by affiliate program managers as a starting point, while the approaches to motivation of culturally diverse affiliates should be shaped in light of their sociocultural context and with due respect to it.

Friday: Arrive at Your Own Optimal Approach

One vital thing to understand about extrinsic and intrinsic motivators is that they are not to be treated as mutually exclusive elements of affiliate program management but rather as complementary components. Even when working with a superaffiliate who is strongly motivated from within, you should remember that they still appreciate personally geared bonuses and commission increases. It is just that bonuses and prizes alone are not enough to keep such people motivated. On the other hand, there is another side of the spectrum, where you have new affiliates that exhibit low levels of professional or psychological maturity. With these affiliates, starting with extrinsic—attractive and achievable—rewards is the way to go. Keeping in mind Herzberg's advice (about helping them develop a "generator of their own") is a must, though. Otherwise, the more expensive your prizes and the larger your giveaways become, the more that will be expected for the same performance.

There is a belief that rather than offering cash prizes, one of the most effective ways to incentivize affiliates is to offer them "money-can't-buy" types of rewards (such as VIP tickets to concerts and sporting events, international trips and cruises, computers, and other expensive prizes). These are definitely great, but they are still extrinsic motivators (just a bit more expensive!), and external incentives like these always lose in comparison with those that produce a real and lasting motivation. It's good to use them as a starting point and a stepping-stone on the way to fostering intrinsic motivators within affiliates but not as ultimate motivators of any sort.

In Chapter 18, you will find practical ideas on how to get started with extrinsic motivators. Feel free to take them and use them as they are or adapt them to your own context. But along the way, remember that external rewards are not your end goal; you are aiming at cultivating intrinsically motivated affiliates.

Month 4: Advanced Management and Analysis

V

During the next few weeks you will focus on slightly more advanced topics. Allow me to underscore that regardless of coming in closer to the end of the book, the things we'll discuss in this last part are absolutely vital. Affiliate program managers cannot afford to ignore these questions if they are seriously interested in the growth of their affiliate programs. So, do give the next four chapters the attention they deserve. It'll save you a lot of potential headache in the future.

Week 1: Study and Learn to Deal with Parasitism and Problematic Affiliates

Although this part's title is "Advanced Management and Analysis," most of the things I am going to talk about this month are so crucial that I wish I had a way to include this chapter earlier in the book. However, because of the step-by-step, instructional nature of this book, anything earlier than this chapter would have been too early.

This week you will develop a systematic approach to evaluating affiliate applications; I'll also discuss the problems of affiliate parasitism (the importance of which cannot be overemphasized) and discuss coupon and content theft.

15

Chapter Contents

Monday: Monitor Red Flags in Affiliate Applications
Tuesday: Learn About Affiliate Parasitism
Wednesday: Educate Yourself on Adware and Toolbars
Thursday: Police Trademark Violators
Friday: Learn About Coupon Theft and Copycat Sites

Monday: Monitor Red Flags in Affiliate Applications

As I was working on this book, a new affiliate program manager emailed me a question:

> *I am new to the title of "Affiliate Manager" and I'm having a hard time discerning what classifies an affiliate as a "good" or "bad" affiliate. Do you have a "list" of what to look for when it regards accepting/declining affiliate applications? I don't know what I'm looking for.*

Immediately it struck me that this simple yet extremely important question isn't something that is systematically answered anywhere. I talk about what's acceptable and what's not, but there really isn't a checklist of the things to look for in "bad" affiliate applications. So, I took a stab at compiling such a list. It consists of some red flags you should watch out for while reviewing affiliate applications:

URL-Related Mismatches and Problems If there is a mismatch between the category in which the affiliate website is listed and the category it truly belongs to (or the listed title of the website and its the actual title), this should raise a red flag. Additionally, you want to be aware that some affiliates use a popular site's URL when filling out their affiliate application. If there are reasons to suspect that it is not their actual URL, ask them to verify it (generally, a message sent to and from an @theirURL.com email address should do).

Trademarks in URLs If you see an applicant use another merchant's trademark in their domain name, check whether this is permitted by the other merchant. If it's not, this should raise a red flag. In Figure 15.1 you can see general information on two affiliates who once applied to a program I managed on Commission Junction. One application came from the United Kingdom, while the other one came from Serbia.

Both iPhone and Travelocity are registered trademarks that belong to Apple Inc., and Sabre Holdings Corporation, respectively.

None of these applications were for Apple's or Travelocity's affiliate programs. But does this mean there is no reason for concern? Quite the contrary! If they are squatting on trademarks of other merchants, there is no guarantee that they won't do the same to you. I declined each of these affiliate applications and suggest that other affiliate program managers handle such situations in a similar manner.

Nonsense Descriptions of Promotional Methods It isn't unusual to see an affiliate profile that in the field designated for promotional methods says "I love [affiliate network name]" or some other nonsense of this kind. It is then apparent that the account was set up by someone who needed to open it quickly and didn't bother much about the content (as long as all mandatory fields were filled out). I recommend double-checking on such an "affiliate" prior to letting them into your program.

Email Spammers This one was suggested by one of the affiliates I work with, Denis Westphal of Convergence Companies, and I believe it is a good one. When you see

nonsensical sounding domain names—for example, urheenbusser.com, peagon
.org, agualolo.com, elaylstinger.com, and similar—this may be a sign that a typical
email spammer is applying to your program (Figure 15.2). Another warning sign
is that the domain was registered less than a month ago. Spammers churn through
domains very rapidly.

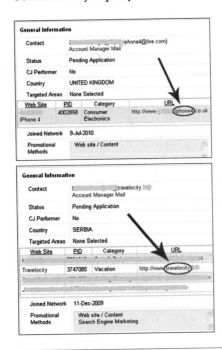

Figure 15.1 Affiliates using merchant trademarks in their domain names

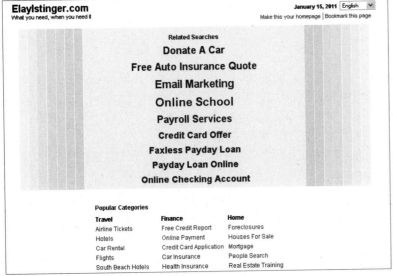

Figure 15.2 It isn't unusual for a spammer site to look like this.

Incompatibility of Affiliate's Promotional Methods and What Works for Your Program A good example of such incompatibility would be a loyalty affiliate's business model, which, as illustrated in Chapter 1, "Understanding Affiliate Marketing," doesn't always work with all types of affiliate programs.

Another example is a virtual currency affiliate. At one point during my management of Volusion's affiliate program, I had such an affiliate join our program and had to learn the lesson the hard way. Within just the first month in the program, they became the most productive affiliate aboard. When I analyzed their referrals at the end of the year, I found out that more than 95 percent of them canceled their accounts within the "free trial" period. The model that the affiliate had in place presupposed immediate credit of the virtual currency to his users' accounts; and with the high payouts, their virtual currency payouts were generous by extension. The affiliate program, however, had a 60-day locking period, and having found out that the vast majority of the sales they had referred were canceled within a matter of days, I reversed the affiliate's commissions and dug deeper into the type of traffic they had been sending us. It was then that I found out that this particular model does not work well with that affiliate program. Just as in the example with loyalty affiliates and "free sample" merchants, the end user's motivation is not tied to the product/service the merchant is selling but to the rewards they are receiving from the affiliate (cashback, reward points, virtual currency, or anything else). Make sure you fully understand your prospective affiliate's core marketing model before you accept them into your program. When unsure, ask.

Inappropriateness of Content This is something that should be spelled out in your program's agreement, but even if it is, do not presuppose that it will save you from inappropriate websites applying to your affiliate program. Many affiliates do not read program agreements. On a regular basis I have explicitly "adult" websites apply to DaySpring .com (a Christian merchant) affiliate program.

You have specified what content is unacceptable in your affiliate agreement, but be open to refining the list as you encounter more and more affiliate sites (it'll range from websites promoting pornography and violence to a plain ol' "banner farm," which will add no value to your brand/company).

Inaccessible/No Website, or Attack Sites You want to personally visit every website you approve into your program. At times when there is *no website* listed on the affiliate account, reach out to the affiliate to clarify how exactly they are planning on promoting you. Although I believe that every serious affiliate must have at least a web page, an absence of a website is not a reason for decline.

If a website is *inaccessible* at the time you attempt to view it, try again within 24 hours, and if it is still not up, it's a red flag.

Attack sites, however, are a separate issue. Essentially, these are websites on which dangerous scripts are run. I remember reviewing one particular affiliate site;

when opened in Internet Explorer, it resolved just fine. However, when trying to access it in the Mozilla Firefox browser, I received a warning notifying me that the website had been "reported as an attack site" and therefore "blocked" from viewing.

A good way to check affiliate websites for malware is by seeing what Google's Safe Browsing Diagnostic says about the website. Introduced in May 2008, this free service is a great tool that affiliate program managers can (and should) use. Upon the tool's launch, Google wrote the following in its blog:

> We've been protecting Google users from malicious web pages since 2006 by showing warning labels in Google's search results and by publishing the data via the Safe Browsing API to client programs such as Firefox and Google Desktop Search. To create our data, we've built a large-scale infrastructure to automatically determine if web pages pose a risk to users. This system has proven to be highly accurate, but we've noted that it can sometimes be difficult for webmasters and users to verify our results, as attackers often use sophisticated obfuscation techniques or inject malicious payloads only under certain conditions. With that in mind, we've developed a Safe Browsing diagnostic page that will provide detailed information about our automatic investigations and findings.

Just go to http://google.com/safebrowsing/diagnostic?site=URLofWebsiteTo Check.com, and you'll know whether they're kosher or not.

Figure 15.3 shows the Safe Browsing Diagnostic tool's report I received about the affiliate that Firefox red flagged for me.

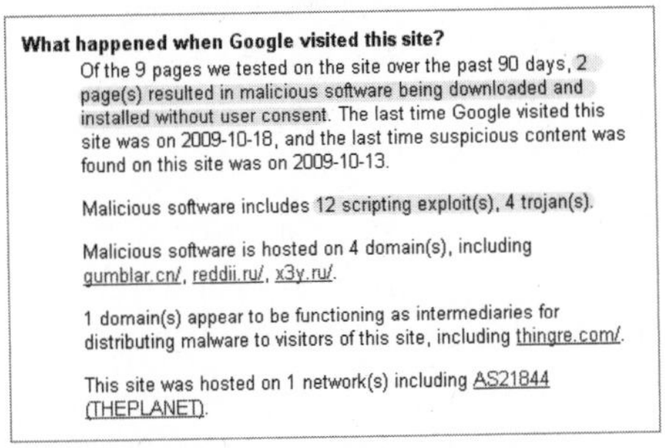

What happened when Google visited this site?
Of the 9 pages we tested on the site over the past 90 days, 2 page(s) resulted in malicious software being downloaded and installed without user consent. The last time Google visited this site was on 2009-10-18, and the last time suspicious content was found on this site was on 2009-10-13.

Malicious software includes 12 scripting exploit(s), 4 trojan(s).

Malicious software is hosted on 4 domain(s), including gumblar.cn/, reddii.ru/, x3y.ru/.

1 domain(s) appear to be functioning as intermediaries for distributing malware to visitors of this site, including thingre.com/.

This site was hosted on 1 network(s) including AS21844 (THEPLANET).

Figure 15.3 Google Safe Browsing Diagnostic's report on an affiliate website, highlighting mine

Make sure you thoroughly check on your future affiliate partners prior to approving them into your program.

Affiliate Relying on Adware, Toolbars, BHOs... I will devote time to a detailed discussion of the issue of adware and toolbars in the rest of this chapter. In essence, these are affiliates who distribute downloadable applications that may interfere with most of your online marketing channels, affiliate program included. Figure 15.4 one of the most frequent ways adware "reminds" you of itself (or the need to click its link) while you're shopping.

Figure 15.4 iGive pop-up, which displays after the automatic redirect

Lack of Response If you have contacted the affiliate trying to clarify their application and haven't heard from them within 72 or more hours (do give them enough time to reply, and, when possible, follow up), you may decline their application.

Negative Feedback It is beneficial to check whether an affiliate has been mentioned in various affiliate forums, blogs, or other feedback systems (see Figure 15.5 for an example). If strong negative feedback has been left about the affiliate by other program managers or affiliates, you'll want to carefully consider what others are saying.

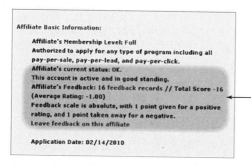

Figure 15.5 ShareASale's feedback system allows merchants to leave feedback for affiliates and for other merchants to view while doing their due diligence.

Although some will argue that other things (such as an email address on a free email service or foreign country residence) should raise red flags, I do not believe these to be reasons for serious concern. They should definitely prompt a more comprehensive review, particularly if an application is coming from a country where you've experienced a high incidence of questionable affiliates, but they shouldn't imply that an affiliate must be declined right away. You want to be diligent and cautious but not to a degree of missing valuable opportunities.

Finally, as discussed at length in Chapter 10, "Week 4: Final Brushstrokes," when you have to send that denial email, make sure it is worded in a way that doesn't burn bridges but gives every affiliate a chance to reply and be reconsidered.

Tuesday: Learn About Affiliate Parasitism

The term *parasite* describes an organism that lives in or on another living organism, existing at the host organism's expense. In the affiliate marketing industry, the problem of parasitism is almost as old as the industry. What is especially noteworthy in this context is that such a relationship often exists without the mutual agreement (or awareness) of all participating parties.

While stemming from the classic definition, affiliate marketing parasitism is somewhat of a synergy between biological and social parasitism. I've defined the former already; now let's look at the latter. Social parasitism can be defined as "a mode of existence based on extraction of wealth from producers without assisting them in any way to produce it" (*The Uses of Comparative Sociology*, University of California Press, 1969). In a moment, you'll see that this definition fits our context almost perfectly.

Affiliate marketing parasitism often involves a mode of generating revenue by employing technological and strategic methods that *hurt* the advertiser and/or its other affiliates, the overall development of its affiliate program, and other online marketing campaigns. Regardless of the form or methods used, a parasitic affiliate is essentially one that reaps the fruit of someone else's work.

Three Types of Parasites

Some limit the term parasite to include only downloadable applications that intrude on the user's shopping experience by facilitating cookie settings or swaps on the customer's machine, regardless of the original source of traffic. In reality, it goes beyond just software. It is my firm opinion that *any* affiliate marketing behavior or methods that interfere with any other channels of marketing that a merchant (or its affiliates) may be employing should be deemed parasitic.

There are three main categories of parasitic affiliates to be aware of:

Adware and Toolbars These are the downloadable applications that I referred to earlier.

Trademark Violators These are affiliates who take advantage of a merchant's trademarks (primarily in paid search campaigns but also in domains—by cybersquatting and typosquatting methods I discussed in Chapter 9, "Week 3: Research and Develop Program Policies").

Coupon and Content Thieves These affiliates take other affiliates' content or exclusive coupons and present them as their own.

I'll talk about each of these categories in greater detail throughout this chapter. As the industry and technology develops, you are likely to see newer forms of parasites emerge, but these three have existed for quite some time.

Program Agreement

On November 3, 2010, Wal-Mart affiliates received a notification of an update to Walmart.com's affiliate terms and conditions. The core of the message read as follows:

You May NOT:

* *employ, use or place any web browser add-ons, toolbars or pop-ups on your website.*

* *engage in any direct or indirect relationships with ISPs and/or mobile carriers that results in the delivery or act of address bar keyword and URL error trafficking (e.g., a user mistypes a web address in the ISP's address bar or search bar, and, as a result, is redirected to a web page that contains a Qualifying Link that directs the user to sites like Walmart.com).*

* *without the prior written approval of Walmart.com, use any Trademark, or any Licensed Material in an advertisement that is not created or provided by Walmart.com in any way that might suggest or imply or mislead or is likely to mislead a visitor to your website into believing that Walmart.com, Wal-Mart Stores or any related entity was the creator or sponsor of such advertisement.*

* *employ, use, or receive any direct or indirect benefit from, any "cookie stuffing" methods (e.g., use of "cookie stuffing" to cause LinkShare's tracking systems to conclude that a user has clicked through a Qualifying Link—and to pay commissions accordingly—even if the user has not actually clicked through any such link).*

I find two things especially amusing about this: the coverage of different types of parasites that mirrors the categories I just discussed (with an addition of cookie stuffers to the list) and the fact that up until November 2010 Walmart.com did *not* have this detailed clause in its agreement.

I have already discussed affiliate program agreements in Chapter 9, but it bears repeating—a separate section of the agreement prohibiting parasitic affiliate behaviors in your program is a must. At the time I'm writing this book, multiple online merchants—including many from the Top 500 Internet Retailer List—lack such a clause in their program agreement. First, this makes them significantly more vulnerable to rogue affiliates; and second, it makes it harder for affiliate program managers to fight such behaviors. After all, if it hasn't been prohibited in the first place, how do you enforce it? I believe that every merchant should mimic Walmart .com in prohibiting all of these activities.

Cookie Stuffing

Walmart's agreement made reference to cookie stuffing. So, let's spend a little time on this important subject as well.

Cookie stuffing is a practice known by many names. These include *cookie dropping*, *forced clicks*, and *cookie sprinkling*, but all stand for the same blackhat marketing method used by affiliates to record tracking cookies on the end user's machine, without the prior consent of the user and with the purpose of creating an impression that the customer/user referral is to be attributed to the blackhat affiliate's marketing.

While looking into the problem of cookie stuffing, an acclaimed expert in the area, Ben Edelman, starts from the essence of how the affiliate marketing mechanism works, and only after that does he get to the core of the issue. At www.benedelman.org/cookiestuffing/, Edelman writes the following:

> *Affiliate tracking systems are intended to pay commissions to independent web sites ("affiliates") when users click through these sites' links to affiliate merchants. Merchants are not intended to pay commission when users merely visit affiliates' sites. Instead, commission ordinarily only becomes payable in the event that a user 1) visits an affiliate's site, 2) clicks through an affiliate link to a merchant, and 3) makes a purchase from that merchant.*
>
> *However, some affiliates use "cookie-stuffing" methods to cause affiliate merchants' tracking systems to conclude that a user has clicked through a tracking link (and to pay commissions accordingly) even if the user has not actually clicked through any such link. If the user subsequently makes a purchase from that merchant—immediately, or within the "return days" period specified by the merchant's affiliate program— the affiliate then receives a commission on the user's purchase.*

Essentially, what happens is an abuse of the system by taking advantage of the technological imperfections and the "last-cookie-gets-the-credit" rule.

Edelman gets into greater detail and examples, and if you want to get a full picture of how bad things can get, I highly encourage you to take a few minutes to carefully study his article and watch the videos he offers to back up his observations.

It is important for me to emphasize here that cookie stuffing affects both the affiliates in the program that has the cookie stuffer on board and the merchant's overall online marketing. With other affiliates, the blackhat affiliate overwrites their tracking cookies that have already been recorded on the customer's machines (though pop-ups, toolbars, and so on), hijacking the commission that legitimately belongs to other affiliates. With merchants, on the other hand, the cookie stuffer cannibalizes the other marketing channels that the etailer is employing. Cookie stuffers hurt all channels—affiliates, merchants' own SEO and PPC achievements, and other online marketing endeavors.

In conclusion, by keeping a cookie stuffer aboard an affiliate program, you let them hurt the program's healthy development and distort the metrics of your other online marketing campaigns (making you overspend too!). The only method that works here is spotting them and booting them from the program. Some of the indicators that cookie stuffing may be occurring include things such as pop-ups, toolbars, poor site quality but referrals still coming through, iframes, and multiple redirects. Also, when in doubt, consult with other affiliate managers (for example, at ABestWeb.com or in the Affiliate Program Management group I run on LinkedIn), or contact experts like Kellie Stevens of AffiliateFairPlay.com.

Just as the online space itself, affiliate marketing parasitism is multifaceted and *continuously developing*. It is therefore important that both affiliates and merchants constantly educate themselves on the topic so they can monitor the landscape for newly evolving threats and fight them collaboratively.

Wednesday: Educate Yourself on Adware and Toolbars

There is nothing wrong with toolbars or any other browser add-ons as such. The problem arises when affiliates are employing toolbars and other adware in a way that plugs them into the sales channel regardless of how the end user gets to the merchant site (via organic search, another affiliate's link, a merchant's paid search campaign, or even a direct type-in).

In late 2009 I published an article at Econsultancy.com where I used an example of one particular adware affiliate (Figure 15.6). I demonstrated how its pop-up cannibalizes every one of the seven marketing channels I tested. You can find the "Toolbars, Pop-Ups, and Parasites in Affiliate Marketing" article at http://econsultancy.com/us/blog/4525-toolbars-pop-ups-and-parasites-in-affiliate-marketing. It contains some interesting comments and important videos, which together with the videos at http://youtube.com/eprussakov, vividly demonstrate both the magnitude and the depth of the problem.

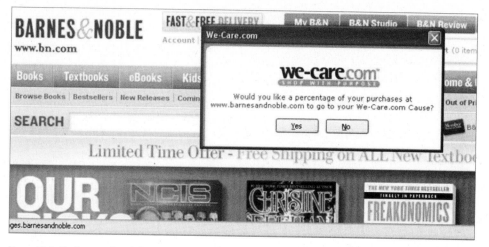

Figure 15.6 We-Care.com "reminder" pops-up on a direct type-in of the Barnes and Noble URL into the address bar.

In my experiment with the previously mentioned adware, I have seen it cannibalize the following channels, popping up regardless of how I got to the merchant's website. If you are involved in any of the following channels and have toolbar/adware affiliates in your program, I highly recommend ceasing your partnership with them. To exemplify the severity of the problem for each marketing channel, I am listing cases/ examples of confirmed pop-ups that I registered when writing the Econsultancy article:

- Affiliate marketing (confirmed: Kmart link on CouponCabin.com, BarnesAndNoble.com link at SunshineRewards.com, PacificPillows.com link at Shopping-Bargains.com)

- Organic SEO (confirmed: Crocs.com, Diamond.com, Newegg.com, PetSmart .com, Zappos.com)

- Paid search (confirmed: AbeBooks.com, Apple Store, EntirelyPets.com, TheFlip.com)

- Direct type-in (confirmed: Amazon.com, Blair.com, Ice.com, Expedia.com, OfficeDepot.com)

- Comparison shopping (confirmed: BlueNile.com through Shopzilla.com)

- Banner advertising (confirmed: RadioShack.com ad on USAToday.com)

- Twitter links (confirmed: links posted @DellOutlet, @BareNecessities, @theFinishLine)

The caliber of these brands whose online marketing efforts are being cannibalized by adware affiliates makes it almost hard to believe that this is really happening.

However, it *is*, and I encourage you to read my article (`http://econsultancy.com/us/blog/4525-toolbars-pop-ups-and-parasites-in-affiliate-marketing`), as well as watch my YouTube videos on the problem. It is a serious matter, and as an affiliate program manager, you must be well-educated about it.

What Parasites Are and How They Work

This group of parasites includes browser-helping objects (BHOs), plug-ins, toolbars, pop-ups, pop-unders, and stand-alone applications that cause affiliate cookies to be overwritten or affiliate links to be intercepted or redirected, thereby removing the possibility of proper credit being given to an affiliate in the instance of a commissionable activity.

Adware can be either bundled with another application (such as the Dealio toolbar that can be installed with the Weather Channel's desktop application) or exist as a stand-alone application or plug-in.

Among the more widely spread adware and spyware operators (and distributors) are 180Solutions, Direct Revenue, Dollar Revenue, Gator (Claria GAIN), Targetsaver, TopMoxie, Zango, and WhenU. Toolbars and browser plug-ins that I have observed to interject themselves into the online user experience have been produced and distributed by such affiliates as CoolSavings.com, Ebates, FreeCause.com, MyPoints.com, OneCause.com, ShopAtHome.com (ShopAtHomeSelect.com), UPromise.com, and We-Care.com, among others.

Five groups are frequently involved in a parasite-affected affiliate transaction: end user, affiliate whose cookie gets overwritten, merchant/advertiser, parasite, and affiliate network. Harvard-based expert on spyware, Ben Edelman, in his 2004 report titled "The Effect of 180solutions on Affiliate Commissions and Merchants" (available online at `www.benedelman.org/spyware/180-affiliates/`), pointed out that although parasites and affiliate networks normally benefit from the parasitic activity, the former three (end users, affiliate, and merchant/advertiser) always suffer. Analyzing 180Solutions' parasitic activity, Edelman wrote this:

1. *Users suffer from 180solutions' activities. Users' affiliate commissions do not reach the affiliate (if any) that 180 users selected intentionally (e.g. to support a particular website) or implicitly (e.g. by using that site and clicking through its links to recommended merchants). This redirection harms users—especially when they are thwarted in their explicit goal of directing commissions to particular affiliates. To the extent that 180's activities take money from merchants, and merchants ultimately increase their prices to cover their costs, users—even users without 180 software—indirectly fund 180.*

2. *Legitimate affiliates suffer from 180solutions' activities. Legitimate affiliates lose commissions on purchases by users with 180 software installed.*

These losses are particularly serious to the extent that affiliates rely on these commissions—e.g. to support their Web hosting and development costs, or to make Web publishing a job rather than a hobby.

3. *Merchants suffer from 180solutions' activities. Merchants suffer in at least two distinct ways from 180's activities.*

    a. *180 cookie-stuffing causes merchants to pay commissions to 180 even when users reached a merchant's site directly or through some source other than an affiliate link. If a user typed in a domain name after seeing an ad on TV or in print, the merchant has already "paid for" acquisition of that user via the offline advertising. If a user arrived at a site via a sponsored link from a search engine, the merchant incurs a cost for that user's visit via payment to the search engine. Nonetheless, 180's affiliate cookie-stuffing causes the merchant to pay again—to pay twice for a single user and a single purchase. 180 cookie-stuffing therefore increases the cost of acquiring new customers, reducing the returns to merchants' advertising both online and offline.*

    b. *180 cookie-stuffing causes merchants to pay commissions to 180 even when commission is properly payable to another affiliate. By reducing the earnings of other affiliates, 180's activities cause merchants to lose affiliates or to recruit worse or fewer affiliates. This in turn reduces the effectiveness of the merchant's overall affiliate program.*

I would like to draw merchants' attention to the third point. Not only do parasitic affiliates hinder an affiliate program's growth by overwriting any other affiliate's cookie, but they are also cannibalizing other channels of online marketing that the merchant may be using (from paid search to organic search results and direct type-ins).

Also, it is important to mention that although all major affiliate networks restrict parasitic affiliate behavior, it isn't unusual for some of them to advocate such affiliates at the same time. So, relying entirely on the network, even if in its terms of service it prohibits such behavior, isn't something a merchant can afford. Every affiliate manager must carefully prescreen all affiliates on the approval stage and then also closely monitor them once in the program.

For further self-education on the subject of adware and spyware, I highly recommend visiting Ben Edelman's website at www.benedelman.org, as well as publications by Kellie Stevens of www.affiliatefairplay.com. As mentioned, I also have a couple of videos on the subject at www.YouTube.com/EPrussakov. Additionally, any related seminars, blog or forum posts, and articles are a must-read for all affiliate program managers.

What Affiliates Think

In early 2009, ShareASale, an affiliate network famous for its antiparasite and pro-affiliate stand, was contemplating a possible change in its terms of service to start allowing some affiliates to use toolbars, establishing a process to ensure that all toolbars allowed into the network would be nonharmful to other affiliates. At that time, an affiliate started a poll to find out other affiliates' opinions on whether the affiliate network should allow toolbars among affiliate and/or merchant sites. More than 86 percent of affiliates voted against toolbars (Figure 15.7).

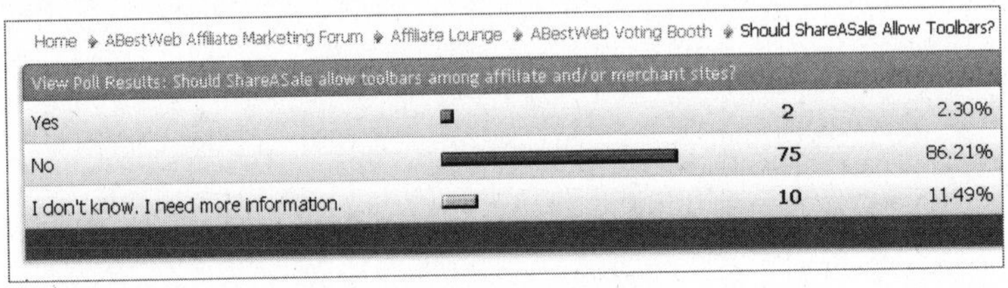

Home ❖ ABestWeb Affiliate Marketing Forum ❖ Affiliate Lounge ❖ ABestWeb Voting Booth ❖ Should ShareASale Allow Toolbars?			
View Poll Results: Should ShareASale allow toolbars among affiliate and/or merchant sites?			
Yes	■	2	2.30%
No	▬▬▬▬▬▬	75	86.21%
I don't know. I need more information.	▭	10	11.49%

Figure 15.7 The vast majority of affiliates are against toolbars.

The results of the poll demonstrate an important point. Affiliates are *so strongly* opposed to parasites that they don't even want to see nonparasitic toolbars allowed.

Also, remember that by having *any* toolbar affiliates aboard, you'll also limit the true developmental potential of your affiliate program (many smart superaffiliates will simply not join your program).

Thursday: Police Trademark Violators

I have already touched upon the subject of trademark violations while discussing affiliate program policies and agreement. Frequently referred to as *trademark poachers*, trademark violators are essentially affiliates who either exclusively or, along with other keywords, bid in their paid search (or PPC) campaigns on merchant's trademarks, URLs, and variations and misspellings of these. The parasitism in this case is classic—affiliates run their PPC campaigns with the sole purpose of diverting the trademark traffic to go through their links and ads first. The goal is to set an affiliate cookie on the end user's machine and, should the user place a sale or create a lead, earn the commission on that.

Although there are exceptions—merchants with unknown brands or those that consist of generic terms like DownPillows.com or Calendars.com (where you can restrict PPC bidding on the domain name but probably not on the individual words), for example—it is normally in the merchant's best interest to restrict trademark bidding and police it. I discussed both the subject and the wording of the affiliate program agreement (addressing PPC search restrictions) in Chapter 9. So, today you'll look at the tools that can help you police trademark bidding—to enforce your program rules effectively.

The tools that can help you in the policing task can be split into two groups: those offered by affiliate platforms (either your affiliate network or your in-house software solution) and those offered by independent vendors.

Platform-Based Tools

To my knowledge, AvantLink is the only affiliate network that offers a tool for its clients. The Paid Search Review tool is available free of charge and appears merely as another reporting option in the merchant's interface. As Figure 15.8 illustrates, AvantLink can report observations of trademark bidding happening in other affiliate networks.

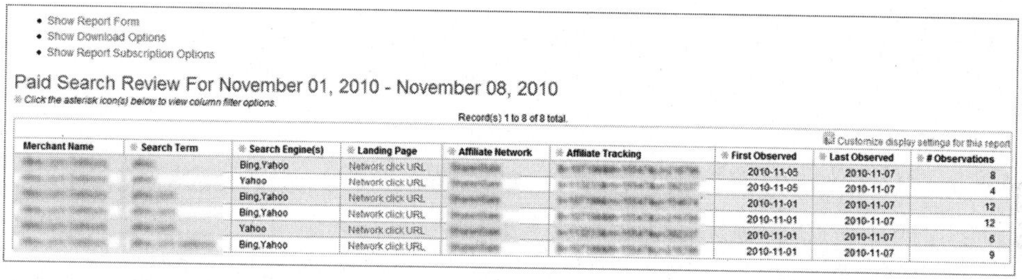

Figure 15.8   AvantLink's Paid Search Review tool in action

The tool monitors the merchants across the major paid search platforms for certain keywords, regardless of what network they're in. Upon catching a violator, AvantLink reports on the exact search term, the search engine, the affiliate network and affiliate tracking, and the number of times the violation has been registered, as well as the first time one was observed and the last time too.

Independent Tools

You can use a number of third-party monitoring to police affiliate compliance with your paid search policies. Here are five such tools:

iTrademarkBidding   This is a free, open source solution for monitoring trademark bidding. The solution uses proxies in most U.S. states to monitor trademark bidding on three major search engines: Google, Yahoo!, and Bing. "The information is recorded every hour allowing you to know who was bidding on your keywords." It was this solution that was the inspiration of the AvantLink tool. You can find more information at www.itrademarkbidding.com.

Brandverity PoachMark   Developed by Andy Skalet and David Naffziger, graduates of University of Colorado at Boulder and MIT, respectively, PoachMark was built exclusively with one aim in mind—to meet the paid search compliance need. This excellent piece of software counters the techniques used by more sophisticated blackhat affiliates (such as referrer laundering, geotargeting, dayparting, and ID obfuscation). As shown in Figure 15.9, in the output, the affiliate manager gets the affiliate's ID along with all of the associated data to facilitate an educated decision.

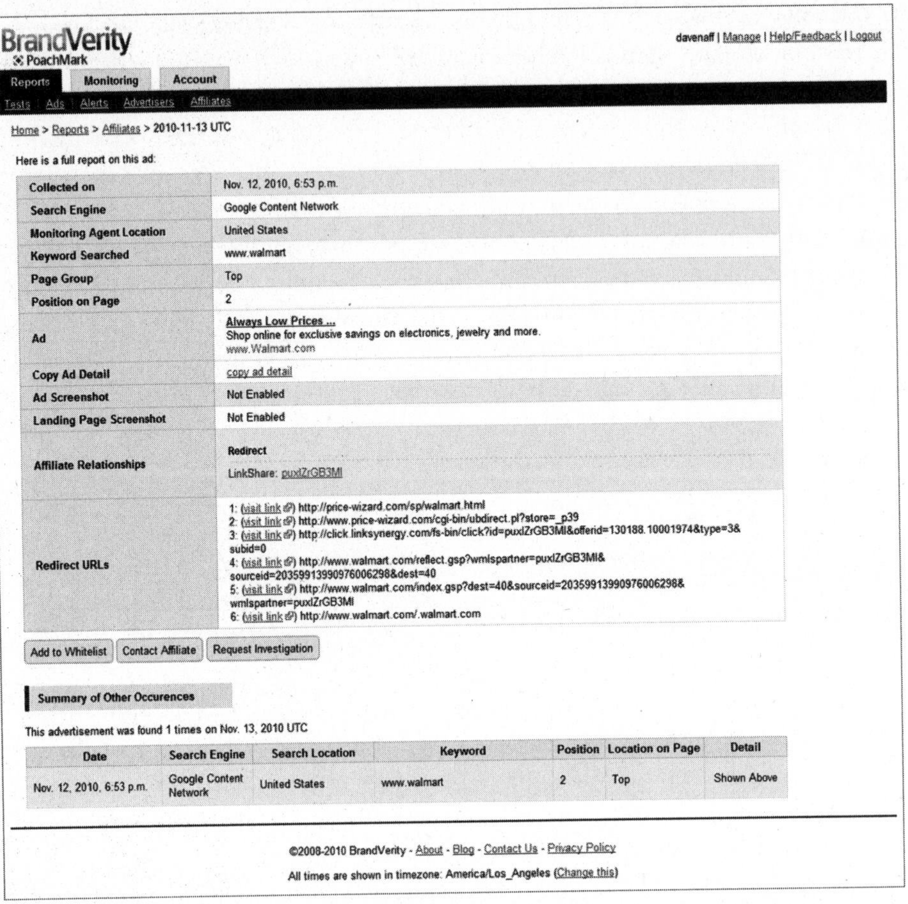

Figure 15.9 A PoachMark report demonstrates how a LinkShare affiliate is bidding on "`www.walmart`."

BrandVerity also manages two important databases: PoachMark Pool and the Affiliate Watchlist. The PoachMark Pool is a shared resource that provides participants with deeper insight into the activities of blackhats across the programs of other Poachmark Pool participants and is a free opt-in service for all PoachMark customers.

The Affiliate Watchlist, on the other hand, contains the websites and IDs of the most abusive affiliates. BrandVerity customers nominate affiliates for inclusion, and affiliates are added once a BrandVerity Advertising Abuse Analyst has thoroughly reviewed the data collected on the affiliate and the techniques the affiliate used to conduct their abuse. Full details on each abusive affiliate are available to PoachMark Pool participants. The Affiliate Watchlist is provided free to all PoachMark customers. I highly recommend BrandVerity's products to all affiliate program managers. You can learn more about BrandVerity at `www.brandverity.com`.

The Search Monitor Founded in 2003 by a group of search marketing enthusiasts, The Search Monitor was part of the original team that pioneered KeywordMax, the first bid management tool to automate keyword bidding based on financial goals. Right now The Search Monitor focuses "real-time competitive intelligence to monitor brand and trademark use, affiliate marketers for compliance, and competition on paid search, mobile search, organic search, local, social media, and shopping engines worldwide in every language." The Affiliate Monitor, `http://www.thesearchmonitor.com/affiliate_monitor`, can be effectively used to police affiliate marketers for compliance with affiliate program terms and conditions, not only with restrictions pertaining to keyword bidding (Figure 15.10). This tool also allows you to police direct linking ad copy rules and keyword rank. With reporting, you have the choice of viewing it online or receiving email reports. Everything is "100 percent customizable on the fly to meet your rules and requirements," while the "setup is easy and includes bulk imports of keywords." You can find more information at `http://thesearchmonitor.com/affiliate_monitor`.

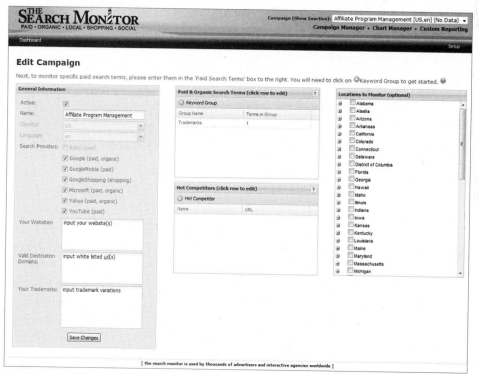

Figure 15.10 The Search Monitor's setup screen for editing your trademark policing campaign

brandwatcher This U.K.-based service "offers you the ability to monitor pay per click activity on AdWords, Yahoo!, and MSN in the UK 24/7/365, helping you protect your brand name, trademarks, products, and reputation as well as identifying and reporting unauthorized affiliate activity" (Figure 15.11). It offers a number of packages, which provide automated monitoring of anywhere between 1 and 20 keywords every hour. Merchant categorization, archiving of the violators' ad copies, spidering to identify affiliate redirects, monitoring of both brand and generic keywords, and many other useful tools are available for British merchants. You can find more information at www.brandwatcher.co.uk.

Figure 15.11 brandwatcher.co.uk home page

AdGooroo Trademark Insight Like the other tools, Trademark Insight provides 24/7 automated brand monitoring by identifying advertisers that are bidding on or using your brand terms (Figure 15.12) in their ad copy. Each license enables merchants to monitor up to 200 variations of a single trademark on 8 search engines in 46 countries. You also have the option to view copy and the average position of competing ads and identify the ad servers and individual affiliates in infringement. For more details, see www.adgooroo.com/products/trademark_monitoring.php.

The array of available PPC policing tools is certainly vast. Most of these tools have automated alert systems and are truly essential to leverage the affiliate manager's time. Choose one today, and make the policing of affiliate paid search rules compliance your regular routine.

In conclusion, if you are prohibiting affiliate utilization of your registered trademarks in their domain names, there are tools to police cybersquatting. One tool that is good for policing such affiliate behavior is CitizenHawk. Its unique technology "identifies instances of cybersquatting that infringe on a company's trademark, sends notices of fraudulent activity to domain owners, interrupts the flow of money being paid to cybersquatters, and automates legal action to get fraudulent sites stopped for good." You can learn more about them at www.citizenhawk.com.

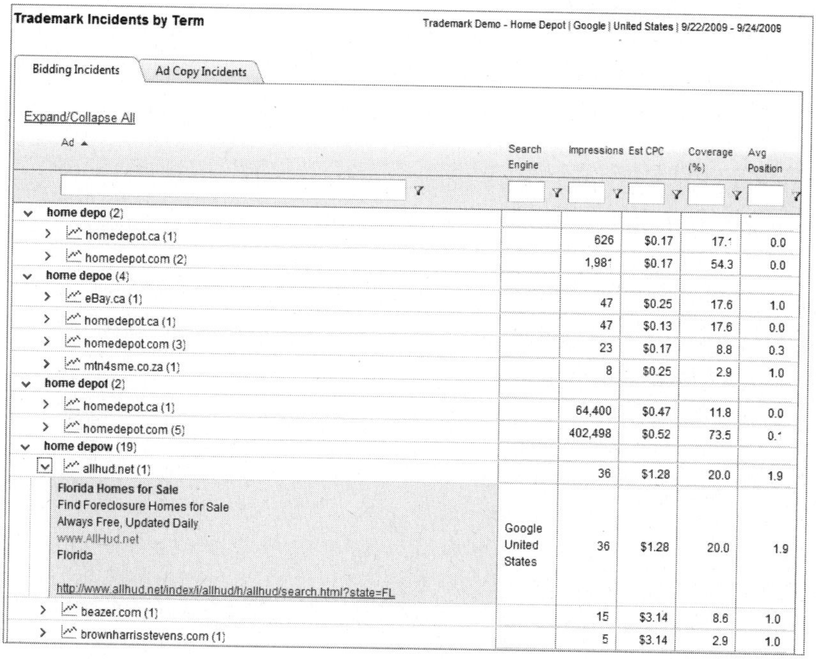
Trademark Incidents by Term
Trademark Demo - Home Depot | Google | United States | 9/22/2009 - 9/24/2009

Bidding Incidents | Ad Copy Incidents

Expand/Collapse All

Ad	Search Engine	Impressions	Est CPC	Coverage (%)	Avg Position
home depo (2)					
homedepot.ca (1)		626	$0.17	17.1	0.0
homedepot.com (2)		1,981	$0.17	54.3	0.0
home depoe (4)					
eBay.ca (1)		47	$0.25	17.6	1.0
homedepot.ca (1)		47	$0.13	17.6	0.0
homedepot.com (3)		23	$0.17	8.8	0.3
mtn4sme.co.za (1)		8	$0.25	2.9	1.0
home depot (2)					
homedepot.ca (1)		64,400	$0.47	11.8	0.0
homedepot.com (5)		402,498	$0.52	73.5	0.1
home depow (19)					
allhud.net (1)		36	$1.28	20.0	1.9
Florida Homes for Sale Find Foreclosure Homes for Sale Always Free, Updated Daily www.AllHud.net Florida http://www.allhud.net/index/i/allhud/h/allhud/search.html?state=FL	Google United States	36	$1.28	20.0	1.9
beazer.com (1)		15	$3.14	8.6	1.0
brownharrisstevens.com (1)		5	$3.14	2.9	1.0

Figure 15.12 Trademark Incidents by Term drill-down report by AdGooroo Trademark Insight

Friday: Learn About Coupon Theft and Copycat Sites

Coupon theft is a subject I haven't touched upon yet. This type of parasitism has also been a long-standing problem, especially for affiliates who are receiving exclusive deals from merchants. Coupon parasites seek to cash in on unique affiliate-merchant relationships, featuring other affiliates' exclusive coupons on their sites, on Twitter, or via other means.

The Problem

The essence of the problem is as follows:

- You run XYZ affiliate website.
- A merchant gives you an exclusive coupon code (one available only through you) for a 20 percent store-wide discount.
- You upload it, start ranking well, and begin converting sales for the merchant.
- A competing affiliate steals the coupon code and posts it on their site.

You now have to chase down the merchant's affiliate program manager (or the affiliate network representative you're working with) to get the thief to remove the coupon code from their site.

Of course, there is no guarantee that they will do so, and then the exclusivity of a coupon loses all its meaning.

The Solution

You can do something on a larger scale, especially if the merchant's affiliate program is run on a popular affiliate platform (in-house software or affiliate network). The solution is actually logical and simple, and I am surprised that at the time I am writing this book, the only affiliate network that offers such a tool is buy.at.

In August 2009, buy.at pioneered a new functionality, which I covered in my blog when it was new. The product allows merchants to assign exclusive coupon codes to specific affiliates, but in such a way that even when the exclusive coupon code is used on another affiliate's site, it is *the original* affiliate who gets the credit for the sale. Here is how buy.at described this technology:

> *Buy.at's OfferCentral technology provides merchants with full control over voucher code communication and distribution.*
> *Above and beyond similar technologies, this system enables merchants to hand pick select affiliate(s) to promote a unique offer code and set end dates. Further, merchants are given the ability to reassign commissions if an unauthorized affiliate uses another's unique code.*

Figures 15.13 and 15.14 show the buy.at merchant interface and demonstrate how setting up the code and selecting a unique set of affiliates (or single affiliate) work.

This simple yet highly effective solution works well for all parties involved in the process: The affiliate always gets their commission, the affiliate network collects its fee and relieves itself from acting as a mediator in interaffiliate disputes over exclusive coupons, and the merchant gets the sale. I sincerely hope that more affiliate networks will follow buy.at's example and start offering a similar tool for its clients.

To be fair to affiliate program software solutions, I must also mention that some of them offer a similar functionality. For example, in early 2009 PostAffiliatePro made it possible for its merchant users to generate exclusive affiliate coupons (Figure 15.15) that are tied to specific affiliates only.

Should any affiliate steal the exclusive coupon code—from the original affiliate's website, Twitter feed, or any other way—they will not profit from it, because all-exclusive, coupon-specific commissions are always credited to the original affiliate's account. It's a simple yet extremely effective solution to the problem.

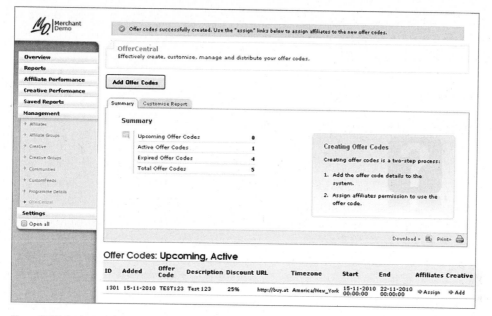

Figure 15.13 Setting up a coupon code in buy.at's OfferCentral

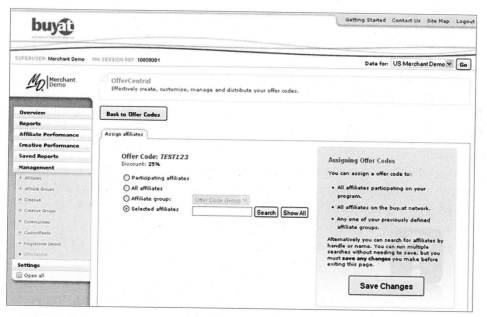

Figure 15.14 Assigning an exclusive coupon to select buy.at affiliates

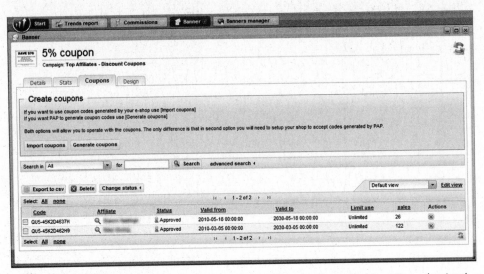

Figure 15.15 A PostAffiliatePro merchant reviews reporting on the redemption of two exclusive coupons, each assigned to a unique affiliate.

Copycat Sites

The problem of SEO hijacking or web scraping is probably as old as the Internet itself. Copycat websites or clone sites have been webmasters' headache for a long time. Stories of direct clones ending up ranking higher than the original are a sad reality. Although there are ways to stop web-harvesting bots from scraping a website—such as blocking by IP addresses, blocking by traffic volume, or even putting together JavaScript code to block them—stopping a real person (not a bot) requires a real person or sometimes more than one.

As an affiliate program manager, you want to join forces with your affiliates to help them fight the "competitors" that are stripping their content, switching affiliate links to their own, and *without adding any value to the merchant* earning commission.

Be it coupon thieves or copycat "affiliates," be prepared to work hand in hand with your good affiliates to assist them in fighting these parasitic techniques. Authentic empathy always goes a long way.

Week 2: Master Affiliate Program Analytics and Optimization

It is interesting that you do not see much written about affiliate marketing analytics, whereas if there is one industry that relies on analytical data especially heavily, it is affiliate marketing. Additionally, I do not see many quality articles on the importance of ongoing testing and optimization or competitive intelligence. This week you'll focus on all of these and beyond.

16

Chapter Contents

Monday: Understand What KPIs and Metrics to Focus On
Tuesday: Split Test to Improve Conversions
Wednesday: Explore Alternative Tracking Solutions and Compensation Models
Thursday: Engage in Ongoing Competitive Intelligence
Friday: Analyze Progress and Stay Informed

Monday: Understand What KPIs and Metrics to Focus On

When analyzing your program's performance, you want to clearly understand what key performance indicators (KPIs) and metrics are to be measured and focused on. You will start by looking at the KPIs that will be helpful both to merchants with affiliate programs that are managed by an in-house or external affiliate manager and to affiliate program managers themselves.

KPIs for Advertisers/Merchants

Let's look at affiliate program performance through the eyes of a merchant who looks both at the affiliate program performance and at the performance of the program's manager.

When analyzing how well your affiliate program is doing, especially how well it is managed, I recommend focusing on the following performance indicators:

Affiliates Recruited I recommend breaking this KPI down into *three* parts:

- The number of new affiliates recruited into your program (within any given period of time)
- The quality of the websites they run (measured by traffic rank, demographics, niche focus, and so on)
- The type of affiliate (refer to Chapter 1, "Understanding Affiliate Marketing," for details)

Reviewed altogether, these three dimensions will give you a good picture of your affiliate program's affiliate recruitment.

Activity Index You want to also know how many of your affiliates are truly active in the program. After all, a recruited but stagnant affiliate is not making any impact.

Before you start figuring out your activity index, you want to decide what will constitute activity for you. There are three basic ways to define activity: as a display of links (Figure 16.1), as a referral of traffic (website visitors), and as conversions (sales or leads). Once you've decided what exactly you're measuring, calculate the *activity index* as the percentage of affiliates active in the program over a given period of time.

This is not to say that if you define desired "activity" as conversions you should ignore the other two types of activity altogether. Instead, keep your finger on the pulse of all activity in your program, aiming to get more and more affiliates to demonstrate the *most desired* activity.

Activation Inactive affiliates need to be motivated to get active. So, look at the number of previously stagnant affiliates *activated* within a given time period. Make it your affiliate program manager's goal to focus on activating nonproducing affiliates. Motivation and activation are just as important as recruitment. Read more about the good ways to handle it in Chapter 14, "Week 4: Affiliate Motivation."

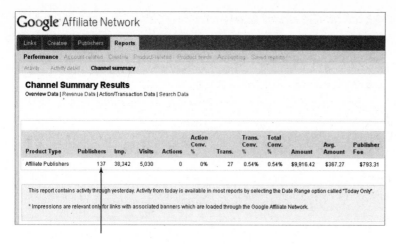

Figure 16.1 Among other data, Google Affiliate Network's Channel Summary report displays the number of affiliates who display your creatives.

Traffic Look both at the tendencies in traffic increase (Figure 16.2) and at the exact month-to-month (or week-to-week) comparisons of the hits/clicks volume referred to you by your affiliates.

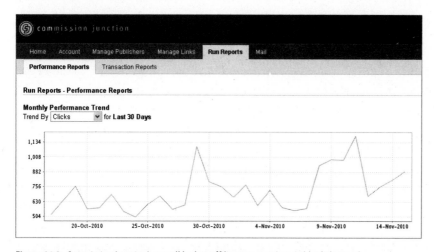

Figure 16.2 Commission Junction's overall look at affiliate program's monthly clicks trend

In some cases, it is also good to analyze the number of impressions of merchant's creatives/links. Affiliates will do a lot of branding for you. In some cases, when it is high-quality branding, developing additional personalized remuneration mechanisms may be of mutual benefit. However, in most cases when choosing between impressions and clicks, I recommend focusing on measuring the latter.

Transaction Volume Finally, the increase in affiliate-referred sales or leads is your most tangible KPI. When analyzing the sales increase, focus on the monetary figure (Figure 16.3)

and new customers referred (by all means, remunerate sales to returning customers, but instituting an additional bonus for new ones is always nice and keeps affiliates motivated). When analyzing leads, look at the numbers *and* quality of those leads.

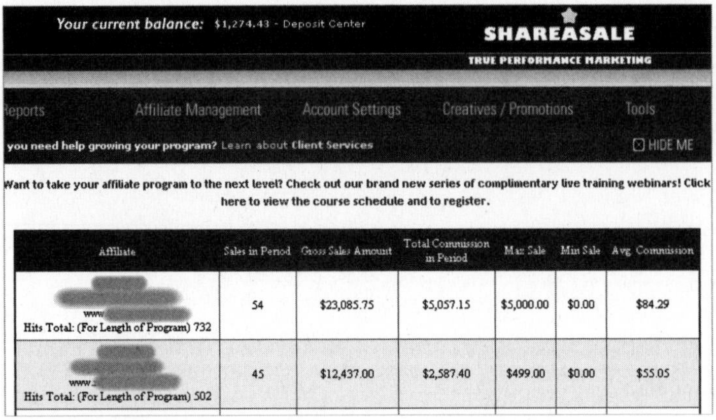

Figure 16.3 When reviewing your ShareASale reports, focus on the gross sales amount as opposed to the number of sales in a period.

Although some would also like to include an affiliate program's conversion ratio (CR) in the list of KPIs by which an affiliate program manager should be judged, I would argue that frequently CR has very little to do with either the affiliate or the program manager's performance. CR—if defined as the ratio of affiliate-generated qualified actions (sales, leads, and so on) to the total number of affiliate-referred visitors to your website—is something that is heavily dependent on the landing pages, the overall usability of the merchant's website, and the competitiveness of the offer (I will discuss this subject in greater detail tomorrow). It is for the same reasons that you should not include earnings per 100 clicks (EPC), average order value (AOV), or any other KPIs that are contingent on factors other than the performance of your affiliates or your affiliate program manager.

Tuesday: Split Test to Improve Conversions

Also known as *A/B testing* or *bucket testing*, split testing is a method of marketing testing whereby the performance of two versions of the landing page (or web page elements) are tested against each other. The end goal is to determine which one performs better (Figure 16.4) —yielding lower bounce rate and better conversions (sales, leads, subscriptions, sign-ups, and so on)—and then go with the better-performing page (or page element). One of the first companies to try A/B testing in the ecommerce space was Amazon.com, which through testing various versions of its add-to-cart button (along with countless other variables) achieved higher conversions rates and increased average order value. You can find more information at http://grokdotcom.com/2008/02/26/amazon-shopping-cart/.

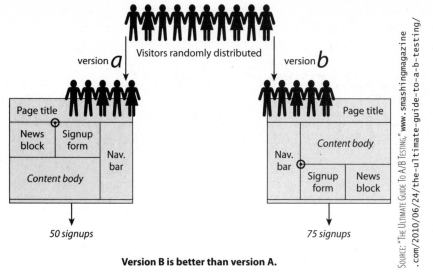

Source: "The Ultimate Guide To A/B Testing," www.smashingmagazine.com/2010/06/24/the-ultimate-guide-to-a-b-testing/

Version B is better than version A.

Figure 16.4 A/B testing illustration by Smashing Magazine

Per Internet Retailer's 2008 survey of the top 500 online retailers, who were asked whether they were engaged in either multivariate or A/B testing, 76.7 percent of the surveyed merchants replied negatively (source: "Website Design and Usability Guide" by Internet Retailer, as quoted at http://grokdotcom.com/2008/02/08/website_redesign/). Just think about it for second: More than three-fourths of the world's leading online merchants were not engaged in any kind of testing in early 2008!

The situation has been improving on the overall ecommerce landscape, but not so much in affiliate programs. Testing is an area that is all too often ignored by merchants and managers who run affiliate programs. At best, affiliates are offered the same landing pages for years; at worst, all affiliate-referred traffic goes to the merchant's home page.

Although you may certainly engage in more complex kinds of testing (such as multivariate testing), I recommend starting with at least A/B testing. You won't regret it when you see the results.

Conversion Optimization

More than once I have heard merchants complain that affiliate marketing doesn't work for them because the conversions they are seeing are extremely low. Now, although the quality of the affiliate-referred traffic has a lot to do with it, affiliates will seldom send you massive amounts of traffic that doesn't convert. For most of them, this traffic isn't free and costs them their time, energy, money, or opportunity. So, when they don't see good conversions, they either take their campaigns down or funnel the traffic to another merchant.

When I'm talking about conversion, you must understand one fundamental truth. The responsibility for conversion of affiliate-referred traffic is always a shared one. On one hand, affiliates should work on making it a targeted traffic, while on the other, merchants should ensure that their own websites actually convert. I have seen affiliate programs with zero conversion rates, and not because the affiliate-referred traffic wasn't right! In some cases, the merchant's offer just wasn't competitive or enticing enough to produce results, while in others the merchant had major shopping cart problems that prevented safe and speedy checkout. When there is no (or low) conversion across different affiliates in one program, there is always an internal (read: merchant) problem to look for.

In early 2010 I launched an affiliate program for an established brand that was a recognized leader in its vertical. I set up its affiliate program on a solid platform, recruited a good number of highly targeted affiliates, but regardless of the number of visitors these affiliates were sending to the merchant, the traffic wasn't converting well at all. The average across-the-program conversion rate was ranging from 0.8 percent to 0.9 percent, while I really expected to see something in the range of 2 percent to 3 percent. So, I worked closely with the merchant on optimizing the landing page where affiliates were sending their traffic, and although there was still room for improvement, the difference from the original page's performance was too obvious not to notice.

As Figure 16.5 illustrates, after tweaking the landing page, I reaped a nearly threefold conversion increase (from 0.86 percent to 2.47 percent). Consequently, the improvement in average affiliate EPC naturally followed—growing by more than 250 percent (or more than 3.5 times), this meant that the average affiliate went from earning $36.02 on 100 clicks reffered to this merchant to $127.02. This improvement was possible based on nonexpert advice, folks! I am an affiliate marketing consultant and program manager, not a landing page optimization expert. Yet even with my purely commonsense suggestions, such as keeping it simple and focused, ensuring there are strong and clear calls-to-action (CTAs) above the fold, using imperative verbs in the copy, and reinforcing the product's strong points and the risk-free nature of the purchase, I was able to see considerable improvements. Needless to say, the company has never gone back to the previous version of the landing page.

Sales	Leads	Clicks	CR	EPC (USD)
52	0	2,102	2.47%	$127.02
35	0	4,081	0.86%	$36.02

Figure 16.5 Landing page improvement yields higher conversion and EPC (see first row data vs. the second).

If you're serious about your online business, you'd better be really serious about split testing and conversion rate optimization.

What to Test

So, what do you want to test as an affiliate manager? I believe there are some basic variables you should be paying attention to and that you should do split testing on each them constantly:

- Affiliate banners
- Landing page headlines
- Calls to action
- Landing page style and layout
- Images
- Descriptive copy
- Pricing and promotional offers

With all of these variables, you want to experiment with the wording, placements, colors, and sizes. The end goal is the survival of the fittest to convert best. Everything else should be treated as ballast, which you can dump to allow you to fly higher.

Headlines—The Biggest Opportunity for Conversion Rate Improvements

(This was adapted from an AMNavigator blog post from July 2010.)

Regardless of whether you're marketing products, services, or anything else, your landing pages contain several common elements. The first element that every visitor and search engine sees is the headline.

At one point I came across an interesting article that described how the author's split testing of headlines *doubled* his conversion rate and earnings. The content, and all other elements of his landing pages, remained the same. He played only with headlines, and the increase in conversion rates ranged from 20 percent to 122 percent. Spending less than an hour of his time on everything, he increased his income from one given affiliate page from $600 to $1,600 a month.

Upon reading about this experience, I spent a bit more time researching. I found that headlines, or the first line of text that web page visitors read upon landing on a page, are believed to offer the biggest opportunity (namely, about 80 percent of the opportunity) for improvements in conversion rate. I therefore recommend that you spend time split testing various headlines, keeping the ones that produce the best response rates.

The doubling of conversion is actually not that unusual while A/B testing headlines. In fact, some landing page optimizers testify to instances where a headline change alone increased conversion from 300 percent to 500 percent. This is pretty amazing, and I'm surprised you don't see more affiliate marketers writing about it. Or maybe this is just one of those secrets marketers who know what they're doing just prefer not to share?

How to Test Effectively

Now that you know what you want to test, let's briefly answer the "how" question. First, I'll cover the tools that will help you make your A/B split testing easily measurable and sensible. Second, I will touch upon an idea that you may find helpful as you engage in split testing; and finally, you will look at the additional resources to follow up split testing and landing page optimization.

A/B Testing Tools

Unfortunately, as of late 2010, I know of no affiliate program platforms (neither networks nor in-house software) that will help affiliate managers split test their creatives or landing pages. Therefore, you'll want to use external tools. Thankfully, there's no deficit of these.

A number of different solutions will help you (and your affiliates) test the different versions of your landing pages. The following are the most popular tools at the time I was writing this book. URLs where you can find out more about these tools are also included.

- Google Website Optimizer: `http://google.com/websiteoptimizer/`
- Visual Website Optimizer: `http://visualwebsiteoptimizer.com/`
- LiveBall: `http://ioninteractive.com/liveball-landing-page-software/`
- A/Bingo: `http://bingocardcreator.com/abingo`
- PickFu: `http://pickfu.com/`
- Vertster: `www.vertster.com/`
- Unbounce: `http://unbounce.com/`
- SiteSpect's A/B Testing: `www.sitespect.com`
- Fivesecondtest: `http://fivesecondtest.com/`
- Vanity: `http://vanity.labnotes.org/`

Go Beyond Small Things

In 2008, an advertising and social media blogger, Andrew Chen, came up with the term *local maximum*, which Joshua Porter describes in his article "The Local Maximum" (`http://52weeksofux.com/post/694598769/the-local-maximum`). It basically means a point at which you've hit the limit of the current design and it is as effective as it's ever going to be in its current incarnation. This happens when, while engaged in split testing, you test only one of the previously mentioned page-specific variables at a time. Once you've hit the ceiling, you have nowhere to go, and without a major shake-up, you won't make any big gains, according to Porter ("Why A/B Testing Isn't Just About Small," `http://blog.performable.com/why-ab-testing-isnt-just-about-small-changes/`).

To pull off a better design than that achievable at your local maximum (Figure 16.6), you need to go beyond the testing of single design elements and test the entire page as a variable. Page-level testing is a major strategic change, but there are case studies that truly justify it, and it is definitely worth keeping in mind.

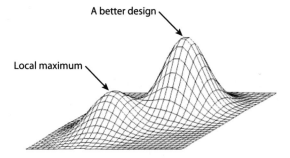

Figure 16.6 Local maximum vs. a better design

Source: Performable.com: "Why A/B Testing Isn't Just About Small Changes," `http://blog.performable.com/why-ab-testing-isnt-just-about-small-changes/`

Resources

For further education on the testing and conversion optimization, read (and listen to) the material by the following companies and individuals:

- ABTests.com
- Anne Holland
- Bryan and Jeffrey Eisenberg
- Eric J. Hansen
- ion interactive
- Tim Ash
- WiderFunnel
- Unbounce

This list is merely alphabetical and shouldn't be treated as a ranking of any kind.

Happy testing!

Wednesday: Explore Alternative Tracking Solutions and Compensation Models

Whether you implement any of them or not, it is good to at least familiarize yourself both with alternatives to tracking and with optional compensation patterns. Today you'll look at both of these topics.

Cookieless Tracking

Although in the vast majority of cases affiliate program tracking relies on cookies (see Chapter 4, "Week 2: Understanding Tracking and Reporting"), a number of platforms do not solely depend on them for tracking. Tracking can also be tied to the end user's IP or be URL-based (when affiliate IDs are being embedded in each URL) or can incorporate a number of other solutions (for example, Flash cookies and ETags to track clicks and JavaScript code to track transactions) that aren't tied to cookies.

Here's a brief list of some software providers and affiliate networks that support cookieless affiliate tracking:

Software

- 1AutomationWiz
- AffiliateTracking.com
- DirectTrack
- HasOffers
- LinkTrust
- Post Affiliate Pro

Affiliate Networks

- AffiliateFuture
- oneNetworkDirect
- Webgains

Backing your cookie-based tracking with alternative solutions will give your affiliate program a competitive edge in the eyes of affiliates.

Alternative Compensation Models

The default payment model that works in most affiliate networks and affiliate programs is commonly known as the "last click wins" model. It's been the prevailing compensation model since the dawn of affiliate marketing and remains such at the time I was writing this book. It essentially says that the last affiliate who referred the customer should get the commission.

However, there exists a line of argument that when the "last click wins" model was invented, consumer paths to the point of checkout were significantly more linear than what they have become with time, and in the present age of multi-touchpoint ecommerce, it may not necessarily be the best affiliate payment model.

Split Commissions

When considering the multi-touchpoint nature of the presale process, merchants are often encouraged to think in the direction of multiattribution, or compensating multiple affiliates who may have influenced the end user's purchase decision.

The majority of current affiliate networks are sticking to the "last click wins" model as the best out of the ones available. But some platforms (for example, the MoreNiche affiliate network in the United Kingdom and the Post Affiliate Pro affiliate program software) are advocating split commissions and offering merchants tools to support them.

The question of conversion attribution is as old as the existence of referral traffic, and the global consensus on the subject is far from reached. As is apparent from Figures 16.7 and 16.8, which are taken from Econsultancy's 2009 Affiliate Census reports, not all affiliates are entirely happy with the current state of things.

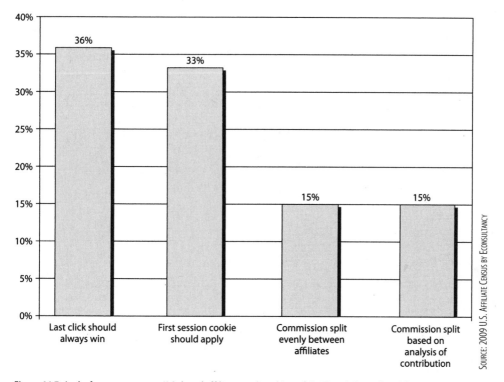

Figure 16.7 Lack of consensus among U.S.-based affiliates on the subject of the "last click wins" model

Of course, as someone said, "There are three kinds of lies: lies, damned lies, and statistics." From what I've seen, most affiliates still strongly believe in the "last click wins" model. But since in this chapter I've decided to cover more advanced possibilities, I'll briefly talk about split commissions.

There is an idea of remunerating both the last-referring affiliate *and* the affiliate who initially introduced the end user to the brand. It seems to be fair at its core, but numerous questions linger. For instance, how do you know who really introduced the customer to the brand when the real introduction could've happened beyond the affiliate program's cookie life? And on what grounds are you assuming that the first and last affiliates played the most significant roles in the consumer's decision-making process? And if you want to pay the affiliates who played their roles between the first and the last ones, how can you effectively measure the value of their participation in the preselling? All of these are semi-rhetorical questions. I encourage you to actively monitor any developments in this direction to be able to make educated and well-weighed decisions on the subject. At the end of the day, you want to do what's best for you and be fair to your affiliates.

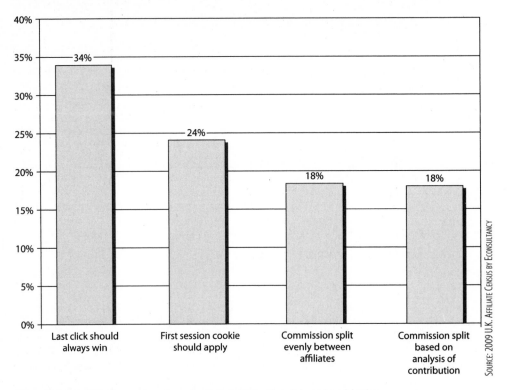

Figure 16.8 U.K. affiliates are not unanimously satisfied with the "last click wins" model either.

Quality Click Pricing

In September 2009 eBay implemented a revolutionary affiliate compensation model, christening it *quality click pricing* (QCP). It essentially meant moving from its previous CPA model to a CPC model. QCP was created to do something previously unprecedented, namely, to take into account the *incremental* value of that traffic to eBay (in other words, whether a sale happened as a direct result of the publisher's actions) and reward the affiliate accordingly (according to the August 19, 2009, article "Announcing Quality Click Pricing" at eBay Partner Network Blog).

eBay Partner Network (eBPN) stated that this new affiliate payment model would be better for affiliates because of the following advantages:

- Commission structure will be simplified.

- Payout will be more closely aligned with traffic quality, which will allow eBPN to pay more to those affiliates who are driving high-quality traffic.

- Publishers will be rewarded for multiple sources of value in addition to sales, such as revenue from advertising on eBay pages and PayPal transaction revenue.

- EPC will be visible the very next day and will be more stable on a day-to-day basis.

eBay also wrote that for many affiliates "this change will mean that [their] payout will increase." Some, however, will start making "less money than under the previous payment structure and will need to make some changes to [their] campaigns in order to see better rewards."

Over the next two years this unique idea was recognized by the online marketing community, helping eBay win such prestigious digital marketing awards as the Innovation in Affiliate Marketing 2009 award by Econsultancy and Exceptional Merchant 2010 award by Affiliate Summit.

The thoughts at the foundation of QCP were originally brought up in the *Search Engine Marketing Journal* (where I serve as the senior editor for the "Affiliate Marketing" section), and I remember reviewing the eBay team's "The Coming Evolution in Affiliate Marketing: A Focus on Quality" white paper prior to its publication in the February 2009 issue. My thoughts on it haven't changed since then. I understand eBay's desire to focus on the traffic quality but would love to see more flexibility and collaboration with affiliates on resolving conflicting opinions.

In spring 2010, I polled affiliates to find out whether the QCP model has worked better or worse for them, and as Figure 16.9 shows, about one-third of affiliates haven't noticed any change in income, 9 percent have noticed better earnings, and the vast majority (63 percent) of eBPN's affiliates have registered a decrease in earnings. One could argue that with the introduction of the QCP, eBay has encouraged the more productive affiliates to produce more, cutting its expenses on the less valuable affiliates. Only access to internal information would allow us to judge how affiliate-friendly such a model is. A lesson to learn, in my opinion, is this: By all means perfect your affiliate compensation model, but keep both your own *and* your affiliates' interests in mind at all times.

Also, it is important to understand the uniqueness of the situation that led to QCP. Prior to QCP, eBay had a very high per-lead payout based on the lifetime value of a customer. However, the lifetime value can vary tremendously depending on the methods the affiliate is using and the quality of their traffic. For the vast majority of merchants (the ones who pay a percent of sales), however, this will not be an issue. So although it is good to know about it, a model like QCP wouldn't be necessary in most cases.

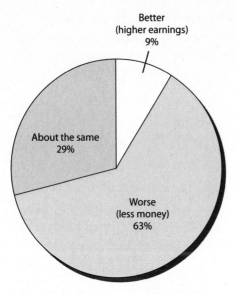

Figure 16.9 How QCP influenced affiliate earnings

Other Options

Although the previously described models require robust and not always quickly available platforms to support them, you can start doing certain things right away (while contemplating going the routes). Here are just a few ideas:

- Institute an additional bonus (to be paid on top of your regular commission) for referrals of new customers.

- If you aren't yet offering tiered commissions (increasing with the cumulative sales volume referred by affiliates), do look into it. More than likely, your competitors are already doing it. Also, remember to be both realistic and generous.

- When a potential affiliate is more familiar with display ads and is hesitant to try themselves in the capacity of your affiliate, offer them a [smaller placement fee] + [commission] option for a trial period. Renegotiate terms, based on results, once the trial period is over.

Stay open to opportunities and be flexible in your work with promising affiliates. In my personal affiliate program management experience, entrepreneurial flexibility has paid off more than once.

Thursday: Engage in Ongoing Competitive Intelligence

I talked about competitive market analysis and intelligence tools during the very first week (in Chapter 3, "Week 1: Perform Competitive Marketing Analysis"), but the focus back then was very different from what I'll cover today. Back then, you were just getting a sense of your strengths and weaknesses, trends, threats, and opportunities. Today you want to briefly recall what I talked about on Friday of week 1 and dive deeper into the amazing ocean of competitive intelligence.

Why?

Why do you want to engage in competitive intelligence in the first place? My answer is, to educate yourself and gain practical insight into how you can improve our affiliate program further. I like how Seena Sharp put it in her book, *Competitive Intelligence Advantage* (Wiley, 2009), when talking about competitive intelligence advantages. She writes this:

> *Companies often downplay intelligence, believe their competitors to have access to the same data and even the same information. Well, everyone also has access to a wide array of fruits and vegetables, yet many don't eat them or eat very few. Access does not translate into action. Your competitive advantage includes executing good analysis of the right information and then figuring out what all of this means for your company.... Those who seize the opportunity and develop an effective plan that can reasonably be accomplished have a significant competitive advantage.*

She also emphasizes that the real point of competitive intelligence is to learn and to act and to not merely gather data or develop information. All of this is crucial to keep in mind, and just as it was with your SWOTT analysis (see Chapter 3), while reviewing your discoveries, remember to look at them through a prism of *practical* application. You're doing this to pick up data that can be immediately turned into competitive advantages of your own.

How?

How exactly are you going to retrieve information on competing affiliate programs? For details, you want to go back to the "Develop Competitive Intelligence Strategy" section of Chapter 3, but to refresh your memory with a quick list, try the following methods:

Join Affiliate Programs Sign up for competing (and related) affiliate programs as an affiliate—to receive their newsletters and to keep up-to-date on what they're doing.

Friend and Follow Them Of course, you don't want to do it from your corporate Twitter and Facebook profiles, but you can follow them as an individual—to see what they're doing through social media. If they have blogs (corporate or affiliate program ones), subscribe to their RSS feeds as well. If they are active on forums, follow them there regularly too.

Become Their Customer Join their customer-oriented email list. If it requires buying something from them first, do it.

Set Up Automatic Monitoring In addition to the more than dozen of tools mentioned in Chapter 3, consider also employing such tools as Xinu Returns, PostRank, Website Grader, SEMRush, and Trackur.

Employ Traffic Measuring Tools Some examples are Alexa, Compete.com, Hitwise, and Quantcast.

Also, don't limit yourself merely to the tools and methods mentioned here. New services come up all the time. Keep your eyes and ears open to learning and your mind open to embracing new opportunities.

What?

Remember Sharp's advice about good competitive advantage? She wrote that it includes executing good analysis of the right information and then developing an effective plan to implement the necessary steps on your way to competitive superiority. Naturally, for effective work in this direction, you should clearly understand what exactly that "right information" is.

With affiliate program competitive intelligence, the task is much narrower than that which was prescribed by Christopher West and quoted in Chapter 3. You do not need to analyze "every aspect of [our] rival's activities and performance." You can focus on things directly related to affiliate marketing activities or performance. Splitting the objects of your observation into these two groups—activities and performance—you want to monitor, analyze, and draw conclusions from the following:

Affiliate Program and Related Performance

- Best-performing creatives
- Key performance indicators (for example, conversion ratio, EPC, reversal rate, AOV, and so on)
- Conversion rates of specific types of affiliates
- Wording of text links
- Best-selling products/services

Affiliate-Oriented vs. Customer-Centric Promos

It isn't unusual for merchants to mix the two; and whether this is done intentionally or accidentally, affiliates always appreciate a clear distinction between these promos.

The traditional meaning of sales promotions has always implied giving "consumers a short-term incentive to purchase a product" (*Sales Promotion Essentials* by Don E. Schultz, William A. Robinson, and Lisa Petrison [New York, 1998]). These are what I like to call *customer*-centric promotions.

Affiliate-Oriented vs. Customer-Centric Promos *(Continued)*

Affiliate-oriented promotions, on the other hand, aim at motivating affiliates (generally, through immediate extrinsic motivators) to sell a product/service.

Although it is extremely important to keep affiliates updated on the sales promotions (or customer-centric campaigns) that they are running, advertisers must word their newsletters in a way that does not suggest mistaking affiliates for customers. On numerous occasions I have heard affiliates complain that immediately upon joining a merchant's affiliate program, they also got added to the merchant's customer mailing list.

By all means, keep your affiliates informed about the hottest offers to market, but don't forget that you're talking to affiliates. Don't just copy and paste (or forward) your customer-centric email to them. Craft one that's explicitly geared to affiliates and one that helps them succeed with selling what sells well and doing marketing in a way that motivates the customer to purchase.

Affiliate Program Activities

- Customer-centric promos and coupons
- Commission structure changes
- Bonuses and tiered commission increases
- Affiliate-oriented promos
- New partnerships
- New tools
- Any program enhancements

Walmart's Exemplary Advance Affiliate Equipping

Year after year, affiliates have to deal with the lack of advanced notice from merchants on upcoming promos and important sales-related activity. Merchants don't equip affiliates with the necessary tools and information for marketing merchants effectively. The situation is truly paradoxical. You would think it is in every merchant's best interests to equip their affiliates (be it with data, coupon codes, new creatives, sales notices, or anything else) well in advance so that they have enough time to plan for marketing the merchant better.

However, time and again you see merchants notifying affiliates of sales and promos (which often last between two to five days) one or two days into the promo. Now, I understand that most merchants do not want affiliates to start promoting their deals and promos in advance (because people will simply not buy until the date the promo/sale starts). However, giving your affiliates at least a few hours (preferably, 24 hours) of *advanced notice* is a must—if, of course, you care about them marketing your deals—especially during busy shopping seasons.

Continues

Walmart's Exemplary Advance Affiliate Equipping *(Continued)*

I would like to give Walmart credit for what it did for its affiliates in the fourth quarter of 2010. On November 5, Walmart announced a Holiday Campaign Calendar—a tool to help affiliates "keep organized and up-to-date" on all of Walmart's holiday campaigns in November and December 2010. The merchant's affiliate newsletter continued explaining that from this campaign calendar affiliates would see all the campaigns on the site, see when they would receive banners, see key shipping dates, and more. Here you can see how the December calendar looked.

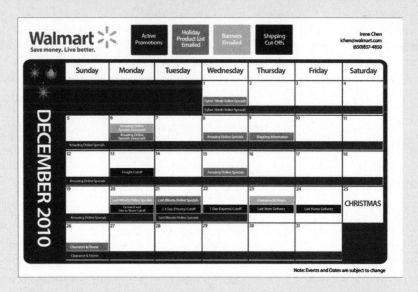

This was definitely a great strategy that other merchants and affiliate program managers should borrow and use—not only during holiday shopping seasons but over the entire calendar year. No one knows your product and target niche better than you do. You know what sells best during what times. So, let affiliates know about it too, and the earlier, the better.

Again, do not limit yourself *just* to the things I've listed here; constantly widen your investigation scope. Your goal is to be more competitive than they are. This requires aggressive and diligent ongoing competitive intelligence. It isn't hard to do if you know what you're after, why you're doing it, and how to handle it effectively. Now that you do, get going with it, and you'll soon learn that it's actually quite a bit of fun.

Friday: Analyze Progress and Stay Informed

There are two levels on which you want to analyze progress when it comes to your affiliate program: its immediate context and its broader industry-wide level. It is equally important to stay on top of things on both levels, and today you'll see how.

Monitor Affiliate Program Performance

I recommend instituting a schedule of regular reporting between the affiliate program manager and the merchant, regardless of whether the program's manager works within the company or has been hired on an outsourced basis. My experience shows that weekly meetings/calls work best for everyone. The merchant is then constantly in the loop on what's happening in their program, what works and what doesn't, what problems require resolutions, and what opportunities remain untapped.

During your weekly reviews of the affiliate program's activity, ask your affiliate manager to report on the following:

- Hits (or clicks)—how many times the affiliate ad was clicked during any given time period
- Sales (number)—how many sales have been referred by your affiliates (if you're paying for leads, have them report on the number of qualified leads; if it's both leads and sales that you remunerate, review both)
- Sales ($ volume)—monetary volume of sales driven in
- Conversion ratio—percentage of click-throughs that converted into sales or leads
- Commissions—total amount paid in commissions over any given period of time
- Active affiliates—the number of active affiliates in the program
- Recruited affiliates—both the number and any important highlights (superaffiliate, content sites especially strong in your niche, and so on)

Since some affiliate platforms report on these, some merchants also like to see such metrics as impressions (or how many times affiliates showed your ad) included in affiliate program performance reports. I wouldn't focus too much on this metric; it is frequently skewed because many affiliates mask their links, so the true number of impressions is almost never correctly reported.

Reusing the previous list of things to report, have your affiliate program manager report not only on a shorter time period (for example, a week) but also on a longer one (for example, month-to-date, quarter-to-date, or even year-to-date) to get a better perspective on where you are and where you're heading.

In addition to the previous items, analyze everything else I have talked about: the affiliate program's key performance indicators, how successful your creatives and landing pages are, what works for your competitors, what threats and opportunities there are, and where you are in the achievement of your short- and long-term goals. Treat your affiliate program as a serious marketing campaign that requires your ongoing attention. Only *then* will it yield fruit.

Be on Top of Industry Trends and Developments

On February 17, 2010, Drs. Foster and Smith terminated their relationship with all Virginia affiliates. The notification received by affiliates read that the relationship was terminated "due to business reasons connected to the pending bill SB 660" (the so-called "Amazon Bill" which was proposed to levy taxes on online transactions for out-of-state web retailers if the consumer was referred to them by a Virginia-based affiliate). Five days later they shut their affiliate program down completely in fear of multiple states passing tax laws, which would oblige merchants to collect additional tax on sales driven in by affiliates from specific states. With this step, Drs. Foster and Smith have written themselves into the history of affiliate marketing as the first major brand affiliate program to shut down entirely because of such a reason. Virginia never passed that bill SB 660. Neither have Maryland, Connecticut, New Mexico, and a number of other states that were also considering it.

Yes, there are states (for example, New York, North Carolina, and Rhode Island) that collect such a tax (once affiliate-referred sales exceed a certain threshold), but together with this, there are tools provided both by affiliate platforms (Figure 16.10) and external vendors (Figure 16.11) that merchants can use to effectively take care of this.

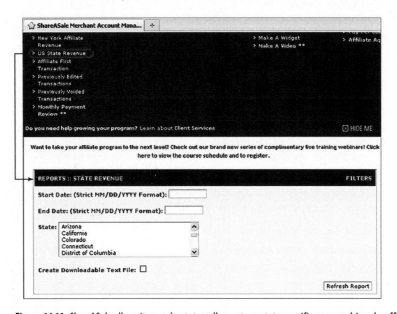

Figure 16.10 ShareASale allows its merchants to pull reports on state-specific revenue driven by affiliate traffic.

The previous example, however, illustrates a point much bigger that one concrete case of hasty affiliate program closure. From 2008 through 2010, I have seen such merchants as Amazon and Overstock either remove state-specific affiliates from their programs or announce their plans to do so as soon as a new state jumped on the affiliate nexus bandwagon. Following these announcements, and Drs. Foster and Smith's example, some of the smaller merchants would likewise remove state-specific affiliates from their programs. However, in many cases, Overstock and Amazon would make these strategic steps (especially with announcements of potential removals) in attempts to influence state governments, not because of any tangible losses already incurred. To make *educated* decisions on such important issues, you as an affiliate program manager must stay on top the current industry's news and developments.

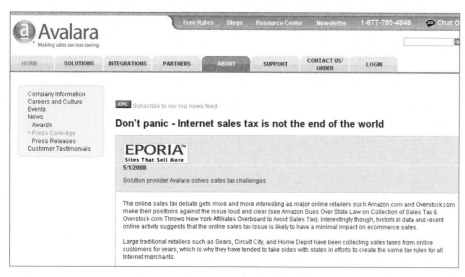

Figure 16.11 Avalara helps merchants automate online tax collection and reporting.

Make it your professional goal to always stay informed on everything related to the affiliate marketing industry. At the very basic level, it will ensure that you don't miss anything important (be it new tax legislation or a cool tool to enhance your affiliate program). However, aim beyond the basics, and do everything you can to perfect your expertise to the level higher than that of the other guy.

Here are just a few ways to stay on top of things:

- Attend digital marketing conferences.
- Follow the industry's thought leaders.
- Educate yourself through books, podcasts, webinars, and so on.
- Follow industry associations.
- Read (and participate in) forums.
- Follow top blogs (don't limit yourself to just affiliate marketing blogs, but monitor other digital marketing ones, especially from AdAge's Power 150 list, because it's all interwoven).
- Monitor trends.
- Subscribe to the industry's leading print publications.

Unlike more static industries, affiliate marketing—just like any branch of digital marketing, which is all closely tied to the technological progress—requires an *ongoing* education. You can't just read a book and know everything you have to know. Good education is never an event but a lifelong process. Therefore, continuous education is your key to success. With this in mind, make a concrete goal, and set aside at least half an hour every day to continue self-educating even after you're finished reading this book. As the famous American philosopher, psychologist, and educational reformer John Dewey put it, "Education is a social process. Education is growth. Education is not a preparation for life; education is life itself." I couldn't have said it better myself.

Deadliest Mistakes
to Avoid

Time flies—you have already come to the home-stretch of the journey called Affiliate Program Management: An Hour a Day. *In the concluding two chapters, I will provide you with two important compilations to wrap up things: the mistakes frequently committed while running affiliate programs and affiliate program promotion ideas.*

In this chapter, I will outline 40 mistakes you want to avoid while managing your affiliate program. Although what follows by no means represents a complete list of mistakes one may commit, my choice of the number has a meaning. In biblical symbolism, 40 is generally emblematic of a period of trial followed by blessings. Keeping this beautiful picture in mind, let's go through these mistakes now—with the goal of avoiding them later and reaping good fruit as a result.

17

Chapter Contents

Mistakes, Errors, and Lessons to Learn

Comedian Sam Levenson is known for saying that one must learn from the mistakes of others because we simply can't possibly live long enough to make them all ourselves, as quoted in *The Truth about Thriving in Change,* by William S. Kane (FT Press, 2008). In the context of affiliate program management, this statement would have to be slightly reworded. I'd say that you must learn from the mistakes of others precisely because you can make them all yourself, burying your affiliate program in the process.

Now, don't get me wrong. It is OK to commit errors, and I have certainly made a fair share of them myself on my route toward becoming an award-winning affiliate program manager. However, it is important to recognize the difference between an error and a mistake. Per Orlando A. Battista's definition, "an error doesn't become a mistake until you refuse to correct it," as quoted by Paul Resnik in *Everything You Need to Know to Manage Your Own Small Business* (Wiley, 1998). Yes, it is *that* simple. Just like in a school test, you may commit an error while working on it, but when you're double-checking it, you should correct it. Otherwise, it will turn into a mistake that will take points off your final grade. It is exactly the same in the affiliate program. It is best to avoid errors altogether, but if you have committed one, you want to take care of it fast. I like the advice Chris Brogan gives in this regard. In *Trust Agents* (Wiley, 2010), he wrote about a lesson he learned during his brief work at a restaurant:

> *When a customer complains about something, follow the three A's: Acknowledge, Apologize, Act.*

The same applies to affiliate program management. But to help you avoid some of the most frequent, and altogether most deadly, mistakes, I'm writing this chapter.

I'll split all mistakes into two groups: those committed by merchants and those made by affiliate program managers. Altogether I'll cover 40 common mistakes to avoid while running an affiliate program. These are by no means the only ones, but they are some of the deadliest ones—those that you really do not want to make.

As Otto von Bismarck put it, "Any fool can profit from his own mistakes. The wise man profits from those of others," as quoted by Anthony St. Peter in *The Greatest Quotations of All-Time* (Xlibris Corp., 2010).

15 Mistakes Committed by Merchants

A merchant is someone who runs and manages a website that has an affiliate program. Some of the following mistakes may also be at times committed by affiliate program managers, but by and large, they are made by merchants. Sometimes it happens because merchants have a limited understanding of the importance that the affiliate channel really has, while in other cases, it occurs because merchants do not fully comprehend the consequences that some of their actions (or lack thereof) may have on their affiliate program.

For obvious reasons, in what follows I will not be calling out any merchants by name, and wherever examples of real mistakes are provided, I'll omit the merchant names.

Mistake 1: Leaky Websites

Leaks are external links within your website that lead to sites that do *not* credit your affiliates for the work they perform. They come in all sorts of shapes and forms, but the essence is always the same—the merchant benefits from them, while the affiliates who refer traffic to the merchant do not.

Some of the most common types of leaks are as follows:

Telephone Number/Live Chat You are making it possible or even encouraging the end user to place their order by phone or via an instant chat system, bypassing affiliate tracking.

AdSense Units You are "monetizing" the traffic that is being sent to you by affiliates, but affiliates do not get any compensation for it (because the only one Google is paying in this case is you).

Affiliate Links/Amazon Widgets Although it may seem obvious to some, there are merchants that do not see how having these on their sites hurts their affiliate program. Reason? It's the same as for AdSense units!

Links to "Network" Stores/Sites If you have a "family" of web stores and are interlinking them (see Figure 17.1), make sure your affiliate platform tracks transactions across all of these stores—so if an affiliate refers a customer to one online store of yours but the shopper makes a purchase from another one you've linked to, the affiliate still gets compensated.

Figure 17.1 Kmart's network of stores is a great example of several online storefronts interlinked.

Links to Other Merchants I understand the benefit of link exchanges, banner swaps, and other types of link partnerships, but look at things through your affiliates' eyes: If the traffic they refer can go to another merchant that does not compensate them for their work, it's a leak.

If you absolutely must have some of these leaks, make sure they are invisible to affiliate-referred traffic.

Mistake 2: "Autopilot" Approach to Affiliate Program

I covered this problem extensively in Chapter 5, "Week 3: Evaluate Program Management Options." Flee from "automatically steering" your affiliate program. It cannot be run on autopilot or cruise control. It *must* be managed. Otherwise, it may become a gateway to all sorts of unwanted "marketing" activity, which will not only hinder the healthy growth of your affiliate marketing channel but also cannibalize the other channels of digital marketing that you are involved in (see Chapter 15, "Week 1: Study and Learn to Deal with Parasitism and Problematic Affiliates," for details).

Mistake 3: Unclear or Absent Program TOS

Your program's terms of service (TOS) agreement is one of the best defensive mechanisms to deal with "predators" (more in Chapter 5). Make sure you have a good one in place. Refer to Chapter 9, "Week 3: Research and Develop Program Policies," which was devoted to developing an affiliate program agreement.

Mistake 4: Nonexistent PPC Policy

Although paid search rules and restrictions that merchants want their affiliates to abide by are an integral part of the terms of service agreement, it isn't unusual for a merchant to have the agreement in place but to not be clear on what's permitted and what's forbidden for PPC affiliates to do while aboard their program. With this thought in mind, I'm singling this one out as a mistake of its own. It is one of the most important parts of your agreement. Don't leave it out!

Mistake 5: Embarrassing Commission Rates

With larger etailers, it isn't unusual to see commission rates ranging from 1 percent to 4 percent. Following them by example, some smaller merchants set their commission rates significantly lower than they could in reality afford. For help in deciding on the optimum commission/payout rates, see Chapter 6, "Week 4: Finalize Payment Models and Cookie Life." Do not skimp on how much commission you pay your salespeople. With the larger and more well-known brands whose affiliates enjoy conversion rates as beautiful as 10 percent or even 20 percent, lower commission rates still attract affiliates. The strategy of low commission/payout rates may not necessarily be the best idea, though.

Mistake 6: Short Cookie Life

Again, looking at some of the larger brands (see Table 17.1), some merchants think one to three days is enough of a cookie life for an affiliate program.

5 hours or less	12–24 hours	3 days
Sephora.com (4 hrs)	Nordstrom.com (12 hrs)	Apple iTunes
Toys R Us, Babies R Us	Enterprise.com (23 hrs)	Champs Sports
eToys.com	Chase.com (23 hrs)	Dell
Miles Kimball Company	Amazon (24 hrs)	ESPN Shop
ShopNBC.com		Foot Locker
		Walmart

Note: Data collected on December 20, 2010.

As shown in Chapter 6, the data on end-user cookie retention rates, as well as distribution of affiliate-referred orders by return days, speaks in favor of building affiliate-friendly cookie duration terms by setting cookie life at 90 days or more.

Mistake 7: Insisting on Home Page Links

Links on the affiliate's home page may or may not get you some good traffic. If/when an affiliate suggests a different page within their website for your links, carefully consider their reasoning. Their home page may not always be a good place for your ad to show. Your goal is to have your links on web pages with intense and highly targeted traffic. At times, this may mean pages other than the home page.

Mistake 8: Insisting on Promotion of Best Sellers

Inform your affiliates of your best sellers, and create respective banners, text links, or other ways for them to feature these best sellers. However, do not insist that they promote them. Some affiliates may not want to focus on the best sellers, because other affiliates are already pushing them actively. Some affiliates would rather go with the other items you sell, and that is absolutely fine. Affiliates often know best what fits their websites. Offer your help, but do it gently.

Mistake 9: Commission Drops

A smart affiliate program manager will warn a merchant not to do this, but some merchants will still do it. Here is an example of an email text one merchant sent to their affiliates:

> As a _valued_ [Merchant Name] affiliate partner, I wanted to let you know that we are currently working to make our program, and our partner-ships, _as successful as possible_. In order to continue _to support the success of our current partnership_ we are unable to continue to offer you a flat 4 percent commission on all goods. Starting at the end of February, our new offer will be lowered to 1.5 percent on all goods. [underlining mine]

Speaking of how much you value your affiliates and want to support the success of your partnership while doing exactly the opposite is paradoxical and illogical. In fact, it is destructive to your relationship/partnership (Figure 17.2). Think and calculate your expenses thoroughly *before* you launch the program, and not after it has picked up, and you're trying to increase your profit margin at the expense of your "valued affiliate partners." Unless, of course, you want them to turn around and switch their links to your competitors.

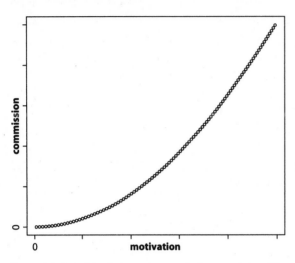

Figure 17.2 Commission/payout amounts are in direct correlation with affiliates motivation to work for you.

Mistake 10: Lack of Advanced Notifications

Whether it is seasonal promotions, coupons, or any other announcements and/or enhancements to your affiliate program, give your affiliates enough time to prepare for the changes. At the time you become aware of these, give your affiliates the courtesy of also letting them know. With promotions, send out one advanced announcement describing it about 10 days before the promo. Then, send another one a few days before the promo begins. Not all affiliates can set dates in their databases. Notify them duly.

Mistake 11: Late Payments

No excuses. "We can't pay you until they pay us" is never an excuse to withhold payment from your affiliates. This always reminds me of the way salaries were, and still are, paid in the former Soviet Union: People work for months without pay, not getting their January paycheck until July. No "Soviet Union excuses" in affiliate marketing, please!

Mistake 12: Changes That Affect Affiliate Links

If you delete a product from your website, either keep the affiliate thumbnail image on your server or have it replaced with a default "Sold Out" image. This way, the websites of your data feed affiliates will not have "broken images" until they update the data feed. The same advice applies to all other changes within the merchant website that may affect affiliate websites. Things that may seem small to the merchant (such as changing the size of your thumbnail images from 120×120 to 100×100 or rounding up the prices from .95 to .00) will cause a major headache for your affiliates. If you persistently make changes that affect thousands of their links and fail to notify them of these changes in advance, they will drop your program sooner than later. If things like these are not under your control as an affiliate manager, let your employer read this paragraph, stressing the importance of the point in question.

Mistake 13: Tampering with Tracking Code

Everyone in your company who has access to the pages that contain the tracking components of your affiliate program must be instructed on the importance of these pieces of code. More than once I have seen web designers and SEO folks delete or mess up the affiliate tracking pixels on the merchant side. This immediately resulted in untracked transactions and major problems with the affiliate program. Never let anyone tamper with your affiliate program's tracking code.

Mistake 14: Unrealistic Goals for Commission Increases

Figure 17.3 shows a "performance incentive" plan one affiliate program put in place.

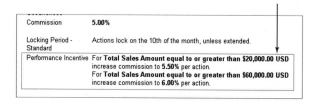

Figure 17.3 Example of a less-than-motivating tiered commission structure

By my estimates, their AOV must be around $650. This means that to qualify for 0.5 percent of the commission increase, an affiliate would have to generate close to 31 orders (for a fairly expensive product) within one month. To get a 1 percent commission increase (from 5 percent to 6 percent), you would have to generate over 92 orders over one-month's period. That's a challenging task, to put it mildly. It's not entirely unrealistic, but I wouldn't call such a performance incentive motivating, especially for beginning affiliates. You want to be setting reachable goals—be realistic and encouraging.

Mistake 15: Asking for Something You Cannot Return

One of the ideas that may work wonderfully for the development of your affiliate program is asking a noncompeting merchant from a related vertical to join your affiliate program and place the link on their "thank you" page. If you are selling chewing gum, it could be a dental care merchant; if you are selling sports equipment, it may be a sports shoes merchant; and so on. However, prior to asking another merchant for something like this, put yourself into their shoes. Would you agree to a proposal like this? If so, under what terms? If you are willing to join *their* affiliate program and put their link on your "thank you" page, then word your proposal respectively. Show them the benefits they will get from it, quoting the average number of daily/monthly sales you get. Then explain that you are willing to do this if they also do this for you in return. If handled properly from the start, this recruitment method could be very beneficial for both parties.

25 Affiliate Program Management Mistakes

An affiliate program manager is someone who manages the merchant's affiliate program. Regardless of whether they are based in-house or outsourced, the mistakes I'll talk about are committed by both. Some are more deadly than others, but all are good to avoid. I will start the numbering at 16—to continue the count started in the previous section.

Mistake 16: Managing Affiliates

As mentioned numerous times throughout the book, the job of affiliate manager is actually not to manage affiliates. In fact, the very term *affiliate manager* frequently leads to having managers who treat affiliates like employees and attempt to manage them, when, in reality, their job is to manage the affiliate program. It has been said that a perfect job is one that gives you the freedom to live your life the way you want to live it. Keep in mind that affiliates are in this business exactly because of their appreciation of the freedom this work gives them. Flee from employee–worker associations in your emails and newsletters. Treat your affiliates like *business partners*. Respect their freedom, and honor their devotion to your affiliate program, and they will appreciate it in return. Refer also to Chapter 5, "Week 3: Evaluate Program Management Options," Chapter 13, "Week 3: Program Management," and Chapter 14, "Week 4: Affiliate Motivation," to read how exactly to work with your affiliates.

Mistake 17: Assuming You Are Smarter Than Affiliates

One of my favorite definitions of affiliate marketing belongs to Chris Sanderson of AMWSO. He says that affiliate marketing is "the art of doing a merchant's marketing better than they can and profiting from it." It is a bad mistake to presuppose that just because you're at the helm of an affiliate program, you're smarter than those who drive sales through it. In the vast majority of cases, affiliate managers will have a lot to learn from their affiliates, especially the more successful of them.

Mistake 18: Assuming All Affiliates Are Prone to Fraud

Having heard and read about rogue affiliates, some managers start assuming that all jumps in traffic and sales should be immediately tied to fraudulent or prohibited affiliate activity. This is one deadly mistake.

Here is a communication string between an affiliate manager and an affiliate that occurred after the latter started driving sales to the former:

> *Manager: I wanted to let you know that we strictly prohibit direct linking to our website from search engines. Please update any campaigns or otherwise we will not be able to continue working with you.*
>
> *Affiliate: We are not doing any direct linking to [merchant URL here]. What makes you think we are?*
>
> *Manager: Great! We didn't. We just saw your sales pick-up and wanted to ensure you knew our keyword policy.*

The assumption was clear from the start. There was also a threat to discontinue the relationship. Once the manager received the affiliate's reply, they didn't apologize and, actually, sounded plain stupid. Do not let this happen to you. Remember Oscar Wilde's words, "When you assume, you make an *ass* out of *u* and *me*."

Mistake 19: Terminating Inactive Affiliates

This is actually one of the biggest mistakes an affiliate program manager can make (and it isn't unusual for an affiliate network to *encourage* merchants to do this). Inactive affiliates do not hurt you in any way. Ask yourself, *why* they are not active and what have *you* done to motivate them to become active with your program?

Some affiliate managers don't terminate affiliates but send out what I call get-active-or-we'll-remove-you-from-the-program messages. Belief in motivation by threat stems from the misunderstanding that you are there to manage affiliates (and not the program). One manager once wrote to an affiliate to "opt into the lower-commission offer immediately, or we will have to remove you from the program." Another one emailed inactive affiliates this: "If your site has not generate a sale by [date here], you may be removed from the [merchant] affiliate program." Both were top-brand online retailers. Needless to say, the results were very different from what those managers may have expected—one affiliate removed herself from the program right away, switching the links to their competitor, while another one complained about this in public. As written earlier (see Chapter 14), threats are actually *counter*productive and always demotivating.

Mistake 20: Practicing a "One-Size-Fits-All" Approach

Repeatedly throughout this book—and especially when discussing the contingency theory—I have written about taking an individualized approach to affiliates. Yes, it is hard to handle, but it is worth every moment, and you want to do your best to approach each affiliate, keeping their unique situation in mind.

Mistake 21: Believing Money Is the Best Incentive

Money is not the best incentive, and people are more strongly motivated by interesting work, challenge, and increasing responsibility. Motivate by presenting opportunities, and reread Chapter 14 every once in a while.

Mistake 22: Being Impersonal

Get personal with your affiliates. Find out their names, and make sure they know yours. Find out when their birthdays are. These would be great days to present them with gifts, commission increases, bonuses, or something of the kind. Do not alienate yourself from them by presenting yourself as an XYZ.com's Affiliate Program Management Team (a mistake too many managers commit). It will not give you the desired respect and trust. The sequence is always in reverse: First you want to gain trust—not through impersonal presentation but by work. Respect and mutual amiability will then naturally follow.

Mistake 23: Belated Approvals

If membership to your program is available by manual approval only (which I highly recommend), please remember that you must look through those affiliate websites and either qualify or disqualify them from joining your affiliate program. Do not delay the approval decision of any affiliate application for longer than 3 business days; and by all means, aim at reviewing all outstanding applications within 24 hours.

Mistake 24: Untargeted Recruitment Emails

If you are contacting a particular website with a proposal to join your affiliate program and your recruitment email is geared toward websites in a specific vertical, filter your list of targets carefully before emailing that proposal. Otherwise, you may end up sending affiliate recruitment emails for a makeup merchant to websites that specialize exclusively in motor oil sales. Needless to say, you may not be treated seriously even if that particular affiliate happens to have a skin care website as well.

Mistake 25: Use of Email Addresses Based on Free Servers

Some affiliate managers think about getting an email address from a provider like Hotmail, Yahoo!, Gmail, or another free server. Some may think that it's safer for recruitment; others may just want a separate email account for affiliate program management. Whatever your reasons may be, it is a *bad idea*. First, affiliates will not take you seriously if you have a free email address. Russians say, "When you meet a man, you judge him by his clothes; when you leave, you judge him by his heart." Your email address is the "clothing" that they will look at first. Do not let it obstruct their way of knowing your heart with regard to affiliate marketing. Second, some spam filters will simply block your newsletters and promos if they have a combination of a free email and a subject that looks suspicious. As mentioned earlier, if at all possible, get an @CompanyName.com email address. If you have to start a separate website and then have an @CompanyNameAffiliates.com address, that is fine too. These look much more professional and trustworthy. If you are an OPM, a ClientName@OPMcompany.com email would be another way of doing it.

Mistake 26: Not Responding to Affiliate Emails and Questions

Years ago a merchant that approached me with a proposal to manage their affiliate program made it explicit from the start that he would fine me $10 for every unanswered affiliate query. This may seem rigid, but all affiliates would agree that it is just. The affiliate manager is there to provide *full* support for their affiliate program. Affiliates send you their questions and expect a response. They turn to you for help. Do not turn away from them, or the next thing you'll see is them turning away from your affiliate program. Make it a rule to answer any affiliate email (or query that comes in any other way) within 24 or 48 hours.

Mistake 27: Failing to Maintain an Ongoing Communication Channel

Besides responses to ongoing support questions, you want to communicate with affiliates through circulars and follow-up calls regularly and on different levels. The most frequently preferred channel of communication is email, followed by the affiliate program's blog. Phone is one of the least preferred ways affiliates want to be contacted. Read more about methods of communication and frequency in Chapter 12, "Week 2: Plan Your Affiliate Communication."

Mistake 28: Informing Affiliates of the Obvious

One of the biggest challenges of affiliate management is that you, as the affiliate manager, have to market to the marketers. Be careful and selective with what you say and when you say it. Do not let your emails state the obvious. If your company makes its best sales during the fourth quarter (Q4) season, remember that most everyone else's do, too. If you want to communicate that to your affiliates, communicate it to them differently. Quote the statistics: "During November and December our company makes 54 percent of the year's revenue." This would sound much better than "Now is the time to push us, because it's our best sales time." Also, if they hear these Q4 stats from you a few months in advance, it is much better than informing them of this in the beginning of November. Calls like "Join us today, because now is the best sales time for us" may also not work as effectively as you want. Even if they join you in October to November, there is little chance of them sending you considerable sales within a month or two of signing up (unless they already have well-optimized sites for your product sitting on the shelf waiting for you—which is highly unlikely).

Mistake 29: Ignoring Affiliate Suggestions

Although the previous point relates to your communication with affiliates, this one has to do with reacting to their suggestions. Let your affiliate program be a two-way street: Don't just communicate to them but also respond to their proposals. Every suggestion you receive from an affiliate should be treated seriously and replied to as such. Some affiliate managers take offense when affiliates point out errors or suggest that something should be done differently. Do not ignore *constructive* criticism. With their help, you will be able to transform your program into the best affiliate program in your industry. I've seen this happen more than once. Heed what they say, and try to accommodate every reasonable proposition. Not every single proposition will be sound and/ or feasible, but many will be. Do not repeat the mistakes of most affiliate networks, which, unfortunately, tend to ignore affiliate feedback. Be different! Be there for them, and it will eventually reflect in the sales they send you.

Mistake 30: Low-Quality Answers to Questions

When you are asked a specific question, give a specific answer. If you do not know the answer, dig into it, find out the answer, and then reply to your affiliate. It is a widely known fact that the best way to learn something is to teach someone else about it. When you receive questions you do not know the answers to, celebrate! They are *your* opportunities to grow.

You may also devote part of your monthly newsletter to educating your affiliates on more advanced issues. These may include working with data feeds, working with parasites, optimizing your CTR in PPC bidding, and many other topics. You can fish them right out of the questions you get from your affiliates. Including such a section in your regular newsletter will make it an interesting read, not only for "newbie" affiliates but also for the more advanced players of the affiliate game. It is obvious that most of the more advanced questions will require more than one paragraph, but do not overload your newsletter. Use the *educating paragraph* to give a brief introduction into the matter, as well as the benefits of this knowledge to affiliates, and then give a link to an article on it. It is best that you compile the article yourself, because it will help build you up in the eyes of the affiliates. If you are not able to write a full article on the question, you can always put together a creative, intriguing introduction, followed up by the major questions on the topic and the external hyperlinks to web pages that give the respective answers.

Mistake 31: Asking Affiliates How They Can Do Better

Do not *ask them*, but propose your help working shoulder to shoulder *with them* to bring their affiliate performance to the top level. Do not promise them what is not under your control, but ensure they know that you are willing to help.

Mistake 32: Selective Helping

This is yet another mistake connected with helping your affiliates. Some merchants and affiliate managers practice selective helping—communicating more willingly with their superaffiliates and not as much with the "newbies." This is a serious error. I have had a "newbie" turn into the second best-performing affiliate within five months of signing up! Divide your help and goodwill equally among all your affiliates, and watch yourself succeed in ways you never thought possible.

Mistake 33: Typos, Spelling Mistakes, and Code Errors

This mistake may be of two types: language mistakes (misspellings, improper grammar, incorrect URLs, and so on) and code errors. Since the first type is self-explanatory, let me elaborate on the second one in more detail here. What do I mean by code errors? If your affiliate network or your in-house software has a function of "short codes," this is *wonderful*! Short codes help you put together beautiful personalized newsletters; I myself extensively use short codes to correspond with affiliates. However, be aware of the risk they may carry. What I will say now may seem too basic for you, but trust me, errors like these discredit affiliate managers daily. Do not type these short codes unless you really know what you are doing. I always recommend cutting and pasting to avoid emails that start with "Dear [affiliate_first_name]" simply because you forgot to hit that Shift button to enter the proper {affiliate_first_name} short code. The legendary Willie Sutton wrote, "Success in any endeavor requires single-minded attention to detail and total concentration." Regardless of his vocation, I must agree.

Mistake 34: Insisting on Phoning

I discussed this when touching on the methods of contacting your affiliates in Chapter 12. In general, affiliates are very protective of their privacy and extremely defensive of their freedom. Insisting on calling them may have more of a negative effect on your relationship with them. Yes, mention your contact telephone number in every affiliate newsletter and every piece of outgoing email, but do not insist on setting up a call of any kind unless they have initiated it.

Mistake 35: Termination of Affiliate Accounts Without Notice

While reviewing your affiliates' performance statistics, you may notice that a particular affiliate is sending you many clicks but few, if any, sales. This may lead you to suspect such an affiliate of fraudulent behavior. Suspicions are fine; however, remember they are only *suspicions* unless proven to be fact. While you are looking into the clicks history, contact the affiliate directly. Talk to them. They may well be in need of your help with conversions, may feel frustrated about the situation, and may appreciate suggestions on how to improve their performance. Talk to them before you do anything.

Mistake 36: Dryness and Blandness

Cultivate creativity. Being an affiliate manager implies motivating others (I will talk more about this in Chapter 18, "Affiliate Program Promotion Ideas"). If your communication and the whole creative inventory reflects a dry, bland, and boring style, do not expect them to follow you. You are to be their source of enthusiasm and inspiration: Let this be your mission if you really want them to sell for you. Keep in mind that many affiliates get dozens of private offers on a daily basis from other affiliate programs. Some of these propositions may well be your competitors'. Make your affiliate management style stand out—through contests, commission increase offers, bonuses, large end-of-year prizes to the best performers, professionally created banners and readiness to custom-make banners of virtually any size for individual affiliates, and so on—and you will be listened to.

Mistake 37: Unkept Promises

When you promise your affiliates something, keep your word. If you have to, write everything down to remember what was promised to which affiliate and exactly when it was promised. If you do not follow your words up with actions, the automatic conclusion will be that you are an affiliate manager/program that does not keep promises. Word like this can spread like wildfire, and your reputation could go up in smoke.

Mistake 38: Ultimatums

Some affiliate program managers may word their affiliate correspondence in such a way that their email messages sound like ultimatums, containing demands (as opposed to suggestions) for activation or sales of a particular number or monetary amount. This most certainly is not a display of professionalism. In fact, it will only make you appear amateurish and desperate. Do not demand from your affiliates, say, to produce at least one sale within the next month, threatening to remove them from your affiliate program. This will *not* motivate them, but it will most certainly do you a disservice. Not only will these affiliates drop your program before you even think of analyzing their end-of-month statistics, but they will also let others know of such practices, harming both your own reputation and the reputation of your affiliate program.

Mistake 39: Showing One Affiliate's Site to Others

Never do this without getting prior approval from the affiliate whose website's URL you want share with other affiliates. Remember that affiliates compete with each other, and as in any competition, there are a lot of unethical practices involved, one of them being site copying. Unless you have received the affiliate's "go ahead" on sharing the website's information with another affiliate, do not do this.

Mistake 40: Failing to Admit Mistakes

I started with this, and I'll finish with this. Global research has found that regardless of the geographical location, the one most admired characteristic in leaders is *honesty*. I cannot overemphasize this. If there is a mistake to own up to, admit it, apologize, and act to correct it.

Affiliate Program Promotion Ideas

18

In this final chapter of the book, you will find more than two dozen practical ideas on affiliate program promotion. I have used them all and have seen some other affiliate managers build up quite successful campaigns based on these ideas. I hope you will find them helpful and be able to use them to take your affiliate program management to new heights.

Chapter Contents
Why Share Ideas?
Practical Ideas to Promote Your Program

Sharing Ideas

One of my favorite pieces of wisdom says, "If you have an apple and I have an apple and we exchange these apples, then you and I still each have one apple. But if you have an idea and I have an idea and we exchange these ideas, then each of us will have two ideas." This quote belongs to Ireland's most famous playwright and one of the world's most influential thinkers, George Bernard Shaw.

Shaw put this in the best possible way. I am a strong believer in sharing ideas. Ideas, in all their intangibility, are what move marketing. Ideas unleashed into the world change the world. The best ideas turn into *ideaviruses*—thanks to Seth Godin for a beautiful book on this called *Unleashing the Ideavirus*, (Hyperion, 2010). The good ideas turn your own work, and the work of those under your guidance, into fun. An affiliate once told me how much she appreciates the component of fun in the promotions I run for the affiliate programs I manage. She said, "If I can't have the fun, I don't want to play." Ideally, in your management work, you should strive to turn everyone's routine tasks into work that is pleasurable. Do not underestimate the power of fun. Speaking from experience, I can testify that when your affiliate management style is undergirded by original, out-of-the-box thinking, this makes life fun, and you'll be on the road to success.

How does one cultivate the idea-generating spirit? You may be reading this thinking, "This is just not me. I am not an idea generator. I have no talent for this." And you may be right. Neuroscientific concepts on brain lateralization applied to marketing tell us that most marketers are either right-brain or left-brain dominant. The right-brainers are the best fit for creative work, while the left-brainers are better at performing analytical tasks. Combinations of both in one individual are rare or even extraordinary. Now, turning to the comments of those who struggle with creativity in marketing—those left-brain marketers of the affiliate world—let me tell you: Do not despair! Learn from the ideas of others, modify them to fit your context, synergize them with your own thoughts, and then polish and tailor them to work for your specific needs. Remember the words of the wise Irish dramatist, and take it even further— take my idea, couple it with yours, and produce a third one that becomes a synergy of the two. Keep "idea breeding" regularly, and you will inevitably succeed.

My ideas are no secret. I believe in growing the affiliate marketing industry by sharing ideas—posting them Internet-wide on various message boards and forums. I've put the ideas together in this chapter for you to use. Yes, you've heard me right: Be my guest! Use them, transform them, customize them. Make your affiliates' lives fun, and the avenues of their gratefulness paved with affiliate sales will be endless.

The ideas in the following sections are not arranged in any specific order. Many of them are totally unique, while others are inspired by marketers working in industries other than affiliate marketing. Still others are modified versions of what I have seen other affiliate managers using. I hope they will help you manage your own affiliate program.

Better Base Conditions for Select Affiliates

This was one of the first ideas I had when I started managing affiliate programs: Offer better base conditions for select groups of affiliates. They could be affiliates who belong to a particular forum or an online community. Let's say the base commission of your affiliate program is 10 percent and it has the cookie life set at 90 days. Offer 12 percent instead of 10 percent, or offer 120 days of cookie life to those affiliates who sign up for your program through a specific link, through a specific online forum, or during a set period of time from the official launch date of the program. Not only can you play with the commission rate and the cookie days, but you can also offer particular monetary per-sale bonuses. These bonuses may be lifetime or time restricted. Commission and cookie life increases are always for life.

> **Note:** Taking this idea further, you can apply it to private offers you send to those affiliates you know already send traffic to your competition.

Free Domain Giveaway

Everyone loves gifts. Those affiliates who are at the beginning of their affiliate marketing career appreciate them more than anyone. Contests are motivational and productive, all at once.

Merchants are often much better equipped to come up with effective domain name ideas. Come up with a few domain names fitting your merchant's products better, and then register them. If you are having a hard time coming up with the names, ask the company's management or their marketing team for help/ideas. Domain names should be picked with a goal in mind, and your ultimate goal is to have affiliates use them for the websites that send you sales. Once you have registered these domains, announce a free domain giveaway where you will be transferring the ownership of the domains to those affiliates who have performed a particular action (for example, joining your program by a set date; putting together a comprehensive data feed–based website featuring all your products on it; or incorporating your affiliate program's banners, links, product pictures, or descriptions into the content of their website).

Depending on what your affiliate program promotes, you may choose to classify the domains you give away into different categories. For example, a cosmetics affiliate program's manager may think up and register domains fit for data feed–based sites that sell only the merchant's cosmetics, as well as domain names for content-based websites. These websites, may, for example, be devoted to articles on skin care and the like and also allow your affiliate to promote your products and/or links on the side.

 Note: Make sure you state all restrictions in the conditions of the giveaway, or you may end up having an affiliate promote your competitors' products beside yours on the domain name you have purchased!

Arithmetic Progression Bonuses

The way of remunerating your affiliates using this method is not new. You pay bonuses on every sale. The pattern of calculating bonuses, on the other hand, is one that I have never seen used by other affiliate managers. This pattern is based on an arithmetic progression. You set the common difference and then increase each new bonus by that difference. For example, if your common difference is 5 and you are willing to pay a $10 bonus with the first sale, the second sale bonus would then be $15, while the third sale bonus would be $20, and so on.

As with any "per every sale" bonus method, this one would work best for newly launched programs, as well as for programs that are in need of revitalizing.

 Note: Ensure that the conditions of such a bonus campaign clearly list the time period during which the bonuses will be paid. Also, do your math and preliminary research (you could really use those left-brain marketers here) so you do not run bankrupt as a result of the campaign.

Cobranded Version of a Good Affiliate Tool

There are plenty of useful affiliate tools, such as software applications, scripts, and the like, that make affiliate life easier, helping promote your products more efficiently. One of them has been put together by the CEO of the Fourth World Media Corporation, a talented software developer and a good friend, Richard Gaskin. The piece of software I am referring to is, of course, the world-famous WebMerge.

The idea that came to my mind in October 2005 is one of which I am particularly proud, and I will tell you the reason why shortly. I had approached Richard with an idea of making a custom version of WebMerge to fit a particular data feed. WebMerge is a wonderful universal tool, excellent for integrating most any affiliate program's data feed into the affiliate website. However, there are at least two reasons an affiliate thinks twice before ordering it from the Fourth World. First, affiliates have to do their homework before they can really utilize the software with data feeds from various merchants.

Second, the cost of the software—however modest it is—may be deemed a substantial investment by some. The idea was to make it both more affordable and more applicable. The result was the cobranded special edition of WebMerge—WebMerge RL: Russian Legacy Edition. It turned out to be more than 55 percent less expensive than the full version ($44 instead of $99), and it still allowed room for the upgrade to the full version if the affiliate felt comfortable using it with the Russian Legacy's data feed. This unique software piece is still available at www.fourthworld.com/products/webmerge/rl.html, and you are more than welcome to try it yourself.

I mentioned that I take special pride in this idea. Let me tell you why. Ten months after the launch of the WebMerge RL, the ShareASale affiliate network launched WebMerge: ShareASale Special Edition.

Segment Your Products

It is no secret that many affiliates like to "specialize," or work in particular verticals and build websites on a select number of topics. Let's say one likes children and promotes only sites related to babies, parenting, and education, for example. Another may have a few websites with good home-and-garden traffic, and this affiliate, of course, would be great for selling kitchen-, garden-, and home-related merchandise. The list could go on, but my point is the following: If the merchant whose affiliate program you promote carries an inventory that allows you to segment it by products related to various topics, set aside some time to do the segmentation. You will then be able to offer your affiliates some practical advice on how to market those specific groups of products on their websites. Such segmentation works wonderfully for merchants selling collectibles, memorabilia, books, magazines, and so on. Once you have performed the segmentation and grouping of products into topical categories, project the results of your research to the affiliates, telling them how they can use this information. Such homework of yours will tell your affiliates you really care. When they see you treat them with understanding and show them your sincere desire for their success, they will respond accordingly.

Learn to Celebrate

Celebrate everything with your affiliates. Put together a calendar of dates important to the company that is running an affiliate program, and celebrate these dates with your affiliates. Good examples of such dates would be the date when the company was established (call it "Our Company's Birthday"), the date when the affiliate program was started (you may call it "Affiliate Program's Birthday"), or the date when a particular long-term promotion or bonus type was introduced into the life of your affiliates.

If you sell ink, dig into the history, and you will find out that ink was developed by the Chinese some 5,000 years ago. They used it for blackening the raised surfaces of pictures and texts they carved in stone. You could use such a beautiful picture to precede your next promotion campaign and then you could use it to elaborate on the next 5,000. As an example, 5,000 could be used to translate into 100 bonuses of $50 each to add up into the total prize fund of $5,000. You could give these bonuses for every batch of $500 in sales that an affiliate sends you. Announce it to your affiliates and then sweeten the deal by clarifying that this promo is nonexclusive of all or any other promos run by your program! The number of $50 checks to be given away is exactly 100, and this promotion campaign is not limited by time (in other words, it is to be run until the last check is given out). In addition, the number of bonuses to be given out per affiliate is also unlimited. The number of $50 checks an affiliate may receive is tied only to the number of $500 batches of sales they send to you. This has been tried and proven effective. Use it confidently. If your number isn't as large as 5,000 and you have to base your campaign on the number 154—that is fine, too. Staying with the ink affiliate program example, you can give out 154 ink cartridges to all affiliates who show you a 154 percent sales growth within the next month. The numbers do not have to be round for you to use them effectively. Any anniversary is just a reason for you to make the life of your affiliates more fun. Motivate them to do more for your affiliate program in a fun way, and they will appreciate it.

If you are an outsourced affiliate manager, running several affiliate programs and posting around various affiliate forums, celebrate every round number of posts reached by you on any given forum. Let's say you've reached your 500th post. Run a cross-program promotion with a common prize fund of $500 (see the one described in "Cross-Program Promotions").

Note: If you run your ideas by your merchants first, you will be surprised at how many of them will be supportive (both emotionally and financially) of such promos. If you are an outsourced program manager, be prepared that sometimes you will have to invest your own funds into campaigns like the ones quoted under this idea. However, do remember to run the idea by the merchant first. It may save you a buck or two that you will be able to invest into affiliate recruitment, for example.

Run "Happy Weeks"

The Happy Weeks idea came to me while thinking about the Happy Meal concept pioneered by the McDonald's Corporation in 1979. For more than 30 years the idea has been working well for its developers. Renowned motivational speaker Warren Greshes—the author of a premier audio/video program *Supercharged Selling: The Power to Be the Best*—while speaking at a convention, once referred to the Happy Meal concept by stating this:

> *Kids wanted the toy.... Kids wanted the box. You know why? Because kids don't buy food. They buy fun. They figure they can get food anywhere.*

What is your Happy Meal? What is it that you're willing to do for all your customers, your clients, your prospects that no one else is willing to do? How are you differentiating yourself from the competition?

You know my stand on the component of fun in marketing. So it occurred to me one day that since none of us really ever fully grows up, we could all use a little extra happiness every week, and my affiliates are no exception. I then started running Happy Weeks for all of the affiliate programs I managed. Each Happy Week was meant to be different, to be joyous, and to incorporate fresh ideas of affiliate motivation. It was a challenging task, but it definitely paid off. Since the idea of Happy Weeks is more of a concept, a promotional framework, or even a philosophy, if you will, it may encompass any or all of the ideas in this chapter.

Classic "Happy Week" Idea

This idea will probably work best for the very first Happy Week you run for your affiliate program—each day of the working week (read: Monday through Friday) should be attached to one letter in the word *happy*. Then let the focus of each day correspond to the letter that is attached to it. Here is how I did it for an affordable jewelry affiliate program:

Monday: "H" for Homework The following question was asked: Did you know that there is a characteristic by which cubic zirconia (CZ) simulated diamonds actually prevail over natural diamonds? Which one is it? Prizes were given away. The correct answer was that CZ contains more fire (or flashes of rainbow colors) than natural diamonds.

Tuesday: "A" for Ambition A Merriam-Webster dictionary definition of *ambition* was quoted: "an ardent desire for...," "a desire to achieve a particular end." Screenshots of affiliate statistics were presented. They testified to a great conversion of the affiliate program for a particular type of affiliate—coupon sites. Affiliates (especially the coupon ones) were motivated to work more closely with the program.

Wednesday: "P" for Prize Generate 5 sales within the next 24 hours, and I will credit your affiliate account $50! The program was still very new, and we had to run promos like this to motivate affiliates to be more aggressive.

Thursday: "P" for Prize Again As expected, only one affiliate came close to the previous goal but not close enough to reach it. So, we simplified the requirements, calling for 4 sales within 24 hours for the same prize of $50.

Friday: "Y" for Your Chance The following call for action was posted on Friday morning: "Put up our links and send $150+ in sales by the end of the weekend, and I will credit your affiliate account a $20 bonus on top of your regular commission."

In another affiliate program's Happy Week promo, I used the first "P" for *Potential*, while the second one was for *Proliferated Commission*. On the Potential day, we asked affiliates to look through our inventory and guess what product category had the best-selling potential. On the second "P" day, we promised them that whoever sent in two or more sales within the following 24 hours would get a twofold commission increase for the rest of the month. It was posted on the 15th of the month, so the offer was quite attractive.

An A-B-C-D-E Idea

The very first Happy Week I ran for RussianLegacy.com—an online gift shop I founded and owned between 2001 and 2006—had each day of the workweek follow a letter of the Latin alphabet. Each letter of the alphabet attached to the day of the week and stood for the way that particular day was named. For example:

Monday: "A" for Adjustment(s) Day I asked affiliates for their feedback on our affiliate program, calling on them for advice on adjustments that would help make the program better.

Tuesday: "B" for Bonus Day I promised each affiliate a $20 bonus on all $150+ sales generated during that day. Each time the bonus was awarded, I provided affiliates with the screenshots of those affiliate transactions. Nothing inspires better than picturesque testimonials.

Wednesday: "C" for Coupon Day I announced the Coupon of the Week (its expiration date was set exactly a week after the date it was posted), and made it a substantial discount coupon on an expensive category of items on which I had a nice profit margin.

Thursday: "D" for Domain Day I announced two domain names to be given away: SovietGift.com and RussianGiftBasket.com. These domains had to be used for quality data feed–based websites, but the domain giveaway was not limited only to Thursday; Thursday was just the day I used to announce the giveaway.

Friday: "E" for Easy Cash An announcement was made that everyone who generates a cumulative value of $400 or more in affiliate sales from Friday through Sunday would get a $100 check on top of their regular commission. Because sales volumes naturally drop down on weekends, this campaign was meant to motivate better affiliate promotion activity during the weekend.

The A-B-C-D-E idea may, of course, be used for other time periods, such as each week of the month or each month of the year. The concept is easy to follow, and affiliates said they were looking forward to learning what the next letter of the alphabet would stand for. It adds an element of intrigue to the promo, capturing the affiliates' attention and keeping them interested until the end of the campaign.

A 1-2-3-4-5 Idea

This idea is very similar to the previous one, with the only difference that each day of the working week is tied to a number reflecting the order each workday occupies in the week:

- Monday—1
- Tuesday—2
- Wednesday—3
- Thursday—4
- Friday—5

I will give you two examples of how you can use the numbers. I ran the 1-2-3-4-5 Happy Weeks for two programs simultaneously: one for RussianLegacy.com and the other one for the jewelry merchant mentioned earlier. These campaigns were run not only at the same time but also at the same place (at a popular affiliate marketing forum). So, I had to use my imagination to keep the promos different for each of the affiliate programs. Here is what I did:

Jewelry Merchant's 1-2-3-4-5 Happy Week

- Monday: "One affiliate that generates the most sales at [Merchant's name here] between now and the end of this month will receive an additional $10 performance bonus." This was announced on a Monday that happened to be the 29th day of a 31-day month.
- Tuesday: Two announcements were made about upcoming enhancements to the client's affiliate program.
- Wednesday: I announced that there would be three levels of commission increases starting from that moment until the end of the next month on larger gross monthly sales sent to us.
- Thursday: "The first four affiliates who reach a threshold of $1,000 in the current month will get a $50 bounty on top of their commission." This is in addition to the already increased commission announced the day before.
- Friday: "The first five affiliates who show a five times growth in the current month over the previous month will receive a $50 prize check each."

RussianLegacy's 1-2-3-4-5 Happy Week

- Monday: One huge discount/coupon was announced giving affiliates a $200 discount on one particular item. This offer had two main advantages to affiliates: The coupon was not available to customers in any other way but through affiliate websites, and the affiliate commission on this item amounted to almost $50.
- Tuesday: We would announce two pieces of good news on important improvements to the program that affiliates had asked for.

- Wednesday: "Three color" contest for the best affiliate idea on how to promote Russian Legacy's products in an original way, utilizing the three colors of the Russian flag. Prize: choice of Russian Legacy's merchandise ranging from $25 to $31 in price.

- Thursday: The first four affiliates who reach a threshold of $1,000 in the current month will get a $50 bounty on top of their commission.

- Friday: Every fifth sale bonus—awarded on every fifth sale during the current month.

Once again, just as with the A-B-C-D-E idea, the 1-2-3-4-5 principle would also be a wonderful fit for either the 4 weeks of the month or the 12 months of the year.

Colors Idea

Along with numbers and letters of the alphabet, you can use colors (for example, colors of the rainbow) in your affiliate promos. The number of the colors in the rainbow matches the number of the days in the week. I find this very convenient. Each color has a meaning. Play with the symbolism of color, and make another week, month, or year in the life of your affiliates a little more fun. Here is an example of a color-based campaign that I ran for one of the merchants (it lasted one workweek):

Monday: Red Red is the color of energy, war, danger, strength, power, determination, passion, desire, and love. We focused on power, determination, passion, and desire, which are the characteristics of affiliates that an affiliate manager enjoys working with the most. I offered a 90-day to 365-day cookie life increase plus a $5 bonus to all those that put together a nice data feed–based website (at least two-thirds of the data feed had to be used) within 10 days of the announcement.

Tuesday: Orange Orange is known as the color of enthusiasm, fascination, happiness, creativity, determination, attraction, success, encouragement, and stimulation. Hence, Tuesday was the encouragement/stimulation day; I showed everyone a screenshot of the best program's affiliate (keeping his name and website address secret, of course), seeking to motivate others by his impressive statistics.

Wednesday: Yellow Yellow is the color of sunshine and the color that's associated with joy, happiness, intellect, and energy. I used this day to show everyone a yellow product, introducing a whole line of products affiliates often overlooked; but with the nice meaning the yellow color has, you may certainly use it differently.

Thursday: Green Green is the color of nature. It symbolizes growth, harmony, freshness, and fertility. Green has a strong emotional correspondence with safety. Dark green is also commonly associated with money. What better chance to stress the main idea of the week: to get as many people as possible to start using our data feed. I told affiliates that I would throw in $50+ worth of the merchant's products as a prize for all those who integrate our data feed into their sites within 16 hours of this announcement (and this was to happen on top of the already-promised cookie life increase to 365 days and the $5 bonus).

Friday: Blue Blue is the color of the sky and the sea. It is often associated with depth and stability. Interestingly enough, dark blue—associated with depth, expertise, and stability—is a preferred color for corporate America. So, I focused on stability and announced to all affiliates that the merchant is officially going free of fourth click. (See the sidebar "GoldenCAN vs. PopShops" in Chapter 8, "Week 2: Data Feeds, Coupons, and Plug-Ins," on GoldenCAN letting affiliates own 100 percent of their traffic and sales.)

You can also use the remaining two colors of indigo and violet for Saturday and Sunday. Indigo symbolizes intuition, meditation, and deep contemplation, while violet stands for interchange or unity. Both colors' meanings are excellent for asking affiliates for a weekend analysis of your program and coming up with suggestions for improvements.

If it suits your affiliate program, you can also use the meanings of different flowers (this would work wonderfully for flower-sending merchants), picking up 5 or 7 for the week, 12 for 12 months of the year, or 28–31 for the days in the month.

Lingua-Symbolic Idea for One Week

Being a professional linguist (I have both a bachelor's degree and a master's degree in linguistics), I have always been fascinated by correlations between the meaning of words and their origin. I was brought up in a country that speaks a Romance language; I was born and raised in Kishinev, Moldova, where Romanian is the language of the state. Years before even thinking of studying linguistics professionally, I noticed that the name of each day of the week is tied to the name of a celestial body. Monday is "luni" in Romanian, and "Luna" is the moon, for example. Tuesday is "miercuri," which, of course, relates to Mercury.

Later, in the university classroom, I found out that the seven-day system we now use is based on an ancient astrological notion—that the seven known celestial bodies influence what happens on Earth and that each of these celestial bodies controls the first hour of the day named after it. This system was brought into Hellenistic Egypt from Mesopotamia, where astrology had been practiced for millennia and where seven had always been a propitious number. In A.D. 321, the Emperor Constantine the Great grafted this astrological system onto the Roman calendar. He made the first day of this new week a day of rest and worship for all and imposed the sequence and names of the days shown in Table 18.1. This new Roman system was adopted with modifications throughout most of Western Europe.

Celestial body	Latin	English	Italian	French
Sun	Solis	Sunday	domenica	dimanche
Moon	Lunae	Monday	lunedì	lundi
Mars	Martis	Tuesday	martedì	mardi
Mercury	Mercurii	Wednesday	mercoledì	mercredi
Jupiter	Jovis	Thursday	giovedì	jeudi
Venus	Veneris	Friday	venerdì	vendredi
Saturn	Saturni	Saturday	sabato	samedi

As you might have already guessed, the Happy Week was based on the names and meanings of planets corresponding to days from Monday (lunedi) through Friday (venerdi), and it went like this:

Monday: Moon Day If there was one day that the affiliate marketing world proclaimed the day of industry, it would probably have been Monday. So many of us in this industry are true "children of the moon" (coding in moonlight until 3 or 4 a.m. and getting our best inspiration for sites' promotion, PPC methods, content associations, and affiliate promo campaigns all by the light of the stars). The basic planetary association connected with the moon has to do with reacting to something. My call was as simple as 1-2-3: Put up one link by Tuesday, send two sales by Friday, and get a threefold commission increase on all sales this week. I had a winner before I posted the next day's post.

Tuesday: Mars Day Mars is traditionally associated with asserting, making things happen, expressing positively, and fighting for things (especially beliefs). I called affiliates to "make things happen"—join our affiliate program, put up links, and receive the $10 activation bonus that was advertised in the welcoming email.

Wednesday: Mercury Day Mercury is often called the communication planet. So, I had a Communication Wednesday, when I communicated to affiliates what problems had been resolved and what new features had been introduced to the program since the last week.

Thursday: Jupiter Day Jupiter is traditionally associated with maturing, developing, and growing. To motivate everyone to develop and grow in the capacity of [Merchant name here] affiliate, I made a special deal for all affiliates who had generated zero sales before that day: I committed to pay them doubled commissions on all sales generated between that Thursday and the beginning of the next week.

Friday: Venus Day Venus is connected with marking something as different, in other words, valuing. I communicated to my affiliates that I wanted to single out one affiliate—the one who generated sales for the highest total amount by the end of Sunday (by

11:59 PST). That affiliate was promised to be "valued" and "marked as different" by getting a $20 bonus payment in their affiliate account.

As with all other ideas, feel free to modify this one to fit your own situation and goals.

Sliding Scale of Commission Increases

I already touched upon this idea in the framework of the 1-2-3-4-5 Week I ran for a client of mine, and I'll elaborate on it here. I believe this idea deserves special attention, because it fits best into periods much longer than a day or a week. This idea may be used well within a period of one month, half a year, or even a year. The idea is simple: You offer your affiliates higher commission levels on larger sales sent to you. The commission increases they get kick in with a fairly small amount of sales sent in—something achievable and realistic. Affiliates—especially those who send you zero hits/sales—do not get motivated by promos calling on them to "generate $5,000 in sales during the next month." Look at it from their point of view. Provide testimonials demonstrating the achievability of the task (if possible, backed up with screenshots that have affiliate names and details blanked out, of course), and make it attractive and motivating.

If you have started running a program for a merchant with a large profit margin (for example, inexpensive jewelry, certain publications, and so on), talk to the owners of the business or whoever oversees the affiliate program management, and offer them a sliding scale of commission increases as a promo that could jump-start the program. I had a merchant with the base commission set at 10 percent that agreed to cut his own profit for the sake of jump-starting his program. So, we ran the following one-month campaign:

- Send a total of $500 in sales—get an 11 percent commission on all of them
- Send $1,000 in sales—get 12 percent in commissions
- Send $2,000 in sales—get 13 percent commission on all of them

A month down the road when the sales did pick up and I remembered the success of the previous offer, I raised some of the qualifying amounts, also offering more attractive commission increases:

- Send a total of $500 in sales—get a 12 percent commission on all of them
- Send $1,500 in sales—get 13 percent in commissions
- Send $2,699+ in sales—get 14 percent commission on all of them

I was basically offering a 20 percent increase of the default 10 percent commission if they reach $500 in sales, a more than 33 percent increase for $1,500, and a 40 percent increase for $2,699+ in sales.

I am convinced that one way or another, the commission increase idea will work for *any* affiliate program. Be prepared, however, that some merchants may consider it as an additional expense—an expense they "didn't expect." One merchant (with whom I was negotiating while discussing the possibility of taking on the management of his affiliate program) even called this commission increase idea "hidden charges." That was the last time we talked. Be forewarned, you may need to open the merchant's eyes to the fact that any marketing is always an investment, not just an expense article on their balance sheet. Be ready to show the advantages of running a flexible, performance-rewarding affiliate program, one that respects its affiliates and knows how to show it.

Bonus Weeks

Besides offering performance bonuses to affiliates who reach particular goals within one month, one quarter, or one year, remember to run bonus weeks. They work well, but the conditions of bonus weeks have to look extremely attractive. Affiliates must be motivated enough to set everything else aside and start putting up the links to your program and your coupons or start setting up PPC campaigns, leading traffic to you. If you can afford to give away $100 for $499.99+ in weekly sales, this would be a very nice incentive. If you can't, see whether you can afford to live with a $50 bonus for $399.99+ in weekly sales or $100 bonus for $699.99+ in sales or something similar. Talk to the merchant, and try to make the bonus as attractive for the "end user" (your affiliate) as possible, yet do not undercut the merchant's profit so much that it turns the affiliate program into an unprofitable venture.

Growth Tied to Commission

Do not concentrate on giving away only cash bonuses. Many affiliates would much prefer a commission increase to a bonus. So, since your ultimate goal is your program's growth, why not stimulate that growth by offering higher commissions to those who show they can have an impact on it? Run a campaign like this one: Every affiliate who shows you a twofold growth in weekly sales (compared to your weekly average and based on the last eight weeks' performance) this week/month will get a twofold commission increase for the entire following month. You may also throw in a $10 cash bonus for everyone who reaches the twofold growth goal. Set the exact deadline when this offer expires and when you will analyze the outcome of the promo. When/ if you have any winners, congratulate them openly (through newsletters and forums). Testimonials of other people's successes can be a great form of encouragement.

Offer Tripled Commission

This may sound unreal to some merchants, but if you are not offering a 25+ percent commission to your affiliates, why not run a tripled commission campaign once in a while? Although you may make it as short as a three-day campaign, I do not recommend anything shorter than one week. You may offer the tripled commission in the following cases:

- To affiliates that show you the growth that justifies the campaign (you will need to sit down with the merchant to agree on the calculations)
- To all affiliates on all sales of $XXX.XX or larger
- On select products to which you want your affiliates' attention drawn

Again, when you have winners, make sure you share their achievements and awards with others. I had an affiliate earning 36-percent commissions on the program with a default commission of 12 percent. However, since she was earning it on items that the company made more than 55 percent on, the merchant didn't mind.

You can certainly also run double commission promotions and attach cash bonuses to whatever pattern you decide to go with. If you do a double commission promo, it may be a good idea to tie that to a double increase in sales over a particular period of time. For example:

> *Every affiliate that shows a twofold growth in weekly sales (compared to your weekly average and based on the last eight weeks' performance), in the course of any week during the following four weeks will get a twofold commission increase on all sales generated during that week (a "Happy" one for you, to be sure!). And to make your life even sweeter, I will also throw in a $20 cash bonus into every affiliate who shows me the growth by next Monday.*

This should be communicated to affiliates on Sunday or Saturday to give them one full week to work on trying to increase their sales twofold, aiming at getting not only the commission increase but also the cash bonus. The period during which you run this promo may be of any length: five weeks, six weeks, and so on. Make sure you let them know if you are willing to reward every week that they show the growth and, if so, how the growth will be calculated (in other words, comparing to what weeks). Do not make it overly complicated, though. Word it clearly and attractively. If needed, use bullet points.

Play with the general concept of tripled or doubled commissions to generate your own variations. Be creative, and make the work pleasurable and the goal rewarding.

Run a Lottery

There are two ways to communicate the largest sale amounts within your program to your affiliates: Tell them the numbers up front or tell them the numbers up front but in such a form that it will make them remember those numbers (or at least the ranges of numbers). In the beginning of October 2006, I came up with an idea of running a lottery.

I picked the five largest amounts of sales that occurred within one affiliate program over a period of 10 days and invited my affiliates to take part in the following contest:

During the period of the last 10 days our affiliate program has seen XXX sales. Some of them were too beautiful not to quote, but instead of simply showing you the numbers and the commissions paid out, I thought it would be nice to do it the fun way. Let's have a lottery!

Here are the amounts of the top five sales:

$178.55

$188.64

$244.95

$315.34

$340.45

<u>*Task*</u>*: Kindly put them into the correct chronological order.*

<u>*Condition*</u>*: One guess taken from each affiliate.*

<u>*Prize*</u>*: $50 sent to each winner via PayPal (you will be sent $52.50 so that the PayPal commission charges are covered by us).*

<u>*Deadline*</u>*: October 9, 10:08 a.m. EST.*

The lottery will be run for one full work week. I am looking forward to your guesses. Remember, the number of $50 bills to be given out is unlimited.

To find out how many possible variations of five entry sequences there could be, you need to find the factorial of 5. The factorial of a number is the product of all the whole numbers, except zero, that are less than or equal to that number. To find the factorial of 5, you would multiply together all the whole numbers, except zero, that are less than or equal to 5:

$5 \times 4 \times 3 \times 2 \times 1 = 120$

Hence, there were 120 different ways of answering the question posed in our contest. This secured us well enough yet gave every participant a realistic enough of a chance to win the prize. In this lottery we had seven participants, and only one came close to the actual sequence, guessing the following:

$315.34

$178.55

$244.95

$340.45

$188.64

However, unfortunately for the participant, the last two had to be swapped for him to earn his $50 prize. We had no winners.

Theoretically, you may run a lottery based on 12 numbers. However, considering that the total number of possible sequences is more than 479 million, I do not recommend it, regardless of how large a prize you offer. A lottery based on seven numbers with a large prize would probably be the largest I would run. The factorial of seven is 5,040.

Let Them "Test-Drive" It

If you are selling a product/service that can be used by affiliates, let them "test-drive" it. If it is multidomain hosting, you do not have to offer affiliates full 10- or 20-domain packages but can create a custom affiliate package with a hosting capability of two or three full domains. If it is gum, send them a sample to try once they send in their first or second sale. If it is coffee, send them coffee. If you are printing business cards, print a certain quantity for each affiliate free of charge.

You do not have to do any of these "test-driving" promotions just for the sake of the test-driving. In fact, I believe they should never be detached from your ultimate goal—to get your affiliate program to generate sales. When you are giving anything away for free, there is a very big chance that the giveaway will diminish the value of what is given away. It may also lead some to assume that the quality of what is being given away is not as high if it is free. This latter possibility will ideally be waived once they actually try it (again, I am assuming you are selling a quality product), but to stress the value of your products/services, attach an affiliate action to the "test-drive." It may be a sign-up for your affiliate program and putting up one or two quality links on their website; or the "test-drive" may be attached to the first or second sale.

If you are selling furniture, fireplaces, or any other bulky and expensive products or services (travel, for example), neither the sign-up and activation nor the first sale bonus structure will work for you. However, this does not mean you should completely disregard this idea. Think further, and I am confident you will be able to modify it to fit your context. Take this idea and make it conditional on your affiliate reaching a particular monetary amount in gross sales sent to you. For example, if you are in the travel vertical, you could be giving away round-trip airfare tickets or trips for two. Just imagine what a promo that would be! Do the math, calculate what will work for you, and go for it.

Offer 100-Percent Commissions

Needless to say, promotions that have "100-percent commissions" in the title look attractive. If you are promoting an affiliate program for the manufacturer of a product or a direct supplier of a service (not a subcontractor or reseller), such offers may be possible to run from time to time. They are especially great at the start of your program, when affiliates may not know the company or the product well and you want to make your program announcement have a strong impact. I did these for manufacturers of chewing gum and web-hosting suppliers, and I must admit, they did pay off. Not only did I get many new sign-ups, but I also got plenty of activations and sales (in other words, formerly idle affiliates got their links up in an effort to achieve the goal).

You may offer 100-percent commissions on every second (or any other number) sale, sales above a particular number of sales within a set period (for example, all sales after the tenth one in the course of the current month), or even all sales within a period of time (for example, three days or a week). Do whatever you and the merchant deem reasonable and practical.

Run a "Free Graphics Help" Week

If you think it is feasible, you should run an ongoing graphics support campaign, providing your affiliates with banners of any size, shape, or color. However, I do understand that some affiliate programs may not have the resources to do this. If you do not, run at least one Free Graphics Help Week. At this time, you take in requests for any sized banner (preferably an unlimited number of banners per affiliate, because they will not ask you for banners that they will not put to use immediately), promising to get the banners back to them within a set period of time. The reasoning behind this idea is as follows: Affiliates may not be promoting you because the creatives you are supplying them with by default do not fit the spots they have assigned to merchant banners. You are then losing potential sign-ups and also have those who are "on the list" (that is, those who have joined the program) but cannot use the banners you are offering. Your goal during this week (again, it may be a month or any other period of time) is to get the stagnant affiliates supplied with the banners in sizes they need and also to attract new affiliates by the offer.

Award "Every-Third-Sale" Gifts

Do not take this literally. These gifts can be for every second sale, every fourth sale, every fifth sale, and so on. The idea is to discuss with the merchant the thought of giving away gifts after every Xth sale (if you are working as an in-house affiliate manager, things may be simpler for you, because you will know the internal situation in the company). The idea may not be right for the merchant straightaway, but when they are clearing all stock—be it after Christmas, another holiday, or just because they got in a new collection—this will be a great way to use the products. Explain it as an investment. You are not just giving away the merchant's products; you are essentially awarding gifts that, with the merchant's markup, cost them much less than they cost at the merchant's website.

I ran this for one merchant as an Every-Third-Sale Gifts campaign and announced that the gifts given away were worth $20+. The merchant did not really spend more than $7.50 on each of them, but a $20 gift is obviously accepted better than one that is worth only $7.50. It is a good way to stimulate sales, and it also allows the merchant to get rid of certain items. Additionally, it is an original way to award your affiliates. You are giving away $20 gifts instead of the $7.50 cash bonus that would basically be an equal deal for you (but not for the affiliate!).

Cash for Everything: CAIs, FSBs, and So On

CAI stands for *cash activation incentive*, while FSB is the *first sale bonus* abbreviation. It is a good idea to constantly run these for your program. They should be announced right in the first email each affiliate gets from you—the approval email. I have discussed these before (without abbreviating them), so I will not spend much time on them here. What I want to suggest is that every once in a while you run a Cash for Everything Week. Such promotions obviously catch an amount of affiliate attention that can be beaten only by a 100 percent commission offer. During the Cash for Everything Week, give away CAIs to those who haven't put their links up yet, FSBs, second sale bonuses (SSBs), and bonuses for every sale. You may synergize this idea with the arithmetic progression bonuses idea and give away $5 for two links, $10 with the first sale, $15 on top of the second sale, and so on. The common difference does not have to be 5. It may be anything you want it to be. Also, you do not have to run such campaigns for a week. You can make it a one-day, a three-day (the absolute minimum I recommend), or any other length campaign.

Cross-Program Promotions

Cross-program promos work well both between programs managed by different affiliate managers and between programs managed by one OPM. I have already referred to them while addressing the question of affiliate recruitment. Here I would simply like to give you two examples: an example of a cross-program promo between two programs managed by different affiliate managers and an example of a promo an OPM/AM that manages several programs.

Between Programs Managed by Different AMs

20-percent Cross-Program Commission Increase

It is our pleasure to announce our first-ever cross-program promotion, where every affiliate who generates a total of $499+ in sales between <Campaign Start Date> and <Campaign End Date> in both ours and <Company Name> affiliate program will get a 20-percent lifetime *commission increase in both programs. For example, if you are on a commission level of 10 percent, we will raise it to 12 percent for you.*

Important: Once granted, the commission increase will also apply to all sales generated between <Campaign Start Date> and <Campaign End Date>.

Between Programs Managed by One OPM/AM

5000th Sale = 100 * $50 Bonuses Cross-Program Promo

To announce the 5,000th affiliate sale received this year across all affiliate programs we manage, we would like to celebrate in a special way with all of our current and potential affiliates. We have 100 bonuses of $50 each (to make the total prize fund of $5,000!!), and they will be given out in our Cross-Program Promotion Campaign. To get yours, generate $500 in sales in any of the following programs we manage:

<Program #1> <Respective Sign-Up URL>

<Program #2> <Respective Sign-Up URL>

<Program #3> <Respective Sign-Up URL>

Important:

This promo is nonexclusive of all and/or any other promos run for the participating programs! The number of $50 checks to be given away is exactly 100, and this promotion campaign is not limited by time (that is, we will run it until the last check is given out).

The number of bonuses to be given out per affiliate is also unlimited. This means the number of $50 checks you may receive is tied only to the number of $500 batches of sales you send for each of the previously listed programs.

The numbers used in these samples may be changed around to suit your own situation. The general idea of the first type of cross-program promo is both to encourage your affiliates to generate more sales and to raise your affiliates' interest in another affiliate program. It is best if the two programs are somehow related. For example, if you are running a collectibles affiliate program, a good match would be a flower delivery program. If you are managing a gourmet products program, a kitchen utensils merchant with an affiliate program may very well be interested in running a cross-program promo with you. The second type of promo, on the other hand, aims at attracting affiliate attention to the full list of programs you manage. Both types of promos can have an excellent response if run at the right time and in the right manner.

Dynamic Scripts

This idea is not new, but it should certainly be mentioned. The idea of creating scripts that let affiliates keep their websites up-to-date—without having to do much work on their end—always gives any affiliate program a considerable advantage in the face of its competitors. Such scripts may help affiliates import your whole inventory into their websites or else choose what products to import. Some dynamic scripts may focus on your specials or price-drops only, while others may give affiliates a chance to display a dynamically updating list of the merchant's best sellers right on the affiliate website. Having a good PHP programmer within a reachable distance will help your affiliate program satisfy the needs of your affiliates both quickly and efficiently. Do get a few dynamic scripts up for your program.

Commission-Beating Policy

Do you see how online and offline merchants run price-matching and price-beating campaigns daily? Why not run an on-going commission-beating campaign for your own affiliate program? Here is how you can word it on the page with the description of your program:

> *a) Find an immediate competitor of ours that offers a better commission.*
>
> *b) Contact us at <Affiliate Manager Email>, and present one of the following:*
>
> *URL with the advertised commission*
>
> *Screenshot of the base commission*
>
> *Email copy of commission offer*
>
> *Scanned copy of printed commission offer*
>
> *Description of a private offer (be prepared to provide proof)*
>
> *c) We will beat the competitor's commission by 20 percent.*

You can offer a commission-beating pattern or not specify the percentage by which you are going to beat the competitor's commission at all. It is up to you—but having it there makes your affiliate program look serious about the promise.

Before you offer this, analyze all possible ways how this could not work, and then make it work! Do your own competition analysis, and if it shows that certain merchants offer higher base commissions, analyze their prices and come up with a formula where you would still be offering your affiliates better conditions. Make sure you word your commission-beating proposal clearly yet eloquently.

Exclusive Coupons for Select Affiliates

This idea is not a new one either but is definitely worth a mention. To begin with, all coupons offered to your affiliates should, by definition, be exclusive—not available anywhere but through your own marketing. No direct visitor of your website should be able to find these coupon codes; they should be available only through affiliate websites.

Having exclusive coupons for select affiliates, on the other hand, implies that you are creating private coupons and making their codes available/known only to the affiliate for which they were created. This technique works very well when you know to which affiliates you should offer such coupons. This is not an idea for public announcement, but with proper contacts in the affiliate world, it can help you accelerate your program.

Time-Sensitive Private Offers

This is something I ran for one of our clients, and it worked quite well. The idea was to make one announcement a week, targeting affiliates working in different spheres every week. The announcements were made via all methods available to us: our own database of affiliates, online affiliate forums, and the client's pool of affiliates (those who have already joined their program but were not promoting it actively). The essence of each announcement constituted publicizing the merchant's intention to offer higher affiliate payouts to those that work in specific areas. If you are selling backpacks, you would want to target affiliates with travel and sports traffic; if your product is gourmet foods, you would be interested in working with those affiliates who have holiday-related traffic, as well as those who are food-related. Make your offer time-sensitive, and do not announce exactly what you are willing to offer. Just ask them to contact you, letting you know where they can place your links, and assure them that they will not be disappointed by the offer. "Will not be disappointed" means a considerable commission increase. Make it worth their while. Do not offer 1 to 2 percent commission increases; a 50 percent increase is normally adequate to get them motivated.

Free Content Help

When speaking of different types of affiliates, I mentioned content affiliates, or those affiliates who build content-saturated sites and feature merchants' banners, links, and/or products on the side. Many of them are great writers of that content. They enjoy doing it, and what they write reads well and attracts visitors. However, not all affiliates have great writing skills. Some outsource copywriters can do the work for you. To save them the money and get them to prioritize your affiliate program's promotion over others, why not offer them free content help? By doing this, you provide them with the text they can use on their websites to promote your program "between the lines," and you will end up with a good selection of articles you could post around the Internet. It is a known fact that submission of articles to various ezines and directories helps you with the search engine optimization of your own website. It is an excellent incentive for you to run a continuous Free Content Help campaign for your affiliates. Write one article a week and publish it on the Internet, giving your affiliates access to it, too. At the end of the year you will have 52 articles published all around the Web, helping you with your search engine positions and also sending you visitors. In addition, you will have all of these articles available for affiliates to use on their websites.

It's important to restrict your Free Content Help campaign by a condition that affiliates can publish your articles only at their own websites so that you and your affiliates do not end up publishing them in the same online directories and ezines.

Activation Incentives

Affiliate activation is a topic that deserves special attention (see Chapters 12, "Week 2: Plan Your Affiliate Communication," and 14, "Week 4: Affiliate Motivation"), because it is a well-known problem for every affiliate manager. I do not know of a single affiliate program that has at least one-third of all affiliates sending hits and sales. The reality is normally as dreadful as already mentioned—less than one-sixth of all affiliates that any given program has on board are actively contributing to the life of the program. Let me give you practical examples of two activation incentives that I use daily: cash giveaways and cookies and commission increases.

Cash giveaways or bonuses presuppose immediate monetary remuneration for an action performed by an affiliate. You can give away cash for links put up on the affiliate website (smallest amounts), for data feed import (larger amounts), and/or on top of their first or second sale's commission (largest amounts).

Cookies and commission increases can also be used as a powerful activation incentive tool. If your budget does not allow you to give away cash bonuses right away, offer your affiliates cookies increases, commission increases, or a combination of both. In one affiliate program I manage, affiliates often request access to merchants' data feeds. This is always a good sign, because it shows they are planning on using the data feed. However, experience shows that, just as with affiliate sign-ups, affiliate requests for data feed access may not mean much unless you motivate them to get active with that data feed. When I approve affiliates for data feed access, I send each and every one of them a message that is worded along the following lines:

> *Dear <Affiliate's Name>*
>
> *Congratulations! You have just been approved for FTP access to <Merchant's Name> data feed.*
>
> *Please let me know as soon as our products are up on your website.*

PROPOSAL: If you add at least half of the data feed to your website by <Date, Month, Year>, we will raise your cookies life to 180 days. If you add at least two-thirds, you will get 365 days of cookie life and an additional $10 bonus in your affiliate account.

Looking forward to hearing from you!

Best regards,

Geno

<Merchant's Name> Affiliate Program Manager

Once I introduced such data feed–approval emails, the number of affiliates who actually imported the data feed into their websites rose from 8 percent to 47 percent. The effect was obvious, but it still left room for improvement. If you send out follow-up emails to those who never claim their activation "prizes," you will increase the effectiveness of your activation endeavors even more.

Turn a Sale into a Contest

In July 2006, an affiliate sale came in through RussianLegacy's affiliate program. The sale was for $521.85. It was not your usual sale, though, because it consisted of a large number of a single product. All of a sudden, I was reminded of the words of Dr. Vernon A. Magnesen:

We learn:

10 percent of what we read

20 percent of what we hear

30 percent of what we see

50 percent of what we see and hear

70 percent of what we say

90 percent of what we say and do

Ninety percent of what is not only spoken but also done is remembered by the initiator of the speech and action. That is why I ran a contest two hours after this interesting sale came in. The conditions were simple:

We have just had the following sale come in:

<Screenshot of Affiliate Transaction> (with the sale amount and the large commission paid on it underlined)

Guess what was purchased, and get one of them yourself!

Within just 24 hours we had close to 50 guesses, and none of them hit the mark! Not one! The order was for 300 hand-painted keychains (shaped like nesting dolls), and not one affiliate could guess it. Did it ruin the contest? Not at all. We achieved the higher goal: A large number of affiliates browsed the merchant's inventory of 3,000+ products (that's your action) and voiced their guesses (that's your speech). One of the affiliates admitted, "Smart idea, Geno. I never would have spent that much time digging through your site."

Glossary of Abbreviations

Ad: advertisement May be in the form of text, banner, Flash, video, or any other method that is displayed on the Internet.

AM: affiliate manager Person in charge of the management (and sometimes organization) of a company's affiliate program.

AOV: average order value A metric that reflects the average value of a purchase. Calculated by dividing the total value of orders within a given period of time by the number of orders.

ASP: Active Server Pages A Microsoft technology for dynamically generating web pages that contain one or more scripts that are processed on a Microsoft web server prior to the page being displayed to the end user. The idea is somewhat similar to *SSI. See* www.asp.net.

ASP: application service provider A third-party entity that distributes software applications or software-based services via a network or the Internet. Affiliate networks may be referred to as ASPs, because their features are accessible over the Internet by merchants and affiliates alike. ASP may also stand for *affiliate solution provider.*

AW: Affiliate Window The United Kingdom's first and largest affiliate network, owned by Digital Window Ltd.

B2B: business to business A way of exchanging products or services *or* a transaction that takes place between businesses, rather than between a business and a consumer.

B2C: business to consumer A way of exchanging products or services *or* a transaction that takes place between a business and a consumer, rather than between one business and another.

BHO: browser helper object A DLL that allows its developers to customize and control the end user's Internet Explorer. BHOs have access to all events and properties of each browsing session. Parasitic affiliate behavior is often closely associated with BHOs.

Bot: robot A software application that crawls the Internet with the purpose of indexing websites and web pages.

CAC: customer acquisition cost The cost associated with convincing a website visitor to become a customer for your product/service.

CB: callback A way of interviewing somebody after a product usage. The term may also refer to any repeated attempt to contact a potential responder after an unsuccessful first-contact attempt.

CGI: Common Gateway Interface A way of transferring information between an Internet server and a CGI program. CGI programs are also often referred to as *scripts* and may be written in such programming languages as C, C++, Java, and Perl.

CJ: Commission Junction Affiliate Network One of the major affiliate networks. The company has a presence in the United States, United Kingdom, Germany, France, and Sweden. *See* www.cj.com.

CPA: cost per action Also sometimes spelled out as cost per acquisition, a payment model where an advertiser pays for each qualifying action made by the end user in response to an ad. Such qualifying actions normally fall into one of these categories: sales, completions of registration or other website forms, and confirmation of the end user's interest in the advertiser's product/service.

CPC: cost per click A payment model where an advertiser pays for each click on an online ad.

CPI: cost per interview General marketing term calculated as the full number of completed interviews divided by the budget allocated for the interviewing project.

CPL: cost per lead A payment model where an advertiser pays for each new qualifying lead. Here are some examples of leads: email addresses, completed surveys, and various online forms. This payment model is normally tied to the completeness and verification of the leads.

CPM: cost per thousand Cost per *mil* (or 1,000) impressions (or showings). This may imply anything from the amount charged per 1,000 banner impressions to a copy of a newsletter sent to 1,000 subscribers.

CPO: cost per order A payment model where an advertiser pays for each new qualifying order.

CPS: cost per sale Total advertising expense divided by the total number of sales received as a result of such investment. The result of this mathematical operation helps merchants determine the cost that has to be incurred to make each sale possible.

CPV: cost per view See *PPV*.

CR: conversion rate or conversion ratio The percentage of visitors who take the desired action (purchase, subscription, form completion, and so on).

CRA: customer relationship analysis/analytics The processing of data about customers and their relationships with the merchant in order to improve the company's future sales/services and lower cost.

CRM: customer relationship management Improving customer service and general interaction with customers by means of relevant methodologies and software applications geared at bettering customer understanding and increasing customer satisfaction and loyalty.

CSS: Cascading Style Sheets A data format that, when added to HTML, helps separate style from structure. It gives both web developers and end users of websites more control over how web pages are displayed, and it reduces HTML file sizes. Using CSS, web designers and end users may create style sheets that determine how such elements as headers and links appear. The style sheets may then be applied to any web page. *Cascading* refers to the fact that multiple style sheets may be applied to the same web page.

CTR: click-through rate or click-through ratio A metric used to measure response to advertising. CTR reflects the percentage of website visitors who click a particular link. This percentage is calculated based on the average number of click-throughs per 100 ad impressions.

DLL: dynamic link library Defined by Microsoft as "an executable file that allows programs to share code and other resources necessary to perform particular tasks."

DPSC: Dynamic Product Showcase Creator A tool created by AffSolutions that allows affiliates to generate a JavaScript code that retrieves a merchant's product information that affiliates can then insert into their websites. The code enables affiliate tracking and real-time updating of product information (AffSolutions also offers a static Product Showcase Creator for several merchants). This works only for merchants subscribed to this service. You can find a full list of these merchants at www.afftools .com/psc/directory.html.

EPC: earnings per click An important metric used for reporting merchant or affiliate performance. Although the abbreviation stands for earnings per click, this is often misleading. In reality, EPC numbers more frequently reflect EP*H*C, or earnings per *100* clicks sent by affiliates to the merchant's website. The formula for calculating EPC is EPC = Profit ÷ Clicks × 100.

EPM: earning per thousand Earnings per mil (or 1,000) link impressions.

FFA: free-for-all (link lists) Lists of hyperlinks where anyone can add a link to their website, not having to abide by any qualifications.

GAN: Google Affiliate Network One of the major North American affiliate networks, formerly DoubleClick Performics. Rebranded to GAN soon after Google's acquisition of DoubleClick in 2007–2008. *See* www.google .com/ads/affiliatenetwork/.

IM: instant messaging A way of instant text communication between two or more people via an offline or online-based application. IM may also stand for *instant message* or an *instant messenger*. The most popular instant messengers are AIM (AOL's instant messenger), YIM (Yahoo!'s instant messenger), MSN Messenger, and one of the pioneers of the industry, ICQ. Skype has an IM embedded in its application and allows not only for voice communication but also for messaging in real time. Instant messengers are excellent for staying in touch with your affiliates worldwide.

LS: LinkShare Affiliate Network One of the leading affiliate networks. *See* www.linkshare.com.

LTV: lifetime value A marketing metric that aims to reflect the total amount a customer may spend with a company during their lifetime. Sometimes also abbreviated as customer lifetime value (CLV) or lifetime customer value (LCV).

MLM: multilevel marketing A pyramid sales system within which salespeople not only receive commission on their own sales but also receive smaller commissions on the sales of the people they convince to become sellers. Such multitier programs are generally not welcomed in the affiliate marketing community.

O(A)PM: outsourced (affiliate) program manager An affiliate manager who performs program management outside the company's premises or on an outsourced basis. The less frequently used abbreviations include OAM and APM. Most frequently abbreviated as OPM.

ODP: Open Directory Project The largest human-edited directory on the Internet. Google and thousands of other websites are using its data throughout the Web. This is sometimes also referred to as DMOZ.

PFI: pay for inclusion Also sometimes abbreviated as PPI (for pay per inclusion), a search engine marketing model in which website owners pay a search engine to be listed in search results. Some search engines support it, not distinguishing between paid listings and organically achieved search rankings, while others label PFI listings hidden advertising, demanding that paid search results be clearly marked as ads.

PFP: pay for performance An Internet marketing model based on delivering sales or other measurable performance.

PID: profile identification A Commission Junction affiliate's unique ID number assigned to every website an affiliate lists in their profile.

PM: private message An internal forum or other online community means of communicating between the members of the forum/community.

PMA: Performance Marketing Association Nonprofit organization established "to connect, inform and advocate on behalf of this growing industry." You can learn more at www.performancemarketingassociation.com.

POP: point-of-purchase The location where the product/service is actually purchased. This may refer to both a physical location and the online equivalent.

POS: point-of-sale *See* POP.

PPA: pay per action Another way to refer to a *CPA* model.

PPC: pay per click An Internet marketing model in which website owners pay only for targeted clicks. When search engines' PPC campaigns are concerned, you pay only for clicks coming from searchers looking for the keywords that you bid on. The main provider of such a model is Google (with its Google AdWords), but other search engines (Yahoo! and Bing) as well as Facebook are also in the game. In Britain there's Espotting.

PPCall: pay per call A marketing payment model where remuneration is due only when qualifying calls are received by the advertiser.

PPCSE: pay per click search engine Search engine that supports PPC campaigns, allowing the search results to be ranked according to the bid amount received. Advertisers are charged according to the classic PPC pattern—or only for the clicks that occurred.

PPI: pay per impression An Internet marketing model in which payment is calculated based on the number of impressions an ad receives.

PPL: pay per lead An Internet marketing model in which payment is due only when qualifying leads are received by the advertiser.

PPS: pay per sale An Internet marketing model in which payment is due only when qualifying sales are received by the advertiser/merchant.

PPV: pay per view One of the newer techniques where the advertiser pays every time their website is viewed by a visitor. It often uses pop-up windows, generated by adware installed on the end-user computer. When this book went to press, no mainstream affiliate networks (in other words, not subaffiliates or so-called CPA networks) allowed linking from PPV traffic.

PR: PageRank Google's patented method for ranking web pages based on a complex technology (*see* www.google.com/technology) that weighs each web page on a numerical scale of 0 to 10. The purpose of such measuring is to define the relevance and importance of any given web page within a set of the web pages to which it is hyperlinked. Google's PR of a web page has an immediate effect on organic ranking of the latter in search engines.

PSC: Product Showcase Creator Static version of AffSolutions' DPSC.

PV: page view There are two ways to define a page view, depending on the context. One defines it as a single web page viewed by a web user through a browser. The other way characterizes every file as either having a text file suffix (.html, .text) or as having a directory index file as a page view. The latter definition helps estimate the number of authentic documents transmitted by the server, which is helpful for website statistics. Images, CGI scripts, Java applets, or any other HTML objects (except all files ending with one of the predefined page view suffixes, such as .html or .text) are not considered page views.

ROAS: return on advertising spending A metric used to measure the revenue generated for every dollar spent on advertising.

ROI: return on investment Originally a finance term, a measure of a company's profitability. It is equal to a fiscal year's income divided by common stock and preferred stock equity, plus long-term debt. In the investment and business analytics world, the ROI measures how effectively the investment is used to generate profit. In ecommerce, the term retains its financial sense, but more often than not, its definition is simplified to the evaluation of the money earned (or lost) against the amount of money invested.

RON: run of network An online advertising term that designates a type of Internet promotion where banners, images, media, or text ads appear on a network of websites.

ROS: run of site An online advertising term that is defined as a type of Internet promotion where banners, images, media, or text ads appear on a web pages within one website.

RSS: Really Simple Syndication (*previously* Rich Site Summary) A file format originally developed by Netscape. On one hand, it allows webmasters to put the content of their sites into a standardized format (an XML file called an RSS feed, web feed, RSS stream, or RSS channel); on the other hand, it lets users subscribe to their favorite websites and view/organize the content through RSS-aware software applications. As such, RSS provides a way for websites to dispense their content outside of a web browser. The RSS technology has basically provided the world with a better technique by which users can stay automatically updated on their favorite websites. RSS supports news feeds, events listings, news stories, headlines, project updates, excerpts from online forums, and even corporate information.

SAS: ShareASale Affiliate Network One of the leading affiliate networks. Known for its stance against parasites, it strives for tranparency and strong affiliate and merchant support. *See* www.shareasale.com.

SE: search engine A program developed to search for documents by keywords and key phrases. Each request returns a list of the documents where the requested keyword or key phrase is found. Examples are Google .com and Yahoo.com.

SEM: search engine marketing Marketing acts associated with researching, submitting, and positioning a website within search engines with the aim of achieving the best website exposure on these search engines. The best exposure may be achieved by improving the website's search engine ranking, participating in PPC campaigns, or a combination of these and other relative activities (for example, SEO).

SEMPO: Search Engine Marketing Professional Organization A nonprofit organization established to increase people's awareness of the value of search engine marketing through continuous education.

SEO: search engine optimization Acts associated with website altering with an aim of achieving higher website rankings on major search engines.

SEP: search engine positioning Acts aimed at achieving higher *organic* (natural) rankings on major search engines.

SERP: search engine results page The page displayed to the end user after submitting the search query.

SID: shopper identification A parameter that affiliates can add to their tracking URLs to be able to monitor which links produced which sales and/or leads. SID affiliate tracking was originally invented

by Commission Junction (*see* www.cj.com/ downloads/smartrewards.pdf), but it is now also offered by every major affiliate network, as well as by some providers of in-house software. The acronym is also sometimes spelled out as a *session ID*. I believe the time has come to broaden its meaning into a unified *Sub ID*, which would include Commission Junction's *sid*, DirectTrack's *dp*, LinkShare's *u1*, My Affiliate Program's *sub*, GAN's *mid*, ShareASale's *afftrack*, and other link parameters carrying out the same function.

SMB: small and medium-sized businesses Used interchangeably with SME, which stands for small and medium enterprises. In the European Union, enterprises with fewer than 50 employees are categorized as small, while those that employ fewer than 250 workers are considered medium. In the United States, conversely, small businesses refer to those with fewer than 100 employees, while medium designates businesses with fewer than 500 people employed. An interesting fact is that more than 90 percent of all American businesses fall under the U.S. definition of small business.

SMOB: small and medium-sized online businesses An acronym created to designate small and medium online enterprises, as opposed to the online giants (such as Amazon, eBay, and others).

SSI: server-side include A variable value (for example, a page "last updated" date) that a server can include in an HTML file before sending it to the end user who browses the website.

SWOT: SWOT analysis A strategic planning tool aimed at singling out Strengths, Weaknesses, Opportunities, and Threats in the object of study, arriving at an action plan for the proper use of the collected data. SWOT is an excellent way to analyze any marketing or management endeavor, affiliate programs included. The SWOT matrix essentially consists of four quadrants. Each of the quadrants helps the researcher analyze where the object of study is now, where it should be, and how to get there.

SWOTT: SWOTT analysis A variation of SWOT with an extra "T" standing for "Trends." For further details on specifics and application *see* Chapter 3, "Week 1: Perform Competitive Marketing Analysis."

TOS: terms of service Rules and regulations that one must agree to and follow in order to use a service. In the context of affiliate marketing, the TOS acronym is frequently used to designate either an affiliate program's agreement with affiliates or an affiliate network's service agreement.

UBE: unsolicited bulk email Email messages sent to the recipient as part of a larger group of messages, all of which have essentially identical content and are sent out without the prior recipient's permission. In short, UBE is email spam. An email message may be classified as spam only if it is *both* unsolicited and bulk. If they do not want to be accused of UBE, affiliate managers should be careful in the wording of the affiliate recruitment messages they send.

UCE: unsolicited commercial email Another common way to refer to UBE.

URL: Uniform Resource Locator The global address of an Internet resource on the World Wide Web (for example, www.affilinomics.com).

UV: unique visitor A term frequently used when tracking a website's traffic and designating a person who visits a website more than once within a specified period of time. Traffic-tracking software normally distinguishes between visitors who visit the website only once and UVs who return to the site. Unique visitors are different from hits or page views, both of which reflect the number of documents requested from the website. UVs are often determined by the number of unique IP addresses that the site visits come from.

Index

A

H

HalloweenMart.com, 249
Happy Meal concept, McDonald's, 372–373
Happy Weeks
    1-2-3-4-5 idea, 375–376
    A-B-C-D-E idea, 374
    classic idea of, 373–374
    colors idea, 376–377
    lingua-symbolic idea for one week, 377–379
    overview of, 372–373
    promotion idea, 372–379
Harvard Business Review
    "How to Motivate Your Problem People," 300–301
    "Moving Mountains," 286
    "One More Time: How Do You Motivate Employees," 299
headlines, increasing conversion rates, 336
HealthCompare.com, 234–235
Herzberg, Frederick, 299
Hewitson, Owen, 294–295
Hiam, Alexander, 289
hierarchical taxonomy of leadership behavior, 291–292
Hitwise traffic monitoring tool, 44
holiday/seasonal best-seller lists, 209
holiday-specific coupons, 146–147
Home Depot banner, 125
home page, avoiding links to, 355
honesty
    admitting mistakes, 365
    leadership trait, 277–278
"How to Motivate Your Problem People," *Harvard Business Review*, 300–301
how-tos, blog posts as, 239
hyperlinks, 110

I

Impact Radius, media partner directory, 40–41
importing. *See* data feeds, importing options

inaccessible websites, 310–311
inactive affiliates. *See* activation
incentive affiliates, 13
incentives. *See also* extrinsic motivation
    avoiding believing money is best, 360
    calculating commission budgeting in, 99–101
    finalizing overall payment terms, 105
    how not to write affiliate recruitment messages, 230
    offering tiered commission increases, 101
    offering ultimate affiliate contest, 103
    types of monetary, 101–103
income, of superaffiliates, 7
indemnification, affiliate program agreement, 180
independence, affiliate love of, 290–291
independent marketers, affiliates as, 5
individualized consideration, transformational leadership, 282–283
industry trends, 347–348
information, problems with text on mini-sites, 200
in-house affiliate programs
    assessing, 61–63
    how to choose, 63–64
    outsourced vs., 78–80
initial deposit, sample OPM agreement, 87
inspiration, leadership trait, 277–278, 282
instant messaging, as communication channel, 246
instructional section, affiliate program blog, 261–263
integrity, leadership trait, 278
intellectual property rights
    merchant accountability to protect, 171
    sample affiliate program agreement, 176
intellectual stimulation, transformational leadership, 282
internal issues, SWOTT analysis, 35, 39

MOW (Meaning of Working)
International Research Team, 302
Multi-Level Marketing brochure
(Ford), 8
multilevel marketing (MLM), affiliate
marketing vs., 8–9
multitier commission structures, 94
My Favorites widget, Amazon.com, 112
MySQL Product Feed Website
Creator, 141

N

negative feedback, checking affiliates
for, 312
negative keywords, 204–206
Network Solutions, on error traffic, 160
network stores, leaky website from
linking to, 353
network-based solutions
importing data feeds, 142–143
WordPress tools for, 150
newsgroups, affiliate program
agreement, 177–178
newsletters, affiliate
avoid mixing customer with affiliate
promos, 297
format and characteristics of,
250–251
frequency of, 247–250
motivating through, 255–256
previewing, 252, 252–253
proofreading, 251
providing options, 252
sample, 253–255
niches
superaffiliates focusing on, 7
video affiliates focusing on, 15
Nicholson, Nigel, 300–301
Nielsen Norman Group (NNG),
on text links, 118
NielsonOnline AdRelevance Data
Glance, 120–121
NNG (Nielsen Norman Group),
on text links, 118
noncompetition clause, contract
agreement, 84

nondisclosure clause, contract
agreement, 84
nonexistent domain (NXD) errors,
market for, 160
nonexistent links, affiliate program
sign-up, 194
nonreversal affiliate policies, 29–30
notification in advance
avoid not giving, 356
incentive campaign, 295
NXD (nonexistent domain) errors,
market for, 160

O

objectives, affiliate marketing, 267
Objectives-Performance matrix, 267
Obligations, sample affiliate program
agreement, 175–181
On Becoming a Leader (Bennis), 276
100-percent commissions, promotion,
383–384
"One More Time: How Do You
Motivate Employees," *Harvard
Business Review*, 299
one-size-fits-all approach, mistake of,
360
123LinkIt Affiliate Marketing Tool, 151
1-2-3-4-5 promotion, Happy Weeks,
375–376
one-way symmetric communication, 247
online brand monitoring, 270–271
online-based solutions, importing data
feed with, 136–140
on-server applications, importing data
feeds, 140–141
open communication channel, 247
open coupon affiliates policy, 156–158
opinion sites, for affiliate program
promotion, 237
OPMs (outsourced program managers)
affiliate program management,
78–80
contract agreement with, 82–85
feed maintenance, 131–132
in-house solutions vs., 78–80

P